Pro Football in the 1

Pro Football in the 1960s

*The NFL, the AFL and
the Sport's Coming of Age*

PATRICK GALLIVAN

McFarland & Company, Inc., Publishers
Jefferson, North Carolina

This book has undergone peer review.

LIBRARY OF CONGRESS CATALOGUING-IN-PUBLICATION DATA

Names: Gallivan, Patrick, 1957- author.
Title: Pro football in the 1960s : the NFL, the AFL and the sport's coming of age / Patrick Gallivan.
Description: Jefferson, North Carolina : McFarland & Company, Inc., Publishers, 2020 | Includes bibliographical references and index.
Identifiers: LCCN 2020018827 | ISBN 9781476678313 (paperback) ∞
ISBN 9781476640402 (ebook)
Subjects: LCSH: Football—United States—History—20th century. | National Football League—History—20th century. | United States—History—20th century. | Football and war—United States—History—20th century.
Classification: LCC GV954 .G25 2020 | DDC 796.332/640973—dc23
LC record available at https://lccn.loc.gov/2020018827

BRITISH LIBRARY CATALOGUING DATA ARE AVAILABLE

ISBN (print) 978-1-4766-7831-3
ISBN (ebook) 978-1-4766-4040-2

Front cover: (left to right) Vince Lombardi (Photofest), Johnny Unitas (Malcolm W. Emmons) and Joe Namath (NBC/Photofest)

Printed in the United States of America

*McFarland & Company, Inc., Publishers
Box 611, Jefferson, North Carolina 28640
www.mcfarlandpub.com*

Table of Contents

Acknowledgments

I am very thankful for the loving support of my wife, Karen, and my daughter, Annie. They were there with an encouraging word when I needed it most. The same goes for my siblings, Tim, Mike, Kate and Kevin. Tim provided helpful guidance reading an early draft that still needed a lot of work.

I appreciate the assistance of the San Antonio Public Library. The research librarians were calm and helpful as I asked endless questions in the pursuit of knowledge.

Interviews with the men who played the game were conducted. I am thankful for their recollections. Transcripts of interviews conducted earlier were located when the memories faded.

The library of videos in NFL Films contained a wealth of history looking back that this era of football. The Pro Football Researchers Association provided additional view into this golden era of football with their database of research and *The Coffin Corner* magazine.

The history is rich with countless stories. I hope that you, too, will find this era interesting as we take a look back at the nineteen sixties in America.

Preface

I have long considered the sixties as a critical point in American history. The decade featured a war in Southeast Asia, political assassinations and struggles for individual freedom across the nation. Battles waged between races, income levels and generations. Protestors demanded social change. Hair became longer and sexual freedom increased. In sports, integration came slowly to professional teams. Two professional football leagues battled for attention and attendance. Media focus came as televisions became a required piece of furniture in homes across the country.

As a lifetime fan of sports, I was intrigued about how the social and political changes of the world impacted professional football. Today, fans will frequently tune in to sports to avoid the bitter struggles of the real world. My research showed sports were not immune to the struggles of the sixties. Too often the best players did not make the team as choices were made based on race rather than ability. Players were not given the opportunity to even try to make the team at selected positions; instead they were stacked at one position to compete with others of the same race. In short, pro teams looked very different than they do today.

Sure, sports did not face the life and death consequences manifested in race riots, political assassinations and the brutalities of war but they were important on a different scale. Athletes come from neighborhoods across the country and are impacted by all the environmental forces that can be experienced. If their families were victims of discrimination, they came to the game with that set of experiences. Likewise, they may have had family members drafted into military service during an unpopular war or someone testing the social norms of the day.

Just as today, sports teams battled for viewers. Television was in its infancy and programming opportunities came slowly but the public was receptive when they came. Owners of sports teams were not sure how to treat this new medium without affecting attendance at games. The 1958 NFL Championship Game turned heads for fans, television executives and league officials. The exciting overtime ending made it memorable for all who witnessed it.

These factors made this decade so interesting to explore. Many of the key players from the decade have left us so sources of firsthand accounts were limited. My search moved to transcripts of interviews conducted as the time, newspaper accounts and books from the era. The result is contained here. We began the football journey with the 1958 overtime championship and end it with the sport's youth facing off against the veterans, drawing a direct comparison to the struggles between generations in the larger world.

The journey walks us through the struggles of the sixties. When president John F. Kennedy was shot, the nation mourned but football confronted a decision: whether to play and divert attention from the sad news, or stand down and join the mourners. Civil rights affected the players as the struggle included men who faced those issues daily. As the sport increased in popularity, gambling increased. Players were not immune. Young men were drafted to fight the escalating war in Southeast Asia. Players were part of that fight. This story orients us to how football fits into a turbulent decade.

Early in the decade, football was dominated by strong personalities of coaches like Paul Brown and Vince Lombardi. As the decade wore on players such as Jim Brown and Joe Namath took on a prominent role, claiming more of the spotlight. Technological advancement in television, the very technology that enabled many Americans to watch Jack Ruby shoot the accused killer of President Kennedy, helped propel major advances in sports broadcasting of live events. The decade featured many changes in television and the creation of a company dedicated to building the mythology that advanced professional football. These events made the 1960s an especially interesting decade to study.

Introduction

I love history, especially American history during the 1860s and 1960s. So much happened during these decades exactly a century apart. The War Between the States and the emancipation of the slaves were big events during Abraham Lincoln's era. War, assassination, civil rights and an overall change in social attitudes came during the 1960s. "No ten-year period since the Civil War was attended by such upheaval—by assassinations, political protest, war, cultural ferment, riots and other turmoil," wrote the editors of *Time*.[1]

How exactly did the growth of professional football fit into the turbulent decade of the sixties? Looking back, the decade began as a rebirth in America. The United States elected John F. Kennedy president on November 8, 1960. Less than three weeks later, the president-elect's second child and first son was born. One thing was certain: young children would be living in the White House. About the same time, professional football experienced the birth of a new league and a young commissioner took over the National Football League.

Many Americans viewed Kennedy as representing the new generation; he appeared youthful with an attractive wife and family. The media loved him and his young wife. His opponent, Richard Nixon, served eight years as vice president to Dwight D. Eisenhower. Nixon was only 39 years old when he ran as Eisenhower's running mate on the national ticket. In 1960, he was far from new to national politics. Nixon first won election to the House of Representatives in 1946 and to the United States Senate in 1952. Despite the perception as a political newcomer in the 1960 election, John Kennedy had also won his seat to the House in 1946. Due to his more recent emergence on the national scene, many considered Kennedy to be much younger than Nixon. However, Kennedy was only four years younger.

Candidates for commissioner of the National Football League do not run a head-to-head political campaign and they do not make life-and-death decisions like the president. They are both chief executives of major organizations in public view. As the owners of the franchises met to select a new commissioner in 1960, two candidates stood ready. One represented the establishment since he had served as the right-hand man to the previous commissioner. The other was a longtime team executive in the league office. Owners passed on both. They cast ballot after ballot without a winning option. Days later, with little progress noted, a new candidate was proposed.

Pete Rozelle, general manager for the Los Angeles Rams, had served various marketing

President Kennedy, Mrs. Kennedy, John F. Kennedy, Jr., and Caroline Kennedy play with family dogs at Hyannis Port, Massachusetts (Cecil Stoughton, White House/John Fitzgerald Kennedy Library, Boston).

roles in and out of the league prior to assuming control of the team as general manager. He held that job for only three years. After 23 ballots, the NFL finally had their man. Just like the 1960 presidential election, Rozelle's selection came as a surprise to many. Only 33 years old, Rozelle was not very well known. Like Kennedy, Rozelle had a media background. The medium was still new; at the time, network television transmitted signals using telephone landlines tied together with coaxial cable. First sold in the fifties, color television sets were not highly popular until the mid-sixties when reliability improved and the price came down. By 1960, an estimated 500,000 color television sets had been sold in the United States.[2]

Kennedy, who used television to get his message across during the campaign, continued to deploy the new medium during his early days in office. He was the first president to use live televised press conferences, speeches and special appearances as a normal course of his presidency. First Lady Jackie Kennedy gave a nationally televised guided tour of the newly refurbished White House. Kennedy maintained tight control over his television image, ensuring that America did not hear about his womanizing, his health or anything else he preferred stay private.

In 1962, Rozelle negotiated his first television contract, selling CBS the rights to show a full season of games for $4.6 million. His media background helped steer professional football from a game televised sporadically in black and white to a full slate of contests shown weekly in color. When he took over, the college game was more popular but Rozelle engineered a move to the top spot as an entertainment vehicle. Today, nearly all of the most-watched television programs each year are NFL games.

Before he could negotiate that fat television contract, he needed the owners to buy into his vision with a concept called "league think." He said owners should think about what was best for the league as a whole rather than what benefits their individual team most. Each team kept separate books but shared revenue from league sources. His calm, patient demeanor convinced owners to believe that the overall health of the league took priority over the individual team. The concept is similar to the "weakest link in a chain" idea where individuals must think about the overall health of the group. It fosters competition by providing equal footing for all. The agreement was critical to the league's rapid growth during the decade and the years to come.

The comparison to league think came with president John Kennedy's inaugural address. "Ask not what your country can do for you," proclaimed Kennedy, "ask what you can do for your country." They might have been the most quoted words the president uttered during a speech that was loaded with memorable phrases. In the simplest sense, Kennedy was challenging the country to improve their collective state. His speech sought improvement in the whole country and not individuals just as Rozelle challenged NFL owners to think not just of their own interest but also of the entire league.

Both leaders faced some early struggles with issues of race. In 1962, the first African American athlete took the field for the Washington Redskins. Until then, they had zero minorities on their roster. The Kennedy administration sought integration. The team was preparing to move into a new stadium build on federally controlled land affiliated with the national parks system, which put it under Secretary of the Interior Stewart L. Udall's domain. He told the team they could not use the facility unless they followed federal laws, including those pertaining to hiring discrimination. Redskins owner George Preston Marshall said his team represented the South and a segregated roster was fine with him and his fans. It became a crunch point between two strong forces. In the end, the national government had the upper hand. In 1962, a black man, Bobby Mitchell, took the field for Washington.

Blacks and other minorities played professional football early in the century. Considered one of the first African Americans to play professional football, Charles Follis played for a team known as the Shelby Blues in 1904. Other African Americans followed but they were all out of the league by 1934. Again, there are ties to American history. Many blacks, some of them former slaves, participated in government during the Reconstruction period. Hiram Revels and Blanche Bruce served in the United States Senate during Reconstruction during the 1870s. After they left office, there was not another African American until Edward Brooke of Massachusetts joined the body in 1967.

Civil rights were a hot issue during the decade. Populist leader George Wallace stirred emotions on both sides when he won election as governor of Alabama in 1962. A notorious opponent of desegregation, Wallace supported the policies of Jim Crow. Those laws were state and local measures that enforced racial segregation in the South. In his 1963 inaugural address, Wallace said he stood for "segregation now, segregation tomorrow, segregation forever." Martin Luther King Jr. led a march on Washington that same year in which he proclaimed, "I have a dream that one day my four children will live in a nation where they will not be judged by the color of their skin but by the content of their character."

The struggle came slowly across the country. After two seasons in the Canadian

Football League, Art Powell earned a slot with the Philadelphia Eagles as a reserve defensive back and kick returner in 1959. During his rookie season, he finished second in the NFL in kick returns with a 27-yard average. The following summer, the Eagles traveled to Norfolk, Virginia, for an exhibition game. After learning that the black players could not stay at the team hotel with their white teammates, Powell refused to play in the game. None of his teammates, black or white, joined the protest and the team released him.

Looking for new employment, Powell signed with the New York Titans of the American Football League. Head coach Sammy Baugh moved Powell to receiver and Powell rewarded him with four touchdowns in his first preseason game. With the Titans, he combined with Don Maynard to form a potent tandem. Each receiver posted 1,000 receiving yards in the same year twice, in 1960 and 1962. Powell refused to play in another preseason game in 1961 when the Titans played the Houston Oilers in Greenville, South Carolina, after being told he could not stay in the team hotel. Again, no other player joined the protest.

The Titans were facing financial issues in 1962 and needed to cut costs. Even though Powell led the AFL in receiving yards during 1962, the Titans made him available to other teams in the league. He signed with the Oakland Raiders and led the league with 1,304 receiving yards and 16 touchdowns in 1963. The Raiders' preseason schedule included a trip to Mobile, Alabama, to play New York, now known as the Jets. Powell protested the segregated seating plan for Ladd Stadium. This time, three black teammates—Clem Daniels, Bo Robertson and Fred Williamson—joined the protest. They aired their grievances to Al Davis, at the time the head coach of the Raiders, and the Raiders moved the game to Oakland. Powell's struggles were an indication of the changing times. His early protests were solo events but that changed as the decade went on.

The Reverend King led the early struggles for race reform in the decade. Some blacks grew impatient with his nonviolent tactics, which gave rise to more radical strategies. Deeply rooted in the principles of individual rights, the civil rights movement sought basic protection for people who did not have the most basic rights others took for granted. Civil rights riots sprang up across the country, from New York City to Watts, California, and back to Newark and Detroit. They were severe with property damage and loss of lives. Thirty-four people died and 400 were injured in riots at Watts. Violence occurred repeatedly across the country. Several major national civil rights leaders died during the struggle. Malcolm X, the Reverend King, Medgar Evers, and Fred Hampton, a young Black Panther leader in Chicago, died fighting for civil rights.

Violence was always a part of the game of football. NFL Films created lore for the sport with videos that captured and celebrated its violence. *NFL Greatest Hits* and *Big Blocks and King-Size Hits* were two popular titles. Violence drew the attention of the national media and fans. At times, it became too much. Early in his administration, Rozelle faced the violence challenge head-on. *Sports Illustrated* called the 1963 season rougher than ever. "The stretcher has been as important to the game as the football," wrote Walter Bingham in the magazine.[3] The league enacted rules to tighten control with a goal of reducing unnecessary roughness and injuries.

In recent years, Colin Kaepernick received headline attention by kneeling during the national anthem in protest of police violence. Civil rights protests are nothing new in the United States. Four North Carolina A&T students sat at an all-white Woolworth's lunch counter in Greensboro, North Carolina, in 1960. Denied service, the students refused to leave the building. This form of protest spread through the South. The climactic event during the decade of the sixties came in Mexico City during the 1968 Summer Olympic Games when American sprinters Tommie Smith and John Carlos performed a very silent protest seen around the world.

After finishing first and third in the 200-meter dash, respectively, the sprinters took the medal stand for the playing of the national anthem. Australia's Peter Norman finished second. The Americans bowed their heads and raised black-gloved fists towards the sky. They stood shoeless to represent black poverty. Carlos wore a necklace of beads around his neck for those lynched during slavery years. Prior to the start of the event, sociologist Harry Edwards, the founder of the Olympic Project for Human Rights (OPHR), had urged black athletes to boycott the games. Media attention was immediate and negative. Smith and Carlos were sent home from the games. *Time* magazine summed up their protest with one word, "ugly."

The protests were part of an 18-month movement that formed the OPHR. They had four demands: the expulsion of countries supporting apartheid from the Olympics, the removal of IOC president Avery Brundage (who supported awarding the 1936 games to Adolf Hitler's Germany), the hiring of more black coaches and restoration of Muhammad Ali's heavyweight championship title. Ali was a central figure of protest through the decade. An outspoken opponent of the Vietnam War, Ali refused military service. On April 28, 1967, as he appeared before the Armed Forces Induction Center in Houston, Ali refused to step forward when called. That was a violation of selective service laws, which was a felony offense. About five weeks later, the group of athletes gathered to talk to Ali. Each of them may have had their own reason for being there. Jim Brown said he just wanted to hear Ali's reasons for the decision.

Prior to the mid-sixties, athletes were expected to "shut up and play" the game. That began to change as the top athletes in many sports became vocal about political and social issues facing the country. Bill Russell was one of the best professional basketball players, Lew Alcindor (later Kareem Abdul-Jabbar) the top college hoops player and Jim Brown was considered the best in football. All of them were vocal during the stressful sixties. Before the Ali Summit in Cleveland in 1967, black athletes who mustered the strength to point out injustice stood alone. Like Art Powell, who had to protest alone, black athletes before the sixties spoke with one single voice. Men like Paul Robeson laid the groundwork for the protests by athletes in the decade. Robeson, an African American athlete, singer and actor, was an outspoken critic of racism during the 1940s, including challenging president Harry S. Truman to support anti-lynching legislation. Due to his criticism of racism, the House Un-American Activities Committee accused him of being a Communist. The government revoked his passport, starting what would become his eight-year battle to win it back.

The meeting in Cleveland marked a departure as a dozen prominent black athletes gathered to discuss Muhammad Ali's decision to avoid military service. Famed running back Jim Brown came up with the idea of a gathering of black athletes after Ali's managers called him. Former teammate John Wooten helped recruit the guest list, which included prominent football and basketball players. They met at the Black Economic Union office in Cleveland. Not everyone who attended the meeting agreed with Ali's stance. "Truthfully, I didn't feel extremely comfortable with the actions Ali was taking at the time," said former Chiefs running back Curtis McClinton, who was a member of the Army reserves. "But I acknowledged him as a citizen. He had a right to speak his mind and we wanted to support that."[4]

Anti-war movement was the strongest among young people 20 to 29 years old. As the war dragged on, support for the war declined even further among other groups. President Lyndon Johnson appeared destined to win his party's nomination for another term just one short year before the 1968 election. The Tet Offensive early that the year changed that view as anti-war candidate Senator Eugene McCarthy challenged the president in the primaries. In New Hampshire, McCarthy achieved 42 percent of the vote to Johnson's 49 percent, making the president appear vulnerable.

As casualty statistics increased, public support for the Vietnam War declined. Protests in the streets of Washington, D.C., let the nation's leaders know that the troops needed to come home. In 1968, protestors picketed outside the White House as they chanted, "Hey, hey, LBJ, how many kids did you kill today?" The anti-war sentiment contributed to President Johnson's decision not to run in 1968. The public grew weary of the conflict and wanted it to end, much as owners of professional football teams desired ending hostilities. About the same time, some owners of pro teams wanted their money battles with the other league to end as salaries skyrocketed. The AFL signed a television deal with NBC that paid $10 million over two years; money was available to pay big signing bonuses. Joe Namath got more than $400,000 from the Jets. The Packers paid $1 million for the backfield combination of Donny Anderson and Jim Grabowski. Salary inflation was heating up. The leagues announced a merger on June 8, 1966. It would take another four years to get the two organizations to unite their operations and integrate their regular-season schedules. By then, they had played four Super Bowl contests.

Big events dominated throughout the decade but some bookends signaled the beginning and end of the decade. Some look at the Kennedy assassination as that climactic event that highlighted a major change in the country. If you were alive on that day, you can recall what you were doing when you heard the news, much like the Pearl Harbor bombing for older generations and the September 11 attack for the younger generation. On a Friday afternoon in downtown Dallas in November 1963, shots rang out. Riding in a motorcade to a speaking event, President Kennedy was fatally shot by an assassin. Across the country, NFL teams were preparing to play a full slate of games that weekend. When news came out that the president was dead, Rozelle had a difficult decision to make. Teams were getting ready to board airplanes to get to a full schedule of games. Time was short. While the rest of the nation essentially shut down to mourn, the NFL pressed on. The rival American Football League and many colleges postponed games.

Pete Rozelle later named that decision as the one he regretted the most. The nation's chief executive was a huge sports fan known for playing touch football games on the lawn with his family and attending sporting events. He threw out the first pitch for baseball games and religiously attended the annual Army-Navy game. At Harvard, he played freshman and junior varsity football. He swam, mainly competing in the 100-meter backstroke and 300-meter medley relay. Before taking office, he authored "The Soft American" in *Sports Illustrated*, in which he established major points for improved fitness in the country. A year and a half later, he followed it up with "The Vigor We Need" in the same magazine.[5] Kennedy's love of sports was one factor that made Rozelle decide to play the games.

Even more of a landmark event in pro football history was the 1958 title game, which signaled a major change in the sporting world. The game went into overtime for the first time in history so the special ending made it memorable for the television audience. The game lasted into the early evening, which may have been opportune for those catching

President Kennedy and First Lady Jacqueline Kennedy arrive at Love Field the morning of November 22, 1963. Kennedy would be shot several hours later in an event most Americans found unforgettable (Cecil Stoughton/John F. Kennedy Presidential Library and Museum, Boston).

the game as the action heated up. Many of the potential investors point to this game as the thing that made them want to own a professional football team.

These events were not the only connection between football and history. The United States and the Soviet Union battled for dominance on earth and in space during the sixties. This competition between super powers mirrored the competition on the playing field. The Soviets launched the first man, Yuri Gagarin, into outer space in 1961 and the first woman, Valentina Tereshkova, in 1963. The United States appeared to be chasing the Soviets. In 1967, a flash fire swept through the command module during a rehearsal test of an Apollo rocket. Despite the efforts of the ground crew, the three astronauts onboard died. The space program overcame the tragic setback and successfully landed the Apollo 11 mission on the moon in 1969.

"That's one small step for man, one giant leap for mankind," said Neil Armstrong as he set foot upon the lunar surface. The space war in pro football came with an aerial attack designed to attract spectators. As a new league, the American Football League needed customers through the turnstiles and viewers on television. In the AFL's first season, teams averaged more points per game than their NFL counterparts did. These points came from teams more determined to throw the ball. Lionel Taylor posted the first 100-catch season in 1961 for the AFL Denver Broncos. The first player from an old NFL team to catch more than 100 passes was Art Monk of the Redskins, who achieved that milestone two decades later in 1984.

The climactic football event at the end of the decade was Joe Namath's Super Bowl victory with the New York Jets. The United States was the underdog in space to the Soviets just as the AFL teams were underdogs against powerful NFL teams when they faced off on the field. Namath became a key personality of the decade of the sixties. He represented the coming of youth as he took the field against two veterans on the opposing sideline. Namath was only 25; Earl Morrall and Johnny Unitas were elder statesmen at 34 and 35 respectively. Namath's victory came over a veteran Baltimore Colts team that had beaten the Cleveland Browns, 34–0, in the league championship just two weeks before the Super Bowl. The Jets' victory signaled a coming of age for the junior league that that competed for respect from the establish league all decade long.

Namath was not the only influential young man of the second half of the decade. The arrival of the Beatles to America signaled a change in times. An estimated 73 million television viewers, or about 40 percent of the population, tuned into the *The Ed Sullivan Show* when they appeared on the program for the first time in February 1964.[6] Listening to the performance was challenging over the screams of teenage girls in the audience. Perhaps the growth of television helped the Beatles as much as it did professional football. Their haircut style and mod clothing signaled that the Beatles were not your parents' band. Many professional football players in the early sixties looked like modern-day accountants, except for their size. They were clean-cut, as rules prohibited facial hair. As the AFL moved along, rules loosened much like social mores in the country. Players challenged rules prohibiting facial hair. Joe Namath was the poster child for those challenges as he wore the latest styles of clothing and hair.

That was not all! If fans of recent times got tired of seeing Peyton Manning in one commercial after another, those in the late sixties and early seventies must have felt the same about Namath. His ad for Beautymist pantyhose might have brought the most attention, but Namath also appeared in ads for the Hamilton Beach Butter-Up Corn Popper, Franklin Sporting Goods and Ovaltine. Noxzema shaving cream hired a beautiful young actress, Gunilla Knutson, to stand next to Namath and urge him to "take it off, Joe. Take it all off." She was talking about a close shave. Farrah Fawcett appeared in the next ad. Shaving ads were gaining popularity at the same time facial hair was growing in professional sports.

The facial hair many of the Jets were wearing presented an issue with the AFL offices. League president Milt Woodard sent a letter to Jets management asking the team "to conform with the generally accepted idea of an American athlete's appearance."[7] Translation: he was telling them to shave their faces and trim their hair. Namath did not like people telling him what to do, but when Schick offered $10,000 to shave his moustache, he was willing.

Just as Joe Namath appeared on advertising during the decade, politicians showed up in unlikely television programs. Just two month before the 1968 election, Richard Nixon appeared on *Rowan & Martin's Laugh-In*. That program was unlike any other seen to date with a memorable set design and frequent jumping from skit to skit. Nixon's appearance was only about five seconds long but it was memorable. He delivered one of the show's trademark lines, "Sock it to me!"

One thing is certain: The 1960s were a decade of dramatic change, both in professional football and in the country overall. The people, places and events tie football history to general history. This view takes us back to a decade that changed football forever.

Chapter One

Lombardi and Namath

At first glance, it would appear as though the two men had nothing in common. One had long hair and youth while the other wore thick glasses and approached middle age. Not even in your wildest imagination could you find any physical characteristic that they shared. The young man stood tall, athletic and good-looking while the senior appeared short and squat with a timeworn countenance. He stood 5 foot 8 and weighed 185 pounds while the athlete stood 6 foot 2 and weighed 200 pounds.

Their differences went beyond the physical. Women swooned when the young man spoke while men jumped when the old man barked. The young man moved people, especially women. The old man moved men at a high rate and with remarkable efficiency. The old man excelled as a leader while the young man had a knack for bringing people together.

Some differences between the two emanated from generational gaps and others from their very different backgrounds. The older man learned discipline from his hard-working father and compassion from his mother. His adolescent upbringing in the Catholic Church reinforced by the Jesuits at Fordham University laid the groundwork for those principles. His actions were similar to a military man even though he had not served. His closest experience came from coaching at the United States Military Academy at West Point.

The parents of the young man divorced during his teen years. It left a huge impact. Low supervision provided opportunities to go places his parents might have preferred he not go. The divorce provided the opportunity for him to learn a mean game of life in the streets of the small western Pennsylvania town. He learned how to hustle pool to earn spending money. Pool taught him to gamble, on and off the field. It also taught him angles, which proved valuable on the gridiron. It gave him social confidence off the field and risk-taking of a gambler on it.

The old man was Vince Lombardi, coach of the renowned Green Bay Packers. Without a doubt, Lombardi's Packers were America's football team of the sixties. They won numerous championships, attracted media attention and put Green Bay, Wisconsin, on the map. The Packers won five championships in Lombardi's nine seasons leading the club. His teams won three titles in a row—something never duplicated—including dominating the first two Super Bowl games.

The young man was Joseph William "Joe Willie" Namath. He grew up in western Pennsylvania, the cradle of quarterbacks. As a pro, he ran the streets of New York City and brought the Jets their only championship in January 1969 when he shocked the world with a huge upset over the heavily favored Baltimore Colts in Super Bowl III in Miami, Florida. Namath had a penthouse suite on the top of a hill in the cavernous buildings in America's largest city. It was a true bachelor pad in Manhattan richly decorated with zebra and snow leopard skins covering the furniture.

The Lombardi house differed in every way or about as far away from a penthouse suite as you could get. Vince and Marie Lombardi purchased a modest brick ranch home at 667 Sunset Circle in Green Bay, Wisconsin, built in 1959, the year Lombardi came to Green Bay. Win or lose, Lombardi held court behind his homemade bar in the furnished basement. He poured drinks, laughed at his own jokes and even did magic tricks. His children saw it as the only time all week he truly relaxed. "He'd walk in with a big smile," Susan Lombardi said. "Win or lose. He never came in with a grumpy face. He would go behind the bar. 'Well, everybody got a drink?'"[1]

The young man held court at the bar, too. Let us just say he took full advantage of the nightlife in New York City. Frequently seen with a gorgeous woman on each arm, Namath regularly visited the finest drinking establishments in the nation's largest city. He even invested in a bar that nearly ended his football career only weeks after the apex in Super Bowl III.

Vince Lombardi, born the eldest of five children of working-class Italian immigrants in the Sheepshead Bay section of Brooklyn, New York, in 1913, grew up in a family not unlike the other neighborhood families. Namath's father and grandfather came through Ellis Island as immigrants from Hungary just two years before Lombardi's birth. Neither spoke the language but welcomed the opportunities that this new country offered. They settled in western Pennsylvania where the steel mills and coalmines provided opportunities for work.

Joe Namath, the youngest of four sons, entered the world in 1943 in Beaver Falls, Pennsylvania, a steel mill town located 28 miles northwest of Pittsburgh. Both his father and grandfather worked in the steel mills. Growing up, Joe followed the path of his athletic older brothers into sports.

As he entered high school, his parents divorced. Upset, Joe found relief in sports, starring in three sports in high school. He played basketball, baseball and football. He played high school hoops with youngsters from his Lower End neighborhood as the only white starter. His strong throwing arm helped him lead the baseball and football teams into the playoffs. Joe had his own style. He wore his hair slicked back. His usual wardrobe included a varsity jacket and dark sunglasses. In the high school yearbook photo of the baseball team, Joe stands out as the only player in the picture with his shades on. Outside of school, he frequented one of his favorite places, the Blue Room, where he hustled pool. Just like Fonzie in the *Happy Days* television program, Namath turned heads when he entered the room.

Lombardi's early years followed tradition for that time in neighborhoods settled by hardworking immigrants. His working-class upbringing taught him to work hard to get ahead. When Vince began high school, he considered joining the priesthood, but two years later transferred to a more conventional Catholic high school. His circle of friends came from other working-class families in that close-knit neighborhood. Lombardi went to Fordham, a university run by the Jesuits. He loved the structure, order and discipline the Jesuits preached. Fordham allowed no sleeping in or skipping classes and everyone returned to their rooms by the 8 p.m. curfew with lights out no later than 10:30.

Namath attended the University of Alabama where coach Paul "Bear" Bryant suspended him from the football team after he admitted to drinking alcohol. The penalty seemed harsh considering Namath claimed he had just one beer. Coach Bryant, however, had standards and rules he needed everyone to follow. The penalty proved hard on the team. Most of Bear's assistant coaches wanted the head coach to look the other way, but Bryant could not do that. With Namath suspended, Alabama survived a late Miami rally to hang onto a 17–12 victory on the road. Without Namath's strong throwing arm, the Crimson Tide offense sputtered in the Sugar Bowl against Ole Miss. They needed four field goals to win the game, 12–7.

Lombardi taught biology, physics and Latin in high school and coached football and basketball. Although his coaching career moved from high school to college, he did not get a coaching job in pro football until age 41. Another five years passed before he took the helm of the Green Bay Packers. In Lombardi's era, the NFL's strict rules required that its players trim their hair in short military style, prohibited facial hair and demanded sports coats while traveling to road games.

Meanwhile, a new establishment joined professional football in 1960. A group of young millionaires, known as "The Foolish Club," founded the upstart American Football League (AFL). The owners, younger and wealthier overall than the NFL owners, dared to challenge the grand old league. In order to attract fans to their games, they needed to attract top talent. To do so, they relaxed many of the rules compared to the established NFL. Dress codes disappeared, many players wore their hair long, and some even sported facial hair. Jackets on the road? Not these teams.

Immediately, other differences developed between the rival leagues. The AFL liked to throw the ball and take chances. The NFL primarily ran the ball and played solid defense. Strong powerful runners such as Jim Brown and Jim Taylor led NFL offenses. The AFL wanted to open up offenses in hopes of attracting fans to a high-scoring game. In 1965, the New York Jets picked Namath as their first draft choice, which was the first overall by the new league. A perfect choice for the team in the largest city because this new league wanted to pass the ball and Namath could really throw it.

While Lombardi and Namath lived in two different universes, they shared more commonalities than one might think. Both came from immigrant families living in low- to middle-class neighborhoods. They witnessed firsthand their parent's struggle to make ends meet. Their families drove home the fact that getting ahead in the world required hard work. Namath grew up in a poor neighborhood where he had both white and black friends. Lombardi did not get a head coaching job sooner because of discrimination in his opinion. He experienced

Vince Lombardi's strict training led the Packers to five titles in seven years, including three in a row during the sixties. He was generally considered the best football coach in league history (Photofest).

denial of service in a restaurant on at least one occasion due to the dark tone to his skin, made even darker after enduring the hot summer sun of training camp.

Additionally, both men gained considerable fame for their roles in the football world in the turbulent sixties. Lombardi took over the Packers, at the time regarded as the worst team in professional football, and led them to championships in five of seven seasons between 1961 and 1967, including three in a row, a record that stands to this day.

Namath took over as quarterback of a team only a few years removed from bankruptcy and led them to the biggest upset victory in professional football history. An 18-point underdog to the Baltimore Colts, a team that some in media touted as even better than Lombardi's Packers, who had dominated AFL foes in the first two Super Bowl contests. The Colts entered Super Bowl III after completing a 13–1 regular season record and fresh off a 34–0 victory over the Cleveland Browns in the NFL Championship Game. Namath, however, predicted an AFL victory and backed it up with a 16–7 victory despite some people having crowned the Colts champions before they took the field.

Lombardi's and Namath's differences quickly overshadowed the few similarities the two men shared. Lombardi represented discipline, stability and religious virtue. Namath came across as the exact opposite, known for his promiscuous sex and his bachelor pad. Namath freelanced plays while Lombardi made his team run the same play repeatedly until they executed it perfectly.

Social changes happening across the country in the sixties did not exclude sports. Social norms underwent challenges as minorities questioned the separate but equal doctrines that governed many parts of the country. Both men played big roles during the changing sixties. They were definitely among the most influential sports people throughout the decade.

For example, in 1965, Packers defensive end Lionel Aldridge requested to speak with his head coach. A fourth-round pick in 1962, Aldridge served as a valuable member of the Packers defense. "Willie Davis was flashier," said Dan Devine, who coached the Packers from 1971 to 1974. "Nobody was steadier than Lionel Aldridge."[2] Aldridge listened when the coach spoke of the priorities he wanted to see in his players. Family, faith and the Green Bay Packers stood as the announced priorities. Aldridge knew he followed those traits closely. Now he wanted to see if the coach would stick to his principles.

Aldridge fell in love with a woman he wanted to marry. They had met at Utah State and dated for several years. They faced one big issue: Aldridge was black and his fiancée

Quarterback Joe Namath signed a $400,000 contract with the New York Jets in 1965 instead of playing with the rival NFL. In 1969, he led the Jets to an upset victory over the NFL Colts in the first AFL victory in the Super Bowl series (Photofest).

white. At the time, many places had laws prohibiting interracial dating much less marriage. Aldridge knew that many living in nearly all-white Green Bay, Wisconsin, had never met or spoken to a black person. While he did not need Lombardi's approval to get married, he wanted to see what the coach thought.

Aldridge had heard stories about Cookie Gilchrist, a man no longer in pro football. Gilchrist had starred at Har-Brack High School in Breckenridge, Pennsylvania, when he caught the eye of the Cleveland Browns' legendary coach, Paul Brown, who signed him to a pro contract at just 18 years old. Gilchrist did not make it through Cleveland's training camp. Out of a job and without college eligibility due to the signed contract, the running back went to Canada and proved himself worthy of playing pro football. Returning stateside, he reached stardom with the Buffalo Bills in the American Football League. Rumor had it that Cookie's career was shortened after he married a white woman. Lionel's wife, Vicky Aldridge Nelson, picks up the story: "Lionel just wanted to find out what was going to happen if we got married, so he went in and met with Lombardi. From the rumors that I'd always heard about Lombardi, he was always very non-prejudiced—he had one goal in mind, and that was to win. He was very fair. I had not talked to him up until that point, because, again, I was just engaged. Lionel called me and told me that Lombardi said, 'You know what, I don't care who you marry, as long as you keep the Green Bay Packer team clean, and you play good football. Don't worry about it—the same thing won't happen to you that's happened to Cookie Gilchrist.'"[3]

Vicky said that Lombardi's response and reaction to the question made all the difference. She said they would not have married if Lombardi's reaction been negative. The league unfortunately did not prove as tolerant as the coach did. "Yes, the commissioner [Pete Rozelle] came into town and tried to stop it," she said. "And Mr. Lombardi said [to Rozelle], 'Absolutely not. This is my team. My team is who my team is and nobody can tell me what I can and cannot do.'"[4]

Lombardi defied the commissioner and held his ground. Then he received a letter from Vicky's parents. Lombardi responded by telling the parents about his beliefs in religion, family and his football team. In the end, Vicky held Lombardi in the highest esteem. She said Coach Lombardi would check with her to make sure that Lionel treated her well. She considers Lombardi a "racial pioneer" for taking a stand that many others would not take during the turbulent sixties.

There are other stories, too. If you spoke with the players they would tell you about the Vince Lombardi they knew. "There was definitely another side to this man," said defensive end Willie Davis. "He could get teary-eyed talking about life and the reasons for things happening like they do. As the defensive captain, I was sort of the liaison between him and some of the players. A guy came to me—Bob Jeter—he had one of his relatives pass away, and in those days we made so little money, just barely enough to make it, literally, from week to week and through the offseason. This was early on in camp, and he [Lombardi] came to me and said, 'Look, here's airfare for Bobby, and I don't ever want to hear anything else about this.'"[5]

When one hears the name Lombardi, the first image is not a humanitarian who wanted to take care of players. Most picture a screaming man, whom some might even call a lunatic. Players said he never seemed pleased by their performance and always yelled at them to do better. Despite the public image, those close to him say that was not the man they knew.

"He was a different person in person from the way you imagined him with his team out on the football field," said Texas "Tex" Schramm, who ran the Dallas Cowboys for many years and faced off in many critical games against Lombardi's Packers. "Vince was a very kindhearted, sweet person, the kind who would do anything for you even though he was a very important, influential man in the National Football League. He never gave you the impression of being a league big shot in our committee meetings or on a personal basis. You talk about a guy that can be dogmatic or whatever you want to call it, he could be, but he was never that way. There was no feeling of animosity or feeling of friction involving the members."[6]

The person who knew him the best, his wife Marie, felt Vince's ups and downs daily. In *Instant Replay*, guard Jerry Kramer's diary of the Packers' 1967 season, he described how Marie learned about traveling with the team. "Marie Lombardi joined us at a team dinner before one game last year, and the desert was apple pie," Kramer wrote. "Marie asked the waiter if she could have a scoop of ice cream on her pie, and before the waiter could answer, Vince jumped out of his seat, red in the face, and bellowed, 'When you travel with the team, and you eat with the team, you eat what the team eats.'"[7]

Those who got to see Lombardi in settings other than the sidelines of a NFL contest saw the great coach as a well-rounded man. "Everyone thinks Vince is fierce, hardboiled, temperamental and ruthless—when in truth he's just a bunny!" said Ethel Kennedy, widow of Senator Robert F. Kennedy.[8]

In the book, Kramer summed up the wide array of emotions that his teammates felt about their coach. He called Lombardi a "cruel, kind, tough, gentle, miserable man whom I often hated and often loved and always respected."[9]

On the other hand, Namath's situation stemmed from a different background. Like many other kids growing up, Namath had a best friend who lived across the street, a boy named Linwood Alford, who was black. Only three when his father died, Linwood saw John Namath, Joe's dad, as a father figure. The young neighbor remembered John Namath leaving for work. "If he kissed Joe goodbye, he kissed me goodbye, too."[10] While they lived across the street, the families remained close. During the summer, John Namath often took the boys swimming at Morado Pool near Geneva College. Although the pool banned blacks, "Nobody saw anybody black in there but me," said Linwood. "I think Joe's dad had something to do with that."[11]

Then, Linwood recalled the time when Joe's mom caught six-year-old Joe with his face covered in brown shoe polish. Joe told her he wanted to look like Linwood. His boyhood friend said Joe never thought of himself as black or white. Later with the Jets, Namath would interact with all players, regardless of color, unusual behavior for the era. Sportswriters covering the Jets saw firsthand how Namath interacted with his teammates.

"I had seen Namath come into a dining room at training camp, check out the tables and sit down at a table composed entirely of black players," wrote Paul Zimmerman, who covered the Jets for the *New York Post*. "Most teams, no matter how close they are, break down into some loose kind of black-white arrangement at meal times. A couple of black players come in together and finds a table. Then a couple more join them. Before long, it becomes an all-black table, and the one next to it becomes predominantly white. To a casual observer, it would give the appearance of a segregated dining room. But, I have seen Namath plunk his tray down at one of those all black tables, and then a few white players join him and soon it became a mixed table. I have seen this happen too many times to assume it is accidental. The same thing on buses. I've seen Namath integrate a little knot of black players by his presence."[12]

Offensive tackle Winston Hill, a black teammate on the Jets, recalled his seasons playing with Namath. In Hill's opinion, Namath did more for race relations than anybody else on the team did. The common denominator between the Lombardi and Namath came from their color blindness in regard to race. In an era in our country when that attitude was not the norm, both Lombardi and Namath worked in their unique ways. The two had the ability to bring people together, not tear them apart.

Maybe it stemmed from his contemplation of the priesthood, but Lombardi saw his role on Earth as more than a football coach. Sure, he earned his living as a coach, but he wanted so much more out of the relationships he had with the thousands of young people he encountered in his role.

"Winning wouldn't be enough to get me back in the game," he said. "But it's how I feel when I hear that a [Paul] Hornung or a Forrest Gregg or a Boyd Dowler is doing well. You never really let go of these guys, you know. I just heard the other day about a kid I used to coach in high school. I heard he is in trouble. I heard he's drinking, doing a lot of heavy drinking." Lombardi paused for a second before continuing. "It's corny and it'll sound awful in writing, but you just feel bad when you know you couldn't get through to a kid like that."[13]

When Lombardi lay in the hospital shortly before his death in 1970 and word spread about his health, players traveled to Washington to see him and thank him for his contribution to their lives. A proud man, Lombardi did not want them to see him in such a weakened state, but he appreciated his players taking the time to visit. All he asked for in return was their prayers.

Decades later, quarterback Bart Starr still got emotional telling a story about the other side of Vince Lombardi. After the coach had moved to Washington in preparation for his new position as head coach and general manager of the Redskins, he returned to Green Bay for a visit. The Starr family had moved into a new house and invited the former coach over to see it. Bart's wife, Cherry, proudly showed him around the house and the coach stopped to compliment her on her decorating.

"We owe this all to you," she responded to Lombardi.

"He actually walked over and hugged Cherry, hugged me," Bart Starr said. It appeared as though the coach was getting emotional. "And then he walked out. 'We always wondered at that time if he knew he had cancer.'"[14]

An extremely emotional man, Lombardi's shouts came out just as easily as the tears. The temper got all the attention, but the sympathetic emotions always brewed just under the skin. Lombardi used his temper to excel as a coach, but also his position as a coach to help people. "It is this temper that keeps me on edge and allows me to get things done and people to do things," said Lombardi. "It is ineradicable, but it must not be irrational. I coach with everything that is within me, and I employ that temper for a purpose."[15]

Strange as it might seem, that same grumpy old football coach also had a take on the subject of love. "We all have to have a little love for each other," said Lombardi. "If you don't have it, forget it. Love is the answer to everything."[16]

Lombardi admitted privately to friends that he attended morning Mass every day on the way to the office to keep his temper under control. Also through Mass and his deep faith in God, Lombardi learned to love and care for fellow human beings. "He had the reputation of going to church every day," said center Bill Curry, who joined the Packers in 1965. "I didn't believe it so I went to Bart Starr and I said, 'Bart, tell me the truth, there is no way that coach goes to church every day.' 'Oh, no,' he said, 'he goes to church every day. He goes to Mass every single morning. The one thing you realize when you've been working with this man about three weeks, you are going to realize that this man needs to go to church every day.'"[17]

Lombardi claimed his players as family. When Vince coached at St. Cecilia High School in New Jersey in the 1940s, one player really was family. His younger brother Joe played for him. Vince worked very hard not to show favoritism toward his younger brother. He went so far that, by the end of the season, the brothers were not speaking. When it came time for Joe to make a college choice, Vince had moved on to serve as the freshman coach at Fordham University. Joe went to St. Bonaventure instead of Fordham for that reason. "I'm not going to play another year for that mean sonofagun," he said.[18]

Despite his tough, hard-driving coaching style, Lombardi took his role of molder of men seriously. He drove them hard to get the best out of them, but was not afraid to share some bible lessons if the situation proved right.

The Packers lost to the Rams in the next-to-last regular season game of the 1967 season. The Packers played well, but the Rams stayed right with them. When Los Angeles blocked Donny Anderson's punt, it gave the Rams the ball back with one last opportunity. The Rams made the best of it by scoring with 34 seconds left, which clinched a 27–24 victory. Some in the media called the Rams the best team in the NFL. They had won their last eight games, including the victory over the Packers. They averaged close to 30 points on offense and only allowed 14 on defense.

The regular-season ended with the Rams winning the Coastal Division title and the Packers taking the Central Division and faced off for the right to play in the championship game. During the practice week, Vince read to the team the text of St. Paul's First Epistle to the Corinthians. "Do you not know that the runners in the stadium all run in a race, but only one wins the prize? Run so as to win," read Lombardi quoting the ninth chapter, twenty-fourth verse of the Old Testament.

Lombardi introduced the concept on Tuesday or Wednesday before the game. The rest of the week, Lombardi would urge his players to "run to win." They did. In the rematch, the Packers scored a 28–7 victory over the Rams, earning them the right to face the Cowboys for the NFL championship. That game, played under adverse weather conditions at Lambeau Field, earned the name "Ice Bowl" from sports fans across the country. "Heart power is the strength of this world," Vince Jr. quotes his dad as having told audiences, "and hate power is the weakness of the world."[19] Lombardi functioned as a compassionate leader; he created an environment in which the players had compassion for one another. Lombardi built a team and believed he needed to drive the players hard to get them to perform at a level close to perfect as possible.

Many said that Lombardi drove his men too hard. He wanted them to perform at their peak of physical fitness, but also worked them hard to provide them a common target. His treatment provided a rally point that all players shared. They bonded together as a team because they all saw the head coach as their common enemy. Lombardi pushed the idea that a player must give one hundred percent commitment on every play to avoid letting down his teammates. It provided a strong motivation to work towards that goal of perfection.

"And love one another!" Lombardi said during one of his offseason banquet talks. "The love I am speaking of is loyalty, which is the greatest of loves. Teamwork, the love that one man had for another and that he respected the dignity of another the love that I am speaking of is charity."[20]

That talk of love sounds like something you might imagine coming from Namath's lips, not Lombardi's. After all, Namath as a ladies' man spread love all over the streets of Manhattan while Lombardi, in contrast, had the reputation of a manic head coach who drove his players too hard. Despite their very different personalities, Lombardi and Namath served as professional football's two leading men in the complicated decade of the sixties. One came in like a lion and the other ended the decade like a lamb.

These two men were central figures in the football world of the sixties. Namath symbolizes the struggles of young people during the decade as they sought social changes against the authority figures represented by Lombardi. The decade brought many hope for the future but riots, assassinations and war came along to dampen that youthful optimism.

Chapter Two

Crisis Brings Change

PHILADELPHIA (AP)—Commissioner Bert Bell of the National Football League died of a heart attack Sunday, leaving a void the men he served say they never really can fill.

The 65-year-old Bell collapsed in the seats in the very stadium in which he started his rise from college player to czar of professional football. He was watching a league game between the Philadelphia Eagles and Pittsburgh Steelers, teams he once owned and coached.

He was pronounced dead 10 minutes later in University Hospital, a stone's throw from Franklin Field, where thousands once cheered him as Penn football captain.

Around the league owners and coaches paid homage to the man under whose guidance the league prospered beyond anyone's wildest dreams. Professional football under Bell became respected as a major sport.

George Halas, a pioneer of the pro game, probably summed up best the feelings of his colleagues when he commented: "Bell was a great leader, a genius in fact."[1]

The proud, traditional National Football League left the stability of the fifties and entered a new decade. On October 11, 1959, commissioner Bert Bell died while watching a football game between the Philadelphia Eagles and the Pittsburgh Steelers at Franklin Field. Ironically, Bell had a close relationship to both the Steelers and Eagles during his long tenure with the NFL. He owned part of the Philadelphia Eagles in the early days of the league. Then after selling his interest in the team, he bought a share of the Pittsburgh Steelers, where he worked with his close friend Art Rooney.

Bell's position as commissioner provided him with a reserved seat in the press box, but he made other plans for any game he attended. Customarily, he purchased his own tickets and sat among the fans in the stands. Because of Bell's actions during his long reign as commissioner, his sudden death forced changes in professional football.

Under Bert Bell's leadership, the league grew during the forties and stabilized during the fifties. Many of the improvements are around today. The common player draft serves as the best example. Today, everyone knows that the team with the worst record receives the first choice in the selection of collegiate players. Prior to becoming commissioner, Bell owned the perennial cellar dwellers in Philadelphia. As the owner of a losing team he watched as the strong teams of the day—the Giants, Bears and Packers—consistently recruited the better players to their teams. "The good get better and the poor get poorer," he thought as he attempted to compete against the stronger teams. At the league meetings during the spring of 1935, he declared things needed to change.

Bell's theory held that the league was like a chain. Pro football is only as strong as the weakest link. He said his teams were among the weakest links so he understood from firsthand experience. He had an idea. To his fellow owners, Bell proposed that teams select eligible college seniors in reverse order of their on-field success. The last-place team would select first and the first-place team would select last.

The owners approved the proposal that became the basis for the draft format we see today. The team with the worst record selects first and so on until the Super Bowl champion makes the last selection in each round. They hoped to provide the weaker teams with an opportunity to improve and thereby challenge the stronger teams. This became the basis for Bell's mantra as he repeatedly proclaimed, "On any given Sunday, any team can beat any other team." He wanted to provide each team the opportunity to challenge for the title. Pro football today stands alone as a sport where the fans of every team view the beginning of a new season with optimism as they challenge for the crown. Today's fan owes that optimistic spirit to Bert Bell.

In order to generate interest and maintain it all season long, Bell also took steps to make league races compelling. He wanted the maximum number of teams challenging for the title as the season progressed. Making the races competitive helped increase the gate. In the days before television, teams made most of their money from people buying tickets and attending the games.

Bell took control of the playing schedule personally. He created it each season right at his kitchen table, which he used as his home office. When Bell owned a team during the forties, the stronger teams scheduled the weaker teams early in the year to stack up wins, hoping to guarantee a winning record. Bell had a better idea. When he created the schedule, he reversed that strategy.

"Weak teams should play other weak teams while the strong teams are playing other strong teams early in the year." He said. "It's the only way to keep more teams in contention longer into the season."[2] Keeping more teams in contention longer in the season generated more interest among fans that created more box office receipts. Current NFL leadership follows a similar rule, scheduling division opponents during the last couple of weeks of the year to increase significance of those contests.

The opening weekend of the 1950 season brought the best example of matching two powerhouse teams early in the season. During the late forties, the National Football League faced competition from the All-America Football Conference. NFL hardliners pointed to the fact that within the AAFC's brief life, one team, the Cleveland Browns, had won all four league championships. They said the level of talent proved so low that one team dominated the rest. That could not happen in the NFL, they said. Then, after just four seasons, the AAFC ceased operations in 1949 and their Browns, Baltimore Colts, and San Francisco 49ers joined the NFL.

Therefore, Bell matched the defending AAFC champion Cleveland Browns against the reigning NFL champion Philadelphia Eagles in the opening game of the season. Many NFL veterans figured that the Browns would get a lesson in "real" professional football. In their first game as an NFL team, the upstart Browns came away with a 35–10 upset over the Eagles. To further establish their position as a superior team, they won the NFL title their first season in the league with a 30–28 victory over the Los Angeles Rams.

Bell was a true football fan. He had to be excited to see the matchup between the Colts and the Giants nearing the end of the fifties in what would be later considered a game for all time in one of the best settings for sports.

The sun shone in Yankee Stadium as the two top teams prepared to battle for the 1958 championship. The temperature, surprisingly mild for a late December day, sat above freezing under a clear sky. Giants players and fans looked at the bright side of the weather conditions. At least it was not snowing as it had two weeks before in the final regular-season game against the Cleveland Browns. As the season wound down, the hometown Giants felt they could not catch a break with the weather. Winter had come early to the Northeast, forcing the Giants to play critical games down the stretch in bad weather. The sunshine provided a welcome change.

The Giants had needed to put together an impressive string of victories in order to get into the title game. They won their last four games of the regular season and a playoff game before they got the invitation to the title game. They played every one of those critical games down the stretch on a frozen field. They won each one, including two against the Cleveland Browns, both played at Yankee Stadium. The first, played in a snowstorm, saw Pat Summerall kick an unbelievable 49-yard field goal through the snowflakes with two minutes remaining to win. There was no snow the following weekend during the rematch playoff game, but it was bitterly cold.

Summerall seemed an unlikely hero to play in any sport. Better known to today's generation as a broadcaster working with John Madden, in those days he earned a reputation as one of the most dependable kickers and occasionally saw action as a backup end. Early in his life, a career in professional sports looked remote for Summerall due to a birth defect in his foot.

"I had a rather unfortunate childhood," Summerall recalled. "I was born with a clubfoot—the right one. It was turned around backwards. At that time, the way they treated it was by breaking both bones in the bottom of the leg and just turning the foot around. The doctor told my mother afterwards that I would be able to walk but would probably never be able to run or play with other kids. As time passed, however, through nature's help and the good Lord's help, it got better and better. And as it turned out, that was the foot I used to kick with—although that was way down the road."[3]

By the time high school rolled around, Summerall played football, baseball, and basketball and ran track for the Lake City (Florida) High School track team. "I ran the 100 in about 10.1, which at that time was considered pretty good."[4] That summer, he also played tennis. At 15, he hitchhiked 350 miles to Fort Lauderdale to play in the Florida 16-and-under boys' tennis tournament. He won. Not bad for someone whom doctors thought probably would not even walk.

Summerall began his pro career with the St. Louis Cardinals, whom he considered a "low-rent" team. He happily joined the perennially contending Giants to get the opportunity to play in big games. He came to New York to replace 39-year-old kicker Ben Agajanian, who retired after the 1957 season. Summerall could play end, but the Giants saw him as primarily as a kicker. His hopes of seeing action in games that mattered finally came true.

That 49-yard field goal nobody thought Summerall could get through the goalposts at the end of the 1958 season enabled the Giants to play in the postseason. It was outside his usual range and the field covered with snow. Vince Lombardi, then an assistant coach with the Giants, greeted Summerall as he ran off the field, "You know, don't you, that you can't really kick it that far?"[5] In all, the Giants beat the Browns three times in 1958, the last two on those consecutive Sundays in December at Yankee Stadium. That last win earned them the Eastern Conference title and a spot in the championship game.

During the buildup to the contest, the media framed the game as one in which the powerful Giants faced the upstart Colts. The Giants had won the title in 1956, which moved them into the focus of the media. Frank Gifford, with his movie star good looks, led the offense. Gifford grew up in Southern California and his Hollywood aura followed him to New York. Much like Namath later, Gifford lived as a man about town, especially hitting all the key nightclubs in the city. He and his wife, Maxine, a former Miss California, regularly showed up at Toots Shor's and P. J. Clarke's, two of the hottest nightspots in the city. Even in those days, he seemed destined for a career in the movies or on television.

Yet, Summerall had the look of a football player. "My nose was broken eleven times," he said. While in college, a plastic surgeon and fan of Arkansas football made him a deal. "If you beat Texas this week, call me when you get through with football and I'll fix your nose for free," the doctor told Summerall. That seemed a tall order since the Razorbacks had not beaten the Longhorns in a long time. "I kicked a field goal with ten seconds to go and we beat Texas, 16–14," recalled Summerall. "When I retired I called him and he did the operation. I always thought that was a very honorable thing to do."[6]

The Colts had a young quarterback named Johnny Unitas who appeared destined for greatness. At age 24, he led the Colts into the biggest game of his young career. Unitas's story sounded like fiction. An unknown college player who played semipro ball with the Bloomfield Rams for six dollars a game, he worked a construction job during the week. The 1957 season was Unitas's first full season as a starter. He finished first in the league in passing yards and touchdown passes, leading the team to its first winning season. The Newspaper Enterprise Association named him the Most Valuable Player in the league that year.

Unitas looked like a typical working-class employee somewhere on Main Street USA. The only thing missing was the lunch box at his side. "Nobody ever gave John anything," said John Steadman, sports editor of the *Baltimore News-Post*. "He worked for everything."[7]

The Pittsburgh Steelers originally drafted the former Louisville signal caller in the ninth round of the 1955 draft; the 102nd player selected during the process that took 30 rounds and saw 360 selections. The Steelers' head coach was future Hall of Fame offensive lineman Walt Kiesling. It did not take Kiesling long to pass judgment on Unitas. He did not see him as smart enough to play quarterback in the NFL.

During their history the Steelers had Sid Luckman, Earl Morrall, Len Dawson, Jack Kemp and Bill Nelsen on their roster at one time or another. This list of quarterbacks shared a common trait: each of them achieved a high level of success after they left the Pittsburgh Steelers. "I'd say we were experts on quarterbacks at Pittsburgh," recalled Art Rooney in a *Sports Illustrated* article. "We had them all, and we got rid of every one of them. We had Johnny Unitas in for a tryout, but our coach then, Walter Kiesling, let him go. Kies said, 'He can't remember the plays. He's dumb.' You had to know Kies. He was a great coach, but he thought a lot of ballplayers were dumb. We were arguing about a guy one day, and I said, 'I don't care how dumb he is. He can run and he can pass and he can block. If he can do those three things, he doesn't have to be a Rhodes Scholar.' But all Kies said to that was, 'He's dumb.'"[8]

The veteran players with the Steelers began to call Unitas "Clem," short for Clem Kadiddlehopper, a character made famous by Red Skelton in short comedy sketches in his television variety show. It certainly was not a nickname you would give a Rhodes Scholar. Looks can be deceiving; many of the veterans thought after one glance they were looking at a player who would not make the team.

Unitas never got a chance to take a snap in live action during the preseason. The only recognition Unitas got happened when two Chinese nuns appeared at Steelers training camp. With all the other quarterbacks tied up with drills, a photographer asked Unitas to pose with the nuns. The picture of Unitas showing a nun how to grip a football appeared in newspapers across the country. When the preseason camp ended, the Steelers cut Unitas and all he had for his time with the Steelers was the photo with the nuns.

The Baltimore Colts signed Unitas before the 1956 season as a backup to George Shaw, who had been chosen with the team's bonus pick at the top of the 1955 draft. Initially, Shaw clearly had the starter position with Unitas as the backup. Just four weeks into the season that changed when Shaw suffered a season-ending leg injury against the Bears in Chicago and Unitas came into the game. Shaw never got his job back.

Now at Yankee Stadium, those gathered for the game considered it one in which the league's most potent offense, the Colts, faced the top-rated defense, the Giants. The Colts had numerous offensive weapons with receiver Raymond Berry, tight end Jim Mutscheller and running backs Lenny Moore, L. G. Dupree and Alan Ameche. The Giants had the game's top defense statistically during the 1958 campaign. The Colts ranked second in total defense. Clearly, the 1958 championship was a good matchup.

Despite the fact that betting circles favored the Colts by three and a half points, in many ways fans considered the championship game a David versus Goliath story. The blue-collar Colts representing small town Baltimore had to travel to the big metropolis of New York City to face the celebrity Giants. It was the media darlings versus the regular guys. Broadway versus Main Street. Johnny Unitas, who easily passed as a regular guy, led the Colts. He wore his hair in a crew cut and looked like the neighbor next door.

The Giants, a veteran team with experience in big games, won the title in 1956 with a 47–7 thrashing of the Chicago Bears in Yankee Stadium. The stadium hosted the title game again in 1958. Not one known for "win one for the Gipper" pregame speeches, Weeb Ewbank, the Colts' diminutive coach, came up with a good story to fire up his troops. "In fourteen years I heard them all," defensive end Gino Marchetti said. "Win one for Mother. Win for Father. Do not disappoint all these people watching on television. Weeb really put it to us."[9]

In the locker room before the game, he named nearly every player on the Colts roster and told a story about how some team turned their backs on them. He labeled them all a bunch of discards from other teams. He made his message clear: the Colts comprised the group that nobody wanted. He included himself in that classification.

"We were a team that nobody wanted," Unitas said later. "I was a quarterback no other team wanted, we had a coach that the owner really didn't want and I'm thinking we can win a championship. We were truly a team of football orphans that found a home together."[10]

Ewbank's talk should have inspired them but it did not appear, at first, to have the right impact. One might have expected the team to charge off to an early lead, motivated by the coach's speech. That did not happen. The game, nicknamed "The Greatest Game Ever Played," did not start out that way. Neither offense generated any traction right away as both teams played sloppy in the first half. The Giants received the opening kickoff, but quickly had to punt. On the Colts' first drive, Sam Huff sacked Unitas, who fumbled. The Giants got the ball back and Don Heinrich fumbled. Carl Karilivacz intercepted a Unitas pass intended for Jim Mutscheller. Three of the first four drives ended with a turnover.

The Colts got the ball back and produced the first big play of the game as Unitas threw to Lenny Moore for a 55-yard gain. Soon that Colts drive stalled and they settled for a field-goal attempt. Steve Myhra, successful on only four of ten attempts during the season, missed the goal posts. One of the Giants jumped offside so Myhra got a second chance. Sam Huff blocked the second kick and the game remained scoreless.

At 6-foot-1 and 230 pounds, Giants defensive coach Tom Landry believed Huff was ideally suited for the newly created role of middle linebacker. Landry thought that Huff had the instincts and movement skills to play that upright middle linebacker position. He inserted Huff into the lineup in that spot as a rookie. Both Huff and Landry stayed in the Concourse Plaza Hotel, developing a close bond that turned into a lifelong friendship.

"I'd be watching television, and the phone would ring," said Huff. "It was Tom. 'What are you doing?' he'd say, and I'd reply 'Oh, nothing.' Then he'd say, 'Well come on up and watch some football with me.' He had this projector in his apartment, and we'd go over the other team's offense. I learned more football in one season in Tom's room than I had learned all through high school and college."[11]

It seemed like Huff saved his best in the biggest games against the biggest opponents. Those contests motivated him to do his best when playing the best. Every time the Giants faced the Browns, his job entailed stopping pro football's best runner. During the playoff game, the Giants held Jim Brown to only eight yards on seven carriers. Brown had to think Huff lurked in his shadow because he was never very far away. Huff also had great games against the other top fullback of the day, Jim Taylor of the Green Bay Packers.

Landry served as a player-coach his last two years with the Giants. As a player, he did not have great physical skills. Landry could see that he did not have great speed or athletic ability like many of his counterparts. He had intelligence and he understood the game. Landry took what his coaches taught him and brought it to another level. He could see that an offense would only run certain plays out of certain sets, so he developed keys to predict what the opposition offense planned to do.

"Tom was an innovator who invented the 4–3 defense," Giants receiver Kyle Rote said. "He refined it. He established it. I'll tell you something else he did. He started the idea of having separate meetings for the offense and the defense. Under Steve Owen, we all met at the same time. In 1954, we started winning again with our defense. Tom decided to take his guys into another room. I think he figured that if the defense had to sit there while we drew up the game plan for the offense, they'd get discouraged."[12]

Landry fit the stereotypical profile of an engineer—soft-spoken, methodical and studious. He rarely showed any emotion. He had an analytical mind and a need to understand how things worked. That led him to developing the keys to read offenses. "Most of us just played the game," recalled Frank Gifford. "Landry studied it. He was cool and calculating. Emotion had no place in his makeup."[13]

Landry understood that teams ran certain plays out of a standard offensive set. If the player knew what plays are run out of certain formations and he knew the down and distance, he could anticipate certain plays. So, he taught players the things they needed to watch for in order to understand what play the offense would run at them. Landry looked at football that scientific way. He looked at football as an engineer would look at how machinery operates. On the negative side, some thought he viewed the players on his defense as machine parts and not human beings. They said he considered players as interchangeable parts in a big football machine.

"Tom is a warm person, but not with his players," Giants head coach Jim Lee Howell said. "He gets impatient with them, and he doesn't pat them on the back. He expects them to go out there and do their jobs. He's also a perfectionist like Paul Brown [then the Cleveland Browns head coach]. And he's smarter than anyone."[14]

Being unemotional was a strategy for Coach Landry. He said he didn't believe you could be emotional and concentrate the way you must to be effective. When he saw a great play, he couldn't cheer or get emotionally involved. He said he needed to focus on the next few of plays and come up with the strategy for the plays to be called.

Like many who played in his day, Landry served in the military during World War II. After one season at University of Texas, Landry joined the Army Air Corps and served as a lieutenant and B-17 co-pilot. He completed 30 missions aboard Flying Fortress bombers. During one mission, his plane ran out of fuel and had to crash land in Belgium. Landry downplayed the dangers of that part of his life. After the service, he returned to Texas as backup quarterback to Bobby Layne. The next year, he moved to fullback and played on teams that won back-to-back bowl games, the Sugar Bowl in 1948 and the Orange Bowl in 1949. He played one season with the New York Yankees in the AAFC before joining the Giants in 1950.

Back to the 1958 title game, the Giants got the ball back and Charlie Conerly came into the game. All season long, Lombardi made it a standard practice to alternate his two quarterbacks. Don Heinrich played the first quarter with Conerly observing on the sidelines. Then they traded places. The senior of the two players, Conerly joined the league in 1948 after four years of college and three years as a marine in the South Pacific, where he saw combat at Guam and Iwo Jima. He started his professional football career as a 27-year-old rookie. He looked older than the rest of the players then, but as his hair prematurely turned silver and his face bore lines of experience, his classic good looks earned him the role as the first Marlboro man. He never received any payment or mention in the ads. The advertisers just wanted an average guy with good looks to sell men on smoking a filter cigarette. Marlboro cigarettes, first introduced in 1924, spent three decades considered a "ladies' brand." Advertisers selected the male models to convince men that smoking a Marlboro cigarette with a filter was manly.

On his first play of the day, Conerly completed a pass to Mel Triplett. The Giants begin to show their first signs of life on offense as Gifford ran around the left side for a 38-yard gain down the sideline. Then Giants kicker Pat Summerall kicked a 36-yard field goal and New York took an early 3–0 lead. At the end of the first quarter, the Giants had scored three points and the powerful Colts had committed three turnovers. The normally explosive Colts offense managed only one first down the entire quarter.

The Giants opened the second quarter with a mistake of their own. Conerly threw to Gifford in the flat, but he fumbled when Ray Krouse hit him. The turnover gave the Colts the ball in excellent scoring position. Just five plays later, with the ball on the Giants' 20 yard line, Alan Ameche carried the ball into the end zone. With the extra point, the Colts took a 7–3 lead. During the drive, Lenny Moore injured his back when Sam Huff slammed him to the turf. Moore told Ewbank that the pain gave him trouble catching the ball. Ewbank encouraged him to continue to play, as long as he could endure the pain.

"We'll use you as a decoy," said Ewbank. The coach knew he needed the threat of Moore running deep patterns to keep the Giants defense honest. Without Moore, the Colts might have crowded the line of scrimmage. Moore, the 1956 NFL Rookie of the Year, gave the Colts an excellent offensive threat operating on the flank and out of the backfield. He contributed 1,638 combined net yards and 14 touchdowns in 1958 as the Colts galloped towards their first championship. The Giants had to send two men out to cover him.

The Giants could not move the ball so Don Chandler punted to defensive back Jackie Simpson, who dropped the ball. The Giants recovered the ball on the Colts' 11 yard line, putting them in scoring position. On first down, Gifford ran the ball around the left side. Hit by Milt Davis, Gifford fumbled the ball and the Colts' Don Joyce recovered it. Back-to-back fumbles increased the turnover count to seven very early in the game.

In the second quarter, a brief skirmish occurred after Sam Huff tackled Raymond Berry near the Baltimore bench. Weeb Ewbank thought the hit excessive and threw a punch at Huff. The 51-year-old Colts coach, who stood 5-foot-7, charged at the man many considered one of the most physical players in the game. It was a bizarre scene with the short, stout coach challenging the big bad linebacker.

"Huff hit Raymond late," Ewbank explained. "Our equipment man went after him and then I did. I can't fight, but I was pushing and shoving. After the game I saw Bert Bell, the commissioner then, and I apologized for doing that, but Bert said, 'the officials were lousy.'"[15]

"I looked at him and popped him on the chin," said Huff about Ewbank. "If they hadn't pulled us apart, I would have hit him again because I didn't like the way I got him. I wanted to cream him. I was wild."[16]

The Colts went to halftime with a 14–3 lead. In the locker rooms, the coaches planned for the second half. Weeb Ewbank told his Colts they could not let down. He warned the Colts that the opposition had many talented players and not to count them out of the game. The Colts had some good fortune and benefited from two turnovers.

Meanwhile, the Giants coaching staff encouraged their players. Turnovers helped the Colts get their points, they said. Lombardi told the Giants offense that he planned to have Conerly throw the ball more in the second half as the Colts had bottled up the ground game. Landry discussed plans to put more heat on Unitas, who had not felt much pressure in the first half. Landry said they would continue to double team Lenny Moore, still unaware of the speedy receiver's back injury.

The Giants were cornered. The Colts came out with a two-score lead and a desire to put the game out of reach. They moved the ball the length of the field as Unitas threw crisp, on target passes. Their offense clicked, taking only five plays to get to the 1 yard line. They had four plays to move the ball one yard and put the game out of reach. A 21–3 lead would prove difficult for New York to recover from. The Giants' defensive front four stiffened. Two runs up the middle by Ameche and a quarterback sneak by Unitas could not advance the ball. On the critical fourth down Ewbank decided to go for the touchdown.

Unitas had a play in mind. The Colts stood fourth-and-goal on the 3 yard line. In the huddle, Unitas called "Flow 28," an option pass around right end with Ameche carrying the ball but looking to throw it into the end zone, a play they had not showed in a game all season. Unfortunately, Ameche did not hear the call in the huddle and thought Unitas called a standard sweep without a pass option. As tight end Jim Mutscheller slipped off his block to position himself in the end zone to catch a pass, Giants linebacker Cliff Livingston dropped Ameche for a loss at the 5 yard line. Had Ameche looked for the pass, Mutscheller would have scored. Instead, the Giants took over at the 5 yard line.

The goal line stand energized the Giants. Momentum immediately shifted to New York. They had an opportunity and needed to take advantage of it by scoring some points. Two plays netted only eight yards. The Giants faced third-and-two on their own 12 yard line. Conerly thought the Colts would anticipate a safe run. Instead, he faked a handoff and fired a 30-yard pass to Kyle Rote at the Giants' 42. Rote broke free and was clearly headed for a touchdown when Andy Nelson caught him. During the tackle, Nelson knocked the ball from Rote's hands. The ball bounced free until Alex Webster scooped it up on the run and rambled to the 1 yard line. It may have looked like simply a lucky bounce, but as the Giants' top play of the day, it covered 87 yards. Two plays later, Mel Triplett charged into the end zone and Summerall's extra point cut the Colts' lead to 14–10. Now, we had a ball game, as announcers might say.

Alex Webster may have lacked the speed that Gifford and Triplett brought to the game. He did excel on third-down situations. Jim Lee Howell liked to call his number on third-and-short because he would reliably pick up the first down. An excellent receiver and blocker his teammates called "Big Red," Webster had one main weakness; he smoked a lot. He would even sneak a cigarette on the sidelines by pulling his hooded jacket over his head so he could not be seen smoking.

This unsung runner came up with the big run that put the Giants back into the game. The Giants had regained momentum due to the unusual 87-yard play. It had to hurt the Colts defense, who had bottled New York up for most of the day. Now the Giants trailed by only four points. Their strong defensive line had not had much success getting heat on Unitas but the goal line stand turned the momentum. They now had confidence they could stop the Colts' explosive offense.

Conerly led them on a drive mixing up passes to Gifford and Rote with runs by Gifford and Webster. He threw back-to-back passes to tight end Bob Schnelker for 17 and 46 yards. Soon it was first-and-10 on the Colts' 15-yard line. Conerly and Gifford executed a perfect double pump play. Conerly pumped the ball as if to pass to Gifford in the flat, pulling cornerback Milt Davis up aggressively. Gifford accelerated, breaking away from Davis. He caught Conerly's pass along the left sideline and ran into the end zone untouched for the go-ahead score. The Giants now led, 17–14.

One of the interesting battles along the line of scrimmage came between Giants defensive end Andy Robustelli and Colts offensive tackle Jim Parker. The two future Hall of Famers engaged in a fierce battle all afternoon. Robustelli came to the Giants from the Rams in 1956 and quickly made New York's defense one of the best in the league. Social scientists would make judgments on the battle between an Italian immigrant and an African American. Football purists saw two talented players facing off. For most of the game, Parker controlled the pass rushing Robustelli.

"Parker, in only his second year in the league, already had established himself as a superb drive-blocker, but his domination of Robustelli was something different, a performance so smooth, so complete, that it was used as a textbook case for many years," wrote Paul Zimmerman in Sports Illustrated. "He takes an outside rush, you run him around the corner; he goes inside, you collapse him into the pile."[17]

Parker later called it the most perfect game he ever played. Robustelli gave most left tackles fits and was an important member of the Giants who had also played on a championship team with the Rams. "In '56, my wife was pregnant and almost due," he recalled. "It was summer, and I had to report [to Rams training camp]. I called and asked if I could get about an extra five days to stay home. Sid Gillman was the coach, and he said no. He also said he'd fine me for every day I was late. Well, I told him I wasn't coming and a few days later they traded me to the Giants for a number one pick."[18]

Giants vice president Wellington Mara saw an opportunity and made the most of it. In those days player holdouts were extremely rare. When he heard the All-Pro defensive end from Connecticut might be available, Mara called the Rams and acquired Robustelli. He immediately fit in the defense and provided excellent leadership. A veteran player who had won a championship on the West Coast, Robustelli impressed the Giants coaching staff as the missing piece the Giants needed to complete for a title. He immediately gained the respect of his teammates.

"If we had a smart-mouthed kid on the squad," recalled teammate Alex Webster, "Andy would take him alone in a corner and when they came back the kid would be shaking and he'd call everybody 'sir' for the next year or so."[19]

Robustelli grew up in a poor immigrant family in an integrated neighborhood in Stamford, Connecticut. His father was a barber and his mother a dressmaker. Robustelli recalled the family was very poor and that they lived in a house with four black families; his was the only white family.

From those humble beginnings, Robustelli learned the lessons of hard work and developed a toughness that prepared him well for life. Robustelli played college ball at a school that didn't offer scholarships—Arnold College in upstate New York. As a rookie in 1951, he replaced an injured Jack Zilly and started every game for the Rams. He always played the game with great passion. With that passion, he raised the play of those around him. In this game, he had to play against All-Pro tackle Jim Parker of the Colts. Parker's job was to keep players away from John Unitas and Robustelli's job was to harass Unitas. The entire game two talented All-Pros battled for supremacy.

Meanwhile, Colts Hall of Fame defensive end Gino Marchetti felt ready for the challenge. A veteran leader of the Colts defense, Marchetti too, had served in the military. He fought at the Battle of the Bulge in Belgium during World War II. He left high school and enlisted in the Army on his 18th birthday. Marchetti took the war personally. His family emigrated from Italy. When the war broke out, the United States government ordered his mother to relocate and closely monitored her movements since she lacked citizenship papers. Marchetti's patriotism drove him to enlist and his dedicated service earned freedom for his mother.

At 31 years old with a wife and three children, Marchetti lived in Antioch, California, during the offseason. There, he worked with his brothers in the family gas station. Marchetti witnessed middle guard Joe Campanella join his former Ohio State teammate Lou Fisher to open a small hamburger place in July 1956. Alan Ameche opened another restaurant he named Ameche's. Marchetti had worked in restaurants and hoped to one day have one of his own. Carroll Rosenbloom, the Colts' owner, encouraged Marchetti to capitalize on his celebrity and convinced him to go into business in Baltimore, where he had developed a name.

He took the owner's advice and opened a chain of fast-food restaurants along with Ameche and Fisher. Loosely modeled after McDonald's, they gave their restaurants a distinctive name to capitalize on celebrity. Gino's Hamburgers started in Baltimore, Maryland, in 1957 but quickly expanded with more stores. At their peak, they had more than 350 stores before they sold out to Marriott Corporation in 1982. Marriott converted them to Roy Rogers restaurants.

Back in the game, Marchetti watched the Giants line up and started to anticipate the play to come. He figured the Giants would run to the opposite side of the field. They would not want to challenge Art Donovan and himself, who were routinely All-Pros in the league. He wanted to get off the ball quickly, chase it down from the backside and prevent the Giants from getting the critical first down. The Giants faced a third down and four yards to go on their own 39 yard line. A first down would allow them to maintain possession and kill the clock.

The Giants had all three backs—Webster, Tripplet and Gifford—in the game. Conerly handed the ball to Gifford, who started right and then cut hard behind his teammates. Marchetti chased him. As Gifford cut back, Marchetti fought off a block by Bob Schnelker and lunged for Gifford. Both players fell to the ground. Soon, several Colts including Gene "Big Daddy" Lipscomb, the 285-pound defensive tackle, piled on to prevent Gifford from wiggling free and gaining more yards. All that weight came down on Marchetti, who had landed awkwardly. He cried out in pain as his ankle broke. Play stopped as the trainers carried him off on a stretcher.

"We ran a 47 Power on third-and-four," Gifford said. "A running back knows when he gets a first down. I did not even look to the sidelines. I just knew I had it. Then I heard someone yell. It was a frightening yell—you knew someone was badly hurt. It was Marchetti. [It] turned out he broke his leg. They had to stop the game and carry him off the field. The official didn't pay attention to where he marked the ball. When they measured, we were short. I was stunned."[20]

Referee Ron Gibbs spotted the ball. He held his hands about half a foot apart signaling to the Giants bench that Gifford had not made the first down. Gifford said the referee concentrating on Marchetti forgot where he'd put the ball. He said he saw him get confused by what foot he had marked the yard and he put the ball down in the wrong spot.

"There's no question in my mind that I made it," Gifford said. "But before I could even complain about it, Ronnie Gibbs called out 'fourth down.' There was nothing I could do. And complaining about the call wouldn't have made any good."[21]

The officials called it fourth down, spotting the ball inches short of a first down. New York Giants head coach Jim Lee Howell had a difficult decision to make. If the Giants could pick up the first down, the game was virtually over. That presented a tremendous risk because, if they missed it, it would give the Colts the ball back with two minutes to play and excellent field position. Howell played it conservative and sent the punting team on the field.

Did Gifford gain enough yards to achieve the first down? An ESPN special that aired on the fiftieth anniversary of the game used modern technology to determine if Gifford made the first down. They, too, said he got close but that the officials did not err when they marked the ball short of the required yardage.

With Gifford's run short of the first down, the Giants punted to the Colts. They started the drive on their own 14 yard line. Trailing 17–14, they needed to travel 86 yards in about two minutes against the best defense in the league. To make matters worse, the Giants had not allowed the Colts to score in the second half of the game.

The wind picked up trash from the stands and blew it across the playing field as the Colts offense took the field. Unitas calmly came into the huddle and confidently told his teammates they could drive the length of the field to win the game. On the first play, Unitas looked deep for Mutscheller but he overthrew the ball. On second down, Unitas looked for Dupree on a circle route. This time the ball fell short and incomplete. The situation appeared bleak. On third down, Unitas spotted Lenny Moore and threw the ball so low only Moore could catch it. Despite his sore back, Moore brought the ball in for a first down.

The Colts still had 75 yards to go with time running short. Unitas called two plays in the huddle with Berry the first option on both plays. When the game came to critical moments, the extra practice time paid off for Unitas and Berry. Defensive coach Tom Landry anticipated Unitas would look for his favorite receiver so he had linebacker Harland Svare walk out and line up over Berry. The Colts had never seen the Giants deploy their linebackers in such a way during the film study preparing for the game. It was not something they normally did.

Of course, Landry did it for exactly that reason. He knew Unitas was a smart and always well-prepared quarterback so he wanted to try something different. He positioned one linebacker in a spot that he had not done before and wanted to see how they would adjust. Anything unexpected might cause confusion. Landry had to try something Unitas had not seen in the films. He thought he might have the strategy to outsmart Baltimore's receiving duo. Landry figured the best time to deploy this tactic came with the Colts in a hurry to get plays run and time running out.

Unknown to Landry, during one of their many training sessions, Unitas and Berry had discussed that very defensive formation. The two players regularly stayed after practice to work on their crafts. That time together gave them the opportunity to discuss strategies that might come up in unique game circumstances. One day, Unitas said to Berry, "What if a linebacker like Joe Schmidt was standing right over the top of you? What would you do?"

"That has never happened," Berry replied.

"What if he does?" Unitas kept on his receiver.

"I guess I'd give him an outside fake like this, try to make him come after me, then jump underneath him like this."

Unitas nodded that he understood Berry.

It took two years but during the final minutes of the title game with the Colts trailing by three points, Berry looked up and there stood a linebacker. It wasn't Joe Schmidt of the Lions, but Harland Svare of the Giants. Out of the corner of his eye, Berry looked toward Unitas who saw it, too. He remembered the conversation and smiled back at Berry.

Both players had stored that discussion in their memory just in case it ever came up. Just as they had discussed, Berry gave Svare the outside fake and cut over the middle. Unitas put his pass right on the mark and the Colts gained a first down to keep the team advancing toward a tie and sending it to overtime.

"We had a common bond in wanting to do extra work, which just didn't happen very much," said Berry. "It's rare to have players willing to do the 'extra extra.' Unitas and I were both that way. Our work ethic would be extremely significant to our being able to work together so well over so many years. We just did it naturally without thinking about it a whole lot. It allowed us to do things as a quarterback-receiver combination that went beyond the norm."[22]

Unitas and Berry had a connection right from the start. When Unitas arrived at Colts training camp, he noticed something right away. The young receiver carried a football everywhere he went. That wasn't what attracted his attention. He noticed something else about the receiver's hands. There was something unusual about the little finger on his left hand. It did not seem to work along with all the rest. Berry had broken that finger on his left hand in high school.

During his youth, Unitas had accidentally put a .38 slug through the index finger of his right hand while cleaning a pistol. His mother, frequently out of the home working one of her two regular jobs, had purchased a revolver to keep the family safe. One day, Unitas attempted to clean it. He safely removed the clip, but pulled the trigger before checking the chamber. One round fired and went right through his right index finger. Doctors saved the finger but he was never able to bend the first joint of that finger the rest of his life.

Unitas and Berry had a connection with their hands. They both had hand injuries that made them a little different from everybody else. Even before they had met, they had something in common. Over time, their shared work ethic and desire to improve reinforced and solidified the connection.

Raymond Berry, a 20th-round draft choice following his collegiate career at Southern Methodist, wasn't particularly big or fast. Stories abounded about his bad back and poor vision. Since he did not have tremendous athletic abilities, Berry knew he needed to put in extra work to improve his production. His dedication went beyond the extra practice sessions. He continued to search for anything that would help him gain an advantage. He found the standard issue football pants too heavy and too binding so he searched out lightweight material and had his own pants made. He washed them himself so he would not risk losing them. He did whatever it took to find an edge and the lighter material might provide a fraction of a second advantage against the defensive back. That fraction of a second could create an opening.

In the end, Berry was a perfectionist. A sideline exchange summed up how Berry saw the game. During a game in 1957, Ewbank saw something that the Colts could capitalize on. During a timeout, he explained the play to Unitas and Berry.

"That should give us a touchdown," Ewbank said with excitement.

"I'm sorry but I can't do it," Berry said to a surprised Ewbank.

"Why not?"

"Because I haven't practiced it," Berry said.[23]

Down to seconds remaining in the championship game, Unitas again called two plays in the huddle. The Colts could not afford to waste any time. Worst case, they needed about 20 more yards to get into field-goal position and tie the game. The Colts still thought of moving the ball across the goal line and achieving an outright victory. Now Unitas planned a surprise against his wary opponents. He knew that they anticipated a sideline route that enabled his receiver to catch the ball and get out of bounds, thus preserving a timeout. Instead of a down-and-out to the sidelines, Unitas called for a down-and-in pattern. He knew the defense did not expect a pattern run across the middle and it might be wide open. Berry cut to the center of the field and caught Unitas's pass, gaining another 15 yards.

Since the clock did not stop, the Colts went straight to the line of scrimmage. Once again, Raymond Berry's very meticulous preparation before every game paid off. When he walked the Yankee Stadium turf before the game, he found the wet spots. As he approached the line of scrimmage, he saw defensive back Carl Karilivacz standing in one of those spots. Berry knew the temperature drop would make the spot slippery now. Berry ran his route and caught the ball right in that area that had started to ice over. He cut sharply. Karilivacz attempted to catch him, but slipped. Berry ran free towards the end zone, only to end up being caught at the 15 yard line.

Those three passes from Unitas to Berry moved the Colts 65 yards closer to a championship. Only 15 seconds remained in the game. The Colts hurriedly sent the field-goal team onto the field. The center snapped the ball. Backup quarterback George Shaw held it and Steve Myhra kicked it. The ball sailed through the uprights to tie the score at 17 points each. Some fans at home wondered what would happen next. Some of the players on the field were confused with what would happen next. For the first time, an extra period would settle the championship.

A lengthy battle between commissioner Bert Bell and the owners had put the overtime rule into place. It sounds hard to believe today, but some owners had resisted putting that rule into effect. In 1946, the commissioner persuaded the NFL owners to pass an overtime rule for playoff games but the rule had not come into play until the 1958 title game.

In homes across the country, America witnessed this unique event. An estimated 45 million watched the game, more than had seen any other football game in history in part due the rarity of live broadcasts of sporting events. Now early evening on the East Coast, the game approached primetime when even more viewers might discover the close contest's exciting final moments. Pro football moved into a new phase of its life and the 1958 title game launched that move.

The officials called the captains to the middle of the field for the coin toss. Co-captains Kyle Rote and Bill Svoboda represented the Giants. Unitas went out for the coin toss since captain Gino Marchetti lay in the locker room with a broken leg suffered during Gifford's critical run. Unitas lost the toss to the Giants, who chose to take the ball. Future Hall of Fame receiver Don Maynard muffed the kickoff but covered the ball on his own 20 yard line. The Giants took the field hoping to stop the Colts' momentum, score some points and end the game.

Gifford ran four yards on first down. On second down, Conerly's pass fell incomplete. Facing a critical third down, Conerly could not find an open receiver and attempted to run for the yardage. The Colts defense stopped him a yard short of the first down. After only three offensive plays in overtime, they had to turn the ball over to the Colts.

Baltimore, fresh off a huge drive that tied the game, still felt the momentum. Unitas handed off to L. G. Dupree on first down for a gain of 11 yards. Next, Unitas attempted the same long pass to Moore that had worked earlier in the game. This time, Lindon Crow knocked the ball out of Moore's hands. It rolled to the turf incomplete.

On second down, Dupree ran the ball again. The Giants defense stopped him for only a two-yard gain. This set up a critical third down from the 33 yard line. The Giants figured that Unitas would look for Berry again as he ran a deep pattern. Instead, Unitas threw a swing pass to Ameche in the flat. He rambled eight yards and a first down.

Unitas's calm, confident demeanor spread to the entire team. His trademark icy composure and fierce competitiveness spanned his entire career. In his mind, he saw this drive as easier than the last one. Now he had plenty of time. He could mix passes and runs. He did not need to worry about stopping the clock or calling certain patterns to conserve time. With time not an issue, Unitas had the entire playbook available. He did not need to rush.

Dupree got the carry on first down and gained three yards. Unitas attempted to pass but tackle Dick Modzelewski sacked him for an eight-yard loss. That sack put the Colts into a third-and-15 situation. Unitas dropped back to pass and found Berry open about 20 yards downfield. First down. Now the Colts had the ball at the Giants' 44 yard line.

Aware that Landry taught his players to read keys and study film in order to stay ahead of the offense, Unitas called unexpected plays to break the tendencies. Those plays caught the Giants off guard because they did not follow established patterns. "He called his own plays and he was totally unpredictable, which was what made him great," said Pat Summerall. "Coach Landry played defense based on percentages, but you couldn't do that with Unitas. He had the soul of a gambler. On third-and-one, you wouldn't get a running play."[24]

"John would sometimes make calls in games against us that just didn't make any sense at all," recalled Los Angeles Rams defensive tackle Merlin Olsen. "But everyone on his team believed they were brilliant calls. Another quarterback could have called the same plays and ten guys would have looked at him as if he was from Mars. And the plays wouldn't have worked."[25]

Those calls worked against the powerful Giants defense. Sensing the Giants were looking for the Unitas-to-Berry combination once more, Unitas called a trap play up the middle with Alan Ameche. The middle of the field lay vulnerable after the passes to the flanks caused the linebackers to shift outside just slightly in order to stop the outside play. After taking the handoff, Ameche raced 24 yards down to the 20 yard line. Although the Colts were within Myhra's field-goal range, Weeb Ewbank did not want to take that chance. He knew of his kicker's inconsistency so he called for caution while still attempting to score a touchdown. There was not any need to rush. In short, they were not interested in kicking the field goal.

"In overtime, all we were thinking was touchdown," recalled Berry. "People ask all the time, why not just kick the field goal when we got down there, but a field goal never entered our minds. We already had had one blocked that day, so we were just very confident we could take it all the way.... Weeb did not have confidence in Steve Myhra kicking the winning field goal, plain and simple. They blocked one and we weren't even sure how they did it."[26]

On first down, the Colts ran outside for no gain. On the next play, Unitas went to Raymond Berry, who caught the ball falling down. Realizing no one had touched him, he got up and lunged for additional yards. He went down for good at the 8 yard line. The Colts had a first down, but, more importantly, the ball moved closer to the goal, shortening a potential field-goal attempt if they needed to use that option. At that critical moment, television sets went dark.

An equipment failure caused NBC to lose its broadcast signal just as the game moved to its climactic finish. Viewers at home sat at the edge of their seats wanting to see how the game ended. Stan Rotkiewicz, a quick-thinking NBC employee standing on the sidelines, pretended drunkenness and ambled on to the field. Game officials stopped play while security officials worked to get him off the field. The pretend drunk fan weaved across the field in an attempt to take as much time as possible. The delay helped the broadcasters. Meanwhile, NBC engineers traced the issue back to a loose cable. They fixed it and the game came back on the air. Despite not being able to see any action for two and one-half minutes, fans did not miss anything of consequence. When the game came back on, the game remained tied with the Colts threatening to score with the ball near the goal line.

On first down, Ameche gained one yard up the middle. A pass to Mutscheller on the right sideline gained six yards before he slipped on the slick field and went out of bounds. It was third down with one yard to go. If unsuccessful with the touchdown attempt, most fans figured Baltimore would kick a field goal on fourth down. It was sudden death so the first points—regardless how they were scored—would win the game.

Unitas knew that Giants All-Pro defensive tackle Rosey Grier left the game injured earlier so he called a play that double-teamed his replacement, Frank Youso. Grier originally hurt the knee the week before the during the playoff game against the Browns. He told the coaching staff before the game that he could not push off or have the strength he normally played with. Unitas noticed a replacement player along the defensive line and suspected he could take advantage.

In the huddle, Unitas called "16 Power," an off-tackle play to Alan Ameche. The play, common for the late fifties, took the big fullback they called "The Horse" through the center of Giants defense. If he succeeded, it meant sudden victory for the Colts. "In the third period we had been turned back at the goal line on four downs," said Mutscheller. "The Giants assumed we were going to do the same in overtime and jammed the middle. It was off-tackle instead. We blocked down to prevent penetration. Alex Sandusky and George Preas, on the right side, blocked to their inside, and this provided the opening for Ameche to score."[27]

Was it really the greatest game ever for 68 minutes of play? That point is open for debate. You cannot get much more excitement than the way it ended as the first championship game to go into overtime. That excitement generated by the climactic end of the game made it memorable for those watching at home. It also attracted the largest television audience, making the game a breakthrough moment for the league. More people witnessed that one game than any other in history did at the time. The networks liked what they saw, too. Roone Arledge, the legendary name in televised sports and architect of *Monday Night Football*, called the game "a defining moment in the growth of pro football. [After that] the networks all of a sudden woke up and saw that they had to have football."[28]

Famed football writer Tex Maule gushed about the 1958 championship game in his article titled "The Best Football Game Ever Played" in *Sports Illustrated*. He said there were countless high points. Maule's view summed what many Americans who witnessed the first overtime contest felt. The dramatic comeback mounted by the Colts and a thrilling overtime session left fans wanting more.

The "greatest game" featured eight fumbles in all; the Giants had six, losing four while the Colts lost two. Statistics do not tell the whole story behind the game. It became historic as the first overtime game. The ending left everyone who watched it, minus the true Giants fan, feeling they had witnessed a thrilling contest. The fact that the game ended with two two-minute drills, one in regular time and the other in overtime, added to the history. Years later, Giants owner Wellington Mara said Rozelle told him the game was critical. "Pete Rozelle always told me that the reason pro football took off was because that happened just at that time, in that season, and it happened in New York."[29] The game featured 17 future members of the Pro Football Hall of Fame. Many in the national television audience saw it as the beginning of a new chapter for the National Football League.

"After the game, I saw Bert Bell outside Yankee Stadium and he had tears in his eyes," Raymond Berry said. "And I wondered why he was crying. Then I realized that the baby he had been nursing had been born that day."[30]

Chapter Three

The First Star

The 1958 championship game catapulted Johnny Unitas into the national spotlight. He led his team on two impressive drives, one to tie the game and the second to win the first overtime game in NFL championship history. Called "The Greatest Game Ever Played," that contest sparked the increased popularity of football that followed in the 1960s. His calm demeanor during those stressful drives earned him instant media attention.

As professional football turned from the fifties to the sixties, Unitas became the first star of the era. How could he be anything else? He quarterbacked the Colts to two straight championships in 1958 and 1959. His crew cut hairstyle gave him the look of a Norman Rockwell character come to life. Off the field, he looked anything but the part of a professional quarterback. With a slender build, hunched shoulders and black high-top cleats, Unitas did not look like the prototypical tall, muscular quarterback on the field either.

As a child, he suffered through two mishaps. At age seven, he and some other boys tried to get a shotgun shell to explode. They threw rocks at it until it finally exploded and the lead hit Unitas in the knee. Doctors got most of the fragments out, but ten years later, as he cleaned a revolver it went off, nearly removing his right index finger. Unitas, turned down by all the big schools, settled for a second-tier college. After college, drafted late, Unitas never got to take the field with that team. His professional career seemed over before it had a chance to start.

"He was bowlegged and slope-shouldered, he looked like a physical wreck, but, man, could he play," said Giants linebacker Sam Huff. "One time when I was playing for the Redskins, I called nine different defenses. He beat all nine of them. I didn't want to call any more defenses because nothing worked against him."[1]

The Pro Football Hall of Fame named Unitas one of the three quarterbacks they selected to an All-Decade team of the 1960s, joining Sonny Jurgensen and Bart Starr. Over his career, he led the Colts to three championships and became league Most Valuable Player twice. He played in 10 Pro Bowls and earned a spot on the all-time NFL team. In 1958, as the Colts played in their first championship game, Unitas completed only his third season with the Colts.

Some may not recall that Unitas played the 1958 championship game under a handicap. He needed to wear a special brace to protect his ribs. Earlier in the season, while scrambling against the Packers, he received a hit so hard in the back he suffered three broken ribs and a punctured lung, sending him to the hospital. The situation fostered

Unitas's reputation as a tough player after he returned to action just two weeks later. His heroics at the end of the title game marked the beginning of Unitas's career as a star on the national stage. His life started about as far away from celebrity standing as possible.

John Unitas entered the world May 7, 1933, as the country struggled to get out from under a rough depression. Like many other families in western Pennsylvania, the Unitas family struggled financially. Francis and Helen Unitas, John's parents, owned a small coal delivery business. In those days, coal was the primary way people in that part of the country heated their homes.

In 1938, John's father, Francis, just 38 years old, caught pneumonia and died. At the funeral, family members expressed concern over how Helen could raise four children by herself. Some recommended splitting up the family, sending the kids to live with various relatives. Others suggested sending the kids to an orphanage. Helen refused to hear any of that talk. Determined to keep the family together and with her oldest child only 10, Helen hired a driver to make the coal deliveries. To make extra money, she worked nights cleaning office buildings, leaving the children in the care of a 70-year-old single uncle.

Despite the difficult times, John Unitas grew up and made it through high school. Not a great student by his own admission, John had his greatest success on the football field. In his junior year, James "Max" Carey started as head coach of the Saint Justin high school team. Coach Carey had a big influence on John. Carey's calm demeanor made him unique as a head football coach. While most football coaches of the day screamed constantly on the field, Carey stayed relatively quiet. His demeanor could best be described as businesslike. Carey's calm attitude worked well with Unitas who responded positively to it. His play improved under Carey's quiet teaching.

Carey taught Unitas to make the calls for the offense. He told his young quarterback he would turn those responsibilities over to him under one condition. John needed to be able to explain the logic behind every call he made. That simple request made John learn the game with greater depth than he would have otherwise. He developed great football intelligence. He could see what the defense planned and call something that exploited their weakness.

Despite a solid high school career, John did not receive many offers to play quarterback in college. Most recruiters thought the skinny young man who stood less than six feet tall did not have the size to play at the major college level. Unitas had a tryout for Notre Dame assistant coach Bernie Crimmins, but the player's size hurt him during the audition. He stood about 5-foot-11 and weighted only 135 pounds. Coaches worried that he would get hurt.

Unitas had heard it all before. When he tried out for the high school team, coaches doubted he could play at that level, too. Unitas did not give up. His persistence drove him to become the starter at the high school level and he used that same determination to believe in himself at the collegiate level. He believed he could earn the starting job despite his lack of ideal size.

Like Notre Dame, Indiana University turned him down due to his size. Some suggested his size made him a better fit for Ivy League schools but his academics did not meet those standards. The University of Pittsburgh offered him a scholarship, but Johnny failed the entrance test. Meanwhile, football programs on many college campuses tried to continue the progress made immediately after the end of World War II. Schools such as Louisville had some success with players coming back from the war. Now they struggled to maintain that progress.

Frank Camp, head coach of Louisville at the time, had brought the T formation to the school at a time when many programs still ran the single wing. To assist in the conversion to the T formation, he recruited Frank Gitschier from the coal mining towns of western Pennsylvania to run the offense. Gitschier, who hailed from Sharon, Pennsylvania, had played quarterback at Louisville during his collegiate playing days. In 1949, he led the Cardinals to an 8–3 record.

Similar to his high school career, Unitas's overall college career proved less than spectacular. He had some good games during his junior and senior seasons, but did not capture a national following. His Louisville team lacked talent, a long way from being a powerhouse of college football. Their only winning season came in Unitas's first year. The school did not belong to the NCAA at the time. Only a couple thousand fans attended most games. Unitas had a dream of playing professional football but feared the league didn't see him since he played at Louisville.

Unitas worked hard in the weight room to gain strength. He started college at 140 pounds and ended at nearly 185 pounds. On the field, he practiced ever harder to better his quarterbacking skills. Camp had taught Gitschier the finer points of quarterbacking during his time at Louisville from 1946 to 1949. Gitschier, in turn, passed that knowledge on to Unitas.

The hard work and preparation appeared to have paid off when Pittsburgh drafted Unitas in the ninth round of the 1955 draft. He was the 102nd player selected that year. The Steelers mailed Unitas a $5,500 contract, which he signed immediately. Of course, he needed to make the team before he could earn any of the money. That never happened. The three other quarterbacks in Steelers camp in 1955 were Jim Finks, Ted Marchibroda and Vic Eaton. Two of them, Finks and Marchibroda, would have long NFL careers as players and afterward.

Jim Finks played seven years in the league. After his playing career, he had a successful career in the front office. As the general manager of Vikings, Bears and Saints, he turned losing franchises into winners. In the mid-fifties, Finks started at quarterback for the Steelers.

Unitas recognized the current backup quarterback. Ted Marchibroda played quarterback for St. Bonaventure in the game that earned Unitas the starting job at Louisville. Marchibroda, who finished his career at the University of Detroit after St. Bonaventure gave up football, led the nation in total offense at Detroit. A first-round choice of the Steelers in 1953, he left the league after one season for a year of military service. Upon his return, he joined a crowded backfield at the Steelers with the two rookies.

Other than the experienced veterans, Unitas faced rookie competition. The Steelers drafted Vic Eaton of Missouri two rounds and 24 selections after Unitas. He was the other rookie quarterback challenging for a roster spot. Eaton could also play defensive back and punt so his versatility gave him an edge over Unitas for the last roster spot. Steelers president Dan Rooney had quarterbacked the 1948 North Catholic High School team in Pittsburgh that lost to Unitas while he played at St. Justin's. Impressed by Unitas in high school, Rooney wanted to see him to get an opportunity with the Steelers. During summer camp, however, Unitas threw more to the Rooney boys than to teammates.

The Rooney family had owned the Steelers ever since 1933 when Art Sr. founded the team with the purchase of a $2,500 franchise. Rooney decided to start the team after the repeal Pennsylvania's blue laws. Laws prohibiting business on Sunday would have made it impossible to survive in the NFL. Rooney long loved sports. He played football against Jim Thorpe, led the Middle Atlantic baseball league in batting and boxed professionally. A self-made businessman, he also loved to bet on horses at the racetrack. Art had five sons, Dan, Art Jr., Tim, Pat and John and they all shared his love of sports.

He often stood at the end of the practice field, not tall but impressive just the same. Art Rooney had the look of a man in charge. He had a cigar in his mouth, but never seemed to smoke it. A close inspection proved the end in his mouth a mangled, chewed-up mess. A chunky man with shaggy eyebrows and thick, white hair combed back, Rooney referred to himself as Art, but many others called him Chief. His nickname, never said to his face, came from his resemblance to Perry White, the editor-in-chief of the *Daily Planet* in the *Superman* stories.

Walt Kiesling was serving his second stint as head coach of the club during Unitas's brief time with the team. Kiesling had first coached the team during the World War II era. He returned as head coach in 1954. As a former lineman who had a Hall of Fame career in the 1920s and '30s, he preferred the ground game to a passing attack. He coached the last pro team to run the single wing offense, a run-dominated offensive attack. The Steelers ran an offense where the quarterback needed to call formations and blocking assignments and Kiesling believed the rookie lacked the capability to handle the play-calling responsibilities.

Kiesling would not even let Unitas take any snaps, even in practice. Instead, the young signal caller had to throw to the Rooney children on the sidelines. Unitas threw to Tim and the twins, Pat and John. The boys knew he could throw the ball. "He would tell them to run as far and as fast as they could," said Art Jr., "and he'd hit them on the head with the ball. His accuracy was incredible. I'd watch him throw for hours and it made me sick to think that Kies wasn't giving him a look."[2]

Without even the chance to throw a ball in an exhibition game, the Steelers released Unitas. He got $10 bus fare to get back home. By that time, John and his wife, Dorothy, had one child and a baby on the way, so he hitchhiked home and pocketed the travel money. In another twist of irony, the Steelers held training camp at St. Bonaventure University, the site of Unitas's first collegiate football success. When he got home, Unitas got a construction job and played semipro football for the Bloomfield Rams for six dollars a game. He continued to wait and hope for another shot at the National Football League.

Some might see it as a big step down from an NFL tryout to a semipro team. Unitas was not through with football and, with a young family at home, he needed money. Unitas made $11 an hour to work as the monkey man on a pile-driving crew. His job involved climbing 125 feet up the rig to grease the equipment that created 50 tons of pressure every time they drove the corrugated pipe into the ground.

Cleveland head coach Paul Brown told Unitas he might get an invite to Browns training camp prior to the 1956 season. Then another opportunity came up. The Colts needed a backup quarterback. Head coach Weeb Ewbank heard about Unitas and arranged a spring workout. Unitas was signed after the Colts received a letter from a fan telling them there was a player in Bloomfield deserving a chance. Ewbank, maybe half-joking, accused Johnny of writing it. For confirmation, Ewbank sought the opinion of an old friend, Frank Camp, who saw Unitas play four seasons at Louisville.

Ewbank felt convinced he found his backup quarterback after watching the workout. The coach liked Unitas's poise and the way he threw the football. Ewbank signed Unitas to a contract. Sure, he saw Unitas as a skinny, hunched over, pigeon-toed player, but he also saw a good passer who seemed in control of the team on the field.

That same year that Unitas went 102nd in the draft, George Shaw was the first overall pick as the Colts' bonus selection. Clearly, they planned for Shaw to take the starting position in Baltimore. When Shaw went out at the beginning of the 1956 season with an injured knee, Unitas took over. According to the often-repeated tale, his pro career did not start well. The legend says a nervous Unitas had his first pass intercepted by Bears' J. C. Caroline, who returned it 59 yards for a touchdown. On the next drive, he bumped into his running back and fumbled the ball. He fumbled again on the next drive. In all, Unitas threw two interceptions and fumbled twice. Three Unitas mistakes cost the team three touchdowns. The Bears won, 58–27.

The Baltimore Sun later determined Unitas's debut occurred October 6, 1956, when he came into a game against Detroit Lions on a foggy afternoon at Memorial Stadium. The game came two weeks prior to the Chicago game. Starter George Shaw struggled and Unitas entered the game in the final minutes of a 31–14 loss. He had his first pass fell incomplete. Then he ran 21 yards. Later, Detroit's Jim David picked off his desperate pass as the game ended. History had said and Unitas confirmed that the Bears' J. C. Caroline picked off his first pass, but the newspaper challenged that story.[3]

John Unitas kept his cool and rebounded. He finished the season strong and made the Pro Bowl the next season. The following year, 1958, saw him reach superstar status, leading the Colts on two drives to win the title game.

The Baltimore Colts gave Unitas the perfect opportunity. The roster was full of tough war veterans such as Gino Marchetti and Art Donovan on defense. He needed to prove to them that he could handle the starting quarterback job. "On the bus going back to the airport that day a couple of players told me he wasn't acting like some [rookie] free agent who just got his first chance and blew it. He was acting like 'I'll learn from it.' He was able to will the fact that he was going to be successful. It was just unique. I've never been around anyone quite like him," said Ernie Accorsi of the *Baltimore Sun*.[4]

Raymond Berry joined the Colts in the summer of 1955, the same year the Steelers drafted then released Unitas. Berry only caught 13 passes that first season, but then Unitas joined the Colts in 1956. Berry saw them as two unproven players trying to make a living playing football. Both stood as long shots with Berry a 20th-round selection and Unitas a free agent given a second chance by the Colts.

In three years, Johnny Unitas had taken an incredible, almost unbelievable, journey. From 1956 to 1958, he grew from a man without a job to the biggest name in professional football. This journey started on a dirt football field in suburban Pittsburgh and reached the apex in New York as his team won the title and the attention of millions watching at home.

Prospects looked good for the Colts to repeat as champions in 1959. The key players that paced the offense all returned: Unitas, Berry, Moore and Ameche. The defense did not get the attention that the Giants defense did, but the Colts also had a strong unit. Up front, Gino Marchetti, Art Donovan, Big Daddy Lipscomb and Don Joyce did not give the opposition quarterback much time to pass the ball. Backed by a solid group of linebackers and savvy group of defensive backs, they also didn't give running backs much space to run. Most sportswriters anticipated a rematch between the Colts and Giants in 1959 and they got it. They clearly were the two best teams in the league.

The Giants started the 1959 season with six wins in seven games. They finished with a 10–2 record and possessed a defense near the top of the statistics. The opposition could only manage an average of 14 points against the stout Giants defense.

At midseason, things did not look so good for the Colts. They struggled in November with back-to-back losses. Nearing the midpoint, the Colts had a 4–3 record. Unitas caught fire and set the team back on course. They swept their final five games. Statistically, Unitas threw for 2,899 yards, 32 touchdowns and only 14 interceptions.

The rematch was on. The media touted the game as a clash between two of the best quarterbacks in the league. Thirty-eight-year-old veteran Charlie Conerly would take the field against the star of the 1958 game, Johnny Unitas. The teams played the 1959 championship game in Baltimore's Memorial Stadium. On game day, Unitas went through his usual routine. He arose at 7 a.m. like every other game day and attended early Mass at Immaculate Conception Church. Then, Johnny watched over his two youngest children while his wife took the two older children to church. Upon their return, he left for the stadium.

Some observers had downplayed the Colts' victory in overtime the year before so the Colts wanted to win this game outright and leave no doubt as to the better team. The Colts defense, highly motivated, wanted to prove they could play on the same field with their Giants counterparts. They felt the media had overlooked the strength of their unit in the comparison with the Giants defense.

The first three quarters saw a tight back-and-forth contest. Then, Unitas got the comeback started with his feet rather than his arm. He faked a handoff to the running back and carried the football into the end zone to take a 14–9 lead. The Colts defense stiffened and the offense turned it up another gear. The fourth quarter belonged to the Colts. They scored 24 points in the final stanza to win with by a lopsided score of 31–16.

Unitas and the entire Colts team earned reputations as everyday guys. Many believe that Unitas took on a superhero quality not only based on his play on the field, but by his everyday man attitude off the field. He did not look like the classic American sports hero. Unitas and the other Colts lived just like their fans. They went to church, took care of their children and acted neighborly when spotted across the city. They stopped to talk and even signed an autograph or two when asked.

Weeb Ewbank and John Unitas had a good relationship. If Ewbank didn't rush over to correct a player for a mistake, his quarterback would do it. From the start, Unitas took control of the offense. He saw it as his team out there on the field and he wanted every member of the offense to play up to his standards. If they let down, he let them know it. Unitas called the plays. Very seldom would Ewbank offer a suggestion. Unitas knew his business when it came to calling plays. He liked to set the defense up. He planned ahead for a play call he would save for the right moment. Coaches sending in plays only seemed to disrupt the order of his play calls. Ewbank sat back, let Unitas work and offered suggestions only when needed.

Colts players recall Ewbank, a nervous wreck on game days, meeting with Unitas on the sidelines during a timeout.

"Whad'ya got?" asked Unitas approaching Ewbank on the sidelines.

"Whadda you got?" the coach relied.

"Ah, c'mon, Weeb…"

"Well, John…"[5]

Ewbank would hesitate on which play to call, and Unitas would finally say, "I'll get the first down," and head back on the field. Players recalled that a typical of the sideline conversations between Unitas and Ewbank.

"Nobody was going to call the shots but Johnny," said Lenny Moore. "He proved he

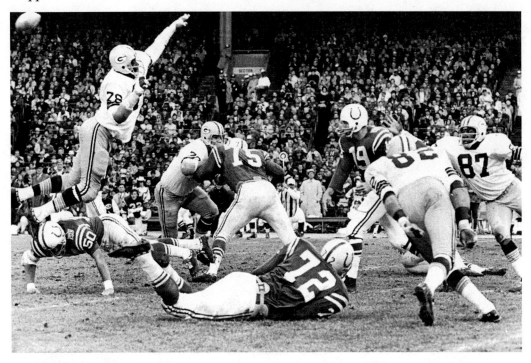

Green Bay Packers defensive end Bob Brown (78) goes after Baltimore Colts quarterback Johnny Unitas (19). Unitas held the record for most consecutive games with at least one touchdown pass for five decades until Drew Brees broke it in 2012 (Photofest).

was capable of being able to handle that. The thing with him is if you thought he was going to do something, he would not do it; if you didn't think he would do something, he would. Unpredictable, and sometimes he would call things right off the wall. All he was doing was playing the defense, setting something up."[6]

After a 7–7 season in 1962, the Colts fired Ewbank. That action disrupted the calm of Unitas's world. Ewbank allowed Unitas tremendous freedom on the field to make calls he felt necessary. Sometimes they came with risk and Ewbank understood the way Unitas played. Unitas's former teammate, 33-year-old Don Shula, replaced Ewbank, thus becoming the youngest head coach in the league.

Shula started his professional career with the Cleveland Browns in 1951 as a defensive back and later played four seasons with the Colts before he left for one last season with the Redskins in 1957. When he moved into coaching, he wasn't much older than many of the players playing for him. His youth made the hire a controversial one. Before his coaching career ended, Shula became the coach with the most NFL victories in history. In 1995, Shula finished his 33rd season as an NFL head coach with 347 career wins, including playoffs. Back in 1963, no one knew the young man starting out in his first head coaching job had that kind of future.

Unitas and Shula had a lot in common. Both Catholics who regularly attended Mass, they had both grown up in immigrant families. Shula's father emigrated from Hungary at age six. Unitas's mother came from Lithuania. Unitas's father died when he was five years old, leaving his mother as the head of the house. Shula had a loving father but, looking back, said his mother ran the house. She was a take-charge woman, he told people.

Their biggest difference involved their tone. Unitas, quiet by nature, stood as an opposite to the loud and direct Shula. That difference sparked the fire. Unitas did not like Shula's yelling. "I'm about as subtle as a punch in the nose," Shula like to say.[7] Over his playing history, Unitas performed best when playing under a low-key coaching style. His early development as a quarterback came under the calm direction provided by Max Carey at St. Justin High School. Frank Camp at Louisville continued in that same manner, as did Weeb Ewbank. Shula gave Unitas his first experience with a coach who was a screamer.

Shula liked to control things. Bob Griese, who played for Shula years later with the Miami Dolphins, saw that taskmaster at work when he took over as coach from George Wilson. "Under Shula, there were assigned parking places," Griese said. "There were assigned seats on the bench."[8] Assigned seats on the bench? That sounds like a coach who controls every part of his players' lives. In fact, he had a list of rules related to off-the-field matters. Shula proved even worse when it came to on-the-field matters. He wanted every player technically sound and every execution perfect.

Shula's management sharply contrasted with the freedom Weeb Ewbank provided his star quarterback. Weeb not only left the play calling to Unitas, but nearly everything done during the game. "On game day Weeb really left if all up to Unitas," said running back Tom Matte. "There was a conflict later on because Shula wanted to control more of the game, and John didn't want anything to do with it. He'd say, 'You run the defense. I'll run the offense, and leave me alone.' They meshed as best they could, but there was always an underlying tension there."[9]

Unitas saw himself as the field general that controlled everything on the field. He called the plays and on game day, he stood in charge. Don Shula, as the head coach, stood as supreme commander in charge of the whole team, including Unitas. That status trumped Unitas. Working together proved a big challenge. Unitas and Shula mixed like oil and vinegar. Both of them had strong Type-A personalities. Unitas would get mad if Shula called a play. "Don would send in something he wanted, and if John didn't think it would work, he wouldn't call it," said Lenny Moore. "They had their differences."[10]

Unitas felt he had complete control on the field. He did not allow any players to speak in the huddle. One incident summed up Unitas's control. In one game, Unitas called six straight plays with Moore carrying the ball. Moore felt winded and told Unitas, "Hey, man, cool it. I'm getting tired." Unitas stared back into the runner's eyes with indignation. "Listen," he said firmly. "Nobody tells me to cool it. I'll run your ass until you die."[11]

Unitas had complete confidence in his ability to read the defense and make the right call. Sometimes he made risky calls hoping to catch the defense off guard. A reporter asked what happened if Shula did not agree with his call. "If he [Shula] doesn't like the plays I call, he has another quarterback siting right there on the bench," said Unitas. "He is paying him good money. He can send him in."[12]

Struggles between coaches and players were not that common during the early sixties. Coaches ran teams as a general would lead his army. Players had little to no voice in anything done with the team as the sixties began. The general attitude among coaches was clear: It was their way or the highway. One of the first man who ruled with an iron fist came to pro football in 1946.

America, as a whole, began the decade in a similar way. Black Americans had few rights in the Jim Crow South. Young adults expressed strong feelings for greater freedom as the decade continued. Protests over sexual freedom, civil rights and the Vietnam War all took center stage during the decade.

Chapter Four

The First Tyrant

The 1962 season had been over for three weeks when Cleveland Browns owner Art Modell called team founder, head coach and general manager Paul Brown into his office. Modell, an advertising executive from New York City, had purchased the team two years earlier for $4 million. Modell reportedly pulled together $225,000 of his own money, borrowed some more and sought the rest from investors. On completion of the sale, he had plunged headfirst into the job by moving to Cleveland and running the team.

Paul Brown, in the mind of many, *was* the Cleveland Browns. He served as the first head coach when the team started in 1946. He built the team from scratch by recruiting all the players. His contributions to the game are endless. Brown made coaching a full-time, year-round occupation. Before he came around, the head coach would head home during the offseason and not return until training camp. He changed that. Brown pushed the mental side of football with film review, classroom sessions, note taking and tests.

Brown, a slender, balding man, took all aspects of the game seriously. He made varied and significant contributions to football. Coaches today follow many of the methods Brown started decades ago.

He introduced sophisticated pass patterns to take advantage of holes in the defensive secondary. His passing attack began the West Coast Offense, according to Bill Walsh, the man credited with creating that offense. "The genealogy of the 'West Coast Offense' started with the legendary Paul Brown, for whom I worked in Cincinnati from 1968 to 1975, and with the offensive genius of Sid Gillman," he admitted.[1] Walsh worked for Paul Brown in Cincinnati when Brown came back to the NFL to start the expansion Bengals. Brown later brought his Cleveland playbook with him to Cincinnati.

Brown innovated changes in many areas, including equipment enhancements (facemasks) and communications systems (helmet receiver to facilitate play calling). Perhaps the first head coach to play such an active role on game day, Brown insisted he stood in a better position to call plays from the sidelines than the quarterback on the field did. The idea seemed radical at the time but quickly spread to other teams. Why do football scouts time football players running 40 yards? Because that is what Paul Brown said to do. He said that was the distance players had to run to cover a kickoff or punt. The league keeps that method so they can compare players from one year to another.

The last thing Paul Brown wanted was an active owner. He achieved success because he controlled everything that had to do with the Browns. As with all the successful coaches of the era, Brown figured control served as an essential ingredient to guarantee success on the field. Paul Brown wanted to direct all the activities and all the individuals in order to mold that group into a team focused on a single goal.

Paul Brown grew up with football in the state of Ohio. He started as quarterback on his high school football team in Massillon, Ohio, a real hotbed for football. They loved their Tigers. Massillon had a tremendous high school football program and a professional team, both named Tigers. After high school, he also started two seasons at quarterback for Miami University in Oxford, Ohio, despite only weighing 154 pounds. His smarts were not limited to playing field; he showed those smarts in the classroom, too. Brown qualified for a Rhodes scholarship as a senior in 1930, but he had married his high school sweetheart, Katie Kester, the year before and needed to find a job. He took a coaching job at Severn School, a prep school in Maryland instead of going to study at the prestigious university in England. After two years, he returned to Ohio to take a job coaching his old high school team.

Brown dominated high school football after returning to home to coach the Massillon High School Tigers in Ohio. Just 24 years old and two years out of college when he took the job, Brown built successful teams. The Tigers went to six straight Ohio high school football championships from 1935 to 1940. At Massillon, his teams outscored opponents by an overall margin of about ten to one.[2] In 1940, his high school team scrimmaged the Kent State University football team. Apparently, Kent State stopped the contest in the fourth quarter after Brown's team scored 50 points.[3]

"It was at Massillon that Brown's innovative nature took root," Ernie Palladino wrote. "Every aspect of Massillon's football program was planned, from how each session of practice would be conducted to classroom lectures and film work. He also made sure that a cadre of assistant coaches would install his system in Massillon's junior highs so the players would already know it when they reached high school."[4] That is the level of control Brown exercised.

After such tremendous success at the high school level, Brown moved to the Ohio State University where he led the Buckeyes to the school's first national football championship in 1942, his second year with the program. They won despite fielding a young team consisting of three seniors, sixteen juniors and twenty-four sophomores because of graduation and military duty.

When World War II started, many football players and coaches joined the war effort. In 1944, Brown received a commission as a lieutenant in the United States Navy and went to the Great Lakes Naval Station where he coached against other service teams and college programs. They finished with nine wins, two losses and one tie during the 1944 season. That record helped the team achieve a No. 17 ranking in the final Associated Press poll. In 1945, they beat a good Notre Dame team, 39–7. Each step in his coaching career only improved his reputation as a top coach. He is the only coach known to have won national championships at the high school, college and professional levels.

As the war wound down, Arch Ward looked to get into professional football. He knew many other business executives who had the same desire. Ward worked as the sports editor of the *Chicago Tribune*, but, when it came to sports promoting, he excelled. He created the Major League Baseball All-Star Game, the Golden Gloves amateur boxing tournament and the College All-Star Game in football where college seniors played the reigning NFL champions. Ward became such a big name in sports the NFL offered him the position of commissioner. He turned it down and, after feuding with some of the

NFL owners, decided to challenge the league instead by founding the All-America Football Conference (AAFC) as a competing league.

Arthur McBride, nicknamed Mickey, loved sports, particularly boxing and baseball. He knew little of football until his son, Arthur Jr., attended Notre Dame and he went to the games to watch him play. After watching, he decided to offer to buy the hometown Cleveland Rams team from Dan Reeves, but Reeves turned him down. When Reeves announced his intent to move his team to Los Angeles, Ward approached McBride with an offer of an AAFC franchise in his hometown of Cleveland and he immediately accepted.

McBride wanted to enter the Cleveland market with a splash, so he hired Paul Brown. The former Massillon High School and Ohio State coach had to be the most popular coach in Ohio. He still had a commitment to the service coaching Great Lakes. That did not stop McBride. He made Brown an offer that started paying him before he left the service. That deal secured his services when the war ended. While still in the service, Brown started looking for talent. He planned to make the Cleveland franchise (at that point unnamed) a huge success. He immediately went to work at building a championship team.

Anyone evaluating the first four years of the team had to admit the Cleveland Browns had success. From 1946 to 1949, the Browns won 47 games with only four losses and three ties. They won four straight AAFC championships. NFL fans, who considered the AAFC a minor league, said that would all change when they joined the National Football League. It did not change. They won their first NFL title in 1950, their first season in the league, giving them five straight championships. That kind of success puts them in the same category as dominant teams from other sports: New York Yankees (1949–53), Boston Celtics (1959–66) and Montreal Canadians (1956–60).

One might have thought Paul Brown owned the team; how else did the team get that name? According to the team website, McBride ran a newspaper contest to select the name of the new team. Many entries suggested he name the team after the popular coach from Ohio who he had already hired to direct the team.

The winning entry suggested the Cleveland Panthers. However, a semipro team called the Cleveland Panthers had operated in the 1920s and still owned the rights to the name despite the fact they no longer played. When Paul Brown heard that former team had perennially lost, he objected strongly. He did not want any association with a name that once belonged to a losing team, never mind that licensing the name would be expensive.[5] McBride authorized a second contest and claimed that many entries came in with a catchy name tied to the boxing champion of the day, and they had their winner. Brown wanted a name that sounded like a champion. "Joe Louis was the best known champion at the time," Paul Brown put forth at the time, "and we received a lot of entries suggesting we name the team the Brown Bombers. So we decided to shorten the name and call the team the Browns."[6] Brown, apparently uncomfortable with the idea of of having a team named after him, stuck to the story for years, but both the Hall of Fame and the Browns organization dispute it today and acknowledge that the team was indeed named after its first coach.[7]

Coach Brown may not have owned it outright, but he ran the team as if he did. Arthur McBride repeatedly said Paul Brown had complete control and did not answer to anyone, including himself. Paul Brown had the ideal situation. He wanted complete control and Arthur McBride wanted someone to run his team. It was an ideal situation for both men. McBride never interfered with Brown, which was exactly to his liking.

When McBride started looking to sell the team in the early sixties, Brown should have known things would change. His introduction to the professional game came with McBride, a laid-back owner who wanted the coach in charge of the whole operation. McBride wanted one man in charge of everything and Paul Brown welcomed that authority. McBride saw himself as a silent partner content with staying in Brown's shadow. Brown did not want any part of an owner who wanted an active role like Modell desired.

Actually, Brown owned approximately 15 percent of the team. Those shares earned him a nice profit; one published report said he received $500,000 for his share of the team when Arthur Modell's group purchased the franchise from McBride.[8] He also received a guaranteed contract worth $82,500 a year for the next eight years. This came about in 1961, a time when professional football really had not achieved the level of success it has today and coaches did not command such big salaries.

A big man in pro football when pro football wasn't big, Paul Brown won seven titles in 10 years after starting the team from scratch. The first four titles came in the AAFC where the Browns franchise began. That league collapsed and the National Football League absorbed some of the teams. The AAFC failed at least in part due to the Browns' dominance. Most critics felt the AAFC played inferior ball and, even though the Browns dominated play in that league, they could not compete with teams in the NFL. The Cleveland Browns quickly put that discussion to rest.

The Browns defeated the NFL defending champion Philadelphia Eagles, 35–10, in the first game of the season. Otto Graham passed for 346 yards and three touchdowns. The Browns went on to finish 10–2 in their first season in the National League. They defeated the Giants in a playoff and played in the NFL championship game against the Los Angeles Rams, which they won, 30–28. The first game and last game the Browns played that year definitely silenced the doubters. They continued to challenge for the NFL title in the next few seasons in the league. They played in the title game each of their first six seasons in the NFL and won championships in 1950, 1954 and 1955.

On the sidelines, Coach Paul Brown stood expressionless looking almost like a professor watching his class take a test. A slender man who always dressed in a neat business suit, he appeared quiet, but he left no doubt that he held complete control. He won those titles by controlling everything. The fifties were an era dominated by military-style coaches who ran programs with strong discipline. Paul Brown exercised even more control than the average head coach did. Players would tell you that the coach virtually ran their lives. He made them wear coats and ties to road games. He established rules such as no alcohol and staying out of bars. Before the season started, he informed the team of the Tuesday rule, which called for abstinence from sex after that day so they would be well rested for the game on Sunday. He said they could not smoke or drink. He wanted them aware of their public image. Above all, they needed to act like professionals.

"If you did your job, he never said a thing," said receiver Dante Lavelli, an original member of the Cleveland Browns. "He never swore at you. If you did something wrong, he'd bore right through you with those beady eyes and tell you off. After he left the practice field, he'd never hold a grudge against you."[9]

Brown believed in organization as the first key to building a successful team. Then, like a military general who drilled his troops repeatedly, he worked his team during practice to make them well prepared for anything they might face. The emphasis on organization and planning stayed with Blanton Collier who coached with Brown at Great Lakes in 1945 and stepped in as the first assistant coach hired when he started the Browns. The two coaches worked together until Collier left for the head coaching job at the University of Kentucky in 1954.

"Everything was planned to the most minute detail," Collier said. "For the first four or five years of the eight I was with him in Cleveland, each player and each coach wrote everything that was in the playbook. I mean, we sat there and wrote down what he dictated to us."[10]

Brown liked smart players. He looked for that quality when he scouted and talked to prospects. Nearly every player on the team had a college degree. For the few that did not have one already, he added a bonus to their contract providing an incentive after they earned a degree.

Brown coveted Bernie Parrish as one of those smart players. A terrific athlete, in 1958 Parrish signed with the Cincinnati Reds to play baseball for $63,000, which was the equivalent of $570,000 today. He played one summer of baseball and figured out that he missed football. Brown met Parrish and saw his combative personality as better suited to football than baseball. He used a ninth-round pick to get Parrish who became a tough cornerback and an important member of the Browns defense.

"Bernie was a cerebral player," said one teammate, linebacker Galen Fiss. "You have to give him a lot of credit for getting our defense to watch more films. He was the kind of guy who took films home at night, which wasn't done that often back then. He'd watch them over and over. He'd track his receiver's tendencies. Before every game, he'd tell us that a certain receiver would go to the sidelines X times, he'd go deep Y times, and he'd go to the post Z times. It reached a point where he forced most of us to watch more film to keep up with him."[11]

Every year at the beginning of training camp, Paul Brown gave a speech. In it, he laid out the rules under which the Cleveland Browns organization would operate for the year. It did not change much year to year. Some of the veterans could repeat the speech nearly word-for-word. Coach Brown started with positives. He told the team they had joined a very successful franchise. In 1958, he told the group that the team existed 13 years and they won division titles in 11 of them. He said they were among the best sports franchises in all sports.

"You must watch how you dress, your language, and the company you keep," he emphasized. "When we're on the road, stay away from that stranger who may want to take you to dinner or to talk to you in the hotel lobby. Maybe he isn't a gambler or after information, but stay away from him anyway."[12] Throughout the talk, he would lay out the rules that the team operated under. He said if he heard of a player drinking, he would call them out in front of the whole team. He continued with the rules.

During training camp, Brown said players needed to be in their rooms at 10 and lights out at 10:30. Sometimes the coaches make a bed check. Anybody caught sneaking out would receive an automatic fine of $500. No exceptions. In short, Brown wanted his players to act in a professional way. He had high standards and he insisted that his players live up to them. In a way, he also had expectations when it came to the owner. Brown did not need or want an active owner getting in the way. Paul Brown controlled everything and he wanted things to stay the same. Despite what he wanted, things changed.

Brown trained his players as if they attended school. They each had notebooks and he expected them to take notes. The handwriting had to be neat. He often collected the books without notice and checked to make sure each player took clear and concise notes that made sense. In the classroom, he assigned seats making it easy to tell at a glance if anyone was missing.

Things in Cleveland started to change in the fall of 1960 when a young advertising executive in New York City heard of a professional football team for sale. Arthur B. Modell, a huge football fan, frequently told his friends that he dreamed of owning a professional team. One of those contacts heard that McBride had put the Cleveland Browns on the market and immediately called Modell. He wasted no time. The advertising executive arrived in Cleveland the following day. He offered nearly $4 million for the franchise with a $500,000 down payment.

Modell formed a syndicate with R. J. Schaefer, owner of the Schaefer Brewing Company of New York, his primary partner. By next spring, that syndicate owned the Cleveland Browns. Modell, the son of a wine dealer who had gone bankrupt during the depression and left his family virtually penniless, stood as a modern-day success story. As a youth, Modell lied about his age to get a job as an electrician's helper to help support the family. After a stint in the Air Force during World War II, Modell returned and worked in the new world of television. He first created a daytime television program aimed at women. After that program ended, Modell turned to advertising. All the while, he built a career and a small fortune. A sports fan, he readily turned his attention to the world of professional football.

Modell came to his new role with a clear desire to take an active role. He put a positive spin on it. He made it sound like he and Brown would share responsibilities for running the team. Modell said Brown would run the football operation while he would run the business end. That talk was not reassuring to someone like Brown, who ran it all. The Modell-Brown relationship did not start on the right foot. Brown saw Modell as a man with zero experience in pro football. He did not want someone with zero football experience encroaching on his turf messing everything up. Worse yet, he did not have time to train a new owner in the business of football.

"It was partly his own pride that caused confrontations in Cleveland when Art Modell secured control of the Browns in the early 1960s," said author Jack Clary. "There is little doubt that Brown resented a newcomer—and a non-football person at that—becoming involved in the day-to-day operation of the team. This was something that had been his domain since the club's founding in 1946 and a position that he was unwilling to share."[13]

Another concern quickly arose. Modell, young and a huge football fan, tended to side with the players. Closer in age to the players and, like many of them, single, Modell frequently went to nightclubs where single young men the players' age went. He often took them to dinner and bought them alcohol. That was an issue. Drinking violated Brown's rules for players. Brown did not want his players drinking and he did not want them to act unprofessional in public. Hanging out in a bar drinking alcohol did not fit the image Paul Brown wanted for his players. The new owner not only took away Brown's control, he made a mockery of his discipline.

Modell moved from New York into a bachelor pad in Cleveland where loud music and plenty of eligible females became the norm. Had Modell been a player rather than an owner, Brown would have talked to him, reminded him of the rules, and issued a fine or suspension. Brown could not do much about his owner's disagreeable lifestyle.

"The cavalier lifestyle of the Browns' new owner troubled Brown," wrote Andrew O'Toole in his biography of Paul Brown. "Modell's freewheeling carousing was one thing, involving players in these antics was quite another. Modell frequently disregarded Brown's wishes and invited players out on the town. Modell flaunted his complete disregard for Brown's ban on alcohol for Cleveland players. This blatant breach of etiquette outraged Brown more than any of the owner's various transgressions."[14]

Sometimes, what Modell said also bothered Coach Brown. At his first press conference, he slighted him when he called Jim Brown his right-hand man. Then he started the bravado by promising a championship. "The new owner saw that as simple huckstering, almost required salesmanship, to drum up interest and ticket sales," Jeff Miller wrote. "The old coach saw it as a noose around his neck in the event that the Browns didn't win a title and fans demanded an explanation."[15]

"Going into training camp in 1962, I had never felt so uncomfortable," said Paul Brown. "The complete control and authority I had once held over [the players] had worn dangerously thin…. The players had begun to react more to what Modell said than to what we tried to tell them."[16]

Jim Brown had his poorest season with the Browns in 1962, and Coach Brown leveled the blame at the feet of his owner. He said part of the reason was his freewheeling attitude of independence fostered by Brown's relationship with Modell. Paul Brown believed in control and discipline. In his mind, those qualifications had helped turn a bunch of individuals into a solid professional football team. Now, his new owner undermined his control and ruined his discipline. To Brown, things had changed for the worse. As the sixties began, attitudes across the country started to change. Over his long coaching career, Brown had always exercised complete control. Now he found that control in jeopardy with a new, young owner undermining discipline.

In his 1979 autobiography, Paul Brown devoted an entire chapter to his falling out with Modell. Brown wrote that the new team owner plotted to get rid of him from the start and intentionally established an atmosphere that sowed discontent among the coaches and players: "During my two years between his coming to the Browns and my dismissal, I lived through a period of almost constant 'intrigue.' Player was set against player; the loyalty of my coaching staff was questioned, and attempts made to find out which ones were 'Paul Brown men'; public criticism of my coaching staff was encouraged among the players and steadfastly carried on by management through the media."[17]

The firing shocked the football world. When anyone thought of the Cleveland Browns, they thought of Paul Brown. This innovative coach developed many of the coaching techniques used by pro coaches today. He started the whole concept of classroom sessions with playbooks, offseason quarterback camps and intelligence testing. These techniques remain today. He called the offensive plays from the sidelines. He would shuttle the plays in by substituting guards as messengers. He did this during an era when quarterbacks routinely called their own plays.

He wanted his players to study the game and his coaches to work as teachers. He deployed six assistants instead of the usual two to facilitate instruction that is more individual. He expected players to take notes, study and know the materials. He gave tests to evaluate the lessons. Some claimed to have seen extensive cheating on those tests. Jim Brown admitted as much in his autobiography, *Off My Chest*. Coach Brown reasoned that if the players needed to write out crib sheets to help them during the test, the repetition in writing the notes helped them learn the lesson.

"Paul understood and respected the way men learned," said Bill Walsh. "He made sure that every one of his players knew exactly what was expected of him, not only in the plays he ran on the field, but in the other aspects of life, too. He put it all right on the table and his methods were proven by his success."[18] Super Bowl–winning head coach Bill Belichick agreed with Bill Walsh. He credits Brown with inventing modern football. Belichick referred to the extensive scouting and the studying of game film. Belichick valued scouting; Brown invented it. In 1962, Steve Belichick, Bill's father, wrote *Football Scouting Methods*, which was regarded as one of the premier books on the topic of football scouting.

Brown used game film to scout the opposition. He believed in gaining whatever intelligence he could on the opposition. He found creative ways to gather intelligence on the opposition even before game film. When he coached in high school and did not have the luxury of game tape, he would send 11 scouts to watch the opposition. Each scout watched one position on the field. The scout responsible for watching the right guard took notes on this one position on each play. It served the same purpose as watching and rewinding the tape to see every player on every play.

Brown did not want to leave anything to chance. He wanted every situation covered in the practice sessions so his players had the necessary preparation when they took the field. He saw a new open substitution rule as an opportunity to get more involved with the play on the field. During the fifties, coaches coached during the week, but the players were in charge during the game. With the quarterback out on the field and substitution limited on Sundays, the quarterback ran the show. Communication between player and coaches was limited to timeouts. Rules opening up substitution of players gave Coach Brown the option of sending in a replacement player with the play he called from the sidelines. To confirm his thinking, Brown stood behind center during practices so he could take the view of the quarterback. How much of the field could he really see? He grew certain he could do better than a quarterback in a cluttered pocket could by gathering all the input from his staff.

"I have a lot of help during games—the other players, a spotter upstairs, the other coaches. I should be able to tell what the situation is much better than the man playing the game," Brown told Jack Newcombe of *Sport* magazine.[19] Brown started calling the plays by rotating messenger guards into the action. The guards carried the play to the quarterback.

In the spirit of continuous improvement, Brown wanted a better way to send in a play from the sidelines without shuttling players in and out of the game. If only he could transmit the play to the quarterback directly, he thought without having to relay the play and make the quarterback wait for the players to run onto the field. He came up with the idea of using a shortwave radio to send the plays into the game. This method would enable Brown to call plays from the sideline without rotating players. The lack of players moving into and out of the game might give the opposition pause wondering who called the plays. Coach Brown figured he could speak into the transmitter and a tiny receiver in the quarterback's helmet would enable the quarterback to hear his words directly.

Paul Brown obtained a shortwave license to operate the radio and tried it for the first time during the 1956 exhibition season. It had mixed results. At times, they had very good reception and other times not. Interference from other local shortwave operators proved disruptive. As with any new technology, they needed to work out some bugs. Brown experimented with the transmitter during preseason games.

The big test came with the regular season encounter with the rival New York Giants. The Browns said the radio did not work well that day. The Giants said they could intercept the transmissions and that forced Brown to give up the new technology. After that game, many of the other league owners, including George Halas of the Bears and George Preston Marshall of the Redskins, went to commissioner Bert Bell and asked him to ban the devices. A telephone poll taken of all 12 teams resulted in the commissioner immediately implementing a ban on their use.

In 1995, the NFL allowed quarterbacks to receive communication from the bench using a small transmitter in their helmet. Teams had tried it during the preseason the previous year. A decade later, in 2008, the NFL expanded the technology to allow one defensive player to have the same capability in his helmet. Brown may have failed with his attempt at transmitting plays into the game, but his method eventually became the norm once the technology caught up. Now it is commonplace to see coaches with headsets and quarterbacks listening for the call to come in. Paul Brown was 40 years ahead of his time.

The question of who was better suited to call plays followed Paul Brown his entire career. In the mid-seventies, sportswriters still asked him about not letting his quarterbacks call their own plays. At press conference after press conference, they asked the same question: Why did he think a coach could do better calling plays then a quarterback on the field?

"Let me ask you one," said Brown back to a reporter. "What's the first thing the quarterback does after he takes the snap?" Brown paused for a second as if to let the reporter answer, but then continued. "He turns his back on the field. Because we know what's coming, all of the coaches, upstairs and down, can concentrate on the point of attack, see exactly what happens and get ready for the next call."[20]

Brown created another device that had longer staying power—the facemask for the helmet. In the early fifties, players did not wear masks to project their faces. In a game late in the 1953 season against the 49ers, quarterback Otto Graham saw his receivers all covered and was forced to scramble. When tackled, he received a hit in the face from a defender's elbow that opened a huge gash. With his mouth bleeding, Graham had to be helped from the field. He needed 15 stitches to the inside of his mouth to stop the profuse bleeding. Once his star quarterback was stitched up, Brown wanted him back on the field but the injured area needed protection. He directed the team equipment manager to put a primitive clear plastic strip on Graham's helmet so that it would serve as a protection for his face. Graham returned to action in the second half, completing 9 of 10 passes in the Browns' 23–21 victory.

The players in the league first used Brown's Lucite design. They quickly determined the facemasks too brittle to wear safely. The Lucite would shatter upon impact, and people would get cut or get the fragments in their eyes. Brown realized the initial design needed improvement, but felt sure about the basic idea. Since the clear plastic could crack and break in cold weather, Brown wanted to attach a single iron bar to the helmet from ear to ear. The bar was devised to keep errant elbows or feet away from the player's face while not obstructing the player's vision. To get this done, Brown contacted a friend who worked for helmet maker Riddell and asked that they manufacture something that stretched across the front of a helmet about as big as his little finger. The helmet manufacturer configured a mask exactly as Brown had prescribed.

After Modell fired Coach Brown, Jim Brown exercised more freedom. When he joined the Browns in 1957, the veteran black players told him to keep quiet and play hard. He said that is how he started his professional career, but it did not last his entire career. "For a considerable time I played the part of the big dumb fullback as well as I could, which is to say with a maximum of physical effort and a minimum of dialogue," wrote Jim Brown in his biography.[21]

Throughout the sixties, many things changed in professional football as they did in society in general. As the game increased in popularity, players became stars. In Cleveland, they influenced the dismissal of a head coach. The accused leader of the player revolt, Bernie Parrish, wrote a tell-all book about it. Things definitely changed in professional sports. Some might consider it ironic that the coach who helped integrate the game ended up ousted at least in part due to a player uprising possibly organized by black players such as Jim Brown. Paul Brown did not view players as black or white. He looked at them based on their ability to play the game. Mike Brown, Paul's son and current president of the Cincinnati Bengals, said he had always had black players on his roster when he coached below the professional level.

"When he coached at Massillon High School, he had many black players on his teams," Mike Brown recalled. "When he coached at Ohio State, he had many black players on his team. When he coached in the service, the same thing was true. When he got to the Cleveland Browns, he looked around and he knew where he had better football players than he had with the Browns. [They were] guys who formerly played for him."[22]

Andrew O'Toole, who wrote an autobiography of the famous coach, did extensive research on his role in the reintegration of the National Football League. He views the Cleveland Browns coach as on a par with Branch Rickey who integrated Major League Baseball by signing Jackie Robinson. Jim Brown, Cleveland's legendary fullback who played six seasons under Brown, said Brown was not an idealist on racial matters.

"Paul was a top business person who was driven to setting up an organization that would be the best in the world, utilizing the best personnel, developing the best devices to win," Jim Brown said. "Color never came into his philosophy—neither positive nor negative. The way he carried his organization was that everybody was afraid of him, so you didn't have any dissension."[23]

When it came time to recruit players to fill his Cleveland roster, Coach Brown looked for players he knew well, regardless of color. In many cases he drew players familiar from his football past in Ohio. In 1945, he went back to his roots to search for players. He even upset his old bosses at Ohio State by signing some players with eligibility remaining. They had left school to fight in World War II so he convinced himself of the legitimacy of signing them to professional contracts despite eligibility left in college.

Brown knew Bill Willis and Marion Motley well from his days coaching in Ohio. Bill Willis had played on the national championship team at Ohio State in 1942. Motley had played for Canton McKinley High School, a rival to Brown's high school teams. He had also played fullback on Brown's team at Great Lakes Naval Training Center.

Willis was an All-American playing for the Buckeyes, a college football powerhouse in those days. He came off the ball scary quick playing in the interior of the defense. Motley, meanwhile, played out of the limelight at the University of Reno before the war. Willis nearly got away from Brown. He had agreed to play in Canada but had not yet signed the contract.

At 6-foot-2 and 199 pounds, Willis played middle guard in the five-man defensive line utilized during the era. His exceptional quickness allowed him the ability to cover the entire field. "I was fairly fast for a middle guard," recalled Willis. "At Ohio State and with the Browns, I used to run the sprints with the backs. I think a lot of times Paul would do that just to embarrass some of the backs."[24]

When Paul Brown welcomed Willis and Motley to his team, he opened a door previously closed to men of color. From 1933 to 1946 there weren't any African Americans playing professional football. Paul Brown had black players on his team at Massillon and at Ohio State. Since he judged players on their ability to play the game, he invited both players to training camp despite the unwritten rule against black players.

The same year, the Los Angeles Rams signed Kenny Washington and Woody Strode. The team had just moved west from Cleveland and looked for a stadium to lease. The Los Angeles Coliseum seemed the most likely place, but the city told the Rams they must have minority representatives on the roster in order to lease the publicly owned facility. The Rams then signed Washington and Strode. It isn't clear if the Rams' lease specifically required minority representation, but it was clearly implied. The city of Cleveland did not require the same from Paul Brown and his team.

Chapter Five

Ground and Pound

A. Philip Randolph, the founder and president of the Brotherhood of Sleeping Car Porters, served as a missionary for civil rights most of his life. In 1941, he organized a march on Washington to demand more jobs for minorities in the defense industry as the country built up for entrance into World War II. President Franklin Roosevelt, worried about the impact of that proposed march, signed an executive order banning employment discrimination in government and defense industries. As a result, Randolph called off the march. Although the military remained segregated, the order opened some opportunities in the defense industry. The order created the Fair Employment Practices Commission.

After the war, Randolph formed the Committee against Jim Crow in Military Service. Those protests helped push president Harry S. Truman to issue Executive Order 9981 banning discrimination in the military. Although some military leadership resisted nearly all of the military had integrated by the end of the Korean conflict.

In 1954, the U.S. Supreme Court struck down the "separate but equal" doctrine that it had defended since the 1890s. The NAACP brought lawsuits to challenge segregation in schools. In *Brown vs. Board of Education*, the court ruled that the separation of school-children "generates a feeling of inferiority ... that may affect their hearts and minds in a way unlikely ever to be undone." In 1955, Rosa Parks, a 43-year-old seamstress, refused to obey the Montgomery, Alabama, law segregating city buses when she sat in a "white-only" seat. In 1960, four freshmen from North Carolina A&T sat a Woolworth's lunch counter where only white customers ate. Waiters refused them service but they remained.

A northern-based organization dedicated to racial equality called Congress of Racial Equality (CORE) organized "Freedom Rides," across the South in 1961. Federal laws prohibiting segregation were not enforced in the South. Riders were physically attacked in South Carolina and Alabama. Local police did nothing. The site of the biggest struggle came in Birmingham in 1963 as thousands of blacks, including children, protested in the streets. Police answered with clubs, tear gas, police dogs and high-powered water hoses. More than 1,000 arrests were made. Progress was slow in coming.

In 1963, Randolph thought the timing right for another march. His goal was jobs for minorities, but he also asked for support of school integration, passage of fair employment legislation and civil rights reform. He hoped the protest might attract as many as 100,000 marchers to the streets of the national capital. When they assembled on the mall, the large number of marchers would send as dramatic a message as the speakers. "Let the nation and the world know the meaning of our numbers," Randolph told the crowd. "We are the advance guard of a massive moral revolution for jobs and freedom."[1]

The protestors gathered on a hot and humid late August day in Washington, D.C. Most folks might have preferred to stay inside with air conditioning instead of outside in the sun listening to speeches on this kind of day. On that day, about 250,000 Americans took to the streets and marched to the National Mall in front of the Lincoln Memorial. They gathered to demonstrate their solidarity against unemployment and to seek racial and social justice. They waited patiently for one of the last speakers to take the podium.

Most came to hear Dr. Martin Luther King, Jr., the son, grandson and great-grandson of Baptist ministers. His words most often quoted came towards the end of the program. He began slowly talking about life as black person in America. Standing in front of the inspiring statute of Abraham Lincoln, he described the "shameful condition" of race relations one hundred years after the president signed Emancipation Proclamation freeing slaves in the United States.

Ironically, Dr. King had not included his famous "I Have a Dream" lines in the prepared text he had brought to deliver to the crowd that day. He had traveled the country speaking to various groups but struggled writing this speech for that day. As the latest in a long line of Baptist preachers, he did not have a problem speaking off the cuff. He decided to deviate from the text and those unplanned words provided the most memorable part of the remarks.

The speech borrowed from many distinctive writings ranging from the Bible to popular music. He used the prophet Amos' version of justice rolling down like a river and righteous like a stream. Towards the end of his remarks, King borrowed from the nineteenth-century patriotic song "My Country 'Tis of Thee" with a line from the first verse: "Let freedom ring." With the Lincoln Memorial as a backdrop, he began the speech with "Five score years ago," echoing the beginning of Lincoln's Gettysburg address "Four score and seven years ago."

Dr. King outlined the plight of African Americans during their journey in the United States and looked to a time when the negative had disappeared. During the years immediately preceding the speech, the civil rights movement began to gain traction. "In three difficult years," wrote the late academic Manning Marable in *Race, Reform and Rebellion*, "the southern struggle had grown from a modest group of black students demonstrating peacefully at one lunch counter to the largest mass movement for racial reform and civil rights in the twentieth century."[2]

Dr. King maintained his philosophy of nonviolence throughout the civil rights struggle. Even as his fellow protestors met with violence, he told people to turn the other cheek and not respond in kind. Even when the violence hit home, as in 1956 when some bombed his house, he remained resolute. Hearing the news, he told people to affirm their policy of nonviolent protest.

Despite concerns of many, the march in Washington that day proved peaceful. Although predominantly black, the crowd included people of all races and backgrounds. The expected large turnout caused concern among law enforcement professionals due to the potential for violence. Despite the large crowd and emotional issues, the environment remained peaceful, just as the Reverend King had preached. The mood in the rest of the country did not always follow that way. "The year before [the march on Washington] had been like a second Civil War with bombings, beatings and killings happening almost weekly," wrote civil rights leader and congressman John Lewis in his autobiogra-

Martin Luther King Jr., talks civil rights with president Lyndon Johnson at the White House. During his administration, the Civil Rights Act of 1964 and 1965 Voting Rights Act were passed into law (Yoichi Okamoto. White House Photographs. LBJ Library, Austin, Texas).

phy, *Walking with the Wind*. "A march would be met with violence, which would cause yet another march, and so on. That was the pattern."[3]

The Kennedy administration found itself in a tough position. Kennedy had won a close election in 1960 with a coalition of northern cities and southern states. As he looked towards a reelection campaign in 1964, he needed to walk carefully so as not to upset any of support groups who voted for him in 1960. Kennedy wanted to hold together a coalition of supporters that included white southerners. It appear a difficult task. Until this point in history, southerners voted solidly for Democrats, but things started changing with many of those changes driven by civil rights movements across the country.

In November 1960, Kennedy won the White House by a plurality of slightly more than 110,000 votes, which was less than one percent of the popular vote. The black vote may well have proven the deciding factor in the race. For example, an estimated 125,000 blacks voted for John Kennedy in New Jersey. He won the state by only 30,000 votes. The black vote in South Carolina, North Carolina, and Texas also proved critical. If Kennedy had lost those three states, the outcome would likely have swung to Richard Nixon.

John F. Kennedy's call to Coretta Scott King, Martin's wife, while her husband sat imprisoned was considered a key factor in the race. Authorities had arrested and then convicted Dr. King of a probation violation during a sit-in in Atlanta. As the Reverend King sat in prison, Kennedy offered his sympathy to Coretta King. His brother, Attorney General Robert F. Kennedy, worked to hasten King's release on bail from Georgia State Prison at Reidsville. Meanwhile, Nixon did nothing. Upon his release, King said he "owed a great debt of gratitude to Senator Kennedy."

"Kennedy frequently claimed that his backpedaling on civil rights was borne of political necessity, and a number of sympathetic biographers and historians have taken him as his word," wrote Nick Bryant in *The Bystander*, a book critical of the president's civil rights positions. "Kennedy's rationalizations were a product of his temperament and his long-standing aversion to even the slightest conflict with members of the southern block. The subsequent justifications put forth on Kennedy's behalf do not stand up in the face of historical evidence. Admittedly, the administration faced a congressional situation that was far from ideal. Yet it was by no means as dire as Kennedy imagined."[4]

Civil rights discussion and actions heated up across the country. In Alabama, Governor George Wallace stood in the schoolhouse door preventing blacks from entering. Wallace drew support from southerners who were fearful of changing times; he pledged to protect the "great Anglo-Saxon Southland" in his inaugural address. This stand may have been rooted in acting than true resistance, but he was making points with his base supporters. His populist appeal rested with working-class men and women, even those beyond Alabama's border who would vote for him in future presidential races.

In Birmingham, tensions grew worse, especially in 1963. In the early sixties, the city earned the nickname Bombingham due to the violent attacks that bombed black homes and businesses. Less than one month after the civil rights march in Washington, in which the Reverend King openly prayed for an America where all races could get along, another tragedy struck Birmingham. At 10:22 on the morning of September 15, 1963, an explosion went off at the 16th Street Baptist Church, tragically killing four young girls attending Sunday school. Members of the Ku Klux Klan planted the bomb.

President John F. Kennedy and First Lady Jacqueline Kennedy pose for a portrait with their children, Caroline Kennedy and John F. Kennedy Jr., on a porch in Hyannis Port, Massachusetts in 1962 (Cecil Stoughton. White House Photographs. John F. Kennedy Presidential Library and Museum, Boston. ID: ST-22-1-62).

Athletes faced the same struggles non-athletes faced in the world. When Syracuse played Texas Christian in the Cotton Bowl in January 1957, Jim Brown could not stay at the team's hotel in Dallas; he slept in Fort Worth. Curtis McClinton, a star running back at University of Kansas, found himself unwelcome at a Houston hotel when his team played Rice in the 1961 Bluebonnet Bowl. His coach kept him out of sight on purpose.

Many of those athletes quietly welcomed the thought of change. The current thinking among many athletes centered on quietly playing the game and not commenting on the social issues of the day in order to keep playing. Although most athletes refused to comment on the protests and politics of the day, a few athletes actually stepped out and joined the protest gatherings. Cookie Gilchrist, a running back introduced to American professional football with the Buffalo Bills, took such a stand.

In 1963, Cookie marched on Washington when the Reverend King delivered his "I Have a Dream" speech. That march and that speech provided the energy to pass the Civil Rights Act (1964) and Voting Rights Act (1965). Gilchrist also found himself in New Orleans when football players staged a protest of their own. As the best players in the AFL gathered at the site of the 1965 All-Star Game in New Orleans, restaurants, jazz clubs and taxicabs denied service to many African American players. Some players even reported having guns drawn on them as they attempted to enter some of those establishments. During a hastily called meeting, players refused to play in a city where they received such poor treatment. A majority of the players voted to boycott the game unless the AFL moved it elsewhere. The game moved to Houston where, ironically they played at Houston's Jeppesen Stadium, which was an AFL facility that restricted black fans to the end zone.

Some say that protest helped provide some level of inspiration for the protests launched by Dr. Harry Edwards and the Olympic Project for Human Rights he founded. Dr. Edwards's movement first called for a boycott of the 1968 Olympics by African American athletes. After the boycott fell through, American sprinters Tommie Smith and John Carlos performed their black glove protest during the playing of the national anthem while standing on the medal stand after their sprint race. Officials sent them home from the Olympic Games.

Gilchrist's professional football career started in the Canadian Football League in the late fifties. Before going to Canada, he had caught the eye of Cleveland Browns coach Paul Brown. He had starred at Har-Brack High School in Natrona Heights, Pennsylvania, and in 1953, Brown signed him to a pro contract at the age of 18. Signing a high school athlete should not have happened since rules did not permit it. Apparently, another team alerted the league office about the signing so Cleveland released him. Despite the great potential Brown must have seen in the runner, Gilchrist did not last long in Browns camp. Since he had signed a professional contract, he lost eligibility to play in college and left for Canada.

He started in the Senior Ontario Rugby Football Union for two seasons. His next step took him to the Hamilton Tiger-Cats of the Canadian Football League, where he helped them achieve a Grey Cup (CFL championship) victory in 1957. Due to his impressive play after his playing days ended, the CFL selected Gilchrist for enshrinement in the Canadian Football Hall of Fame, but he turned down induction, the only player to do so, citing racism and exploitation by team management.

In 1962, he joined the Buffalo Bills of the American Football League. Harvey Johnson, one of the Bills' assistant coaches, had worked in Canada and seen Gilchrist play firsthand. He convinced him to come to the United States and try the American Football League. When American football viewers saw him play, many compared Gilchrist to Jim Brown. Both men had chiseled physiques, ran with power and speed and neither man took any lip from anyone. Gilchrist became the first AFL running back to run for more than 1,000 yards in a season when he surpassed that threshold in 1962. A true jack-of-all-trades, in addition to running and catching the ball, Gilchrist kicked eight field goals and 14 extra points for Buffalo during the 1962 season. It was a productive year for the first-year running back. After playing eight years of professional ball in Canada, he really was not the typical rookie.

Cookie definitely marched to his own beat. During his first game with the Bills, he shocked teammates and coaches when he took off his uniform and headed for the shower at halftime. Some players wondered if he had quit but soon learned of his ritual to change his clothing, take a shower and come out fresh for the second half. In 1965, Gilchrist's independent spirit got him in trouble with hardnosed head coach Lou Saban. The Bills' head coach had played for Paul Brown in Cleveland and adopted his no-nonsense approach to coaching. In a game against the rival Boston Patriots, the Bills fell behind early and switched to throwing the ball in an effort to catch up. Cookie got upset because he was not getting the ball.

"He got mad at Saban, and I guess at me, for not running him," said Jack Kemp, the Bills' quarterback. "It's no secret that he's one of the greatest runners that ever lived, but he also has a temper, and he walked off the field."[5] When he walked off the field, Saban lost patience with his talented but troubled running back. It came as the last straw. Over the previous three seasons, Saban had put up with a lot from his star running back. Gilchrist had arrived late for practices, had run-ins with the law, and disrupted the team. Saban refused to tolerate Gilchrist walking out on the team so he put him on waivers. Team quickly requested a meeting with Coach Saban. They pleaded their case; the running back formed a large part of the team and they thought they could actually win the title if they kept the whole team together. Without him, those chances seemed substantially reduced.

"I went over to Cookie's house," said Kemp, "and I said, 'Cookie this is what happened, this is my explanation. Coach Saban is an old school, blue-collar kind of coach. You offended him by sitting down. You have to come back. We can win the championship, but you've got to apologize to Saban and your teammates.'"[6]

Gilchrist apologized, the Bills recalled the waivers and they went on to win the AFL championship. After the season, Coach Saban traded his star running back to the Denver Broncos in exchange for fullback Billy Joe, the AFL's Rookie of the Year in 1963. Despite his great talent as a very football player, Gilchrist's independent spirit made it difficult for him to follow team rules. That point is evident by the fact that he played for six teams in 12 professional seasons. Cookie's friends offered another explanation. "Cookie was the Jim Brown of the American Football League," teammate Booker Edgerson told the *New York Times* in 1994. "He was the icon of the league. But, the biggest thing about Cookie is that Cookie did not take any mess off of anyone. That's his legacy."[7]

Gilchrist bounced from team to team and ultimately away from football because he had an issue of discipline and following team rules. Was he pushed out of the league due to his activism? Some suggest that was the case since his play on the field could not be argued. Football fans who had not watched an AFL game watched another back that ran with tremendous power and spoke his mind. Years before Cookie burst on the scene, Jim Brown punished would-be tacklers while playing in the NFL for the Cleveland Browns, the team that originally signed Gilchrist.

The Browns finished the 1956 season with five wins and seven losses. It was Paul Brown's only losing season as head coach of the team. From the start of the Cleveland Browns franchise, Coach Brown achieved amazing success with four consecutive AAFC titles. Such success came from the great talent he assembled. For example, Brown had Otto Graham as his quarterback for many seasons, but that era ended with Graham's retirement. He originally left after the 1954 season, but Brown convinced him to come back for one more season. Graham's retirement for good brought the first losing season and a prime selection in the draft of collegiate players.

The Browns had the sixth choice in the first round of the 1957 draft and their coach hoped to draft Graham's replacement. Two quarterbacks interested him the most: Stanford's John Brodie and Purdue's Len Dawson. Other than the two quarterbacks, the draft had more good talent at the top. Green Bay, with the bonus pick, selected Paul Hornung first. Then the Los Angeles Rams stayed home with the selection of Southern California running back Jon Arnett. The quarterbacks Brown wanted went third and fifth; Brodie went third to San Francisco and Dawson went fifth to Pittsburgh.

With the quarterbacks gone, Brown selected the player he felt the best available, the excellent runner from Syracuse, Jim Brown. His impact on professional football proved immediate. Despite his great size, he had great speed and could deliver power with an angry running style. He outran most opponents, but those who got too close received Brown's punishment. He would lower his shoulder and make opponents pay, or extend his arm with a powerful stiff arm that would make the defender shiver.

With his great speed, Brown played a hard, physical game. He dished out punishment to the defender who attempted to make the tackle. When the defender approached, Brown protected himself with a shoulder and free arm. First, he knocked them off balance with a shoulder and then delivered a powerful straight-arm to keep tacklers away. He was not opposed to delivering a powerful blow with his forearm.

Jim Brown understood that he needed to hit first rather than waiting to be hit. That way, the defender never got a good shot on him. He needed to dish out the punishment rather than take it. If a defender should happen to get a good shot in, he never let on that the hard hit bothered him. He decided if he walked back to the huddle the same way each time, the defender would not know if the hit affected him. He called his method of getting up slowly and ambling back to the huddle "getting up with leisure."

Brown did not want the defense to know that their hard hits hurt him. He decided that he would get up off the turf the same way each time. That way they would not know if that particular hit hurt more than any other did. He knew if the defense thought their hits had an impact, it would motivate them to hit even harder next time. By getting up with leisure every play, every game, every season they would never know if they hurt Brown or not. Instead of them messing with Jim's head, he messed with theirs.

"That trademark of Jim taking his time walking back to the huddle came from him realizing, 'If I'm going to be the guy carrying the ball, I want to be able to come back each time with a blast,'" recalled Bobby Mitchell. "He'd come back to the huddle and lean over, and everyone would wonder if he's all right. Then he'd get up to the line and *boom!*"[8]

Perhaps good karma made Jim Brown end up with the Cleveland Browns under Paul Brown. Despite Coach Brown's stated desire for a quarterback, powerful fullbacks excelled in his offense. Marion Motley ran power inside running plays during Cleveland's championship seasons. Brown liked powerful running backs, but it had to do with more than just the running style. He fit for other reasons, too. The Browns head coach was legendary for running a tight ship.

To watch Jim Brown walk around any environment, you saw an independent and strong man. His persona gave off an aura that said no one could bother him and his well-built body suggested no one try. He was an extremely confident man residing in a powerfully built body. At 6-foot-2 and 230 pounds of solid muscle, most men did not care to challenge him anyway. Reading what he thought proved difficult, too. He kept his facial expressions at a stoic, poker face. It made him appear oblivious to the world around him.

Jim Brown developed that attitude as he grew up watching the treatment of other black athletes in the white world of athletics. He saw black stars such as Jackie Robinson, Joe Louis and Jesse Owens go along in order to continue to pursue the opportunity to perform in the white man's world. He told himself he would not do that.

"Jackie had to do it," Brown reflected. "Jackie had to play a role because of the plan that they had, and he made a vow to Branch Rickey, to play that role. That was not his nature. If he did not have to do it for the betterment of the whole, he would not have done it. Joe Louis was a nice man that was kind of like that anyway; Jesse Owens was obviously that way. My attitude was in no way was I going to be that way.... In no way did I ever feel that I would accept discrimination."[9]

From the losing season before he arrived, Jim Brown led Cleveland back to its winning ways as they won nine games to capture the Eastern Division in his rookie season. That year he led the league in rushing with 942 yards on 202 carries in only 12 games. One thousand yards rushing in a season has long stood as the benchmark, but today's NFL backs have 16 games to achieve that standard. Despite not reaching 1,000 yards, Brown led the league in rushing that season. In fact, Brown finished 242 yards ahead of the runner-up, Chicago Bear Rick Casares, even though they carried the ball nearly the same number of times.

Brown bettered his stats in his second season when he set a new NFL rushing record with 1,527 yards and a 5.9 yards average per carry. To top it off, he also led the league in scoring with 18 touchdowns. He broke the previous records for rushing yards and touchdowns in a season, both held by Steve Van Buren, in the eighth game of the season.

He helped the Browns team have a strong 1958 season. Cleveland jumped off to a 9–2 start and only needed a win or tie in the last game against the 8–3 New York Giants to clinch the Eastern Division for the second straight season and Paul Brown's eighth in nine NFL seasons. On the first play from scrimmage, Brown ran 65 yards for a touchdown. He scored just the once as the Giants rallied in a heavy snowstorm to win the game, 13–10. Sam Huff and the stout Giants defense held him in check the rest of the game. That victory set up a playoff game for the division title the next week that the Giants won, 10–0, holding Brown to just eight rushing yards. New York went on to play the Colts in the NFL championship game called the greatest game ever played.

To the media, Paul Brown called Jim Brown "the best draft choice we ever made." The coach entered that 1957 draft in search of a quarterback and ended up with a runner many consider the best ever. Instead of building the offense around the quarterback, as he had done with Otto Graham, Coach Paul Brown built it around the ground game. Over his career, Jim Brown led the league in rushing every year except one. He only missed the rushing title in 1962 when bothered by a sore wrist. It did not keep him out of action—in fact, Brown never missed a game during his career, but the sore wrist may have contributed to missing the rushing title. Brown would not have used the wrist as an excuse; that was not his style.

His teammates knew of the wrist injury but also knew he had not missed a game. Teammates said his wrist hurt so bad that season that Brown often let it hang at his side.

Jim's roommate, John Wooten, said Brown could not even tie his own shoes. Wooten said that he always believed the hurt wrist made 1962 Jim's worst year. When a reporter asked him how he managed to miss only one-half of one game over a nine-year career with every defensive player gunning for him, Jim quickly corrected him. He said he didn't miss a half; he missed a few plays before halftime.

Genetics probably played a part in Jim Brown's physical prowess. Jim's dad boxed professionally and likely passed on Jim's solid build with powerful legs and upper body. Jim's solid chest tapered to a 32-inch waist. During summer camp, head coach Paul Brown lined up the players for sprints. He lined his star running back up against the other speedy Browns in 40-yard, head-to-head races. Running against receivers and defensive backs, Jim Brown won most of those races despite outweighing the other players by as much as 40 pounds.

During Brown's era, pro football had less strict rules than those they play under today, making it a very physical game. In the late fifties, when

Cleveland running back Jim Brown wrestles with a Rams defender. Brown led the NFL in rushing eight out of the nine seasons he played during an era in which pro offenses focused on the ground game (**Photofest**).

Brown started in the league, pro football also had fewer black players than today's NFL. Most teams had only a few men of color on the roster. Those few faced racist remarks and aggressive play more severe than usual. According to reports, Brown took punches to the ribs and kidneys, often in full view of game officials. Under the pile, he had his fingers purposely bent backward.

The physical play only served to stiffen his resolve. On the outside, he presented a cool exterior because he did not want the defenders to see any hurt or anger. His coolness earned him respect from teammates and the opposition. He ran hard and took a beating without complaint or even the hint that it bothered him.

His hands, which were cut, mangled and scarred, became the one place where the beatings drew notice. When he got the opportunity to visit the White House, president Lyndon Johnson noticed the cuts as they shook hands. Other players also noticed the damage. "We didn't wear gloves back then like they do now," running back Leroy Kelly said. "His hands took a beating from hitting all the helmets and being stepped on with those cleats. Yet somehow, those fingers were strong enough to hold the ball."[10]

Brown played unlike any of the traditional fullbacks of the day. Most of them ran up the middle, always keeping two hands on the ball. In many ways, the Browns used him more like a halfback than a traditional fullback. Other fullbacks carried the ball nestled between both hands and arms like a battering ram. They ran short yardage plays and primarily operated as a blocker for the running back. Jim Brown carried the ball with one hand and put the other end of it in the crook of his elbow.

"He was a combination of a fullback and a halfback," said Patriots head coach Bill Belichick. "He had great power and leverage, but he was also very elusive in the open field like a halfback. His quickness, straight-out speed and elusiveness were all exceptional. He was all of 230 pounds. He was bigger than some of the guys blocking for him. I mean, they might have weighed more, pumped up, but Jim's hands, his forearms, and his girth. He was bigger."[11]

To hear him talk, one might have thought Brown wanted to play the game forever. That was not the case. He had dreams of doing something more with his life. After just nine seasons in the league and right before the start of training camp, Jim Brown walked away from football. In London filming the war movie *The Dirty Dozen*, Brown encountered rainy weather, which delayed the filming. Thus, Brown remained in England when his teammates reported to training camp. The Browns wanted him to report to camp so owner Art Modell delivered an ultimatum to the running back. Brown responded to the ultimatum by announcing his retirement. He made the announcement from the movie set in London.

Many observers thought Brown still in his prime when he decided to hang up his cleats. He finished the 1965 season with 1,544 yards in a 14-game season to win the rushing title again. He outdistanced runner-up Gale Sayers, who had just finished a very good rookie season, by 677 yards. While most observers thought he still played the game at a high level, Jim Brown had bigger pursuits in mind. Other than acting, he had a social conscience and he wanted to see things change for those more disadvantaged than he was.

Although the most dominating player of the early sixties, Brown had a great awareness of the social and political climate of the era. He grew up in predominantly black neighborhood on St. Simons Island, off the coast of Georgia. Later he moved north where he mother worked as a domestic. For a short while, they lived in the home of the white family his mother served, but Brown needed to attend school miles away at a high school in the black neighborhood.

Even at Syracuse, where he was one of just a few black players, he remained well aware of the separate but equal philosophy of the day. The team's trip to the Cotton Bowl in Dallas his senior year carried Jim to the Southwest, where he had been. He knew that in the past, college teams traveling south would have to find homes to house their black players because the major hotels would not allow any blacks to stay there.

Selected to play in the College All-Star game under Curly Lambeau with assistance from former Cleveland Browns quarterback Otto Graham, Brown encountered a problem. According to Brown, Graham told him, "you'll never make it in the NFL."[12] According to Brown, Graham said the same thing to Bobby Mitchell, Gale Sayers and Duane Thomas, three black athletes. "Bobby, Gale and I are in the Hall of Fame. Duane was All-Pro. Otto wasn't blind or stupid. It was pure racism," Brown wrote in his autobiography.[13]

Jim Brown was not the only black player to accuse Graham of making less-than-flattering comments. Many others, including many players who are now in the Pro Football Hall of Fame, did the same. "To give you an idea what kind of judge of talent Otto

[Graham] was, he had badmouthed Jim Brown's abilities," said Bob Hayes, who played for Otto in the 1965 College All-Star Game. "He had said the year before that Charley Taylor was lazy and predicted he wouldn't make it with the Redskins and he didn't think much of Gale Sayers, whom he kept on the bench for the entire All-Star game."[14]

Bob Hayes made his name with a gold medal performance in the 1964 Olympic Games in Tokyo, where he earned a new title, "World's Fastest Human." He ran 100 meters in 10.05 seconds finishing a full four meters ahead of the next fastest runner. While that performance seemed spectacular, the relay went even better. When he got the baton on the anchor leg of the 4 × 100-meter relay final in Tokyo the team trailed. He made up nine meters on the field by running or maybe flying over the course in 8.6 seconds.

It nearly did not have the successful conclusion everyone dreamed about. As Hayes prepared for his 100-meter race, he got a tap on the shoulder from the legendary sprinter Jesse Owens. He wanted Hayes to know that he and his wife were in the stands watching. He also reminded Hayes that the United States had lost the same race to the Germans four years ago. "We want it back," Owens told Hayes. Owens worried that Hayes had drawn a bad lane for the race. Hayes had the inside position where the track was torn up from the previous event.

Hayes said he understood and started to get ready for the race. When Owens had approached him, Hayes had set his bag down on the track's infield to put on his spikes. He got the right one on before noticing that his left shoe had gone missing. Hayes later found out that his roommate, boxer Joe Frazier, had knocked the shoe out of Hayes's bag and it fell under the bed while Frazier rifled through the bag looking for gum. Minutes before the race, Hayes scrambled to find footwear. Eventually he found teammate Tommy Farrell who lent him a shoe. Hayes ran in a bad lane with oddly paired shoes, but it did not matter. He ran by the field, winning by seven feet and tying the world record.

"Graham didn't think I was a football player," said Hayes, recalling his own experience at the College All-Star Game. "He dismissed me as just another track star trying to learn how to play football and, as a result, he wouldn't let me return punts. What's strange is that Graham himself had been a two-sport star at Northwestern in football and basketball and went on to have an outstanding career with the Browns."[15]

He also had an explanation for his play during practice before the game. Hayes said many of the other receivers received injuries during the practice sessions leading up to the game and could not practice. Since he remained the only healthy receiver, he had to catch all the passes. Several of his fingers split open due to the extensive use. With sore fingers, he dropped some passes. Graham told the media that Hayes had "9-flat speed and 12-flat hands."[16]

By the time he got to the Cowboys, all that talk fell by the wayside. Bob Hayes proved himself a deep threat the likes the NFL had not seen before. From 1965 to 1968, Hayes caught 212 balls for 45 touchdowns, which equaled one score out of every 4.7 passes caught. Only Homer Jones, who averaged a touchdown every 4.9 catches for the New York Giants, came close.

"There were deep threats and then there was *the* deep threat, Bob Hayes," said former teammate Dan Reeves. "Every defensive back in those days lived in fear of him. Absolutely he changed the game."[17]

Over the years, Otto Graham made some comments that seem to reflect at best an unusual awareness of race and at worst a racist attitude. While training for the 1969 College All-Star game, one of the running backs got hurt. Graham called Tex Schramm of the

Cowboys to inquire about his first-round draft choice as a potential replacement for the injured player. The Cowboys had selected Calvin Hill from Yale in that year's draft.

"We lost a white running back," Schramm quoted Graham having said when he called. "I think it would be best if we replaced him with another white back. Is Hill available?"

"He's available," said Schramm. "But you're going to be surprised when you see him."[18] He then told Graham that Hill was a black man.

As for the 1957 College All-Star Game, the running back many considered one of the best to play the game sat on the bench. Looking back, one finds it hard to comprehend a back of his caliber barely playing in the game. He could not believe that he did not get into the game. It left a real bad taste in Jim Brown's mouth and motivated him to have the career he ended up having. He did not spend the night in Chicago. After the game, he drove through the night from Chicago to get to the Browns training camp in Ohio. In his autobiography, Brown puts a good spin on the experience. He thinks it motivated him to work harder as a pro.

"If I'd played a lot in that All-Star game and had had a good night, or even a fair night, I probably would have stayed in Chicago that night and partied and eased into the Cleveland Browns' training camp at Hiram, Ohio, the next afternoon feeling satisfied with myself. That might have been disastrous. You can begin to count the number of college stars who have failed to make a pro squad because they assumed they had it made.... I did not party in Chicago. Instead, I drove straight from Soldier Field to my dormitory room at Northwestern. I threw my bags into my car and drove all night, muttering darkly about Curly Lambeau. I arrived in Hiram at an early hour in the morning and was ready for practice. I needed no sleep. I was ready for work."[19]

That experience made an impression on Jim Brown. He worked hard at Browns camp and had immediate success at running the ball in the professional ranks. With the ball in his hands, he had control. He could do special things with the ball in his hands, but he also saw the world that existed in that era. He lived it. He knew that some amount of discrimination would come his way. On the field, his brown uniform showed his team but off the field, his brown skin made him a target for discrimination.

"The NFL of the 1950s did not exist in a vacuum," Brown said. "Was there racism? Yes. To the same extent that there was racism in America."[20]

After finishing only his ninth season, Brown surprised the football world with his retirement announcement in 1965. He had won eight rushing titles in those nine seasons. Only 30 years old, most people probably were not surprised that he wanted to do something else; they just wondered why he would leave while still at the top of his game. Brown maintained a high level of play over his entire career. In 1963, Brown set a new record for rushing yards in a season with 1,863. He earned Most Valuable Player honors in 1957, his first season in the league, and in 1965, his last season.

Off the field, Brown had a sense for economics and the business world. Unlike today's players, he took a job in the business world during the offseason, serving as a marketing executive with Pepsi-Cola. That position gave him experience in the business world and an opportunity to see the segregation that existed first hand. That experience led to his founding of the National Negro Industrial and Economic Union, which aimed to help blacks get financing for business ventures.

Jim Brown stayed in the limelight longer than his playing days. Not many athletes can make that claim, perhaps only Muhammad Ali. One could count any others on the fingers of one hand. Many athletes disappear from public view after their playing days are over. The public has remained interested in Jim Brown. He wrote autobiographies in 1964 and 1989. Mike Freeman wrote an unauthorized biography in 2007 and Spike Lee did a feature-length documentary in 2002. In 2015, a full 50 years after he retired, *Sports Illustrated* produced an article titled "Why Jim Brown Matters."

Both Brown and Gilchrist were tremendous athletes living inside talented athletic bodies who dominated their respective leagues. The beginning of the sixties was the era of dominating fullbacks; these two men were two of the best. Both men shared a common interest in making life better for those they viewed as disadvantaged. Up until this point, athletes were expected to keep their views to themselves and play their sport. Nobody wanted to hear their political views. These two men experienced discrimination first hand, which ignited a fuse to take action. They could not keep quiet. The sixties were an era of change and these two men came around at the perfect time.

Chapter Six

New Neighbors

Much like the All-America Football Conference (AAFC) before it, the American Football League came about because the NFL refused to expand. NFL team membership remained capped at a total of 12 teams through the fifties. The list of teams had remained static since 1951 when the Baltimore Colts disbanded after one year in the league. Ownership turned the team back over to the league after financial losses prevented them from going forward. These Colts had played as part of the AAFC, one of three teams brought into the NFL under a merger agreement.

The National Football League continued to grow in popularity with fans and increase in value financially during the 1950s. Despite the gains in popularity, the NFL owners resisted expansion. Numerous executives approached the league and then-commissioner Bert Bell about franchise opportunities but the NFL refused to add teams.

Ole Haugsrud had owned the Duluth (Minnesota) Eskimos in the 1920s and wanted to get back into the league (the Duluth Kelleys, 1923–26, became the Duluth Eskimos, 1926–27, of the NFL). He expressed interest in a new franchise. His signing of Ernie Nevers and taking the Eskimos on a barnstorming tour had helped the NFL through a critical period during those early years. That tour may have lacked the notoriety of Red Grange's tour, but it proved very successful.

When Haugsrud sold the team back to the league, part of the agreement gave him the right to take part of any future team in Minnesota. As the sixties began, rumor had it that the NFL was considering expansion and Haugsrud wanted to exercise that clause. He wanted back in.

He joined a group headed by Max Winter, who had an appropriate last name living in Minneapolis. Winter, a longtime sports promoter and team owner in Minnesota, stood just a shade taller than 5-foot-4. Despite that, he took an interest in basketball in his youth and earned a scholarship to Hamline University in St. Paul, Minnesota. After college, he promoted various sporting events including Harlem Globetrotter games. Winter later served as general manager of Minneapolis Lakers of the National Basketball Association. Under his guidance, the Lakers won three straight league championships. Many consider them the first pro basketball dynasty with six titles in seven years.

The Minnesota group comprised one of several organizations seeking an NFL franchise. The NFL did not give any group an outright negative answer. Doing so would open the door for scrutiny from the government's antitrust division. Leadership of the league just continued to delay. The NFL ultimately set up a committee to look into expansion in 1958, but the committee never met as a group. A group of owners, led by Washington Redskins owner George Preston Marshall, held steadfast against expansion. Marshall opposed expansion because his team, the Washington Redskins, had fans throughout the South and he wanted to maintain that dominance. The Redskins played, at the time, as the southernmost team in the league. Several of the groups interested in gaining an NFL franchise represented cities in the South.

Meanwhile, 26-year-old Lamar Hunt also searched for a sports franchise in the spring of 1958. First he looked into the Continental League, a proposed professional baseball league that Branch Rickey tried to get started. Hunt attended several organization meetings with Rickey where he picked up knowledge on sports leagues. One idea he heard involved Rickey's strategy of sharing the revenue earned from television broadcasts among all teams. That idea stuck with him and he later proposed it with the future American Football League.

Next, Lamar Hunt asked to meet with NFL commissioner Bert Bell to pursue a team. Hunt told Bell he wanted to purchase an NFL franchise. Bell advised him to talk with Walter and Violet Wolfner, owners of the Chicago Cardinals. All through the fifties, the Cardinals had proven a source of difficulties for the commissioner. Their attendance dwindled and they squabbled over territory rights with the Bears and handicapped the NFL's television prospects. The NFL's blackout policy prohibited televising either Chicago team's road games locally if the other team was playing at home.

It was thought that the owners of the Chicago Cardinals, caught up in red ink, might consider a move away from Chicago and its hometown rival the Bears. They wanted to keep all their options open. A vote for expansion would remove potential cities in which to relocate, eliminate potential suitors if they decided to sell and, perhaps, lessen the asking price they could demand for the club.

The Bears' owner, George Halas, wanted the Cardinals to move. He wanted Chicago all to himself. He did not want the competition, even though he won against the Cardinals. If the Cardinals moved from Chicago, it would open the Windy City as a media market for television. The blackout rule prohibited showing games while the home team played so with two teams Chicago TV was always blacked out. While Halas favored expansion, he figured the time had come to add teams and saw it as even more important to do something to prompt the Cardinals' owners to take some action and move out of Chicago.

Meanwhile, acting on Bell's advice, Hunt approached the Wolfner family with a proposal. He wanted to purchase the team outright and move them to Dallas. During negotiations, they ultimately agreed to sell 20 percent, but refused to move the team. Eventually, the Wolfners decided not to sell the team to Hunt or to any of the other men pursuing the team. They had plenty of suitors. Bud Adams of Houston, Robert Howsam of Denver and Max Winter of Minneapolis all went to Chicago in attempt to purchase the team. The Wolfners turned them all down. Instead, they decided not to sell and moved the team to Walter's hometown of St. Louis. The Cardinals began play there beginning with the 1960 season.

Hunt prepared to go ahead with the plans for a new league with eight teams starting play in 1960. Before he announced anything publicly, he sent Davey O'Brien to meet with Bert Bell to seek the commissioner's blessing on the new league. O'Brien had ties to both men. He played for Bell when Bell owned the Eagles and played college ball at Texas Christian University, where he knew Lamar Hunt. In his meeting with Bell, O'Brien did not mention Hunt's name. Bell agreed to meet with the new league's organizers and said he thought a second league could prove successful.

Bell saw an opportunity for expansion in future years. He saw potential for locations like Buffalo and Louisville. Eventually they could look to the Southwest, particularly Houston and Dallas as possible sites along with major Southern cites of Atlanta, New Orleans and Miami. In 1959, Bell believed all owners, with the exception of Redskins owner George Preston Marshall, favored expansion. Bell chose not to bring it up since only one opposing vote would defeat an expansion proposal. He knew Marshall would vote against it.

Eventually Bell went before Senator Estes Kefauver's Antitrust and Monopoly Subcommittee that was investigating antitrust restrictions in sports. Although Kefauver later received notoriety for his investigations into organized crime, at this time he had his committee looking at sports monopolies. The senator had drafted legislation that would apply antitrust restrictions to all pro sports, just as had happened in other industries such as oil and steel. The implications worried the NFL. Moves by Congress could jeopardize some of the ways the league did business. For example, the way they controlled players from the day a team drafted them to the end of their careers. The draft, designed to create and maintain competitive balance, limited competition because once a team drafted a player they held his rights for life. The player had no choice other than not to play at all.

Many of the committee members felt the NFL had a monopoly. Anxious to ask Bell some tough questions, they did not know he had an ace up his sleeve to play when needed. That play came from his conversation with Hunt. Before Lamar Hunt could announce his new league to the media, the NFL commissioner of the established league announced its formation to the congressional committee on July 28, 1959. That single announcement took much of the sting out of the congressmen's questions.

"Bert Bell, the pro football commissioner who is very smart, casually pulled one out of the hat to impress the Senate," wrote Shirley Povich in the *Washington Post*. "He knew that would please the committee, which deplores monopoly. They did not hug and embrace Mr. Bell, but their tone toward him softened because here, surely, was a fine man who stood for what the Senators stood for, pro football for everybody and not merely the little clique of cities lucky enough to be in the NFL."[1]

Hunt, tipped off that Bell might mention the new league, attended the hearing and heard Bell announce the new league. He looked at it in a positive way. The NFL's blessing might well help the AFL. Maybe the upstarts could earn some instant credibility when announced by the long-standing commissioner of the NFL.

Bert Bell just wanted to get Congress off his back. Hunt and his fellow AFL pioneers had not even scheduled the media announcement for the new league yet. In Bell's talk with Congress, he made it sound as though the NFL would welcome a new addition to the professional football world. That attitude appeared in public; behind the scenes, NFL people felt the opposite.

NFL owners had every right to worry. The young, rich men backing the new league had plenty of funding. They seemed well positioned to withstand the rough initial years. Along with Hunt came Bud Adams and Barron Hilton. All three had more money than any current NFL owner did. The NFL faced a real threat. Publicly they said nice things, but in private, they grew concerned that rough times lay ahead. A new league meant real competition for players. Since the competition came from a well-financed group costs had to go up.

Coaches who liked to control things did not like that kind of talk. Cleveland head coach Paul Brown faced the challenge head-on in 1959 training camp. "There's a new league starting," he said. "Don't play any attention to it. It is not going to succeed. It's a bunch of sons of rich guys who don't know anything about football."[2]

He may have predicted failure for the upstart league, but the leadership of the NFL knew better. The men running the National Football League came in when the franchise prices sat in the cellar. In a way, many considered themselves blue-collar owners. That description did not fit the AFL owners. Many in this ownership group were the well-to-do offspring of some of the richest families in the country. Others worked in big business and still others already had ties to sports.

Lamar Hunt, the son of the oil billionaire H. L. Hunt, reportedly the richest man in American in the mid–1940s, had started the formation of the AFL. He grew up in Dallas as a huge sports fan. He earned a geology degree from Southern Methodist University and took a position with the Hunt Oil Company. It did not take long for Lamar to determine he had no real interest in the oil business. He wanted to find an opening in the sports or entertainment business.

Hunt had cultivated a great love for sports from his youngest days. He fondly recalled seeing Sammy Baugh play in the first Cotton Bowl game on January 1, 1937. He would review baseball box scores for hours, play basketball in the drive way and listen to football games on the radio. Like any youth, he memorized baseball statistics and challenged his friends with knowledge of sports. This profound love of sports resulted in his earning the nickname "Games." He captained his high school football team, but never rose past third string at Southern Methodist University. He loved all sports. Later in life, he would own and promote teams in football, basketball, baseball, tennis, soccer, and bowling.

When Walter Wolfner mentioned offers he had received from groups in Houston, Denver and Minneapolis it gave Hunt the idea. If that many groups attempted to acquire that one franchise, why not contact all those groups and form a new league? Hunt sat on an airplane heading back to Dallas when the thought occurred to him. He immediately asked the flight attendant for some paper. She came up with American Airlines letterhead. Hunt starting writing in all capital letters, "ORIGINAL 6; FIRST YEAR'S OPERATIONS."

He continued to sketch out the plan for the first year. Initially, he thought they could start with six teams. Hunt had gained valuable insight into professional sports during the process of pursuing an NFL franchise and from Continental League meetings. He had reviewed the Cardinals' financial statements from the 1956 and 1957 seasons so he knew enough to come up with a profit-and-loss statement for a typical football franchise. He included revenue from ticket sales and costs of the operating the team. He even came up with a likely schedule for the first season.

As a first step, Hunt flew to Houston and had dinner with Bud Adams, who expressed interest in a team in his hometown. Then, Hunt received a commitment from Bob Howsam, the son-in-law of Senator Edwin H. Johnson of Colorado. Howsam had worked with the Continental League that had not played one game before disbanding. His family owned the minor-league Denver Bears baseball team and looked for a step up in competition. Howsam wanted the Denver franchise. Max Winter, an executive in Minneapolis and part owner of the National Basketball Association's Minneapolis Lakers, led the Minneapolis group.

With these commitments, they had four probable franchises. Hunt figured he needed a presence in New York and Los Angeles so he began to search for interest from those locations. His sports contacts recommended Barron Hilton, son of the hotel magnate, Conrad Hilton, in California. They also suggested Harry Wismer, broadcaster of Notre Dame football games, as a potential owner in New York. Both subsequently expressed interest in the Los Angeles and New York franchises. Wismer, one of the leading play-by-play sports announcers in the country, held a minority ownership in the Washington Redskins. Wismer, often described as a combative man, proved unpopular with many sportswriters and, sometimes, even his own partners.

To keep costs down, Wismer operated the New York Titans out of his apartment. The AFL had one of their meetings there and the attendees chose their words carefully thinking the rooms were bugged. "Microphones were everywhere," recalled John Breen, the Oilers' player-personnel director who represented the team at those meetings. "There were so many wires strung underneath my chair, I had trouble standing up."[3]

As a part owner of the Washington Redskins in the NFL, Wismer urged George Preston Marshall to draft black players. Marshall refused and the two men verbally battled over the issue. Once he got an AFL franchise, he crossed the country touting the AFL and denouncing the NFL. "We don't have any ex-bookmakers or dog track operators in our league!" he would tell everyone who would listen. Those statements referred to Tim Mara, a one-time bookmaker, and Arthur J. Rooney Sr., whose family owned racetracks. Both men owned prominent NFL teams.

In what one can only consider bad sportsmanship, the NFL announced a planned expansion after they heard Hunt's group had their first organizational meeting. The NFL announced the addition of two franchises with play to begin in 1961. Not surprisingly, Dallas and Houston turned up as the two cities most rumored to house the NFL's expansion teams. Of course, those cities hosted AFL franchises for Hunt and Adams, the front men for a new league. The action appeared to signal the end of any cooperation between the two groups. The NFL announcement made Hunt even more convinced that he needed to move ahead.

The drive continued to add teams to field the AFL. Ralph Wilson, a lifetime football fan, already owned a small minority piece of the Detroit Lions. He recalled attending Lions games as a young boy. He said he attended his first game in 1934, the year the Lions moved to his hometown Detroit from Portsmouth, Ohio. Wilson vividly recalled that clash between the Lions and Bears. Wilson, on vacation at Saratoga in 1959, he read in the *New York Times* about Lamar Hunt forming a new football league. He called Hunt immediately to express interest in a team. He just needed a city. He first thought of South Florida where he had a summer home.

"I thought of Miami," said Wilson, "but I tried to lease the Orange Bowl and they said they wanted to wait for an NFL team. Hunt suggested Buffalo. I met with the managing editor of the *Buffalo Evening News*, Paul Neville. In those days, you had to have the support from the newspapers or you were dead. I told him I would give the city a franchise for three years if he promised he would write about us every day. He said yes and that was it."[4]

Wilson settled on Buffalo, which had supported an AAFC team and rumored to be a site the NFL would consider when they finally expanded. The Buffalo AAFC team had strong civic support, but still lost money. Oklahoma oil millionaire James Breuil had owned the team. When several AAFC teams folded into the NFL, Buffalo did not, so in an open letter to the city, Breuil explained that his failing health, financial losses, and too many demands on his time made him abandon the Bills (who had the same name as the subsequent AFL team) and accept a minority interest in the Cleveland Browns.

The league appeared all set for franchises when Billy Sullivan, a former Notre Dame publicity director, agreed to join the league with the Boston franchise. Lamar Hunt initially wanted six teams and now he had eight commitments. Things progressed for the men later nicknamed "The Foolish Club" until they gathered in Minneapolis to draft players late in November 1959. The NFL chose that moment to throw their second curveball.

As the AFL founders gathered in Minneapolis, the story of their defection ran as headline news in the *Minneapolis Star Tribune*. Wismer, however, saw the story first as he prepared to join the other owners for a group dinner. Wismer walked into the dinner room in his usual loud manner. He called the event the last supper and labeled Max Winter "Judas" in reference to the apostle who turned on Jesus in the Bible.

Wismer referred to the NFL's announcement that the Minneapolis group would the AFL to join the senior league. George Halas, the owner of the Chicago Bears, had worked behind the scenes to convince the group to join the NFL. It took the AFL two months to find a replacement and that came in the form of Chet Soda, an Oakland businessman, who agreed to host a team in his hometown.

Even though they lost the Minneapolis group, the meeting yielded something far greater. The AFL group announced a cooperative television deal. This deal meant that all teams, regardless of city size or market share, would share equally in the television money. This was something new in pro sports. In the NFL, each team had to negotiate an individual TV deal. Some teams, such as New York and Chicago, made more television money than teams from smaller cities, such as Green Bay and Baltimore. Soon the story spread that all eight AFL teams earned more television money than the NFL champion Philadelphia Eagles did.

Joe Foss, a World War II flying ace and Medal of Honor recipient, became the first AFL commissioner. Foss, the most decorated Marine pilot of World War II, served as governor of South Dakota after his military career ended. Prior to the military, he had a less-than-ideal life. Although raised on a South Dakota farm that lacked electricity, Foss caught the flying bug at a young age when he saw Charles Lindbergh fly his plane, the Spirit of St. Louis.

Foss went to Guadalcanal at the southern end of the Solomon Islands. Captain Foss and his fliers, a band known as Joe's Flying Circus for its acrobatic maneuvers, defended Guadalcanal against the Japanese. Captain Foss downed at least 26 enemy planes, making him an ace five times over. Later, he developed malaria and returned to the United States. President Roosevelt presented him the Medal of Honor citing his "outstanding heroism and courage" on his many air missions. He also received the Silver Star, Bronze Star and a Purple Heart. He later served in the Korean War as well.

Foss may not have had much football experience, but he provided leadership to the new league that he developed over a long and impressive military career. His football experience came during a short term as a backup lineman on the University of South Dakota football team. The new league officially announced his position on November 30, 1959. Although in his mid-forties, he acted like a man much younger, full of energy and vigor.

Many said the former Marine resembled John Wayne, one of his favorite actors. He stood six feet tall with curly hair. Frequently, Foss had a cigar in his mouth; it wasn't always lit but it sat there and he would chew the end. Shooting down 26 enemy aircraft from October 1942 to January 1943, Foss equaled Captain Eddie Rickenbacker's record from World War I. He got his picture in his dress uniform on the cover of *Life* magazine with the caption "America's No. 1 Ace."

When he took command of the American Football League, he saw public relations as his biggest task. His pilot license and private plane came in handy. He crisscrossed the country stopping at every small town Kiwanis and Rotary club in an effort to generate support for the new league. He logged more than 200,000 miles that first year touting the American Football League.

With eight teams ready to play and a commissioner in place, the owners needed to settle on the rules and schedule. They instituted the first 14-game schedule for a professional league. From college football, they borrowed the two-point conversion option after a touchdown. For fans, they decided to put names on the backs of the jersey. The NFL did not have player's names on their jerseys. The AFL picked up the proposal from Chicago White Sox owner Bill Veeck, who had suggested the idea to major league baseball the previous spring.

The group finally kicked off some real action on the field when the Boston Patriots played the Denver Broncos. This game did not feature a passing contest between Peyton Manning and Tom Brady. Instead, Frank Tripucka and Butch Songin called the signals for the teams. With no televised coverage of the contest held on a Friday night at Boston University's Nickerson Field, only the 21,597 people in attendance saw it.

The early years of the AFL proved a struggle. The franchises in the two largest markets, New York and Los Angeles, had hard times. The crowds grew sparse in both cities. The Titans stayed in New York but attendance dropped each season, but the Chargers left Los Angeles for San Diego after one season. When only 5,000 people came to the Chargers' third home game in Los Angeles, Jack Faulkner, an assistant coach, approached head coach Sid Gillman with a suggestion. "Let's save some time today," said Faulkner looking out at the sparse crowd. "Instead of announcing the starting lineups, let's just send the players up into the stands to shake hands with the crowd."[5]

The media did not give the league much credit during those early years. Houston won the title the first two seasons and still could not get respect. "No player on the Houston Oilers could break into the starting lineup of any of the top four teams in either division of the NFL, and only one or two could break into the starting lineups of any team in the NFL," wrote *Sports Illustrated*.[6]

Three teams, the Texans, Oilers and Chargers, dominated the first few seasons. These franchises had solid financing which enabled them to field competitive teams right from the start. Houston won the first two championships in league history. The Chargers played in the title game five of the first six seasons in the league, only missing the 1962 game. The league seemed to hit their stride about the time they played their third championship game. The game pitted the league's first two owners, Lamar Hunt and Bud Adams, against one another in what many considered a battle for Texas. Geographically they sat in the same state (Texas) but, in the AFL Houston represented the "East" division and Dallas the "West."

They played the 1962 championship game at Jeppesen Stadium in Houston, the home field for high schools in the Houston school district and the University of Houston Cougars football team. It also served as the Oilers' home field. With so much heavy use, the field had little to no grass by the end of the season. When Texans coach Hank Stram stepped out of the locker room into the drizzle before the game, he shook his head as he surveyed the field. He knew the field well: on a dry day, the field is like concrete. It was worse when it rained; then it was nothing but mud.

A crowd of 37,981 attended the game, which was not bad for a game played two days before Christmas. The fans looked for a good contest as these two teams had split their head-to-head matchups during the season. Dallas dominated the first half of the game, taking an early 17–0 lead keyed by quarterback Len Dawson along with a strong ground game. The swift-running Abner Haynes combined with powerful fullbacks Jack Spikes and Curtis McClinton to keep the team moving on the ground.

The Pittsburgh Steelers had selected Dawson, a top prospect in the 1957 draft, but they already had Hall of Famer Bobby Layne playing quarterback. He never seemed to get an opportunity and ended up being traded to the Cleveland Browns in 1960. After three years of little activity, the Browns released him. His old college assistant coach, Hank Stram, had a team in Dallas and they gave him a chance. He arrived and everyone thought he had lost the abilities he had shown at Purdue. Rumor had it team owner Lamar Hunt wanted to release him.

"I wasn't very good when I went to Dallas," admitted Dawson, "because I hadn't played in five years and my skills had eroded, but [Hank Stram] knew how to bring that back and he stayed with me awhile. He was the finest quarterback coach I ever had. Some of these other coaches did not know the techniques of the quarterback position. He knew the fundamentals of it. He broke it down from my footwork, how I took the snap, how I turned and he worked on these drills every day."[7]

Dawson had an uphill climb. Cotton Davidson played quarterback that first season. Davidson made the league All-Star Game and earned MVP honors after tossing four touchdown passes in the game. Davidson's prospects seemed bright, but Stram preferred Dawson and, in the end, he got his way. Dallas traded Davidson to the Raiders and Dawson took over the starting job. He led the team to the title game against the defending champion Houston Oilers.

Veteran George Blanda, who had spent time with the Chicago Bears in the NFL before resurrecting his career in the new league, led the Oilers' offense. Blanda seemed like a cat with nine lives. He never really saw eye-to-eye with George Halas as a Chicago Bear. With the exception of the 1953 season, he served as just a kicker in Chicago. At heart, Blanda wanted to do more than kick so before the 1959 season he left the game in apparent retirement. When the new league started, Blanda returned and finally got his chance to play quarterback. At age 33, he became one of the AFL's first stars.

The weather started out with drizzle for the title game, but a front moved through and it started to deteriorate near halftime. "The odd thing that happened is the weather and how it turned at halftime," said Tommy Brooker, a placekicker and end with the Texans. "There were tornado warnings out, the wind was unbelievable. It was awful, the field was so sloppy. It was a wonder that nobody got blown away and that we were able to finish the game."[8]

Despite the lousy weather conditions, Blanda began connecting with his passes in the second half. His 15-yard pass to Willard Dewveall put Houston on the board. Then a field goal followed by Charlie Tolar's one-yard run tied the game. Houston had stormed back and seemed poised to win its third consecutive AFL championship. Dallas hung tough and after 60 minutes, the two teams remained tied at 17 points each.

As the game entered an overtime period, Texans head coach Hank Stram decided if he won the toss, he wanted to take advantage of the strong winds. Usually teams are anxious to take the ball to start overtime, but Stram thought the strong winds would play a big part of the overtime. He wanted his captains to have the wind at their backs if they won the toss.

The wind came out of the north toward the scoreboard clock perched above the end zone seats at south end of the field. As he sent Texans captains Abner Haynes and E. J. Holub out to the center of the field for the coin toss, he yelled his final instructions. He told them to "kick to the clock" in the event they lost the toss. A national television audience watched the coin toss at home where a microphone on the referee let them eavesdrop. "Call it loud," the referee said to Haynes.

"Heads" he said.

It came up heads so the Texans won the toss. Abner Haynes, who had scored both Texans touchdowns during the first half, immediately said the first thing that came to his lips. "We'll kick to the clock," he said. When the referee heard that they would kick, he insisted the Texans stick with that choice. That let the Oilers to choose the direction and they took the wind. The Texans, who had won the toss, now had to kick off into the wind.

The blustery wind rendered both teams ineffective on offense. They traded punts on their first possessions. Dallas intercepted George Blanda for a fourth time in the game, but the Texans could not take advantage. Late in the fifth period, Blanda started getting the Oilers moving. They had reached the Dallas 35 yard line. Despite the windy conditions and already having suffered multiple interceptions in the game, Blanda put the ball up again. His 42 interceptions during the 1962 season is a record that still stands today. He needed at least one more first down to position the ball for an attempt at the winning field goal. Bill Hull intercepted Blanda's pass, ending the drive.

The first overtime period ended without a winner. The Texans survived Abner Haynes's blunder on the coin toss and now would gain the advantage of the wind. When Dallas got the ball back, Jack Spikes provided two key plays to help move the team downfield. First Spikes caught a pass from Dawson for 10 yards and then gained 19 yards on an off-tackle run. With the ball on the Houston 17 yard line, kicker Tommy Brooker came on the field to attempt the game-winning field goal. The center snapped the ball straight back to Dawson, who held it perfectly for the attempt. Brooker took two steps forward and booted the ball towards the post. He reacted immediately, knowing the kick had gone true, ending pro football's longest game. It lasted 77 minutes, 54 seconds.

"The 1962 AFL title game had it all," wrote the *New York Times*, "momentum swings, wild weather, late-game dramatics, a shocking controversy and plenty of star power. The quarterbacks, Dallas's Len Dawson and Houston's George Blanda, later made the Pro Football Hall of Fame."[9]

Much like the 1958 championship had done four years earlier for the NFL, the 1962 AFL overtime contest caught the eye of fans across the country who wanted to follow the excitement of the professional game, but had not seen any action from the new league yet. Fortunately, for the new league, the NFL did not have any games on television that day, which meant the AFL had the television spotlight to itself. It also served to help the junior league catch the attention of the sporting world.

Despite the success on the field, Hunt's team could not match it off the field. They had competed with the NFL's Cowboys for the attention of the Dallas market, but neither team seemed to gain on the other. Both teams inflated their attendance figures to make them sound better, but neither reached an acceptable level.

Lamar Hunt would stop at nothing to create promotions to sell tickets to games. He created a group called the "Spur Club" that ventured around town dressed in red blazers selling tickets. As a complement, he organized a group of schoolteachers called "The Texas Hostesses." He also ran promotions to get additional people to the game. One of them gave free tickets to any barber in town who wore a smock to the stadium. He figured that barbers like to talk and they might talk about the game, making the free tickets an investment towards full-priced sales.

Despite Hunt's promotions, he needed to reconsider staying in his hometown of Dallas. On February 9, a little more than one month after winning the championship, Hunt told a Dallas press conference he planned to move his team to Kansas City.

The announcement caught Dallas Texans players off guard. Receiver Chris Burford had just purchased a house and had started law school in Dallas. "Things just looked great after we beat Houston," Burford said. "It was so good we couldn't wait for the next season to start. We were going to drive those Cowboys out of town. They were getting clocked repeatedly, and we just really felt like we were going to take the town. I think the town was going for us, too."[10]

The national media began to notice the AFL earlier in that 1962 season. In November, the Patriots faced the Bills in bad weather conditions. *Sports Illustrated* writers took notice. A record crowd of 33,247 showed up to watch the two teams compete. "By ignoring the foul, freezing weather and displaying such single-minded fervor over the game, the crowd was saying much about the state of AFL football," wrote Robert H. Boyle in an aptly titled article, "The Underdogs Have Made It." He continued, "Big crowds like the one in Buffalo fairly indicate something team owners have long and loudly contended in public but only in recent weeks believed themselves—that the AFL really has a future."[11]

The article said the AFL owners had begun feeling optimistic about the league's ultimate survival. Just the previous year, many of them felt dejected, but the larger crowds in 1962 got them feeling they had turned the corner. Leadership of the senior circuit ignored the upstart owners in the same way that the establishment shunned youthful protestors who triggered much of the social, economic and cultural change in the decade. While the new league finally gained some footing in the sports world and positive comments in the media, a tough football coach from New York proved he could win in professional football's smallest city.

Chapter Seven

Man of the Decade

A joke making the rounds among football players and fans in the early sixties went like this: A football player died and went to heaven. When he arrived, he saw a team of angels scrimmaging while a short man on the sideline screamed loudly at them. When the player asked St. Peter that fellow's identity, St. Peter replied, "Oh, that's God. He thinks he's Vince Lombardi."[1]

If you close your eyes and imagine what a football coach should look like, you might picture Vince Lombardi. The famous coach, not particularly tall, has a stocky, strong appearance. Sitting atop his barrel chest, his head reveals a face with a strong granite jaw and a toothy grin with a gap between the front teeth. Over his eyes sit tortoise shell glasses. His stance, with both hands on hips, shows he takes this game seriously. He gives the appearance of being ready to explode at any minute. Despite looking like a heart attack waiting to happen, he is definitely a football coach in charge of his surroundings. He stands ready to race on the field at any moment with a teaching point. He refuses to let the finest imperfection go. "Run it again," he would shout.

His rise to greatness coincided with a journey through the sixties. He won acclaim as the NFL's Man of the Decade despite serving as coach and not a player. He held responsibility, at least in part, for the increased popularity of the game during the sixties. Some say he brought about the survival of the Packers in Green Bay. Some wonder what came first, the rise of football as the number one sport in the land, television as the favorite entertainment medium or Vince Lombardi. They may have all grown up together.

On January 29, 1959, at the age of 45, Lombardi accepted the position of head coach and general manager of the Green Bay Packers. It represented his first head-coaching job since high school. He missed out on jobs at Penn, Washington, Air Force and Wake Forest. He may have thought he would get a head coach position if he returned home to his alma mater, Fordham, but they dropped football in 1954. Finally, he received an opportunity to take the top spot.

Vince Lombardi entered the world as the oldest child in a family of five children and lived in the part of Brooklyn known as Sheepshead Bay. The neighborhood comprised an area largely settled by immigrants who had made their homes in working class neighborhoods like that one across the country. Many arrived via Ellis Island, just a stone's throw away. Family was important in this Italian American household. Following the norm of many families of this nationality, as the oldest son his parents put him in a leadership role. They often told Vince what the younger children needed to do and he relayed the message, often in a loud and demanding voice, much like that of his father. This practice helped Vince develop his teaching and leadership skills at a very young age.

His parents had a large influence on Vince. His mother, Matilda, doted on her all children but demanded perfection. Meanwhile, no one dared talk back to Dad—Harry Lombardi. Vince learned about hard work from his father, who had the words *work* and *play* tattooed on the meaty parts of his short fingers at the end of his large, strong hands. Harry Lombardi ran Lombardi Brothers, a meat wholesaler, along with his brother, Eddie. While neither had a particularly good education, they ran this successful business in a competitive industry.

Religion held a very great importance to Vince. He served on the altar at age eight and briefly studied for the priesthood until age fifteen. Vince attended Catholic prep for four years, two short of the six-year program. Throughout his adult life he attended daily mass. His faith, carefully woven through his life, served as a foundation for his success. At daily Mass, he prayed each day for the strength to control his temper. Put simply, Lombardi had strong emotions; he could cry just as easily as he could shout. The temper, however, caused most concern.

Lombardi transferred to St. Francis Preparatory High School, where he played his first organized football. He liked the game right away. He especially liked the toughness of the game. After high school, he attended Fordham University, where he played football for Coach Jim Crowley, a protégé of legendary Notre Dame coach Knute Rockne. He had played as one of the legendary Four Horsemen. Crowley had an enormous impact on the young Lombardi. He ran tough practice sessions where he tolerated nothing less than full effort. Crowley stressed hard, aggressive play from the start of the practice session to the very end. He also wanted his players to play smart. These concepts hit home with Lombardi. They meshed neatly with the hard work message ingrained in him by his father.

Even though Lombardi had made the All-City team as a fullback, Coach Crowley changed his position. He knew Vince as a tough player, but he did not have the speed to play in the backfield at this level. Crowley moved him to guard on the offensive line. Lombardi worked hard at his new position and started as one of the "Seven Blocks of Granite," one of the most famous offensive lines in college football history. As the smallest and least talented player on the unit, Lombardi played hard and tough to make up for his shortcomings.

At Fordham, Lombardi developed the ability to play through injuries. On one occasion, Lombardi continued to play a game against the University of Pittsburgh despite losing several of his teeth in scrappy line play. The coach called on Lombardi to trap the defensive tackle and every time he did, the defender hit Vince in the mouth with his elbow, causing the injury. The days before facemasks made the mouth vulnerable in pileups at the line of scrimmage. Later in life, as Lombardi told the story, he would say his father taught him to ignore the small injuries, telling him the hurt was just in his mind.

All these life experiences—starting at home with his parents, and roiling into the male role models he met along his journey—served to shape the principles Lombardi held dear and served as the corner stones of his life philosophy. It all jelled when he studied under the Jesuits at Fordham. "The fundamental principles that he used in coaching—repetition, discipline, clarity, faith, subsuming individual ego to a larger good—were merely extensions of the religious ethic he learned from the Jesuits," Lombardi biographer David Maraniss wrote. "In that sense he made no distinction between the practice of religion and the sport of football."[2]

After graduation from Fordham, Lombardi worked in business while attending law school at night. To earn extra money, he played semipro football for the Brooklyn Eagles. He lasted one semester at law school when he decided it was not for him. He tried working as a chemist for DuPont Chemical Company for a short time. He even worked for a short time as an insurance adjuster. He wandered through various jobs, struggling to find his place. Lombardi finally found his niche when he tried education. He taught chemistry, physics, biology, Latin, and physical education at St. Cecilia High School in Englewood, New Jersey. His work in the classroom developed in Lombardi the ability to teach, which proved very useful when his career moved from the classroom to the playing field. He set the learning pace by the slowest student in the class. That method may not have followed convention, but it worked well for Lombardi. He developed methods that used repetition to get the student to understand the lesson. At St. Cecilia, he got his first opportunity to coach football and basketball. His teaching and coaching methods worked as his teams won six state championships in the two sports.

Mickey Corcoran, a very successful basketball coach in New Jersey, played hoops for Lombardi for three seasons at St. Cecilia. Lombardi the basketball coach impressed him, even though he admitted Lombardi had never played basketball or coached it previously. Lombardi taught basketball out of a book he had taken out of the library at St. Cecilia. His methods may have seemed old as the book written back in the 1920s.

After a very successful high school career, Lombardi got his first college coaching job with alma mater, Fordham, in 1947. He took a job as an assistant football coach and assistant director of physical education. He worked primarily with the freshman team at first and then moved to the varsity the second year. After the 1948 season, he joined Earl Blaik's team as assistant football coach at the United State Military Academy. Blaik ran one of the most successful football programs in the nation. By the time he retired, Blaik had six undefeated teams in 18 seasons at Army. Lombardi knew it gave him a tremendous opportunity to continue his education as a football coach. Blaik had trained many individuals who were successful coaches. Murray Warmath would go on to win a national title with the University of Minnesota and Sid Gillman an AFL championship with the Chargers. Lombardi wanted to follow in the path of those individuals.

Lombardi's football education continued over the next five years as he learned many coaching techniques from Coach Blaik, who served as a mentor to the young coach. The Army head coach became one of the first to chart plays on the field using play-by-play sheets and game film to analyze the team's tendencies. Blaik and Lombardi spent countless hours watching tape together. That time proved invaluable in Lombardi's development as a coach.

Blaik, known as "The Colonel" during his Army days, gained fame as a tough, stern and disciplined coach. Famous also for running organized and efficient practices, Blaik covered his lessons in a quick but thorough manner so that the future Army officers could get it. He demanded his assistants teach in the same manner and act as tough but fair coaches. Lombardi watched and learned from the master. Blaik proved not just tough on the players; he drilled Lombardi constantly.

"I'd walk into the office at eight in the morning," Lombardi said, "and without so much as saying 'good morning' he would start on me. 'It is third down. The ball is on your thirty. You need four yards. They are in a seven-man defense with the halfback playing up close behind the strong side. What play will you call? Why? Defend it.' The man never stopped thinking about football. He was a perfectionist."[3]

Those training sessions became invaluable for Lombardi as he developed his football strategy skills. Blaik provided a serious training ground for a young football mind. Those years helped him develop his coaching skills and understanding of how to manage a game and run a tight practice.

"I am not for long practice sessions," Lombardi said in his book, *Run to Daylight*, "but I am for an hour or an hour and a half that is meticulously organized and intense, and this, too, is something that I got from Earl Blaik and brought away from West Point. We would arrive at that office every morning at eight and by the time we walked out onto the practice field that afternoon we would have worked out every phase and every time schedule for everything."[4]

He also saw how Blaik would keep it simple while at West Point by seeing practice from the cadet's point of view. Their day was from 5:50 a.m. to 10:15 p.m., the head coach reminded Lombardi. During the day, they crammed concepts such as differential equations, the mechanics of fluids, electrical engineering, and military tactics. He needed to keep his strategy simple so that the players could easily understand it and then execute it at the highest level on the playing field.

Lombardi followed Blaik's example of keeping the game simple when he got to the National Football League. "The game of pro football, when compared with any science, is a simple one," said Lombardi. "It must be kept that way, because as a coach, you are not dealing with the finest minds to come out of our colleges, although some players do have fine minds."[5]

Lombardi's development as a person, teacher and coach came from the influential men who guided him during his life. It started with his father who taught him to work hard and not let little obstacles get him down. Crowley built on the lessons from his father and reinforced the principles of hard work and dedication on the football field. The Fordham Jesuits taught basic principles that Lombardi applied to life and sport. Coach Red Blaik summed them all up and filled in the gaps of how to function as a successful head coach at major college level.

After the 1953 season, Lombardi left Army and jumped to the NFL as an assistant coach with the New York Giants. Wellington Mara, vice president of the Giants, had attended Fordham with Lombardi. Although not that close at school, they had a connection. Jim Lee Howell, head coach of the Giants, operated with hands-off management style. He left the coaching and game planning to his assistants, Tom Landry and Vince Lombardi. Lombardi coached offense and Landry coached defense for Howell's Giants. During that period, the Giants had five winning seasons and a league championship in 1956 when they defeated the Chicago Bears, 47–7.

Landry and Lombardi formed an excellent team. They approached their jobs with a fiery intensity and driving competitiveness. Each man wanted their unit to serve as the driving force behind the Giants' success. Working against each other day after day helped them develop their skills and put them both into position to succeed as future head coaches in the league. Frank Gifford, who played for the Giants during that time, saw "a lot of competition between Lombardi and Landry and I don't know if it ever turned into a friendship. We did not like them [the defense] very much, and they did not like us much. We did not really care. We were cliquey."[6]

In 1959, Lombardi moved to the Green Bay Packers as their new head coach and general manager. Lombardi took over a Packers team he feared had gotten used to losing. After all, they had not had a winning season since 1947. That encompassed 11 long seasons without as much as a breakeven season. Early in their history, they had won many championships under the watchful eyes of Curly Lambeau. Fans watched Arnie Herber drop back and throw to Don Hutson. Championship banners for 1929, 1930, 1931, 1936, 1939, and 1944 hung in the stadium. By the time Lombardi arrived in Green Bay, those days seemed a distant memory. In 1958, they really hit the bottom; they won one game, tied another and lost the other ten to set the worst record in Packers history. The board of directors felt the time had come for a change.

Ironically, even though they only won one game in 1958, seven players on that squad would eventually make the Pro Football Hall of Fame. It makes one pause and consider did the coach make them better players or did all that talent really only win one game in 1958? Did those players lack focus or direction? Paul Hornung and Jim Taylor played in the backfield while Jim Ringo, Jerry Kramer and Forrest Gregg worked on the offensive line. The roster listed Bart Starr and Ray Nitschke but not yet as starters on the team.

"He seemed to have a great ability to reach inside you and turn your motor on," said Jerry Kramer of Lombardi, the master motivator. Lombardi took the assembled talent, added a few additional pieces and began to teach them the game of football. Kramer said he had little sayings that he retained all his life. "The greatest achievement is not in never failing, but in rising again after you fall," Lombardi told the team.[7]

Lombardi had a natural teaching ability. He never turned down an opportunity to pass along a lesson. "My dad owned the hotel attached to the Packers' downtown offices, and I worked in the kitchen doing odd jobs as a kid," said Paul Van, owner of Green Bay's Best Western Downtowner. "One time when I was thirteen, I began filling an order for pancakes, not really knowing all that much about what I was doing. The waitress returned with the order, screaming at me because I had made Vince Lombardi's pancakes with runny middles and the coach was unhappy. When Lombardi found out I was a kid, he came into the kitchen and proceeded to give me a gentle lesson in the proper way of making a flapjack."[8]

On January 29, 1959, the Green Bay Packers hired Vince Lombardi as their head coach and general manager (Photofest).

Players such as guard Jerry Kramer were impressed that the turnaround was quick. The team improved immediately. Players were impressed with Lombardi's organization; every practice session had a flow that guaranteed maximum benefits. Lombardi was a master of detail. He drilled all units, including the special teams so everyone was prepared for anything they might face in the fame. He told them repeatedly that one critical play could decide the game.

Everybody who played for or coached with Lombardi spoke of his demanding nature. He trained his players hard with personal supervision over the grass drills. He made his team strive for top physical conditioning. He told them fatigue would make them cowards. He took players further than they thought possible. His teams excelled in the fourth quarter because their superior physical shape compared to the opposition.

Their 7–5 record in 1959 gave the Packers their first winning record since that 1947 season. In 1960, Paul Hornung set a scoring mark that lasted so long that many thought it would not ever be broken. His 176 points set a league record that stood until San Diego running back LaDainian Tomlinson scored 31 touchdowns for 186 points in 2006. Better yet, the Packers advanced to the championship game in Philadelphia. They faced a veteran Philadelphia Eagles team while the Packers themselves had no other playoff experience. Norm Van Brocklin, approaching his 34th birthday and finishing his 12th season in the league, led the Eagles' offense. Their defense, however, proved just as intimidating.

Chuck Bednarik stood as perhaps the most famous and oldest player on the Eagles roster. Bednarik, one of those old World War II veterans, still played the kid's game of football despite his age. He had flown as a B-24 machine gunner while still a teenager during World War II. He flew 30 missions over Europe for the Army Air Corps in 1944 and 1945. Looking back, Bednarik wondered how any of them survived.

Bednarik, the last of the 60-minute players, starred as an All-Pro center on offense. Then he had to play defense when the starting middle linebacker, Bob Pellegrini, went down with an injury in the fifth game of the season. He had played both ways in his younger days and at 35 years old the coaches asked him to do it again. Playing both ways represented a tremendous accomplishment for a man close to retirement as a player. In fact, he had retired once. The years of playing a very physical game had caught up with him so he decided to retire. Then he and his wife had a fifth daughter making money tight so he came back for one more football season and kept his other job selling concrete.

His building supply job earned him his famous nickname for the gridiron. One might have thought the name "Concrete Charley" came from his violent hits on the football field. It actually came from his life in the cement business. He easily could have earned it with those solid hits on the football field, too. Opponents swore that he hit them with concrete rather than his shoulder. Bednarik played the game hard.

His most famous hit came earlier that season. In a November 1960 game at Yankee Stadium, Giants running back Frank Gifford ran a crossing pattern out of the backfield into Bednarik's zone. The quarterback threw the ball slightly behind Gifford, who turned his head and reached back for the ball. Bednarik saw a clear target, lowered his shoulder and caught the running back right on the chest. The shot took Gifford off guard and he coughed up the ball. Then, he collapsed to the field. A picture taken that moment became one of the most famous of the era.

"Bednarik caught me from the blind side and really nailed me," Gifford said in his autobiography. "I must have glimpsed Chuck just before he unloaded as I tried a quick move that only made me more vulnerable. It was a great shot, and down and out I went. I actually don't remember any of this."[9]

"It was one of those typically tough games between the Giants and Eagles in the middle of November," recalled Bednarik. "I had just hit Gifford when that picture was taken. He was doing a down-and-in pattern, and I saw him coming; I just hit him high in the chest about as hard as I could. His head snapped, and he went flying one way and the ball went flying another. Since I was following the ball, I did not know where Gifford had gone. One of our linebackers, Chuck Weber, was scrambling to get the ball."[10]

As Gifford lay unconscious on the turf, Bednarik waved his arms and jumped in celebration. To some it seemed like poor sportsmanship. From the stands, Bednarik appeared to celebrate over a fallen opponent. The photograph of Bednarik's stance over the prone Gifford is one of the most famous pictures from the history of professional football. Fans asked Bednarik to sign copies at card shows years after the fact. People did not understand the fumble gave the ball back to the Eagles, virtually ensuring victory and a spot in the playoffs for the first time in more than a decade. That was the real reason for Bednarik's excitement, which he took time to explain to Gifford after the game.

Gifford left the field on a stretcher and went by ambulance to the hospital. They labeled it a concussion, but he missed the rest of the season and the all of the next. He even announced his retirement and took a broadcasting job in New York. Years later when Gifford started dating his third wife, Kathie Lee, he figured he needed to warn her. He reminded her that he played professional football for twelve years, made All-Pro at three different positions and Most Valuable Player once, and was elected to the Hall of Fame. "But of all the things you're going to hear about me, the word you'll hear most often is 'Bednarik,'" said Gifford.

"Bednarik?" she asked with a blank look on her face. "What's that—pasta?"[11]

No, it was not pasta, but the cement salesman who hit as if he wore concrete for shoulder pads. Kathie Lee soon learned the whole story. It was not as much a shock as Gifford's first wife, Maxine, had during the game. She saw the hit from the stands and made her way to the locker room to check on her husband. She arrived at the door of the Giants' dressing room when the team physician leaned out and said, "I'm afraid he's dead." She immediately started crying. Later she learned that the doctor referred to a security guard who had suffered a heart attack during the game. They took the guard to the locker room for treatment, but he had not survived the attack.

They played the 1960 championship game on Monday afternoon since Christmas Day fell on Sunday that year. Despite playing one the road in Philadelphia's Franklin Field, the Packers were favored. Neither the Packers nor Eagles had played in a title game since the forties.

Green Bay trailed by only one score late in the game when Bart Starr led the team on what he hoped to make the game-winning drive. Despite starting on their own 35-yard line, the Packers drove deep into Eagles territory. With time running out, Starr mixed short passes with runs to move the Packers down the field. Time was running out. With only 12 seconds left, Starr tossed the ball to Jim Taylor.

Taylor, along with Jim Brown, were considered the toughest fullbacks in the game during the early sixties. As one of the first players in the league dedicated to weight training, Taylor used the rare practice to strengthen his core body. He said it helped him avoid injury and improved his inside running. Lombardi's two-a-day workouts were notoriously tough, but Taylor would get up early and work out with weights before the morning practice. Before his football career, he worked as a roughneck on an offshore oil rig. Tough work like that prepared him for the rigors of the football field. On the field, he prided himself on his ability to gain tough inside yards and break away from tacklers.

Starr looked first to Max McGee deep but found him covered, so he dumped the ball to Taylor in the left flat with the hope that the tough runner could get into the end zone. The mushy turf made cutting difficult, but Taylor turned up the field. He needed to avoid tacklers or run them over. Taylor got close to the 10 yard line before Eagle defenders closed in. He first met defensive back Bobby Jackson, who slowed him down enough for Chuck Bednarik to join in. Together, the two Eagles pulled the Packers runner to the turf. Taylor's run stopped just nine yards short of the winning score. Under the pile, Taylor struggled to regain his feet in the hopes the Packers could get off one more play. Bednarik would not let him get off the ground. He remained on Taylor as he watched the seconds tick off the clock. When he saw zeros on the clock, he let Taylor get up. The Eagles won the game, 17–13. In the locker room after the game, Lombardi told the disappointed Packers they would not lose another playoff game while he was coach and they did not.

The Packers had dominated the game's statistics. Green Bay earned 22 first downs compared to just 13 for the Eagles. Green Bay outgained Philadelphia, 223 to 99, in rushing yards but fell just short even on passing yards (178 to 197). If one looked at just the statistics, they might think the Packers the victors, but the Eagles pulled it out. It left a huge chip on the collective shoulders of the Green Bay Packers.

In just two seasons, Lombardi had turned a bunch of underperformers into a team that could challenge for the title. He did it with hard work, a tough training regimen and a continuous pursuit of perfection. Lombardi's goal aimed to get his team in better shape than the rest of the league. None of the Packers liked training camp but the thing they disliked the most Lombardi called grass drills. The squad assembled and began running in place. When the whistle sounded, the players flopped on their bellies, and then hopped up again. Lombardi urged them on all the time. "C'mon, lift those legs," he yelled. "Lift them. Higher. Higher."

Lombardi personally supervised the grass drills. He worked the players about twenty minutes or so; the players said it felt like it lasted for hours. Afterwards, they would have intense and physical full contract scrimmages. Players said the tough training camps got them into better shape than the opponents they faced during the season. Their physical conditioning helped fuel fourth quarter comebacks.

They dominated play during the 1961 season and overpowered Lombardi's old team, the Giants, 37–0, in the title game. Their third victory over the Giants that season was played in front of 39,000 people at Green Bay, which comprised about half the usual population of that small Wisconsin town. The following year, the Giants kept the score closer, 16–7, as the same two teams returned to the title game. *Time* magazine proclaimed football the top sport in American in its December 21, 1962, edition. Lombardi appeared on the cover with the headline "The Sport of the '60s."

"No other sport offers so much to so many," the editors of *Time* wrote. "Boxing's heroes are papier-mâché champions. Hockey is gang-warfare, basketball is for gamblers, and Australia is too far to travel to see a decent tennis match. Even baseball, the sportswriters' 'national pastime,' can be a slow-motion bore: finger resin bag, touch cap, look for sign, shake head, shake again, check first, big sigh, wind up, and finally pitch. Crack! Foul ball—and the fans could be halfway to Chicago by jet."[12]

Lombardi took this fan-friendly game and boiled it down to its simplest level, blocking and tackling. Lombardi believed in playing sound fundamental football and physical play. Opposing coaches expected a difficult game when they faced a Lombardi-coached team. "His system was not very innovative," Landry continued. "It was a tough, hard-nosed, fundamental type of football. His strength didn't lie there. It lay in his ability to get people to perform better than they thought they could. No one was better than Vince in that area that I've ever seen."[13]

Lombardi predicated his offense on a sound running game with a sprinkling of short passes thrown in. The strong running game formed the key component. Lombardi believed in power. He wanted his team to overpower the opposition with more blockers than they could defend. He would mass blockers at the point of attack in order to outnumber and run over the defense. His favorite play combined all of that strategy.

"Every team arrives at a lead play, a bread-and-butter play," said Lombardi. "It is the play that the team knows it must make go and the one opponents know they must stop. Continued success with it, of course, makes a number one play because from that success stems your own team's confidence. And behind that is the basic truth that it expresses a coach as a coach and the players as a team. And they feel completely satisfied when they execute it successfully."[14]

The Green Bay power sweep—Lombardi's signature play—followed this concept. Two guards pulled around the end and joined with the fullback in leading interference for the halfback. It massed power at the point of attack, a concept Lombardi learned during his playing days. That is a rather simplistic description of the play. After John Madden, who would become a Hall of Fame coach, heard Lombardi lecture for eight hours on that single play, he figured he did not know anything about football.

Lombardi believed in keeping it simple and performing with perfection. In an attempt to reach perfection, his team drilled the same basic plays repeatedly. Lombardi figured repetition would bring them to perfection, or as close as humans could get to perfection. This method came from Lombardi's teaching background. He knew that repetition makes things sink in. If they did it enough times, the players would not have to think during a ballgame, they could just react to what played out in front of them.

Lombardi preferred a simple, well-executed offense but he was far from a simple man. He inherited a strong work ethic from his father. His family brought him his love of God. His religious background also drove his intolerance of bigotry. During his first year in Green Bay, he set down the law that he would not tolerate any infractions of bigotry. "If I ever hear nigger or dago or kike or anything like that around here, regardless of who you are, you're through with me," Lombardi told the team. "You can't play for me if you have any kind of prejudice."[15] Due to his darker skin, Lombardi may have felt some personal connection to the black players who faced the brunt of the racial prejudice. Privately, he may have believed that his Italian heritage delayed his opportunities as a head coach.

Lombardi's actions spoke volumes more than his words. He brought in Emlen Tunnell, a black defensive back whom he knew from his years with the Giants. He wanted Tunnell to spread his defensive concepts on the field and be a leader for the younger black players he hoped to bring to Green Bay in future years. Tunnell took the tougher path through life. He suffered a broken neck in 1942 at the University of Toledo that many thought ended his football career. When World War II started, he attempted to enlist in the army and navy but they turned him down. Instead, he joined the Coast Guard and served until 1946. Leaving the military, he went looking for a spot to finish college.

In the military, he met Jim Walker, who had played tackle for the Iowa Hawkeyes just before the war. Walker told Tunnell tales of black stars such as Duke Slater and Ozzie Simmons who had played for the school. Knowing he had a chance to play, Tunnell enrolled at the University of Iowa and immediately helped the Hawkeyes as a substitute running back on offense, also playing defensive back and returning kicks.

In the summer of 1948, Tunnell hitchhiked to the office of the New York Giants and asked for a tryout. The Giants had never had a black player on their roster before, but

Tunnell thought he would ask for an opportunity since he had heard that the baseball Dodgers recruited Jackie Robinson to play for their organization. He received a tryout, impressed the coaches and signed a contract. Tunnell soon stepped up as a key member of the Giants' defense, specializing in an ability to intercept the ball. He ended his career with 79 picks, the all-time career record at the time.

Tunnell opened new doors for men of color. He was not just the first black player with the Giants. After retiring as a player, Tunnel became the first African American to serve as a regular fulltime assistant coach in the league since the early 1920s. The first black player selected to the Hall of Fame, Tunnell also had the honor as the first selected as a pure defensive player.

"When I got to Green Bay, there wasn't a colored family in town," Tunnell recalled later. "I really didn't have a place to live.... Well, [Lombardi] called up a hotel in town, told them he wanted a special rate for me and gave them my name. Then he stopped. 'Oh, yes.' He added. 'The player is a Negro. That won't make any difference to you, will it?' Only he didn't make that a question. It was a statement. I spent many happy hours in that hotel, and I got along just great with the people. Green Bay is a great place to live."[16]

That upbringing uniquely qualified Tunnell to integrate the pro football team in the NFL's smallest city. In those days, the nearly all-white Green Bay had a nearly all-white Packers team. The roster had only one black player when Tunnell joined the team. The new coach wanted to change that. He needed a model citizen with tough skin willing to endure some struggles in the journey. He needed a leader who could mentor younger players. He found all of that in Emlen Tunnell.

Lombardi had zero tolerance for discrimination. Lombardi had experienced discrimination first hand himself. Lombardi believed he lost some jobs because of his Italian heritage. Lombardi's own experiences made him an advocate against discrimination. He spread the word among Green Bay restaurant and bar owners that if they did not welcome his black players, he would make the establishment off limits for all of his players.

When his team traveled to the South to play exhibition games, they faced discrimination at hotels. The black players could not stay with the rest of the team due to Jim Crow laws. That disturbed the color-blind Lombardi who insisted that his players act color blind when it came to their teammates. Willie Davis, the black defensive captain of the team, had frank discussions with the coach about race during the sixties.

"He felt that because he was Italian, he'd been held back for a long time and that's the way it was for Negroes now. He said, 'If you really want something'—and he felt I did—'you can have it if you are willing to pay the price. And the price means that you have to work better and harder than the next guy.... He was not bitter when he talked about his past. I think he used it with me to show that he had great empathy for the problems of blacks all over."[17]

Lombardi arrived in Green Bay as the nation opened the door on the turbulent sixties, when racial clashes erupted across the country and civil rights legislation was debated in Washington. Only one black player wore a Packers jersey when Lombardi got there. He left nine seasons later with 14 black players on the Green Bay roster.[18] For most of the sixties, NFL rosters had 40 or fewer players.

Lombardi's own experiences dealing with discrimination helped shape his liberal attitude in dealing with social injustice. He felt his Italian background and his darker complexion subjected him to discrimination. He did not want others treated that way.

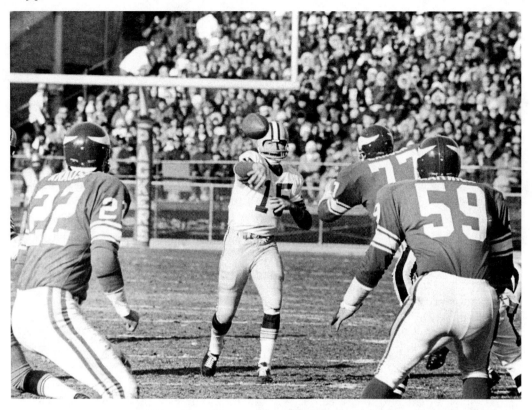

Bart Starr (15) fires a pass between Minnesota Viking defenders during a game in the early 1960s. Starr, a 17th round draft choice, led the Packers to five championships (Photofest).

He also felt strongly on the equal treatment of people due to sexual orientation since he had a gay brother.

Lombardi's Packers dominated the decade of the sixties. His teams consistently won due to their sound, consistent play. The 1962 Packers may stand as Lombardi's best team. They scored more than 30 points in eight contests that season and by year's end had outscored their opponents 415–148, averaging more than 19 points more than their opponents in each game. The defense, led by middle linebacker Ray Nitschke, stifled opponents while the offense, led by the backfield of Paul Hornung, Jim Taylor and Bart Starr, all three future members of the Pro Football Hall of Fame, outscored them.

The Packers of 1962 were a talent-laden team. In 1962, half of the starting lineup, 11 players, made one or more of the All-Pro teams, recalled Jerry Kramer years later. He remembered six players as unanimous selections to every All-Pro team: himself, tackle Forrest Gregg, center Jim Ringo, fullback Jim Taylor and linebackers Dan Currie and Bill Forester.

That season, the Packers went undefeated through six exhibition games and the first 10 games of the regular season. During that 10-game winning streak, they scored 31 or more points six times and posted three shutouts. Their ninth win came against the team that had defeated them for the 1960 title—the Philadelphia Eagles. In a game as one-sided as the 49–0 score indicates, the Packers had 37 first downs to the Eagles 3 and 628 total yards to 54.

His team's performance prompted Lombardi to place a sign above the door leading into the Packer's locker room. It read, "The Green Bay Packers, the Yankees of Football." Lombardi wanted to build a dynasty like the famed baseball team. His message had a psychological aspect, too. They would play the 1962 title game in Yankee Stadium, the home the baseball franchise shared with the Giants. He wanted to keep his team motivated for the contest. They had beaten the Giants in the 1961 title game by 37 points and he did not want an overconfident club suffer a letdown.

The Packers won the 1961 title playing on their own field at City Stadium, which the city later named Lambeau Field. Three Packers stars—Paul Hornung, Ray Nitschke and Boyd Dowler—had to get leave from the Army in order to make the game. Hornung made the most of it. He scored 19 points and picked up most outstanding player of the game honors. That victory came as the first of five titles for Lombardi's Packers over a seven-year span. The Packers won, 37–0.

The 1962 title game featured a repeat for the Packers and Giants. Extremely poor weather conditions in Yankee Stadium forced all the participants to endure terrible conditions. Camera operators had to warm their cameras over bonfires in order to keep them from freezing. The wind chill made it feel colder than single digits due to gusting winds swirling up to 40 miles per hour. The ball fell off the kicking tee three times before the opening kickoff.

Two Packers had strong performances in the game. Jim Taylor led the bruising Packers ground game, earning 85 tough yards on 31 carries. Every yard he gained came at a cost. Nearly every one of them ended with a hard hit by Sam Huff immediately followed by another hit on the frozen turf.

"If Taylor went up to get a program, Huff was supposed to hit him. Wherever Taylor went, Huff went with him," said guard Jerry Kramer. "I remember sitting next to Jimmy on the way home and he had his topcoat on. He never took it off. He had it over his shoulder and the guy was shivering almost all the way home. He just got the [heck] beat out of him that day."[19]

Ray Nitschke paced the Packers' defense, which totally stymied the Giants' top-ranked offense. The middle linebacker recovered two fumbles and deflected a pass for an interception. In fact, the Giants' only score came as the result of a special teams play, a blocked punt recoved in the end zone. The media selected Nitschke, finishing his first season as a full-time starter, as the game's MVP. Just hours later, Nitschke appeared on the television game show *What's My Line?* The game show involved a panel that asked questions of a guest in attempt to guess their occupation. Nitschke wore thick glasses that may have made him appear more like an accountant than a football player. Despite his calm off-field attire, two Giants fan panelists, Martin Gabel and Bennett Cerf, recognized Nitschke.

As the Packers began their ascendance, the Giants, yet unaware, started a dry period in their history. After winning the 1956 title, the Giants lost championship games in 1958, 1959, 1961, 1962 and 1963. The luster wore off after the 1963 season in which Y.A. Tittle earned the NFL MVP award after leading the Giants to an 11-win season. In 1964, they seemed to get old all at once and suffered through a two-win season. Unfortunately for "Big Blue" fans, they did not have another winning season for the rest of the decade.

The 1963 season did not go so well for the Packers. In a way, it seemed like a case of history repeating itself for Lombardi. A cheating scandal involving members of the football team at West Point happened while Lombardi served as an assistant coach there.

Players involved left the school. Army suffered through a two-win season. They had lost only three games over the previous seven seasons. Army football stood at the pinnacle when the scandal erupted. Now similar adversity hit the Packers after two consecutive titles. Favored to win a third straight championship, the Packers had problems when the NFL suspended Paul Hornung for gambling.

The 1963 season presented a significant challenge. Hornung was a key player in the Green Bay's offense. His suspension left the Packers seeking a third consecutive championship shorthanded. The season started poorly as the champion Packers lost to the College All-Stars in the annual preseason game in Chicago. Losing to a team of college kids playing in their first professional game came as an insult to Lombardi. It seemed like an omen for the coming season. In the season's sixth game, things got worse when Bart Starr broke his right wrist as he tumbled out of bounds. Now, the season tested Lombardi's theory that football's central flaw was that one player, the quarterback, carried too much importance.

The Bears upset defending champion Packers in the opener as they intercepted four Bart Starr passes. The Bears' defense held the Packers to just 150 yards passing with only 77 on the ground. That victory gave the Bears a tremendous lift and they marched to four more victories before losing to the 49ers, 20–14. After losing to the Bears, the Packers started an eight-game winning streak and the two old rivals stood tied for first place when the rematch came at Wrigley Field. The Bears did even better in the second game with a 26–7 victory.

The two victories over the Packers put the Bears in the driver's seat in the Western Division. They managed to survive the rest of the season and finished as division champions with a date to play the New York Giants for the NFL title. The Giants had only missed the postseason twice between 1956 and 1963. That 1963 season cost the Packers the opportunity to win three straight titles.

By 1967, the Packers seemed a driven team. They won two straight titles and were primed for another run at three straight championships. Since the start of training camp, Lombardi had talked about making history by achieving that goal. He reminded the team that it had never happened before and they had a second opportunity to do it. They missed their opportunity in 1963. They dominated throughout the season; they lost only two games by a total of four points. Lombardi wanted to win three straight titles more than any other goal. The stress of chasing titles wore on the coach.

Jerry Kramer compared Lombardi's appearance to that of a president after two terms. He enters office young and tireless but, at the end of the eight years, looks grey and tired. Kramer saw the same in his head coach. Lombardi looked older than his years due to the stress, workload and his health.

He suffered from arthritis, especially in his hip. His wife, Marie, worried about his heart because on occasion he complained of chest pains. He had given up smoking three years earlier, but still suffered occasional dizzy spells and nearly blacked out in the locker room a few times. He found it necessary to take an evening nap and occasionally one in the afternoon to keep up the work schedule.

According to some reports, Lombardi had considered stepping down as coach for about a year. He had discussed the decision with his wife, Marie. He told her he felt he could no longer handle both the coach and general manager jobs. Now he faced a difficult decision. In the car ride home from the Ice Bowl victory over the Dallas Cowboys, Vince Jr. recalled his father telling him that he had just coached his next-to-last football game.

Deep down, Lombardi may have known his health was not good as he attempted to reduce his workload. After winning the third straight title in 1967, he retired as head coach. Lombardi retained the general manager title and passed running the team onto his chief assistant, Phil Bengtson.

Having Bengtson, defensive coach for nine years under Lombardi, move to the head coaching job did not seem like a big change according to guard Jerry Kramer. The players knew Bengtson had a different personality than Lombardi, but most thought the team would continue to play well for the new head coach. The strong Packers defense, coordinated by Bengtson, paced the team's success for years. In the end, though, it proved very difficult to replace a legend. Bengtson's Packers lost seven games and won only six with one tie in 1968. The previous three years the Packers lost only nine games and won 38 including playoff games.

Teams that dominate their sport for years often get favorable press for a period and then some negative reports start to come out, and so it was for Green Bay. The Packers dominated football for most of the sixties. The media darlings of the early sixties saw press that was more negative as the decade ended. One article, in particular, really affected Lombardi.

In January 1968, an unflattering feature article on Vince Lombardi hit the newsstands. A fellow New Yorker and a freelance writer named Leonard Shecter wrote "The Toughest Man in Pro Football" for *Esquire*. The article depicted Lombardi as a man who constantly cussed out his players and ignored their physical ailments and pain. When he saw it, Vince became furious. "Am I like this?" he ranted, throwing the magazine down. "Am I really like this?"

Lombardi had granted the writer access to practice and granted an interview at the beginning of training camp in July 1967. Shecter's observations sounded bad to the readers of the magazine. The article painted a picture of Lombardi as a hard-driving coach who did not care about his players. One part in particular unsettled those who may never have played the game for a hard-driving coach. During training camp, there was a pileup of players involved in a physical play. Out of the group came a painful shriek. As the players untangled, Jerry Moore, a rookie guard, was crying out in pain. Moore was seen with his hands grabbing at a knee. The writer quotes Lombardi as telling the player to get up.

Shecter also described the "up down" grass drills Lombardi conducted during summer camp, a big part of his intense fitness programs. Such drills stood as a hallmark of his program to have the best-conditioned team in the fourth quarter so that they could preserve victory, even when it may have seemed remote. He would personally lead the grass drills driving his men past the point they would have thought possible.

"It was a drill," Shecter wrote, "best conducted in the summer sun at brain-frying temperatures because sane men will not do it. The crazy men run in place, double time, as hard as they can, while Lombardi shouts at them in his irritating, nasal, steel-wool-rubbing-over-grate voice.... As the drill goes on, the noises they make breathing almost drown out the sound of Lombardi's voice. The breathing becomes louder and somewhat wetter, until it sounds like the ocean when the last waves roll up into the sucking sand. Finally, when they are beyond the point of humanity or sanity, Lombardi lets up. 'All right!' he shouts. 'Around the goalposts and back. Now RUN!'"[20]

Lombardi thought that the article reduced him to the status of yet another brutal football coach. He wanted recognition as a teacher and a leader of men. He deeply cared for his players and considered them his family. Shecter's words hit him hard. After the descriptions of Lombardi as a tyrannical man working his men too hard, came some unflattering personal comments. Shecter compared the coach's treatment of players to a general's ruthless use of troops in battle.

Dick Schaap, who worked editing *Instant Replay* (Jerry Kramer's diary) at the time, criticized Shecter's tone. "There were a lot of truths in it, but it was too far one way," said Schaap. "It may have been one hundred percent truthful, but one hundred percent truthful isn't always the truth. It may have been accurate, but it wasn't fair."[21] Paul Brown, Lombardi's closest ally as a coach, had put in a good word for Lombardi when he sought a head coaching job. He wanted Lombardi to do well. Paul Brown saw the *Esquire* article and it upset him. By the late sixties, Paul Brown had returned to football with the expansion Cincinnati Bengals of the AFL. When Shecter showed up at Bengals training camp at Wilmington College to do a story on Brown, the coach recognized him during a press conference. Coach Brown asked Shecter if he wrote the story on Lombardi. When he answered affirmatively, Brown kicked him out of camp.

The other criticism that stung Lombardi involved the winning at all costs angle. Folks widely quoted Lombardi as having said, "Winning isn't everything; it's the only thing." That line actually came in a John Wayne movie called *Trouble Along the Way*. Screenwriter Melville Schavelson said he heard it from his Hollywood agent who also represented UCLA football coach Henry "Red" Sanders.[22] Many coaches used similar language when urging their forces to play their best so they can win the contest.

The issue comes when people attempt to apply that line universally. The line, "winning is the only thing" runs counter to the good sportsmanship attitude captured by Grantland Rice in "it's not that you won or lost but how you played the game." The media incorrectly attempted to apply that line to amateur sports. The professionals are judged by their wins. Only one team wins the championship each year.

"Second place is meaningless," said Lombardi. "You can't always be first, but you have to believe that you should have been—that you are never beaten, time just runs out on you." At another time, Lombardi made it clear what the type of players he wanted on his club. If any players grew "tired of paying the price winning demands, he will have a one-way ticket on a plane from Green Bay, no matter who he is."[23]

As some began to criticize Lombardi and his methods, the media defined his quote to mean "win at all costs." When they asked Lombardi later, he admitted regret in the use of that phrase. "I wished I'd never said the thing," said Lombardi with more than a hint of desperation in his tone. "I meant the effort. I meant having a goal. I sure didn't mean for people to crush human values and morality."[24] Instead, he felt players should continuously strive for perfection. By chasing perfection, they would do their best and, perhaps, achieve excellence. They would take pride in their performance, regardless of the outcome. The professional game had no comparison to kid's games.

Unfortunately, the statement took added meaning when attributed to a coach with a reputation as a relentless taskmaster who drove his players hard and demanded perfection from them. Everybody knew Vince Lombardi as a disciplinarian with a short fuse. When a man with those qualities speaks with words that suggest he would accept no alternatives to victory, it sounds like he had no limit to the extent with which he would compete so that he would win.

After only year as general manager and not coaching, Lombardi grew restless and bored. He missed the direct interaction with players that he had as head coach. One of his closest advisors thought he needed to return to active coaching. "My wife wants me back coaching," said Lombardi said of Marie. "She told me I was a damn fool to get out of it. She is a fan as well as a wife. Besides, I miss the rapport with the players."[25]

At Super Bowl III, rumors said he had his choice of jobs. The Jets, Eagles, Saints, Rams and Patriots all supposedly expressed an interest in him taking over their professional teams and representatives from Annapolis wanted to talk to him about their head coaching position at Navy. Such offers proved flattering, but one in particular caught Lombardi's attention. He received an offer that included a $110,000 salary and 5 percent ownership of a team from Edward Bennett Williams in Washington, D.C. The opportunity to gain some equity in the franchise appealed to Lombardi. Seeing as too good to pass up, he left for the challenge of turning around the Washington Redskins. In 1969, he led the Redskins to their first winning season in 14 years.

One story displayed how Lombardi never missed a thing, regardless how small. While watching practice, he noticed that running back Larry Brown had trouble getting off the ball at the snap. Once going, he had plenty of quickness and speed. Lombardi ordered a hearing test and doctors said Brown was deaf in his right ear. Lombardi got a hearing aid mounted in Brown's helmet and the running back enjoyed a successful career.

Lombardi saw Washington as the capital of the free world and set his goal to make it the football capital, too. He never got the turnaround completed. He improved the win count from five the year before his arrival to seven wins and two ties in his first season. He had just the one season in Washington. In late June 1970, Lombardi entered the hospital where doctors discovered cancer in his colon. He had surgery to remove a tumor inside a section of his colon. He reentered the hospital one month later and never got well again. Lombardi died on September 3, 1970, just before the start of the football season.

The mood in the country seemed almost as if a former president had died. A memorial Mass at St. Matthew's Cathedral in Washington preceded a requiem Mass at St. Patrick's Cathedral in New York. Football royalty came from all over to say goodbye to the legendary coach. Earl Blaik, Vince's mentor at West Point, came. Chicago Bears owner George Halas, Giants owner Wellington Mara and Pittsburgh Steelers owner Art Rooney represented the ownership of the league.

The Green Bay Packers flew their chartered aircraft from Wisconsin. The Washington team flew in from Tampa, where they had played an exhibition game. Many members of the Giants also attended. NFL commissioner Pete Rozelle welcomed many of the players the coach had touched over the years. Three of them, Bart Starr, Paul Hornung and Willie Davis helped carry the coffin into the cathedral.

Cardinal Terence Cooke, a friend of Lombardi's, officiated. The Cardinal recited from the scriptures a letter from St. Paul, who would describe life-and-death matters in terms of an athletic contest. "For I am already being poured out like a libation, and the time of my departure is at hand," he read. "I have competed well; I have finished the race; I have kept the faith." It was one of Lombardi's favorite verses and one he used to motivate his team before a critical game in route to the third straight championship.

Despite some negative press, many Americans knew him as more than just a football coach. He received many invitations to speak to business groups on management and leadership. His coaching principles easily applied to the business world. He served as the chairman of several charitable organizations and Richard Nixon considered him for vice president until he learned that Lombardi was a Kennedy Democrat.

Lombardi saw character as very important. "Character is just another word for having a perfectly disciplined and educated will," Lombardi told management students at Fordham in 1967. "A person can make his own character by blending these elements with an intense desire to achieve excellence. Everyone is different in what I will call magnitude, but the capacity to achieve character is still the same."[26]

Lombardi used discipline in an attempt to develop the character of his players. He used repetition in the classroom and on the practice field to help players learn tasks so they performed at near flawless levels. Many say Lombardi's true strength came not with his knowledge of the game, but his knowledge of people. He understood what motivated people and used that understanding to bring out the best in his players. He developed people, not just players.

John Madden said he learned an important leadership lesson from Lombardi when as a young coach. In order to keep the team properly motivated, the coach must treat the team the opposite way from how he feels. If the team felt sky high from a big victory, the coach must lean on the players harder that week in practice to bring them down a bit. If the team is down from hard loss, he must pick them up. "The coach," Madden said, "must be the buffer. After a victory, everybody is going to tell the players how good they are. The coach must keep them on an even level."[27]

The players saw this firsthand. During Lombardi's first season in Green Bay, the team suffered a heartbreaking loss to a better team in the final minutes. That defeat stung. The team believed they had a heated postgame talk from the head coach. Instead, Bart Starr recalled, he told them how proud he was of the effort they showed during the contest. Starr said Lombardi knew the best time to criticize, which made his remarks so effective.

"After defeating the St. Louis Cardinals by a huge margin in a preseason game, we walked off the field laughing and slapping each other's backs," said Starr. "When we entered the locker room, however, Lombardi was waiting and quickly brought us back to earth. 'Our performance tonight was a disgrace. The only reason we won is because the Cardinals were even worse. You didn't give a damn about playing your best; you only cared about that damn score.' As he continued his fierce harangue, I thought he must be crazy. When I viewed the game films the next morning, I realized he was right."[28]

Lombardi knew exactly how to handle his players. He understood their personalities and treated them differently because he understood which one could handle the criticism. He knew which ones he could intimidate with his overpowering voice and which ones he needed to pull aside to take corrective action. A read of his 1963 book, *Run to Daylight*, explains how he understood the makeup of the players. He contrasted how he felt he needed to handle two linebackers on the team.

"Ray Nitschke is the rowdy of this team and the whipping boy because he needs it and he can take it," Lombardi wrote. He was fun loving off the field but rough and tough on the field. Previous coaches labeled him as a problem to coach. "When you chew him out he's like a child," continued Lombardi. "He's repentant and never gives you an argument, but then he turns around and does the same thing all over again, and one of the best things that ever happened for Nitschke and this ball club is his marriage. It has settled him down. Criticism stills rolls off him until you wonder if it helps him at all. You don't improve him, but happily he improves himself."[29]

Compare his handling of Nitschke with that of fellow linebacker Dan Currie. They played the same position, but Lombardi would not treat them the same way. "Where criticism just bounces off Nitschke, it cuts so deep into Currie that I have to be careful," Lombardi wrote. "My first year here I read him out in front of the others just once and I knew immediately that he resented it and that it wouldn't help. Even in private you have to be careful how you handle him, but if you tell him he's playing well, he'll go out there and kill himself for you."[30]

The players coming into the league in the latter half of the sixties differed greatly from those starting in the first half. One player in particular, though, received extra media attention compared to the rest. The stories seemed to dwell more on his sex appeal and life style than on his ability to play football. The media was not alone; Lombardi noticed, too. Lombardi saw Joe Namath as the poster child attacking the core values that he saw as necessary for success in America. He saw Namath as the prime example of decaying moral values in American society, especially among the youth.

As the sixties dragged on towards the seventies, Lombardi did not like what he saw. The protests in streets and on college campuses confused him. "I don't know what the devil they're dissatisfied about," he wondered out loud. Lombardi understood issues of race and had no tolerance for prejudice. He thought the social and moral issues threatening society were stretching it to the breaking point.

"To Lombardi, society was decaying," Roy A. Clumpner wrote, "as evidenced by the advent of the birth control pill, the new looseness on morality, the replacement of organized religion with drugs and psychedelics and the hippie cult with their ideas of dropping out and non-competition."[31]

As for the new young players like Joe Namath, he had his opinions. "Joe Namath is an almost perfect passer," said the old coach. Lombardi disagreed with Namath's attitude, public persona and lifestyle. Namath's passing arm impressed him. Lombardi thought the young man was not a positive image for the game of football. His son, Vince Jr., recalled his dad would rant a lot about Joe Namath.

Lombardi viewed structure, organization and discipline as vital to the American way of life. He did not like the change he saw happening. The social changes threatened the world he loved. He welcomed more opportunity for blacks, but the sexual revolution that prompted a loose society greatly displeased him. He did not have to go far to see those changes. Pro football now had a player who appeared as a one-man advertisement for those changes.

Lombardi represented the old generation that possessed and cherished family values. He grew up in a hardworking family where his mother and father stressed those values as he grew up. He believed in the value of religion, authority and discipline. Joe Namath appeared to run counter to all those principles. As his popularity continued to climb, the values in America appeared to crumble. By the end of the sixties, he would become the most popular player in professional football.

Chapter Eight

Can We Just Get Along?

Birmingham, Alabama, represented the front line of the civil rights challenge during the spring of 1963. Protestors organized by the Southern Christian Leadership Conference (SCLC) came to the largest city in Alabama to protest the treatment of minorities. The leader of the SCLC, the Rev. Martin Luther King, Jr., headed the nonviolent protests throughout the streets. Police, led by public safety commissioner Bull Connor, attempted to disperse the nonviolent protests with fire hoses and police dogs.

Associated Press photographer Bill Hudson snapped many pictures of the exchange between the protestors and the marchers. One in particular ended up on the front page of many of the nation's newspapers. The image showed 17-year-old black high school sophomore Walter Gadsden attacked by a police dog as police officers stood by. The dog, with teeth exposed, seemed poised to grab hold of his arm as an officer in sunglasses held the black man by his sweater.

Like many other Americans across the country, president John F. Kennedy saw the picture on the front page of the newspaper. While reading the *New York Times*, JFK reacted emotionally. Appalled, he could not stop thinking about the young man attacked by the dog. Longtime congressional representative John Lewis, who attended the "I Have a Dream" speech with the Reverend King, recalled the meeting. He commented that the ugliness he saw in Birmingham prompted President Kennedy to introduce the civil rights legislation.

Hudson took many more pictures during the riots that spring in Birmingham. Some showed young black people seated on the sidewalk as high-pressure fire hoses struck them. Water cannons first appeared for crowd control in Nazi Germany in the 1930s. The high-pressure water could knock someone off his or her feet at a distance up to 100 yards. In Birmingham, the water hoses ripped clothing and pushed protestors down the street.

Another photographer, Charles Moore, went to Birmingham to take photos for *Life* magazine. Moore, born and raised in Alabama, knew Jim Crow all too well. He returned as a photographer to show the racial struggle happening on the streets. "I don't want to fight with my fists," he said. "I want to fight with my camera."[1] Moore took many photos of the struggle including a series showing two dogs ripping protestor Henry Lee Shambry's clothes. They ripped Shambry's pant leg off and bit him on the arm, leg and hip. Another large photograph, spread over two pages in *Life* magazine's coverage of the Children's Crusade, showed firefighters aiming their hoses and blasting them with a hundred pounds

In this May 3, 1963, file photograph, a 17-year-old civil rights demonstrator, defying an anti-parade ordinance of Birmingham, Alabama, is attacked by a police dog. The next afternoon, during a meeting at the White House with members of a political group, President Kennedy discussed this photograph, which had appeared on the front page of that day's *New York Times* (Bill Hudson; Associated Press).

of water per square inch. *Life* presented the image with the headline, "They Fight a Fire That Won't Go Out."

The pictures of apparently innocent nonviolent protestors, including children, shocked many Americans. In her 2001 book about the civil rights struggle in Birmingham, *Carry Me Home*, Diane McWhorter wrote that the photograph rallied more than national outrage. The photos attracted international attention to American's civil rights struggles. The images from Birmingham combined with those of the broken body of Emmett Till, the abuse of four African American students at a Woolworth lunch counter and the baseball bat-carrying parties awaiting the arrival of Freedom Riders at bus stations changed opinions across the country.

In 1954, the U.S. Supreme Court outlawed segregation in the nation's public schools. Two years later, a boycott desegregated the buses in Montgomery, Alabama. A charismatic leader emerged from the struggles. Martin Luther King, Jr., preached a message of hope and followed a strategy of nonviolence during the protest marches. Despite the Supreme Court decision, progress on civil rights came at a snail's pace.

Kennedy took office in the nation's capital and witnessed firsthand the discriminatory practices of the city's NFL team. On March 24, 1961, Secretary of Interior Stewart L. Udall warned the owner of the Washington Redskins to hire black players or face retribution from the federal government. This marked the first time the federal government took action to desegregate a professional sports team.

George Preston Marshall had owned the Washington NFL franchise since 1932 when they still played in Boston. In 1937, Marshall moved the team to his hometown of Washington, D.C. As the Kennedy administration took office, the Washington franchise stood as the lone NFL team without at least one minority player. Some called him a bigot. To illustrate his stance, he issued one statement. "We'll start signing Negroes when the Harlem Globetrotters start signing whites," he said.[2]

Marshall received an NFL franchise in 1932, when he and three partners purchased the franchise located in Boston. In 1933, the NFL had just two black players, Joe Lillard and Ray Kemp. At season's end, both had left. The Chicago Cardinals did not invite Lillard back for another season due in large part to his inability to get along with teammates. Kemp retired and started a long coaching career. Many believe that Marshall successfully convinced his fellow owners to ban blacks from the league.

The Washington Redskins, or Paleskins, as some in the nation's capital called them, sat as the only NFL team without at least one minority player on its roster as the sixties began. In the mid-fifties, while most of the teams desegregated, Washington and Detroit remained all white. In 1955, the Detroit Lions signed their first African American player, Walt Jenkins. Six years later, the Redskins remained the lone holdout with a 100 percent white roster.

Marshall, an extremely vocal and influential member of the NFL's ownership community, had not participated in the 1920 organizational meeting like George Halas. On his arrival in the league during the thirties, however, his influence came immediately. He quickly moved into a leadership position among NFL ownership, ranking right up there with Halas and Pittsburgh owner Art Rooney.

Washington's baseball and football teams played in a turn-of-the-century stadium. Griffith Stadium, built in 1911, served as the home of the Washington Senators playing in baseball's American League from 1911 to 1960 and a new Senators team which began play in 1961 after the original club moved to Minnesota. It also served as the home field for the Washington Redskins from the day they moved from Boston in 1937. Now Washington built a new stadium to replace Griffith Stadium on public land.

Meanwhile, the Kennedy Administration looked for any opportunity to push their civil rights agenda forward. They followed the tactic employed by the city of Los Angeles in the mid-forties to end segregation in professional football. The Redskins signed a contract to play in D.C. Stadium, which, built with public funds, sat on federal land. The contract included a non-discrimination clause. As property owner for the stadium, the Interior Department could deny use of the facilities to anyone who did not meet the terms of the contract. In this case, Udall said the Redskins' discrimination in their hiring practices—not having a single minority on the roster—violated the contract.

"It is certainly our feeling that here in the Nation's Capital, with the marvelous new facility being built on property owned by all of the people of the country, that we ought to set the very highest of standards in terms of adhering to the policies of this Administration with regard to treating everyone in this country equally," Udall said at a press conference on March 24.[3]

The battle was on. His friends described Marshall as a very confident man with a fiery personality. His detractors called him opinionated and contentious. Either way, Marshall welcomed the fight. He and Udall sparred in the media through much of 1961. Marshall seemed to thrive on controversy. Shirley Povich, a *Washington Post* sportswriter, had pushed for integration of the Redskins for years. Marshall had a similar feud going with Redskins minority owner Harry Wismer. Both Povich and Wismer had long urged integration, but Marshall held steadfast.

Marshall's supreme confidence came from his success as a businessman. A high school dropout, he took over the family laundry business and made it widely successful, Marshall considered Washington, D.C., his hometown. His laundry business thrived with promotions and clever advertising. One particular newspaper ad held a nearly blank page with the words "This space was cleaned by Palace Laundry" at the very bottom. He used the slogan "Long Live Linen." By 1946, he had transformed a small family laundry into a multimillion dollar chain with 57 stores.

Marshall stood about 6-foot-2, with blue eyes, black hair, and a very strong face. Any description of Marshall included some of the following adjectives: innovative, shrewd and flamboyant. All those things and more, he also proved highly controversial. His strong opinions left no doubt where he stood. When he took hold of a business, he did everything in his power to make it better. If he saw an opportunity, he moved on it immediately. He did not shy away from tough decisions and was stubborn enough to maintain his position despite criticism.

Marshall finally gave in as the NFL draft approached in December 1961. The Redskins earned the first pick with their league-worst record. They selected running back Ernie Davis, the first black recipient of the Heisman Trophy as college football's best player. Davis later went to the Cleveland Browns for Leroy Jackson and Bobby Mitchell, two African American players. Mitchell became the centerpiece of the trade for the Redskins. An All-Pro with the Browns, he went on to a successful career in the front office with the Redskins after his playing career ended.

As a kid growing up in Richmond, Virginia, in the fifties, Willie Lanier rooted for the Washington Redskins. As a black kid who played football, Lanier did not have much hope of ever playing for them. Until 1962, they remained steadfast in their refusal to have any minority players on their roster.

In the mid-sixties, Lanier played middle linebacker for historically black Morgan State in Baltimore. In the eyes of many pro scouts, Lanier had three strikes against him: His color, the fact he played for a historically black school and the fact he played middle linebacker. Many said he had zero chance of playing middle linebacker in the NFL because the general opinion at the time demanded the so-called thinking positions (quarterback, center, middle linebacker and safety) needed exclusively white players. Coming from a small school did not make it easier for the scouts to find him. However, scouts from the AFL Kansas City Chiefs found Lanier.

In 1967, the Chiefs brought in two stellar college linebackers who would compete to see who got the job as the "quarterback of the defense." Jim Lynch had captained the 1966 Notre Dame football team that won the national championship. He won the Maxwell Award as the nation's best college football player that same year. The Chiefs selected him on the first round of the draft. Lynch is white.

In the second round, the Chiefs selected Willie Lanier, who played college football at Morgan State University. Lanier had twice earned selection as a small school All-American and MVP of the Tangerine Bowl. Chiefs coach Hank Stram wanted to beef up his defense after losing to the Packers in the first Super Bowl so he drafted two linebackers at the top of his draft.

Both players figured to battle it out during training camp for the coveted middle linebacker job. Lynch, selected to play in the College All-Star Football Classic, headed to Chicago. Meanwhile, Lanier went to Chiefs camp. By the time Lynch got to Chiefs training camp, Lanier had all but won the starting job. At the start of the season, Lanier took the middle linebacker position and Lynch played one of the outside linebacker spots. Along with Bobby Bell, they formed one of the best trios of linebackers in the league. After his career, Lanier entered the Pro Football Hall of Fame in 1986.

Back in Washington, Marshall took an extremely active role as owner and came down hard on his coaches. In a 17-year span, he had nine head coaches. Obviously, he proved difficult to work. He even stood on the sidelines during games. Marshall recommended plays and strategy, and berated players and officials.

Corinne Griffith, Marshall's wife, told a story that summed up Marshall's personality and extreme competitiveness when it came to football. During the 1937 championship game against the Bears, Marshall came down to the field to protest rough play against his rookie quarterback Sammy Baugh, who had been slammed into the Bears bench. A heated confrontation between Marshall and George Halas resulted. They nearly got into a fight at that point.

The two men immediately began cussing each other in voices loud enough to carry to the fans in the stands, including Griffith. Halas told Marshall to get back in the stands where he belonged. After exchanging a few more expletives, Marshall returned to his seat next to his wife.

"What's the matter with you?" he asked his wife. "You look white as a sheet."

"Oh! That was awful!" she replied.

"What was awful?"

"That horrible language. We could hear every word."

"Well, you shouldn't listen."

"And as for that man Halas! He's positively revolt—"

"Don't you dare say anything about George Halas," Marshall interrupted. "He's my best friend!"[4]

That exchange sums up the relationship between the two highly competitive and volatile men. They would fight for their teams, but still considered themselves friends when the game ended. Highly competitive, they could disagree heatedly and remain friends. They resembled two brothers who could fight each other but would not stand for any outside criticism of their sibling.

Unlike major league baseball before Jackie Robinson, blacks had not always found themselves excluded from professional football. During the 1920s, during professional football formative years, several blacks played prominent roles. Fritz Pollard coached and Paul Robeson played for the Akron Pros during the 1920 championship season. Fred "Duke" Slater played with the Chicago Cardinals and Jay Mayo "Inky" Williams played with the Hammond Pros. Pollard, the first black head coach in the league in 1921, joined the Pro Football Hall of Fame in 2005.

With minority players seeing fewer opportunities in the NFL, Pollard formed an all-black barnstorming team. His Chicago Black Hawks club played white teams around Chicago in 1926 and then played against West Coast teams during the winter. Similarly, in professional baseball, blacks played in a separate league and barnstorming teams traveled around the country to find games. In the NFL, segregation happened, not by a rule or law, but by practice.

From 1934 until 1945, blacks were excluded from NFL rosters. The black press reported, "George Preston Marshall, owner of the Boston Redskins franchise, George Halas, owner of the Chicago Bears franchise, and Art Rooney, who owned the Pittsburgh Pirates, had a 'gentlemen's agreement' concerning the exclusion of black football players." Marshall never admitted to the existence of a racial ban. Nor would he admit to personal prejudice. Those who talked with him understood his thinking. In 1957, Ed Linn of *Sport* concluded: "In ordinary conversation, Marshall refers to the Negroes in a manner which leaves little doubt that his objection to them [as players] is based along purely racial lines."[5]

Writers cite the logistical problems that having black players on the team created during the segregation period. Harry March, author of the 1934 book *Pro Football: Its Ups and Downs*, said owners cited logistics as a primary reasons for keeping black players out during the exclusion period. He concluded that hiring blacks created too many hassles such as separate arrangements for lodging, dining and traveling. In contrast, Bears owner George Halas attributed the absence of blacks in the NFL to the poor quality of the college talent pool.

It would appear any argument claiming they could not find any talented black athletes playing college football could be easily refuted. Joe Lillard graduated from Mason City High School in Iowa and attended the University of Oregon in 1930. He proved an immediate triple threat (running, passing, and kicking) as a sophomore in 1931. During the middle of that season, allegations surfaced that Lillard had played semipro baseball during the previous summer. Lillard claimed he was paid to drive the bus. He said he merely filled in as driver on an emergency basis.

Regardless, the school suspended him from the team on October 17, 1931, according to the *Los Angeles Times*. Lillard left school and joined some barnstorming teams. In 1932, he joined the Chicago Cardinals as the only black player in the league that year. Duke Slater, who played for the Cardinals from 1926 to 1931, held that distinction the previous year.

Jack Chevigny, the Cardinals' coach, claimed Lillard "disrupted practice by being tardy or absent, missing blocking assignments in games, and disobeying team rules."[6] Most believe NFL owners may have may have used Lillard's volatile personality as an excuse to ban black athletes. Witnesses to his play say he rarely overlooked a racial slur or dirty play. When he felt wronged, he immediately retaliated. In 1933, the NFL had only two black players, Lillard and Ray Kemp, and both soon left. Kemp believed racism stood as the sole reason for his release. "It was my understanding," he said, "that there was a gentleman's agreement [among the owners] in the leagues that there be no more blacks."[7] Yet ownership denied it. "For myself and most of the owners," said Art Rooney of the Steelers, "I can say there never was any racial bias."[8]

With the approaching depression and the economy worsening, blacks remained excluded. The league reorganized after the 1933 season. That year, Marshall proposed dividing the league into two divisions with a playoff game at season end. Quite possibly the topic of outlawing black players may also have come up for discussion at that same meeting. There isn't clear evidence to support that suspicion, but minority players disappeared from the league after that season.

When Lillard and Kemp departed the NFL in 1933, it marked the beginning of the blackout that lasted until after World War II. This custom continued despite the workforce shortages suffered by NFL teams during the war years. The situation grew so severe that some teams needed to combine rosters in order to play games. The Bears went so far as to bring back Bronko Nagurski five years after his retirement to supplement their depleted roster.

About the same time that blacks left professional football, other blacks started coming into public view in other sports. On June 22, 1937, Joe Louis took the heavyweight boxing title from James J. Braddock. Louis, nicknamed the Brown Bomber, had gained popularity in the press. His success in the boxing ring motivated many young blacks in poor neighborhoods throughout the country to take up boxing in hopes of following in Louis's shoes.

A year earlier, Jesse Owens won international fame for his performance in the 1936 Summer Olympic Games in Berlin, Germany. He won four gold medals for his athletic skills in the 100 meters, 200 meters, and long jump and as part of the 4 × 100 relay team. His victories in the games carried greater significance because they happened in Germany in front of Adolf Hitler, who attempted to use the 1936 Olympics to promote his Aryan views. Those beliefs centered on the racist belief that Germanic people had a more pure Caucasian heritage. Hitler anticipated his German athletes would dominate the games due to this pure ethnic background. Owens dashed that desire with his record-breaking performance in the games.

World War II brought the integration issue to the forefront. American soldiers fought to make sure Hitler's discriminatory practices did not spread and yet they had to fight in segregated units. After the war, several efforts looked to eliminate discriminatory practices in federal employment. Chief among those occurred in 1948, when president Harry S. Truman signed Executive Order 9981 abolishing racial discrimination in the military.

In 1970, Halas told writer and broadcaster Myron Cope that no great black players played at the college level during the years while the NFL kept blacks out of the league. Strangely, during that period, at least nine black players earned All-American honors in college, but none got an NFL tryout. However, it appears some teams attempted to attract black players. Reportedly, George Halas wanted to sign halfback Ozzie Simmons in 1936 and Kenny Washington in 1939 but could not gain the consent of fellow owners.

The war years may have changed perspective. Blacks fought and died for their country, but they could not participate in professional sports along with white athletes. Black athletes played prominent roles in college football. Kenny Washington of UCLA, one of the best players in college football in the late thirties, stood as a prime example. In 1939, he teamed with three other black players on the UCLA team—Woodrow Wilson "Woody" Strode, Jackie Robinson and Ray Bartlett. Robinson, who later broke baseball's color barrier in 1947, could have broken the glass ceiling in football as well. He became the first UCLA Bruin to letter in baseball, football, basketball and track. Meanwhile, Washington led the nation in total offense that year. Bob Waterfield, who would later play for the NFL Rams, called Washington "the best football player I ever saw." Washington earned a spot on many All-American teams. Only a scoreless tie in a tight contest with crosstown rival USC kept UCLA out of the Rose Bowl.

Despite leading the nation in total yardage with 1,370 yards in 1939 and leading his team to an unbeaten season, the NFL ignored Washington. This after he played with the College All-Stars against the champion Green Bay Packers. Jimmy Powers, columnist for the New York Daily News, urged Tim Mara and Dan Topping, owners of Gotham's professional football teams, to sign him.

"He played on the same field with boys who are going to be scattered through the league," wrote Jimmy Powers. "And he played against the champion Packers. There wasn't a bit of trouble anywhere."[9] No NFL owners invited him to play on their teams. Instead, Washington went back to California and played in the Pacific Coast League.

What other explanation aside from racial prejudice could have caused this snub? Why would the owners of professional football continue this practice at a time when they needed to generate publicity and gather fans? Some have suggested football owners simply followed the norm established by the number one sport of the time, major league baseball. The national pastime did not have a single black player in the major leagues until Jackie Robinson started with the Dodgers in 1947. They chose not to risk angering fans who bought the tickets.

As World War II ended, professional football started a growth spurt. Service members returned to the States and wanted to play and watch sports. Some returned to college and played the game. Others looked towards the professional game. As a result, attendance at NFL games nearly hit two million in 1945 and grew by another half million in 1946. While the NFL gained in popularity, it also faced a challenge.

The league faced competition from a new rival, the All-America Football Conference. During the war years, each team in the NFL only had 28 players. During the 1946 season, rosters expanded to 33 players. The champions from the 1945 season, the Cleveland Rams, moved to Los Angeles to provide the league a West Coast presence. They played games at the Los Angeles Coliseum. Government officials said they would allow the use of the facility only if the team integrated. Consequently, the Rams signed Kenny Washington and Woody Strode.

Strode was not an enthusiastic racial pioneer. Asked about his experiences later in life, Strode summed up how he felt with a few words. "Integrating the NFL was the low point of my life. If I have to integrate heaven," said Strode, "I don't want to go."[10]

Strode grew up in the Westwood section of Los Angeles and earned a football scholarship to UCLA. During the summer, Strode and his best friend Washington worked at Warner Brothers Studio. Strode had played with the Hollywood Bears football team when World War II broke out. When he was not unloading bombs in Guam, he played with service teams. After the war, he tried life as a professional wrestler, barnstorming the country as a good-guy wrestler. Movie producers saw him wrestling, which earned a spot in front of the camera. He made movies with many of the top directors of the day. He played a slave in Cecil B. DeMille's *The Ten Commandments* and John Ford selected him to play the title role in *Sergeant Rutledge*. His big role came as the as the Nubian gladiatorial opponent who saves the life of Spartacus (Kirk Douglas) in the movie of the same name.

More strides towards racial equality occurred during the late fifties. In 1954, the Supreme Court struck down school segregation in the Brown decision. The following year, a black woman in Alabama named Rosa Parks refused to give up her bus seat to a white man, causing a rash of protests across the country. On December 1, 1955, after working a long day as a seamstress, Parks boarded a city bus in Montgomery, Alabama, for the ride home. As per the custom, she took a seat in the "colored section" of the bus. Soon all the seats in the white section filled up. As several more white riders boarded the bus, the driver asked her to give up her seat. Parks refused and subsequently went to jail.

The act inspired the Montgomery bus boycott as black riders refused to ride city buses. This form of economic protest proved a success as the bus company depended upon the income derived from the minority riders. It also received national publicity. In the end, a Supreme Court decision ended discrimination.

The sporting world soon began reflecting the changes occurring in society. Branch

Rickey signed Jackie Robinson to a contract in 1945 to play for the Brooklyn Dodgers. Robinson played one year with the Montreal Royals, Brooklyn's highest minor league affiliate, before joining the big club in 1947. In 1946, the Rams signed Washington and teammate Woody Strode. That same year, Paul Brown, creating a powerhouse in the AAFC with the Cleveland Browns, signed two black players, Bill Willis and Marion Motley.

Willis and Motley ran into a real struggle in those early years. Brown needed to leave the two black players behind when the schedule called for a 1946 game in Miami, Florida. The state of Florida had a law prohibiting black and whites from playing on the same field. The team received death threats putting players' lives in jeopardy if they attended the game.

The struggle proved even more personal on the field. In 1946, players wore leather helmets without facemasks. The game then seemed a bit more physical than today. Willis told *USA Today* that he had a special protector on field when he played. Teammate Lou Rymkus told him not to retaliate against cheap-shot artists. Rymkus asked Willis to point out the offenders and he would take care of the rest. Since the retaliator usually was called for the penalty, Rymkus employed a strategy to avoid useless penalties by waiting for the right time. As a 245-pound tackle, Rymkus had the size to back up this role.

As a reflection of the changing time in the sixties, Grambling University in Louisiana sent more players into professional football than any school except Notre Dame.[11] Eddie Robinson coached Grambling from 1941 to 1997 and finished his career with 408 coaching victories and countless professional candidates. Minority players needed opportunity and that came with the right environment starting at the top with the head coach. Two of the most successful coaches of the late fifties and early sixties seemed colorblind when it came to adding players to their teams. Paul Brown brought blacks into the game without the pressure from government. Vince Lombardi, who felt victimized by racial discrimination himself, would not tolerate it among the players on his team.

Vince Jr. said his father told him a story one night at the dinner table. "One night, toward the end of the 1960 preseason, again in North Carolina, he was refused seating by a hostess. Naturally dark skinned, he was deeply tanned after spending many hours in the sun out on the practice field. The hostess mistook him for an African American man and turned him away."[12]

Lombardi took positive steps to make sure the color of the player's skin did not matter. He assigned rooms in training camp with no consideration of a player's color. White guard Jerry Kramer roomed with black defensive end Willie Davis as one of the first interracial roommates in the league. Attitudes changed slowly in society; Coach Lombardi demonstrated his concern that all players received equal treatment following that incident in North Carolina.

When a restaurant in the South made the Packers' four African Americans players enter and leave by the back door, Lombardi made the rest of the team do the same. Lombardi swore he would not put in players in that situation again. Society may have permitted discrimination, but Lombardi forbade it. He laid out the rules for his team at the beginning of training camp every year. Lombardi was clear: If he heard any player utter a derogatory term towards a teammate, that player would be immediately dismissed.

Lombardi took advantage of those limits by drafting and trading for African American athletes. In addition to Emlen Tunnell, Lombardi acquired defensive end Willie Davis from Cleveland. Both players served as leaders during the Green Bay turnaround.

Davis, later defensive captain and a Hall of Fame defensive end, joined defensive end Bill Quinlan and tackle Henry Jordan as one of the three outstanding players Lombardi acquired from Cleveland Browns head coach and general manager Paul Brown.

On the field the first few black players took a beating. They got hit early and often, even if some of the hits seemed to come after the whistle. Under the pile, they could get hands stepped on and faces scratched. "My hands were always bloody," Motley said years later. "But if either Willis or myself had been hotheads and gotten into fights and things like that, it would have put things back ten years. Sometimes I wanted to just kill some of those guys, and the officials would just stand right there. They'd see those guys stepping on us and heard them saying things and just turn their backs. That kind of crap went on for two or three years until they found out what kind of players we were."[13] As civil rights protests grew louder and stronger across the country, the media began paying more attention to minority athletes. A national magazine called St. Louis Cardinals defensive coach Chuck Drulis and linebacker Bill Koman bigots due to the way they treated minority teammates.

Author Ed Gruver wrote that many NFL teams had quotas limiting the number of black players they had on their rosters in the early sixties. He claimed the Redskins' quota sat at two while the Giants' limit stood at six.[14] Bernie Parrish joined the Cleveland Browns in 1959. Despite the fact they were considered a liberal franchise, Parrish said the Browns had unwritten rules about how many blacks the roster could hold. "We were still in that era of the quotas," said Parrish. "In 1959, I believe the quota of black players was seven; then it went to thirteen."[15]

Parrish, a white player, noticed that teams often had multiple black players competing for the same position, a practice called stacking. Walter Beach, an African American from Michigan, joined the Browns the year after Parrish. Parrish and Beach became close friends and they compared notes. "There would be six or eight guys competing for my spot and nobody competing for his," Beach said, referring to Parrish, one of his closest friends. "That's where the stacking concept comes from. They would stack black cats behind each other; that was a reality. If you came to the Cleveland Browns and you wanted to play cornerback, there were going to be five brothers over there behind me."[16]

During the sixties, the opportunities for minority players were limited. Certain positions seemed to be permanently off-limits. In particular, quarterback seemed to be a position where only white athletes could apply. Late in the decade, an injury opened an opportunity for a black player. In 1968, Marlin Briscoe earned a starting quarterback job for the Denver Broncos. Many doubted a black player would ever play quarterback in professional football. Briscoe certainly had the odds stacked against him. The Broncos drafted him in the 14th round despite his standing only 5-foot-11 and weighing 177 pounds. When he entered the Broncos training camp, they had him listed as eighth out of eight on the depth chart. The odds were certainly against him.

Briscoe, nicknamed "The Magician" due to his ability to elude defenders and make plays with his feet, quickly learned the Broncos had drafted him based on his athletic abilities. They believed he would make an excellent defensive back in pro football. Briscoe had confidence in his abilities after he had thrown for 2,283 yards passing as an NAIA All-American at the University of Omaha his senior year. During contract negotiations, Briscoe told the team he would sign if he could get a clause in the agreement calling for a three-day trial at quarterback. At first, the team said no, but Briscoe held out until they agreed. When his opportunity came, he performed well. During training camp, the *Denver*

Post wrote an article about Briscoe and his collegiate career. That article gave him the boost he needed. The sporting public in Denver slowly joined Briscoe's side.

In the third game of the season, head coach Lou Saban put Briscoe in with the Broncos trailing, 20–10. He completed his first pass for a 22-yard gain. On his second series, he led the team on an 80-yard touchdown march. He ran the last 12 yards himself for the score. The Broncos fell short, 20–17, but Briscoe's performance won over many fans. He started the next game against Cincinnati, making him the first black quarterback to start a professional game.

In all, Briscoe started five games that season and saw some action in six more games. His 14 touchdown passes set a Broncos team rookie record. He finished with 1,589 passing yards and 308 rushing yards. He finished second to Bengals running back Paul Robinson for AFL Rookie of the Year honors. Despite a record-setting rookie season, it seemed clear to Briscoe that the Broncos did not want him back as quarterback.

"It was obvious that they did not have me in their plans," Briscoe recalled. "I had gone back to Omaha to finish up six hours that I needed to graduate. At that time, they had acquired Pete Liske from Canada. I heard it through the grapevine that they were having quarterback meetings and I was not even invited, even though I was the starting quarterback at the end of the season. That meant that they did not even have plans for me to compete. That is all I wanted, to be able to compete.... The fact that they did not even invite me to the meetings that was a swipe. It was highly unfair. As a matter of fact, when I found out about the meetings, I flew back to Denver and stood outside the office where they were having the meetings. When they came out, Saban could not even look me in the face. He did not even know I was coming."[17]

Things did not change much once training camp started. "When I got to camp, it was apparent that they had no plans to even let me into the fray. I asked for my release, because I thought that with the success that I had, it would give me an opportunity to play for another team. However, that was not the case. I heard through the grapevine that I was blackballed. [Saban] wouldn't release me right away. He said, 'Wait four days.'"[18]

Briscoe finally won his release, but he wasn't given another opportunity to play quarterback in the league. The Buffalo Bills agreed to sign him if he would agree to a move to wide receiver. Briscoe had not played that position before, but the next season he went to a Pro Bowl as a receiver. His joy turned to sadness as the Bills hired former Broncos head coach Lou Saban to take over the team. Saban traded Briscoe to the Miami Dolphins.

Even though Briscoe did not get the opportunity he had hoped for, others got a chance. In 1969, the Buffalo Bills drafted James Harris as a quarterback. Unlike Briscoe, Harris had the prototypical size to play quarterback in the NFL. Briscoe claimed the honors as the first black quarterback to start a game in professional football. He wasn't, however, the first black quarterback since the reintegration of the league. Willie Thrower of the Chicago Bears has that honor. Thrower, the first black quarterback in the Big Ten Conference, helped Michigan State win the national championship in 1952. Thrower played sparingly for the 1953 Bears, attempting only eight passes all season. Like Briscoe, Thrower was not invited back to the team after one season playing quarterback.

The sixties in American history represented a time of civil unrest across the country. The Civil Rights Act of 1964, a landmark piece of legislation, outlawed discrimination due to sex or race. The law aimed to eliminate racial segregation in schools, in the workplace and at any facilities that served the public. The enforcement component of the act lacked any real strength so change came about slowly. Riots and civil unrest followed as people struggled for change. The same struggles occurred in professional football. Black players wore the same uniforms as their white teammates, but some may have felt they played on a different team.

Johnny Unitas came to the Baltimore Colts in 1956. That same year Lenny Moore arrived. Unitas played quarterback while Moore played running back and receiver. One might think they grew close as friends having started with the team the same year and both playing starting roles on the offense. Unitas would throw it and Moore would catch it, forming a dangerous passing duo.

"I could tell you nothing about the personal side of John because we only knew each other on the football field and in the locker room," Moore said in a comment especially telling of the racial relations of the day. "We never socialized together, not with the black-and-white atmosphere at the time."[19]

Moore said blacks and whites on the team did not socialize because blacks could not go to movies or restaurants. Many hotels were off-limits to a black man like himself. He said those restrictions cut the blacks off from the rest of the team. In his 1994 book, *When the Colts Belonged to Baltimore*, William Gildea examined the painful truth of segregation in his hometown in the late fifties and sixties. "On our side of the color line life was almost idyllic," wrote Gildea. White people in Baltimore "didn't cross that line, didn't even think to cross it, and didn't know the pain being experienced on the other side."[20]

As the sixties moved on, changes came to pro football. Some teams started assigning roommates for training camp alphabetically instead of by skin color or position. Players did not universally accept change. They even had cases in which a player had not ever seen or talked with a man of the other race in his life.

That may well have described the situation as two Chicago Bears learned they would share a room. That duo, Gale Sayers and Brian Piccolo, and their reluctant but growing friendship became the subject of a book by Jeannie Morris titled *Brian Piccolo: A Short Season*. Piccolo recorded his thoughts into a tape recorder starting early in 1970 because he hoped to write a book about recovering from cancer. He never got the opportunity to write that book. His widow turned over the tapes to Morris, at the time the wife of former Chicago Bear wide receiver turned sportscaster Johnny Morris. Jeannie Morris put the book together.

Sayers had the greater celebrity of the two players. As an All-American at Kansas, the Bears chose him as their second first-round choice in 1965, one spot behind Dick Butkus. Brian Piccolo led the nation in rushing his senior season at Wake Forest but still had far less renown than his roommate had. Despite the existence of two professional football leagues at the time, no team in either the NFL or AFL picked Piccolo in any round. He signed on with the Bears as a free agent. When George Halas decided to assign roommates based on position, Sayers, a black man, and Piccolo, a white man, ended up in the same room. The two running backs even wore consecutive numbers, 40 and 41. Despite different personalities, as many who read the book or saw the television movie *Brian's Song* are aware, the two became fast friends.

One could not find two more opposite personalities than Sayers and Piccolo. Sayers always seemed quiet, introspective and way too serious. Conversely, Piccolo, known as "Pic," came across as talkative, extroverted and never serious enough. Sayers, the golden child of the Bears, came to the team as the fourth overall player selected in the 1965 college draft. Piccolo signed with the Bears as a free agent and had a hard, uphill fight to earn a position with the team.

When the Bears' training camp opened, one side of the room belonged to the painfully shy northern black man and the other side to the non-stop talking Italian-Catholic from Florida. It definitely was not love at first sight, but the two players began to appreciate one another. Piccolo would do the speaking for Sayers and the serious former Kansas running back would get his white teammate to focus on playing the game. The biggest changes in their relationship, though, came through adversity.

In the ninth game of the 1968 season against the 49ers, Sayers was injured. He was having his best season as a professional. Bears quarterback Virgil Carter called "49 Toss Left" in the huddle. The play swept to the left with offensive lineman Randy Jackson leading Sayers around left end. Sayers saw an opening and planted his right foot to make a cut and take the run up inside instead. Cornerback Kermit Alexander read the play and came up hard to make the tackle.

Alexander hit him around the knees while Sayers had his right leg firmly planted in the Wrigley Field turf. Fans did not know it at the time, but the blow tore Sayers's knee ligaments. Sayers left the game and, in those days, most feared the injury might end his career. Sayers ran with finesse and made his living making tight cuts and darting runs. Knee surgery, not nearly as advanced as today, created a fear that the Kansas Comet's professional career had ended.

"I was carried off on a stretcher to the locker room and [Bears team physician] Dr. [Theodore] Fox said he would take a closer look at my knee at the hospital following the game," said Sayers. "They wanted to operate on me right away, so they gave me some sedatives to relax me. But I was wide awake on the operating table before they finally put me to sleep."[21]

All the while, Sayers said Dr. Fox tried to reassure him that his knee would heal. Sayers cried, fearing the worst. He underwent surgery and started a difficult exercise regimen to build back the strength in his leg. Meanwhile, Piccolo took his spot on the field. He made the most of the opportunity. He caught seven passes the week after Sayers's injury and then ran for 112 yards two weeks later. He finally earned the starting role he coveted so much. During his recovery from the injury, Sayers found inspiration from the encouragement Piccolo offered. Their friendship deepened.

The 1969 season proved a dark one for the Bears. Team founder George Halas retired. The team rotated between three woefully inadequate quarterbacks and had a mediocre year. Late in the season, it got worse for Piccolo. He had to ask the coaches to take him out of a November game against the Falcons. He felt winded and could not get his breath. He had a persistent cough he could not shake. cough. After the game, an X-ray showed a dark area in his left lung. Following this Piccolo had surgery where doctors removed a malignant tumor. Unfortunately, during the surgery, doctors discovered the cancer had spread. Piccolo began chemotherapy treatments, but his health failed. Piccolo kept his positive attitude despite having to go through additional surgeries. He remained committed to recovery and playing for the Bears again.

That spring Sayers went to New York to receive the George S. Halas Award as the most courageous player. Sayers had Piccolo on his mind. "You flatter me by giving me this award," he said, "but I tell you that I accept it for Brian Piccolo. It is mine tonight; it is Brian Piccolo's tomorrow. I love Brian Piccolo, and I would like all of you to love him too. Tonight, when you hit your knees, please ask God to love him."[22]

When Sayers called Piccolo the next day, he had already heard what Sayers had said in New York the night before. "Magic," Piccolo said using his nickname for Sayers, "if you were here right now, I'd kiss you." To that Sayers said, "In that case, we'll be there tomorrow."[23] Only weeks later Brian Piccolo's struggles with cancer ended. He died June 16, 1970, at age 26 years. His wife, Joy, and three young daughters survived him.

The year after Piccolo died, a tackler hit Sayers directly on his left knee in a game against the St. Louis Cardinals. The injury damaged the knee much like the injury two years before on his right knee. This time he needed to recover without his best friend. Sayers tried to return to the gridiron in 1971, but his legs did not have the same ability to move in superhuman ways as they did before the injuries. In November 1971, *Brian's Song* debuted as a television movie of the week with Billy Dee Williams and James Caan in the lead roles. The movie celebrated how two very different football players from divergent backgrounds became teammates and best friends during their struggle to make the Chicago Bears football team. The film showed what challenging times existed in the late sixties in America. Civil rights and Vietnam dominated the headlines, but these two players developed a strong friendship while fighting to make the Chicago Bears football team.

General Colin Powell said he used the *Brian's Song* film when teaching soldiers to get along regardless of race. It "came out at a time when America was going through a very difficult period," said General Powell. "There was a lot of tension and a lot of racial tension as well. *Brian's Song* came along and it was a good time for America to stop and take a deep breath. These were professional athletes who were at the top of their performance and they did not let race stand in the way. In fact, their differences and their friendship became a badge of honor. The message that it gave us in Korea and how it particularly affected us in the Army was that it was a way of showing us that whether we were black, white, Hispanic or Korean, the only thing that counts is how we get along together. We have to look beyond our differences and build on our strengths."[24]

Throughout the sixties, most lessons on how to get along came firsthand. For example, Bill Curry, a late-round draft choice of the Packers in 1964, grew up in racially segregated Atlanta, Georgia. When he came to the Packers, he shared a football huddle with blacks for the first time. He really wanted his new teammates to accept him but he did not know what to expect. Many Packers stars were black and he was a white southerner.

Across the line of scrimmage every day in practice stood many of the great players he had heard of and watched on television. Great black players such as Herb Adderley, Willie Wood, Lionel Aldridge and Dave Robinson played right there with him. Curry thought they might hear his southern accent and might drive them to embarrass him or maybe even hurt him, ending his chances at a professional career. One evening he walked back to his dormitory room after a long, tough day of training camp. Out of the darkness, Curry heard a voice. "Bill, I would like to talk with you," the voice said. He said it terrified him at first. Who was that and what did he want? He did not recognize the voice immediately but learned that it belonged to Packers defensive captain Willie Davis. At a glance, Davis appeared to be the opposite of Curry. He attended historically black Grambling University. Writers honored Davis as an All-Pro performer during his career. Now he was giving a pep talk to a rookie.

"Bill, I've been watching you in practice and I think you have a chance to make our team," Davis said to Curry. "I want to help you do that! So when Nitschke is snapping

Green Bay Packers safety Willie Wood (24) goes all out to block a field-goal attempt. Wood's interception in the first Super Bowl game gave the Packers momentum they needed to win the contest (Photofest).

your facemask and breaking your nose and Lombardi's screaming in your face and there's blood everywhere and you don't think you can take another step … you look at me and I'll get you through it!"[25]

When Curry looks back, he cannot believe that Davis's unexpected and undeserved act of kindness changed his life. He took Davis up on the offer. When things got tough in practice, he would walk over to Davis, who delivered the mini pep talk he needed to get though the rest of practice. Race riots were happening on city streets across the country but sports presented one opportunity for men of different colors and backgrounds to work together. Curry said Willie Davis shattered every stereotype he had about black men.

Chapter Nine

New Leadership

Many folks saw Pete Rozelle as the John F. Kennedy of the National Football League. Both young men took office early in the decade of the sixties and made their mark right away. Kennedy had a vision for the nation. He challenged the country to reach for the moon before the end of the decade. He set the vision and the country achieved the goal, even though he did not live to see it.

As the sixties began, Americans felt optimistic about what lay ahead in the coming years. In the race for the highest office, Americans had a choice between the current vice president, Richard Nixon, and a fresh face in national politics, John F. Kennedy, the junior senator from Massachusetts. Senator Kennedy won election by a very narrow margin. Although the two men were only four years apart in age, many Americans viewed Kennedy as new and promising agent of change and saw Nixon as connected to the past.

The fabulous fifties had ended and Americans looked optimistically forward to the soaring sixties when astronauts would literally fly off to the moon. As the decade began, America seemed at peace and the prosperity at home enabled American to move to the suburbs, purchase color television sets and travel to the new Disneyland theme park in California.

In the same sense, the 33-year-old Rozelle, named commissioner in 1960, had a vision for the league. His flying to the moon goal was to raise pro football to the lofty status of top spectator sport. Today, that might sound obvious, but it was not then. Baseball still stood as America's pastime. College football was more popular than the professional game. Even horse racing and boxing had more fans.

Rozelle, however, saw glimmers of hope. The 1958 overtime championship game sparked interest in the sport among an audience who may not have considered pro football earlier. Television sales increased through the fifties as disposable income and free time increased among the middle class. Television networks needed new sources of programming and, after the 1958 title game, considered football a good fit for the small screen.

When Rozelle took over the NFL, he inherited a collection of 12 teams that, in many ways, operated more like standalone businesses than one unified body. At the same time, they faced the challenge of a new league financed by some of the richest men in America.

Pundits called Kennedy the television president. Some have said that Kennedy won the White House based on his performance in the debates during the election. On television,

Kennedy appeared cool and suave. He stood tall, with tanned, healthy skin displaying a calm confidence with a quick wit. His opponent, Richard Nixon, did not feel well and he looked it. Pale and tired, his top lip showed every bit of the nervous perspiration gathering there and his five o'clock shadow really showed up on television. Nixon refused to wear television makeup to help eliminate those issues. The 1960 election ended as one of the closest in the nation's history. The slightest difference in perception could have changed the outcome with such a slim margin of victory cast.

Rozelle, on the other hand, served as the NFL's television commissioner. While the medium was still in its infancy, he understood how to use it to its best advantage. Once setting the goal, Rozelle needed to outline the vision. That vision started with the philosophy of putting the league first. He wanted all decisions made with regard to the best interests of the entire league and not just one team. With that thought in mind, Rozelle believed that each team needed to be on equal footing financially. The first step towards this goal had teams sharing revenues equally. Large differences in revenues often caused an imbalance that allowed one team to gain a competitive edge over others, creating a league where some teams could not compete. Reduced competition potentially would cause decreased interest in the league.

The mass appeal of the modern NFL came about due to principles laid out by Rozelle years ago. Professional football fans have the sense that their team has an equal or near equal chance to perform well in the upcoming season. This optimism starts before training camp and seems universal through nearly every fan base during the late summer. Major league baseball fans might not share that feeling of optimism. Baseball teams in major markets have the financial advantage enabling them to get any player and immediately shift the competitive balance. In football, teams commonly climb from last place to first place from one year to the next.

The second principle Rozelle implemented revolved around the idea that NFL football needed to entertain on television. Rozelle had spent three years as the head of public relations for the Los Angeles Rams and three additional years in corporate public relations so his background taught him the increasing importance of the media. He could see the potential of mass media in spreading the appeal of the game. As the decade of the fifties went on, television grew in importance to viewers. Rozelle knew television would constantly grow as a bigger and bigger part of people's lives and the NFL needed to ride along with that growth.

Unlike baseball, football seems ideally suited for television. A rectangle, the football field had a shape similar to the television screen. The action fit nicely on the screen. Baseball played out on a diamond, an irregularly shaped field that did not fit nicely on the rectangular screen. Not all baseball players are visible on screen at one time. The larger, darker football showed up much better than the smaller, white baseball. Despite the bad reception on the black-and-white television sets of the day, you could see the football. The frequent static made it difficult for many people to see the small baseball.

Additionally, the pace of football appealed more to fans looking for a faster game. Football has high-speed action with short breaks in between. Of course, those breaks soon filled with instant replays with different angles to enhance the viewing. In the beginning, it allowed comments on the previous play, forecasts of the upcoming action, or recaps of the game for those who just tuned in. By comparison, baseball followed a leisurely, slow pace on television.

These two principles combined to increase the popularity of the game. Television provided a great source of income for the league and the subsequent competitive balance among the teams helped produce entertaining football. Rozelle convinced the owners of the large markets teams to accept a revenue-sharing arrangement of television income. Throughout the fifties, clubs negotiated individual television deals. That meant the larger markets earned more television money than small market teams, generating a competitive disadvantage.

Limited emergence of football on television came during the fifties. In 1951, the DuMont Network televised the championship game between Los Angeles and Cleveland coast to coast for the first time. The network paid $75,000 for the rights to that game. Viewers saw a good game as the Rams defeated the Browns, 24–17. DuMont continued to broadcast other games as the fifties moved on. The other networks took notice. NBC bid $100,000 to televise the 1955 title game. In 1956, CBS began televising selected games across the country to particular markets. They paid $1.8 million a year for those rights.

The turning point came when the 1958 championship game went to overtime as the nation watched. NBC broadcast the game as Johnny Unitas led his team on two drives, one to tie the game with only two minutes left in regulation and the second in overtime to win the game. The nation fell in love with professional football as Alan Ameche tumbled into the end zone for the win. The excitement of the action captured the nation.

As the sixties began, an estimated 45,750,000 American homes had televisions. That meant that 87 percent of homes had sets versus only 9 percent 10 years earlier. The success of the 1958 title game coupled with the increased sales of new equipment showed Rozelle that the new media could help the game grow. If revenue grew along with it, Rozelle wanted that new revenue shared equally. Rozelle saw that individually negotiated television contracts created a growing chasm between the large market teams and the small market teams that could prove detrimental to the game.

"We had a problem," said Rozelle in an interview years later. "In 1960, when I became commissioner, clubs made their own television contracts, and the small market clubs did not do very well. We had a real strange set up; you had CBS carrying the games of—I think—about eight clubs and they paid $175,000 a year for the Giants, down to maybe $75,000 in those days for the Packers. Then you had one of the teams on the Fox sports network—Sports Network, not Fox in those days—that was a Cleveland team, and they got $175. Then Baltimore and Pittsburgh had just moved over to NBC. So it was all fractioning."[1]

Rozelle felt determined to negotiate one television deal for the whole league. A combined deal would generate the most revenue for all the clubs. Previously, CBS-TV had individual deals with nine of the teams so Rozelle offered them the combined deal first. The network offered $3 million to hold the exclusive broadcast rights to all regular-season games for all teams. Then, Rozelle had to convince the owners of teams in Cleveland, Pittsburgh and Baltimore that they would be better off taking that deal and turning down more money from their individual deals with other networks. He also had to address the major-market teams that could negotiate their own individual deals. Once he convinced the Mara family in New York, he found another obstacle. A combined television deal might violate the antitrust laws in the country.

Once Rozelle sold the owners on shared television revenue, he needed to convince Congress. The revenue-sharing concept that allowed the league to sell the broadcast rights as a whole required a special exemption to the antitrust law. The situation put Rozelle's ability to persuade to the test, but he gained approval of the exemption.

The TV deal is one major difference between professional football and major league baseball. All franchises in the NFL share television money equally. Equal sharing of that income provides equal footing for all teams. Equal dollars provides competitive balance and hope for fans of every team. A fan of the Green Bay Packers can have as much optimism heading into a new season as a fan of the New York Giants because they have economic parity. A fan of baseball's Pittsburgh Pirates might not share the optimism since he may think his small-market, cash-strapped team cannot compete with wealthy ballclubs like the Los Angeles Dodgers, who receive much more television revenue.

"So we did press for an antitrust exemption in Congress, and strangely enough, football is subject to the antitrust laws," Rozelle continued. "Baseball got an exemption way, way back, and we tried to get one ourselves. We could not at that time. We did get exemption from the standpoint of selling our television rights as a package, all the teams at one time, rather than individually. They said it would not be against the antitrust laws, so we got that through and were able then to negotiate a contract with CBS."[2]

After securing agreement among the owners and his antitrust exemptions, Rozelle went about negotiating the NFL's first league-wide television deal in 1961. CBS paid $4.65 million a year for the broadcast rights during the 1962 and 1963 seasons. Under this approach, each team received $332,000. At the time, that revenue exceeded the team's payroll in most cases, so even before selling the first ticket, the team faced a profitable year.

The NFL's television arrangement represented a big deal and a major change for the league. When the American Football League came into existence in 1960, their teams shared television revenue. Although not a completely new idea, no sports league had implemented it. Lamar Hunt had heard about the shared television revenue concept while pursuing a baseball franchise in the late fifties. Former Brooklyn Dodgers president Branch Rickey built the principle of shared TV revenue as part of his plan for the Continental League.

Rozelle laid out his vision for the future of the league with these initial steps as commissioner. He saw opportunity with the beginning of the sixties. After a decade in the job, he reminisced about the beginning. Through the sixties, he completed a transformation of the league building on some concepts inherited from his predecessor and some new ones of his own.

"When I became commissioner in 1960," he said looking back, "the offices were located in Philadelphia. They were not even in Philadelphia, but in a suburb, Bala-Cynwyd. We had four full-time employees and an elderly Kelly Girl. I didn't know what the hell I was doing—I was only 33—but I thought we better move to New York. One of the older employees told me that wouldn't be very wise, since if I stayed in Bala-Cynwyd I wouldn't get bothered like I would in New York, but I figured it was better to be bothered."[3]

Rozelle nearly did not get the job. After Bert Bell died, the NFL had two major candidates to replace him. Most media reports said that either Austin Gunsel or Marshall Leahy would take over as the new commissioner. Gunsel had headed up the NFL's investigative unit before taking over as league treasurer before stepping in as interim commissioner after Bell's sudden death. Leahy, a San Francisco attorney, had done work for the 49ers. He said publicly that he intended to move the league offices to the West Coast if the owners elected him. Leahy missed by one vote in early voting.

"Seven clubs wanted Marshall Leahy of San Francisco, but there was another bloc dead set against him because he wanted to move the office to the West Coast," said Rozelle. "Well, the owners started to feel the pressure. They were down there in Florida for 10 days and could not reach a decision. The newspapers were on them. Tim Mara and Paul Brown came to me. It happened quickly and was a total shock to me. I hardly knew some of the owners before this except to talk to on the phone, and I'd been quiet the 10 days. So they decided let's pick somebody, and that will give us time to look around if he doesn't work out."[4]

After 23 ballots and 10 days of deadlock, Rams owner Dan Reeves and Giants owner Wellington Mara met and discussed nominating Rozelle for the job. Rozelle worked for Reeves with the Rams. Art Rooney told the gathered assembly of tired and frustrated owners if Mara and Reeves supported Rozelle, then he did too. After Rooney gave Rozelle an endorsement, they had a vote and elected Rozelle the new commissioner.

"It was the most ludicrous thing I ever heard of," said Rozelle he learned of his election. "It wasn't ludicrous at all," wrote *New York Times* reporter Leonard Shecter. "Rozelle, with the sort of modern cool and athletic good looks that are so admired in the business community, was exactly what football needed as it emerged from the rough and tumble of professional sports into the slick business of the early sixties."[5]

Replacing Bert Bell presented another batch of challenges. He had served as commissioner from 1946 until his death in 1959. Before moving to the league office, Bell owned three teams—the Frankford Yellow Jackets, Philadelphia Eagles and Pittsburgh Steelers—at different times. Bell's famous line, "On any given Sunday, any team can beat any other team," formed the foundation for Pete Rozelle's philosophy of creating an environment in which all teams had hope for a good season. Some have said Rozelle set up rules so that every team would win as many games as they lost. Critics said that meant every team would finish with seven wins and seven losses.

Bell endured some of the same challenges that Rozelle faced. He had the challenge of a well-financed All-America Football Conference. Early on Bell took a harsh stance against gambling. With television still new, Bell established the rules that blacked out home ballgames to protect the gate revenue. Bell even recognized the NFL Players Association despite many owners' objections. Rozelle had his work cut out for him replacing Bell, but he felt up to the challenge.

Rozelle, born Alvin Ray Rozelle, grew up in the suburbs of Los Angeles, California. At a young age, he took an interest in sports. An uncle nicknamed the then five-year-old "Pete" and the nickname stuck. He served a two-year Navy tour at the end of World War II and went to college upon his return. Rozelle began his studies at Compton Junior College, followed by the University of San Francisco (USF), a private Jesuit school. Rozelle worked in public relations while still a student at USF. Then, after graduation, the university hired him as assistant athletic director. That job led to a position with the Los Angeles Rams, where he worked for Tex Schramm, as publicity director in 1952. He briefly left the NFL for a corporate public relations position, but returned to the Rams as general manager in 1955.

He quickly earned a positive reputation as the Rams' GM. His reputation came not through the traditional roles of trades and scouting, but with his marketing of the franchise and his diplomatic skills in handling disputes between the Rams' owners. Rozelle's management style centered on developing relationships with various people in and outside the organization. Those skills would serve him well as commissioner.

Rozelle had mixed reviews for his tenure as general manager of the Rams. He traded

Norm Van Brocklin to the Eagles and Philadelphia won the championship. In 1959, he traded seven players, a 1960 second-round pick and a player to be named later to the Chicago Cardinals for one player, Ollie Matson. Rozelle knew Matson from his University of San Francisco days. Most would have to say the trade backfired for the Rams as their next playoff appearance came well after Matson retired.

Rozelle's diplomatic and marketing skills, in addition to his intelligence, made him an attractive alternative on the 23rd ballot despite his relative youth. He put those skills to work early on when he convinced the owners to accept equal sharing of the television revenues. He built on his predecessor's "any given Sunday" philosophy and made it stronger. Bell introduced the player draft to equalize talent distribution. Rozelle took that an additional step to equalize the financial structure. Rozelle pushed the "league think" concept in which he wanted owners to think of the league as a whole rather than one individual team.

In later years, the NFL applied this equal sharing of the revenue approach to new ventures such as NFL Films and NFL Properties. Rozelle's marketing background helped him identify and take advantage of every promotional tool. The new commissioner set out to promote the league in every possible way and those two ventures went a long way towards promoting the league.

Promoting athletes differed only slightly from the merchandizing of movie actors. When Roy Rogers, an American singer and cowboy actor, ended his acting career, he looked for other opportunities. He had some experience marketing products with his name on them and he believed people would buy products bearing their favorite team logo. Major League Baseball passed, but the NFL liked the idea when Rogers approached them with the idea of creating the joint effort called NFL Enterprises.

"Merchandising is merchandizing," said Roy Rogers. "There's no difference whether a store is selling a Roy Rogers revolver or a junior St. Louis Cardinal football outfit just like the pros wear."[6]

During Rozelle's tenure as the general manager of the Los Angeles Rams, they opened a team store in 1957—the first professional team to do so—where they sold bobbleheads of Rams players the following year. Two years later, NFL Enterprises opened as a division of Roy Rogers Enterprises. The league owned half the company and Roy Rogers the other half. Standard Oil bought the first product they marketed—glassware with team logos—to give away with gasoline fill-ups at their service stations. Within a year, Roy Rogers lined up 45 manufacturers making about 300 products from cigarette lighters to dolls and clothing.[7]

In 1963, the league took NFL Enterprises in-house and renamed it NFL Properties. That group took over as the league is merchandising unit, making it possible for fans of every team to purchase team jerseys and caps so they could look just like they were on the team. Team jerseys went on sale regardless if the team won the championship or finished in last place. Looking back at old footage of games in the fifties, the spectators wore business clothing. Today, nearly everyone—male or female—wears officially licensed NFL football gear to the game. NFL Properties made this possible.

"We formed NFL Properties to sell program advertising," said Lou Spadia, former president of the San Francisco 49ers. "We hired Larry Kent as the first president and he did a fine job getting the league and team logos on T-shirts, lunch pails, anything. His goal was to get a page of NFL items in the Sears & Roebuck catalogue and he did that. That was back in the days when no one put anything on a T-shirt. I think our equipment man was the first to put something on them. Our players were stealing them, so he stenciled '49ers' on them so it would show through their shirts. One guy got around that by wearing the T-shirt backwards, so our equipment guy stenciled both front and back."[8]

Kent got experience working with Roy Rogers, one of the most popular stars of the day. To capitalize on that popularity, Rogers installed Roy Roger Corrals in major department stores around the country selling children's cowboy clothing and toys. Under Kent's supervision, NFL Properties revenues grew from a paltry $36,647 in 1963 to more than $1.5 million in 1969. It continued to grow to $500 million in 1986 and $3 billion in 1996.[9]

When Rozelle's name went into nomination for the commissioner post, some thought he'd been put forward because the owners thought they could push around a 33 year old. "They will cut you up," one owner allegedly warned Rozelle when he got the job as commissioner. Old-time owners found out right away Rozelle didn't intimidate easily. Take for instance an incident involving George Halas of the Bears, a senior owner in the league who intimidated many people. An early challenge for the young commissioner came when he had to discipline the man who helped found the league.

Halas posed an intimidating presence on the sidelines as he stormed after the officials and barked at them as he ran up and down the sideline. He would chase the action up and down the field; he went into areas where coaches and off-field players were not allowed. Halas hoped his bark would intimidate the officials. Many in the league thought Halas could get away with berating officials in ways others could not. Early in Rozelle's tenure, Halas criticized the officials following the game. Rozelle figured he went too far and summoned the Bears' owner to the commissioner's office in New York City.

"And I remember, I had to call him in, and he flew in from Chicago," said Rozelle in an interview in 1991. He "called me from the airport, and asked if we could meet out there. I said, 'No, I want to see you in my office.' He came in and we talked over whatever the problem was at the time. But he didn't get mad. He was very supportive of me. He had respect for authority and knew they had to have a strong commissioner. Not someone who would do just what was, at the time, the thing to do, but one that would stick to their guns and do what they felt was right."[10]

Both Kennedy and Rozelle faced challenges early on in their tenures. Kennedy stood up to the Russians during the Cuban Missile Crisis of 1962. Rozelle's challenge, while not up to the level of the threat of nuclear weapons launching in the Western Hemisphere, had great importance to the sports world and his tenure as NFL commissioner.

The integrity of the game meant fans could believe the contests are fair; without any hint of a fix. When Rozelle received word of players gambling on football, he immediately ordered an investigation to determine the extent of the problem. Using former FBI agents experienced in the gambling world, Rozelle had investigators monitor players associating with the wrong people. League contracts strictly forbade any association with undesirable characters. The league reinforced the policy with official league notices posted on locker room bulletin boards. Players also heard it personally from Rozelle and other league representatives at the beginning of training camp every year. It was not a secret.

Investigators found players placing bets on football games and turned the information over to Rozelle to determine penalties. They specifically identified Paul Hornung, star running back with the Green Bay Packers, and All-Pro defensive tackle Alex Karras of the Detroit Lions. Hornung grew up in the home of horse racing's Kentucky Derby in Louisville, so he had been around betting for his whole life. Rozelle said Hornung had placed bets of $100 to $500 on NFL and college games from 1959 to 1961, so he suspended him for a year.

Rozelle said Karras had been making significant bets on NFL games since 1958 so he too received a suspension. Five other Lions received fines for betting on the Packers–Giants championship game. Rozelle fined the club itself because coach George Wilson ignored a police tip that some players had met with undesirable characters.

Some fans may remember Karras better for his acting career after his playing days ended. He appeared in movies, television shows and commercials. He played George Papadopoulos, a former football player turned sportscaster and the adoptive father of the title character, a young African American boy, in the 1980s series *Webster*. He spent three years (1974–76) in the *Monday Night Football* booth with Howard Cosell and Frank Gifford. His famous line came when he saw steam rising from the clean-shaven head of Raiders defensive lineman Otis Sistrunk. "He's from the University of Mars," Karras said.

For a defensive lineman, Karras wasn't tall but really strong and powerful with quick feet. These factors made him difficult to run against. Opposing players compared blocking Karras to moving a bowling ball. Off the field, he wore black horn-rimmed glasses everywhere. He took them off when he played relying instead on instinct and feel for the game. He played well as a pass rusher, too.

In 1961, Paul Hornung was called to active duty during the Berlin Crisis. He was released on passes during the weekend to play games. Before the title game, Lombardi did not want to risk a pass so he called President Kennedy to gain his release for the game the Packers dominated against the Giants (Photofest).

"Most defensive tackles have one move, they bull head-on," Doug Van Horn, a New York Giants offensive lineman who had to block Karras, said. "Not Alex. There is no other tackle like him. He has inside and outside moves, a bull move where he puts his head down and runs over you, or he'll just stutter-step you like a ballet dancer."[11]

Other than the suspension year in 1963, Karras missed only one game during his 12 NFL seasons. He made the Pro Bowl four times, got the nod to the All-Decade team, and is considered one of the best defensive tackles of his era. It took until 2020 for him to be selected to the Pro Football Hall of Fame. That might have stemmed in part from his reaction to the suspension. Hornung apologized, but Karras never did.

"I don't like Pete Rozelle," Karras told the *Des Moines Register* in a 1977 interview. "I don't talk to him. I don't know if he likes that or not. I don't think he cares. He suspended me for one season for betting on games, and that was a bull (bleep) rap."[12]

Only seven months after the announcement of the suspension, an event happened that shocked the world. President Kennedy, riding in a motorcade in Dallas, Texas, fell victim to an assassin's bullet. The shocked nation immediately went into mourning. For the next three and a half days, the country watched while the drama played out on television. CBS stayed live with the story for 55 hours, ABC for 60 hours and NBC did more than 71 hours.[13] Americans watched Lyndon B. Johnson take the oath of office with the deceased president's widow standing next to him. On Sunday, they saw the purported assassin shot and killed on live television and on Monday, the sad funeral procession wound its way through the streets of Washington, D.C.

With less than 48 hours until scheduled games kicked off, NFL Commissioner Rozelle faced a difficult decision. They had no precedent for such a tragic event. Rozelle needed to move quickly since it was Friday and teams were preparing to travel to the weekend game sites. Teams usually traveled the day before the game. A quick review of the schedule showed no games scheduled for Washington or Dallas, the home of the White House and the site of the assas-

Commissioner Pete Rozelle suspended Alex Karras, defensive lineman for the Detroit Lions, along with Paul Hornung for the 1963 season in a huge gambling scandal. Several other players were penalized (Photofest).

sination. The Cowboys and Redskins both had road games scheduled that weekend.

Rozelle attempted to reach Kennedy's press secretary, Pierre Salinger, on a plane bound for an overseas meeting. Classmates at the University of San Francisco years before, Rozelle knew Salinger, a very close associate of President Kennedy, would give him sound, honest advice. He reached Salinger during a stop in Hawaii. "Our teams were traveling at the time of President Kennedy's assassination," Rozelle recalled several years later. "I asked [Salinger] what we could do on this. We didn't know when services were going to be, so don't know the day of mourning and so forth. This was on a Friday afternoon. He told me that he thought I should go ahead and follow the team's schedule, play the games. It was my decision. I did check with Pierre, and off the top of his head, he thought maybe we should play the games."[14]

Rozelle needed to start calling the owners to advise them of his decision. He started with the ones he knew best. Dan Rooney of the Steelers told Rozelle he disagreed but would support his decision. On game day, Dan stood atop Forbes Field in Pittsburgh two hours before kickoff waiting for the game to kick off against the Bears. He had his transistor radio with him and on it he learned that a Dallas nightclub owner named Jack Ruby had shot Lee Harvey Oswald, the accused killer of the president.

Charles "Stormy" Bidwell, owner of the St. Louis Cardinals, stopped by the league offices in New York the afternoon of the assassination. Rozelle, Bidwell said, "was shaken, he was sad, like we all were. He was also thinking in terms of what we do. He said, 'You know Stormy, the President was very sports minded and I wonder if he wouldn't want the world to continue and not be going into mourning forever.'"[15]

At least two owners called Rozelle and tried to get him to reconsider playing the games. Cleveland's Art Modell wound up paying for extra security because the visiting team that weekend, the Cowboys, came from Dallas. Eagles president Frank McNamee said he would miss his first game in 15 years because he refused to watch NFL football that weekend even though his team played at home. Philadelphia mayor James Tate tried to get a court order to stop the Eagles–Redskins game. McNamee attended a memorial service for the president instead of the game.

The Kennedy clan had long ties to football spanning nearly the entire century. Joseph P. Kennedy signed Red Grange for his film studio, FBO, which later merged with RKO. Remember that Grange, a big college football star at Illinois, may have saved the NFL with his barnstorming tour in the twenties. Grange recalled the Kennedy patriarch touting the football abilities of his sons, especially young Jack, then only five or six. Carroll Rosenbloom, a friend of Edward M. "Ted" Kennedy, recalled supplying Colts players for the famous touch football games at the Kennedy compound.

The Kennedy clan and invited guests played touch football games at their homes. All four Kennedy brothers played football at Harvard. After suffering a back injury, President Kennedy did not play past the junior varsity for the Crimson. Instead, he swam and played golf. He still liked a good game of touch football with family and friends at the Kennedy compound at Hyannis Port, though. As chief executive, he encouraged Americans to improve their physical fitness in an article he wrote for *Sports Illustrated* magazine. Kennedy's love of sports and pro football in particular, drove many to think he would have wanted the games played. He wasn't the first or only president to throw out the first pitch of the baseball season, or the only one to attend the Army–Navy game faithfully, but he showed a genuine interest in the sports of the day. He had a true love of sport and fitness his entire life, despite his physical issues.

"The physical vigor of our citizens is one of America's most precious resources," wrote Kennedy after his election but before he took office. In his *Sports Illustrated* article, Kennedy proposed a physical fitness program for the nation and asked all citizens to get more active. "Thus the physical fitness of our citizens is a vital prerequisite to American's realization of its full potential as a nation, and to the opportunity of each individual citizen to make full and fruitful use of his capacities."[16]

University of Oklahoma football coach and athletic director Bud Wilkinson, who served on the President's Council on Physical Fitness, faced the same decision Rozelle did. He considered the president his friend. When the tragedy occurred, Wilkinson phoned Bob Devaney, his counterpart at Nebraska. Despite the fact that many schools cancelled games, they agreed to play. The day after Kennedy's assassination, Nebraska beat Oklahoma, 29–20, in Lincoln before a then-record crowd at Memorial Stadium.

Officials cancelled many other college games. The service academies considered canceling the Army–Navy contest, but postponed it one week instead. President Kennedy, who served in the Navy during World War II, had planned on attending the 1963 contest. Kennedy watched the 1962 game in person, splitting time on each side of the stadium to present impartiality as commander-in-chief. The National Basketball Association cancelled some games, but ice hockey went on as usual and the Pimlico racetrack in

Flanked by Jackie Kennedy and his wife, Lady Bird, vice president Lyndon Johnson is sworn in as president of the United States of America by Dallas federal district judge Sarah T. Hughes on November 22, 1963 (Abbie Rowe. White House Photographs. John F. Kennedy Presidential Library and Museum, Boston).

Baltimore stayed open. It was a mixed bag of decisions on cancelling and playing sporting events across the nation.

Rozelle said that athletes have traditionally performed in times of great personal tragedy, summarizing his thinking. He said he could imagine the Kennedy clan playing touch football on the lawn. Kennedy thrived on the competition and football was his favorite game. Rozelle insisted Kennedy would have wanted the teams to play. On game day, Rozelle reinforced his thinking. "Everyone has a different way of paying respects," the commissioner said that day at Yankee Stadium. "I went to church today and I imagine many of the people at the game here did, too. I cannot feel that playing the game was disrespectful, nor can I feel that I have made a mistake."[17]

The rival American Football League had four games scheduled that weekend. AFL commissioner Joe Foss had left the country as part of his Air Force Reserve duties. His second-in-command, Milt Woodard, a Chicago newspaperman and former executive on the golf tour, continued to try to locate Foss. Unable to find his boss to ask the question and with time running short, Woodard had to make the decision. He decided the games should not be played.

After making the decision, Woodard spoke on the phone with his son, Ross, at home in St. Cloud, Minnesota. Out of respect for the president, he decided to cancel the games.

"I made a tough decision," Milt told Ross, "and I'm wondering if I'll have a job on Monday."[18] On Monday, he still had a job. Meanwhile, Rozelle got feedback from across the league. Dan Rooney, owner of the Steelers, told him he didn't think they should play the game.

The Baltimore Colts had already boarded their flight going to Los Angeles for a game against the Rams when they got the news. The news really shocked Gino Marchetti, who had campaigned for John Kennedy as he ran against Richard Nixon for the White House.

"We were flying out to Los Angeles and we just about to Kansas City when the pilot announced to all of us that the president had been shot," said Marchetti. "He's the one guy I met that when I looked him straight in the face, I thought the guy came from heaven. I met a lot of guys in my day, but for some reasons, when I shook his hand, he looked me in the face, and something, a spirit came over me."[19]

During the game in Philadelphia, someone vandalized Eagles backup quarterback King Hill's car. They shattered all of the windows, perhaps because Hill's car had Texas plates. Many across the country associated anybody from Texas as being at least partly responsible for the tragedy. Meanwhile, on the field many of the players found it hard to focus on the game. Fullback Don Perkins said he thought everyone from Dallas was indicted for the shooting. When the Dallas Cowboys arrived at the Cleveland airport, future Hall of Fame defensive tackle Bob Lilly recalled that the baggage handlers would not handle their luggage.

Rozelle decided the seven scheduled games should go on despite the fact CBS would not televise any of them. The networks probably would have preempted the game anyway due to wall-to-wall coverage of the events in Dallas and Washington. It started to look as if Rozelle made a decision no one would interpret as the correct one. Then it got worse. On Sunday morning, Jack Ruby shot accused killer Lee Harvey Oswald on national television before the games on the East Coast started.

Brandt recalled Coach Landry addressing the team as they prepared to leave the locker room and take the field. He stood giving the final instructions at a chalkboard. He had the first offensive play written on the board and all players focused on the coach when a security guard came into the room and interrupted with the news that Ruby had shot Oswald.

While critics attacked the NFL, they applauded the AFL for their decision. Fans who attended the games found the environment surreal. Many of them said it did not seem normal. They had no pregame introductions of the players and no music played but the national anthem. They cancelled all of the halftime performances. Fans cheered but the volume was not as loud as normal.

Rozelle attended the Giants–Cardinals game at Yankee Stadium where he encountered *New York Herald Tribune* columnist Red Smith. "I think you're doing the wrong thing."

"Why?" asked Rozelle.

"Because it shows disrespect for a dead president of the United States who isn't even buried yet."

"There can be no disrespect where no disrespect is intended," said Rozelle.[20]

The debate continues over whether or not Rozelle made the right decision. Not everyone disagreed with the decision. Frank Gifford, who played with the Giants and later found fame in broadcasting, saw it differently. "I have three little Kennedy grandchildren,"

President John F. Kennedy lies in state in the Rotunda of the Capitol Building on November 24, 1963. Kennedy was shot while riding in a motorcade in Dallas, Texas, two days earlier (Abbie Rowe. White House Photographs. John F. Kennedy Presidential Library and Museum, Boston).

he said. "My daughter [Victoria] was married to Michael Kennedy. They don't think that way. They are competitors who get up and fight back. I played enough touch football with them to know they didn't want to sit around on their thumbs. It was a tough decision for him to make."[21]

"It wasn't much fun the rest of the year," said Bob Lilly of the 1963 season. "It [the assassination] kind of killed our [spirit]. You know, we tried and went out and went through our motions. But I don't think we had it. I think the assassination affected the Cowboys for at least another year, as far as feeling guilty about our city. Dallas was kind of a coming star and then all of a sudden, it was tarnished. It took Dallas a long time to get over it. It didn't take the team quite as long. [Don] Meredith and I, as Texans, probably felt it a little more. Coach Landry, too. We were kind of ashamed of our city. It's not the best mentality for playing football. Somehow, emotionally, it did something."[22]

The events of the funeral—the riderless horse, the coffin on a horse-drawn caisson, the great numbers of world leaders attending the funeral, son John saluting his father and daughter Caroline touching his coffin remain timeless images of the tragic weekend.

This generation's "JFK Assassination" historical marker came with the September 11 terrorist attack on the World Trade Towers in New York City, the Pentagon near Washington, and a fourth airliner that crashed in southern Pennsylvania. Today, a generation recalls where they were when the twin towers collapsed. An older generation recalls the Kennedy assassination as that time the clock stopped for a moment. The NFL postponed and rescheduled the games the weekend following that tragic event in 2001. The lessons from November 1963 rang clear; NFL leadership had learned from Rozelle's decision.

Perhaps Rozelle got the last laugh. Even though some considered the Kennedy decision Rozelle's low point on the job, *Sports Illustrated* named him Sportsman of the Year just two months later. Rozelle, in fact, became the magazine's first non-athlete so recognized with the award. "In the year of its most alarming crisis," wrote Kenneth Rudeen, "Rozelle decisively and brilliantly guided a great and growing sport. He bucked the almost universal trend in professional sport by emerging as a strong commissioner—making vigorous decisions, not all of them popular, and proving that he could act independently of the owners who hired him. It is in salute to the sporting phenomenon of our time—professional football—as well as to Rozelle himself that we make this award."

After he stepped down as commissioner, Rozelle had time to reconsider the decision to play the weekend after the assassination. "I think it was a mistake, because it was such a horrendous thing, with follow-up on Lee Harvey Oswald, and so forth," said Rozelle. "It absorbed the nation and put them in a deep sense of mourning. We had teams that had gone to different cities, ready for a game on Sunday. So we did play the games that Sunday. I think it was a serious public relations mistake. I think it would have been much better if we hadn't, of course. I was criticized intensely for that."[23]

CBS, sticking with its around-the-clock coverage of the events, did not televise any of the games. The crowds attending the games seemed somber at first, but picked up as the action heated up. Most fans brought transistor radios with them to games in those days so they learned almost immediately that Dallas nightclub owner Jack Ruby had shot Oswald about an hour before the kickoff of games on the East Coast.

The television president took office in the sixties about the same time as the television commissioner took over the NFL. Professional football exploded on television.

Advertising brought a new revenue stream to professional football the league did not have in the beginning. At first, owners, used to getting most of their profits from ticket sales, did not know what to expect with television. They feared it would ruin the gate. Why would anyone come to the game if they could stay home and watch it free? Rozelle correctly predicted television would expose the game to countless fans that had not seen it before or could not attend in person. That exposure helped interest in the sport to grow.

Cash-strapped owners happily watched the money coming in from television in the sixties. They could see the game increasing in popularity. One November morning in 1963, Cleveland Browns owner Art Modell greeted the commissioner with the news that in just seven regular-season and one exhibition game, the Browns might outdraw the baseball Indians, who played 65 home dates. Modell fell short by a small margin, only 8,000 tickets, but he made his point clear—pro football would soon move into the top spot in American sports.

Rozelle's best skills involved his ability to get along with people. A natural negotiator and politician, he understood diplomacy and deal making, two essential skills need to succeed in that job. "This job is a hybrid," he once said. "It's in between being the chief executive of a large company and being the executive director of a trade association. I inherited a strong constitution and an office that held respect, but the whole thing—no matter what the constitution says—is getting the confidence of the owners."[24]

With one exception, Rozelle did that. He had friction from the start with one man, Al Davis, who ran the Raiders after his short stint as the wartime head of the rival American Football League. Davis openly challenged Rozelle and his league-think concept. In the early days of NFL Properties, the league donated the profits to charity, believing those contributions would boost the image of the league. Davis demanded his share of NFL Properties money come to the Raiders and not to a charity.

Rozelle and Davis never got along. Davis took things personally, believing Rozelle had the job he should have had. Owners named Rozelle commissioner of the combined league while Davis returned to the Raiders. Rozelle got along with all the other owners. Rozelle also worked easily with the politicians in Washington. As the league grew, the situation tested Rozelle's abilities regularly.

Davis joined the AFL from its beginning when Los Angeles Chargers coach Sid Gillman hired him as an assistant coach working with the backfield. Gillman said later that he hired Davis because of his skills as a recruiter. The AFL needed to compete with the more established NFL for players. Davis, a skillful salesperson, could convince players to join the new league. Gillman credited Davis with recruiting three key players to the Chargers—Lance Alworth, Ron Mix and Paul Lowe. All three proved key players as the Chargers challenged each year for the West Division title. In 1963, Davis became the head coach and general manager of the Oakland Raiders. At 33 years old, he stood as the youngest person to hold both jobs in professional football. After taking over a team that had won only one game in 1962, he immediately turned the Raiders around, achieving a record of 10–4 in 1963.

Al Davis entered the world on July 4, 1939, in Brockton, Massachusetts. He grew up, however, in Brooklyn where he developed toughness on the streets of New York. Davis played tough and talked tough. As he grew up, he developed a great love and fascination with military history, especially everything with World War II. He learned about the battles, the strategy and the players. The blitzkrieg tactics of the Third Reich fascinated him; he knew how they liked the quick strike and relentless battle. When it came time to develop his strategy for football, he borrowed all the best strategies from military history. He wanted players with great speed so that he could strike deep into the defense and gather huge chucks of yards in a short amount of time.

The disagreement with Davis was unusual for Rozelle. Throughout his entire career, he came across as someone who could get rich, successful men to do what he wanted and make them believe they wanted it, too. His ability to play the politics of the day made him one of the most successful sports commissioners of all time and all sports.

"He could handle people—difficult people—like a lion tamer, if you will," said Mike Brown, an executive with the Bengals. "People in the league felt he had their interests at heart. He was always fair. He was the perfect leader for the NFL, and I think when you look at the job of commissioner, he gets my vote as the all-time greatest one."[25]

"We were fortunate to have Rozelle come along in 1960—a man familiar with the media—with television and the new era we were moving into," said Tex Schramm, who had originally hired Rozelle with the Rams a decade earlier. "He had a lot to do with the tremendous growth our league experienced from the early 1960s to the present. In particular, he helped boost public awareness of the game. He knew how to deal with the media, with TV and he thought big. For instance, his thinking on the Super Bowl—'Let's do it with class and style and make it the best we can.' As a result, it has become the biggest single sporting event in the United States."[26]

In summary, Rozelle was the right man for the times. The game and the changing times aligned to grow together. The laid-back fifties charged into the sixties—a decade of change. Collectively, Americans grew restless with regard to sports and wanted something new. The older generation may have loved baseball, but the younger generation wanted a faster game with greater excitement. Football offered greater pace, strategy and controlled violence. When Rozelle took over, baseball was the undisputed national pastime. Rozelle changed all that.

Rozelle launched a television strategy to introduce the sport to more Americans. His deals with NFL Films and NFL Properties created lore with the game and linkage for all fans to feel like a part of the team. His vision of the Super Bowl as a weeklong event cemented its status as the number one sport. Today Super Bowl Sunday is the closest thing to a national holiday without the declaration. The 17 most-watched television programs have all been Super Bowl games. Football claimed the perch as the public's favorite sport in 1972 and has held off all challengers since then.

Football played well on television at a time when the medium became an increasingly more important part of everyday life. Rozelle sold the game of professional football when the changing demographics of the nation signaled a different attitude. Rozelle built on those changing attitudes to present his game to the country. He convinced them to love football and, in turn, boost its popularity ahead of baseball.

Comedian George Carlin made a living with his stand-up comedy routines calling out the subtle things in life that made us laugh. He pointed out baseball and football as polar opposites. "In football the object is for the quarterback, also known as the field general, to be on target with his aerial assault, riddling the defense by hitting his receivers with deadly accuracy in spite of the blitz, even if he has to use shotgun. With short bullet passes and long bombs, he marches his troops into enemy territory, balancing this aerial assault with a sustained ground attack that punches holes in the forward wall of the enemy's defensive line. In baseball, the object is to go home! And to be safe!"[27]

Football has often been tied to war with terms such as blitz and aerial attack. However, during the sixties, a protracted war in Southeast Asia raged on endlessly and the public was growing weary.

Chapter Ten

War

When Walter Cronkite turned against the Vietnam War, it seemed like the public followed his lead. Public sentiment against the war had begun to sway when the respected journalist came out with an editorial statement that caused quite the stir. The *CBS Evening News* anchor established a strong reputation for believability, earning the nickname "Uncle Walter." Many people felt they could trust the veteran reporter. Cronkite, long considered the most trusted man in America, came back from Vietnam with the observation that we could not win the war. "It was the first time in American history that a war had been declared over by an anchorman," wrote David Halberstam in *The Powers That Be*.[1]

Cronkite took his role seriously. According to many viewers, he reported the news with impartiality. These happened in the days before politically generated programming labeled news appeared on places like Fox or MSNBC. Every night reports on the *CBS Evening News* included news of the war in Southeast Asia. Reports from the war front lacked the optimism of the official briefings from political and military leaders in Washington. When the Tet Offensive reports came in, Cronkite felt he needed to visit Vietnam to determine the truth for himself.

The decision to go to Vietnam did not sit easy with Cronkite. "He was not entirely easy about making the trip and doing his own special from Vietnam because he knew that he was stepping out of his natural role, that he would be perceived differently by his viewers and that his role would never be quite the same again," wrote Halberstam.[2]

During the half-hour news special *Report from Vietnam* that aired February 27, 1968, Cronkite said he considered the Vietnam War a stalemate. This did not represent the view of a network anchor with no experience outside the studio in New York. Cronkite had previously covered war close up. His first big break came as a United Press correspondent during World War II. He covered the landing of Allied troops in North Africa, bombing runs over Germany and some of the major battles of World War II. Neither a pacifist by nature nor a novice to the brutality of war, Cronkite's Vietnam reports reflected observations made by a studio anchor who knew his business.

Cronkite went to Vietnam to see the situation himself. He had read Associated Press dispatches outlining surprise attacks on South Vietnam strongholds such as Saigon. The series of attacks, later called the Tet Offensive, targeted the U.S. Embassy in Saigon, General William Westmoreland's headquarters and the South Vietnamese general staff offices. The term Tet came from the calendar; it coincided with the Vietnamese version of New Year.

Before he landed in Vietnam, Cronkite's impression had America the victor in the war. He gleaned this opinion from listening to generals and politicians in Washington. The administration of President Lyndon Johnson had optimistically pronounced victory in Vietnam imminent and his generals stated that view publicly. At the time, America had about a half-million troops in Vietnam. Now, Cronkite had fresh dispatches from Vietnam telling him otherwise.

Once he arrived on the ground, he saw a different story. He interviewed General Westmoreland who called Tet Offensive an American victory. The general told Cronkite his forces had defeated the enemy at Hue. Cronkite and his group went to Hue to see for themselves; they found the battle still going on when they got there. Cronkite realized then that military and political leaders provided a less than honest view of the war to the American people. This credibility gap created doubt in the minds of the American people, who had not questioned the war in a widespread way up to that point.

Militarily, the Tet Offensive proved a failure for the Communists, but conversely it had political success. "It shocked the American public, which had assumed that a U.S. Victory was right around the corner," wrote Mike Wright. "In itself this created a 'credibility gap.' How could the American public believe an administration that claimed to see a light at the end of the tunnel of war when, so clearly, the Communists could and would send thousands of troops into South Vietnam, realizing they might die?"[3]

Cronkite's CBS News special surveyed the state of the Vietnam War as the veteran correspondent saw it during his personal visit to the war scene. As he toured the country, Cronkite interviewed generals and troops. After the final set of commercials, Cronkite looked square into the camera and delivered a personal commentary. In his editorial, he made his point clear: based on his observations, the war stood at a stalemate and he urged a peaceful end. "To say

President Nixon, seen from overhead, surrounded by U.S. Army soldiers in green uniforms and camouflage helmets, greeting and talking to individual military troops of the First Infantry Division in Dian, South Vietnam, on July 30, 1969 (White House Photographer Oliver Atkins. The Richard Nixon Presidential Library and Museum).

that we are closer to victory today is to believe, in the face of the evidence, the optimists who have been wrong in the past," Cronkite said. "To suggest we are on the edge of defeat is to yield to unreasonable pessimism. To say that we are mired in stalemate seems the only realistic, yet unsatisfactory, conclusion.... It is increasingly clear to this reporter that the only rational way out then will be to negotiate, not as victors, but as an honorable people who lived up to their pledge to defend democracy, and did the best they could."[4]

The Nielsen rating service estimated some nine million Americans watched Cronkite's CBS News special. The significance of that one battle and the news coverage that followed seems clear. Many historians called the Tet Offensive the turning point of the war. Media coverage of the war changed after that battle, too. Members of the media generally accepted the official reports from the military until that point. After the battle and questions of the credibility of the spokespersons arose, more media outlets made their reports from the field.

Before Tet, the war coverage took on the look of a scoreboard show with daily counts of the war dead shown like the outcome of sporting contests. After Tet, correspondents linked with units in the field brought bloody images back to the evening news programs. The brutal and bloody images of war burst into living rooms across the country.

"Vietnam was American's first television war and the Tet Offensive was American's first television super battle," wrote professor Don Oberdorfer, who covered the Vietnam War for the *Washington Post*.[5] By the height of America's involvement in Vietnam, nearly a hundred million television sets spread across the land reached 16 of every 17 homes and a potential audience of 96 per cent of the population. The expanding medium of television offered an opportunity to view events as they happened across the world. The more they saw, the less favor they found with the war. Key leaders began to speak against it.

By November 1967, American troop strength in Vietnam was approaching 500,000. The casualty reports Americans saw on the evening news totaled more than 15,000 with another 100,000 wounded at that time. The dissatisfaction that began on college campuses now was spreading across the country among the general population. Just before Halloween in 1967, some 100,000 protestors gathered at the Lincoln Memorial. That same year, the anti-war movement gain momentum when a civil rights leader went public with his opposition to the war on moral grounds.

"Somehow this madness must cease," said Martin Luther King, Jr., in 1967 at Riverside Church in New York. "We must stop now. I speak as a child of God and brother to the suffering poor of Vietnam. I speak for those whose land is being laid waste, whose homes are being destroyed, whose culture is being subverted. I speak for the poor of America who are paying the double price of smashed hopes at home and death and corruption in Vietnam. I speak as a citizen of the world, for the world, as it stands aghast at the path we have taken. I speak as an American to the leaders of my own nation. The great initiative in this war is ours. The initiative to stop it must be ours."[6]

The first big-name athlete to have his name forever linked to Vietnam War had burst onto the boxing scene years during the 1960 Olympic Games under his given name of Cassius Clay. Muhammad Ali won the gold medal in the light-heavyweight division. As a youth, he took up boxing by accident. During the winter of 1954, he had just received a new red-and-white Schwinn bicycle for Christmas. He and a friend rode their bikes to Louisville Home Show at the Columbia Auditorium. When they came back outside, they found their bikes gone.

The opposition to the Vietnam War gathered steam as the sixties went on. Veterans for Peace express displeasure with the Vietnam War at the March on the Pentagon in Washington, D.C., in the fall of 1967 (Frank Wolfe. White House Photograph from Lyndon B. Johnson Library).

"I was so upset I went looking for the police to report it," he recalled. "Someone directed me down to the gym run by a local policeman named Joe Martin, who was teaching young boys to box in his spare time. I told Mr. Martin that I was gonna whup whoever stole my bike. I was half crying and probably didn't look too convincing. I remember Mr. Martin telling me, 'Well, you better learn how to fight before you start challenging people that you're gonna whup.'"[7] Cassius Clay followed his advice by joining the gym and take up boxing. He got to the gym early and dedicated himself to getting better. The hard work paid off as Clay improved as a boxer and won numerous Golden Gloves titles on the way to taking the opportunity to box for his country in the Olympic Games.

While in Rome for the 1960 Olympic Games, a Russian journalist tried to trap Clay by asking about civil rights in America. "Tell your readers we got qualified people working on that, and I'm not worried about the outcome," he said. "To me, the USA is still the best country in the world, including yours. It may be hard to get something to eat sometimes, but I ain't fighting alligators and living in a mud hut."[8]

Those comments helped win friends in the media and the country as a whole. He stood up for his country while facing criticism by a Russian journalist. In those days as the Cold War heated up, Americans loved to hear such patriotic words coming from a young man who had worked his way up from humble beginnings.

It was also an era of sensitivity in race relations. Many white Americans proudly cheered on black athletes. Many of the same white fans seemed to favor black athletes who performed well on the field, but kept their mouths shut off it. They did not like those who expressed themselves politically. In this decade, minority athletes who spoke publically would suffer an adverse effect with fan loyalty. When Clay defended the United States with the Russian reporter, he received a positive reaction. Yet, his refusal to serve his country and his comments on the war in general caused a negative reaction with many Americans.

After the Olympic Games, Clay turned pro and won all his fights without attracting much attention until one big fight came along. He won his first 19 professional bouts and he bragged that he could beat Sonny Liston, the reigning champion. Many considered Liston unbeatable after he knocked Floyd Patterson out in the first round. Boxing reporters chalked the young boxer's claims up to typical boastful ramblings. At just 22 years old, Clay boasted of beating the apparently unbeatable Liston. In February 1964, young Cassius Clay got his opportunity.

Sonny Liston had far more experience than Clay. Liston had won nearly double the professional boxing matches of his young adversary. He learned to fight while incarcerated in Missouri for robbing a gas station at age 18. Some boxers refused to enter the ring with him. Boxing writers considered him one of the top heavyweight fighters of all time and did not give the young boxer much of a chance against him.

Oddsmakers listed 7–1 odds that Liston would beat the challenger. Both fighters came into the ring ready for the bout. The boxers threw punches back and forth after the opening bell rang. Clay opened a cut on Liston's left cheek. He dictated the fight until a strange twist happened. Clay's eyes started to burn. Apparently, the medicine used to close the cut on Liston's face got into Clay's eyes. At one point, the pain grew so severe Clay wanted to quit. His corner convinced him to stay in the fight. It appeared to them that Clay had a real opportunity to win the fight if his eyes stayed clear.

More than 50 years later, boxing historians still are not clear about how it happened, but the youngster upset the champion. Liston did not answer the bell for the seventh round and the victory went to brash Clay. Some writers thought Liston hurt his shoulder in the first round or speculated he came into the fight with an injury. The one thing was clear: Liston's fearsome left hook did not show up that night. A debate about Liston's age at the time of the fight has also developed. He claimed to be 32, but others have him at closer to 40 years old. Liston grew up in the backwoods of Arkansas where birth records were not clear.

The boxing world, however, changed on the evening of February 25, 1964, when the young boxer pulled off the upset. The next day, it changed even more. After the fight, Cassius Clay revealed he had joined the Nation of Islam and changed his name. First, he said he had taken the name Cassius X; a few days later, he changed it to Muhammad Ali. The philosophies of Malcolm X, Elijah Muhammad and the Nation of Islam (NOI) appealed to him. NOI taught that white America actively worked to keep African Americans from achieving political and economic success. Further, they thought the best course was to form a separate state that would exclude whites.

They did not subscribe to the nonviolent tactics deployed by Martin Luther King Jr. and recommended followers take any action necessary to achieve their goals. "I believe in the eye-for-an-eye business," Ali told the *New York Post*. "You kill my dog, you better hide your cat."[9] Malcolm X and Ali became close friends; he was at the Liston fight as a guest of Ali. Before they met, Ali experienced his own challenges with discrimination and followed closely news such as the murder of Emmett Till. In 1955, while visiting family in Mississippi, two men brutally murdered the 14-year-old from Chicago after he allegedly flirted with a white woman.

In a decade of change, Muhammad Ali changed professional boxing. He spoke his mind on the issues of the day. To many athletes of the day, the Civil Rights movement and the Vietnam War lay out of bounds. They feared commenting on such issues might take away their athletic opportunities. Not Ali. Black tennis player Arthur Ashe, who fought his own battles with racism and discrimination, said Ali altered perceptions. "Ali didn't just change the image African Americans have of themselves," he said. "He opened the eyes of a lot of white people to the potential of African Americans; who we are and what we can be."[10] He became a forceful proponent of civil rights in America and, perhaps, the first celebrity critic of the war in Vietnam.

When he refused induction into the military, Ali knew he faced a possible prison sentence and the potential loss of millions of dollars. Under oath in federal court, his response to the presiding judge showed his awareness of the financial impact. "If it wasn't against my conscience to do it, I would easily do it," said Ali. "I wouldn't raise all this court stuff and I wouldn't go through all this and lose the millions that I gave up and my image with the American public that I would say is completely dead and ruined because of us in here now."[11]

Media reaction to the Nation of Islam announcement appeared generally negative since many viewed the group as an anti-white radical hate group. In general, the media refused to refer to him using his Muslim name. Some went so far as to declare the Nation of Islam as the black version of the Ku Klux Klan, believing in racial separation and seeing the opposing race as inferior. Ali ruled the heavyweight boxing world for a long period. His public political statements polarized people. Some loved him due to his upbeat personality, corny poetry and celebrity good looks. Others disliked his association with a militant group that seemed, in the opinion of some, to hate all white people.

While Ali worked his way to the championship and defended his title around the world, his draft status changed from 1-A (qualified for induction) to 1-Y (unfit for military service due to low intelligence test scores) back to 1-A (qualified for induction). After the Gulf of Tonkin Resolution passed in 1964, providing President Johnson with the power to escalate the war in Vietnam, standards changed and more men like Ali became draft worthy.

Ali found great success in the boxing ring, but his biggest foe came when he received a draft notice from Uncle Sam. Ali supposedly stated, "I ain't got no quarrel with them Viet Cong." He claimed conscientious objector status due to his religious beliefs and refused to serve in the military.

In 1967, he appeared at the Houston, Texas, draft board but refused to step forward as they called his name. Authorities arrested him and charged him with a felony. One day later the New York State Athletic Commission suspended his boxing license and stripped him of his title. Other boxing commissions soon followed suit. The case eventually went all the way to the Supreme Court, which ruled in his favor. Although Ali may have benefited from America's turning against the war in Vietnam, many Americans viewed him as a loudmouth radical.

His stance against the draft kept him out of the boxing ring for 43 months. His last fight before the suspension came at age 25 when he looked unbeatable. He returned at 29 looking physically diminished. In his third fight back, he lost a unanimous decision to Joe Frazier at Madison Square Garden.

If public opinion did not favor Ali before his stance against the war and his part in it, it only got worse as the war went on. In particular, veterans of the Korean War and

World War II grew upset at his anti-war stance. They had proudly marched off to war when the nation called. Veterans drove public opinion that quickly swung against Ali. They could not understand Ali's opposition to serving in the military and his unpatriotic stance. "As a fighter, Cassius is good," wrote columnist Milton Gross of the *New York Post*. "As a man, he cannot compare to some of the kids slogging through the rice paddies where the names are stranger than Muhammad Ali."[12]

Ali's decision to avoid the draft made big news among the black athletic community. In June 1967, ten top black athletes gathered in Cleveland at the Negro Industrial and Economic Union. Most of them played football, but two basketball players, Lew Alcindor, later known as Kareem Abdul-Jabbar, and Bill Russell, attended. Jim Brown joined John Wooten and Walter Beach from the Cleveland Browns. Willie Davis of the Packers, Bobby Mitchell of the Redskins and Curtis McClinton of the Chiefs arrived at the meeting along with several others. They met to talk with Ali about his military draft decision.

"This was not supposed to be a public meeting," said Bill Russell. "When the news leaked out, it was reported wrong, too. We never went to Cleveland to try to persuade Muhammad to join the Army. We went to offer our help; if he had changed his mind and decided to go in the Army after all, we were ready to say that we had influenced him to do it and we were ready to accept our share of the criticism and insult he would be sure to get from some of the Negro community."

Muhammad Ali had a very complicated view of race, influenced greatly by his treatment as a young man growing up in Louisville, Kentucky. One story in particular illustrates his strong convictions. Many members of the 1960 Olympic team observed how the heavyweight boxer who then went by the name Cassius Clay loved his gold medal. They saw him wearing it constantly all over the Olympic village. He had it around his neck constantly. He slept with it, he went to the cafeteria with it, and he never took it off. The week after the proud boxer returned to his hometown of Louisville, Clay wanted to get something to eat. With his medal swinging around his neck, Ali entered a segregated Louisville restaurant hoping to eat a cheeseburger but they denied him service. Despite his success at the Olympic Games and still proudly wearing the medal, he was just a black man who was not allowed to eat in a segregated restaurant. He walked to the center of a bridge over the Ohio River and threw the gold medal into the water.

Despite losing nearly four years of his prime boxing years due to the battle over his conscientious objector status, Ali returned to the ring in 1970. The time away from the sport had taken its toll. His reactions had slowed some and his feet had lost some of that special magic. But still a terrific athlete he eventually regained his title.

Through this dramatic decade, one cannot overestimate Ali's importance in the changing role of athletes in society. A gifted athlete who generated millions for his sport, Ali earned great respect by other black athletes in all sports. He changed the way the public and the press related to black athletes. Unique among contemporary athletes, he had an engaging personality that seemed impossible to ignore. One can see Ali's influence on more modern athletic figures such as Terrell Owens, Ray Lewis and Deion Sanders. He understood athletics as a form of entertainment and lived up to that aspect with his tireless self-promotion. Ali made white America more aware of black militancy during a time when issues of race emerged into a more public space. Professional boxers were not the only athletes who felt the burden of the Vietnam War. The war affected athletes across all sports throughout the decade. The number of military personnel going to Southeast Asia expanded with greater American involvement.

In the fall of 1967, as a college senior, Bob Kalsu played as an All-American tackle on an Oklahoma Sooners team that had achieved its way to a 10–1 record and an Orange Bowl victory over the Tennessee Volunteers. The next season, Kalsu bulked up to 250 pounds and won a starting job on the Buffalo Bills offensive line. At season's end, he had earned the team's Rookie of the Year award, quite an achievement for an offensive guard. He appeared poised to continue a long, successful playing career.

During his college days at the University of Oklahoma. Kalsu developed the ability to lead other men. He participated in ROTC during college where he received some training but he just seemed to rise as a natural leader in any environment. It came to him just as easy as his stomping, pounding gait that earned him the nickname "Buffalo Bob" during high school and college.[13] Ironically, Buffalo Bob played for the Buffalo Bills.

After a successful rookie season in professional football, many friends recommended that Kalsu try to find a way out of his military commitment. After all, now married with one child, he had to consider his family. Bob Kalsu would not hear that talk. He felt an obligation to make good on his commitment. Due to ROTC, he had earned a commission as a second lieutenant in the Army when he graduated from Oklahoma in May 1968. Despite a looming military commitment, the Buffalo Bills had made him an eighth-round selection. He and his wife married in January 1968 about the same time the Bills made him their choice. By the time Kalsu reported to training camp with the Bills, Jan Kalsu was already pregnant with their first child. They called Kalsu to active duty with orders to Vietnam before his daughter turned a year old.

Kalsu arrived in Vietnam just before Thanksgiving 1969 and received an assignment leading an artillery battery on Firebase Ripcord, which sat on the top of a hill in South Vietnam's Thua-Hue province. They supported the infantrymen of the 101st Airborne Division as they engaged the enemy through the jungles and lowlands towards Hue. The enemy's frequent attacks on the base with artillery, mortar and tear gas made it particularly tough duty. Despite the conditions, Kalsu's men loved working for him as they responded to his natural leadership abilities.

Soldiers considered Lieutenant Kalsu a big guy who loved serving with the troops. "He had a presence about him," said former corporal Mike Renner. "He could have holed up in his bunker, giving orders on the radio. He was out there in the open with everybody else. He was always checking the men out, finding out how we were, seeing if we were doing what needed to be done. I got wounded on Ripcord, and he came down into the bunker. My hands were bandaged, and he asked me, 'You want to catch a chopper out of here?'" Renner could see that Kalsu had been hit in the shoulder. "I saw the bandage on him and saw he was staying. I said, 'No, I'm gonna stay.'"[14]

"I remember this tremendous noise and darkness," recalled private first class Nick Fotias who also served Firebase Ripcord with Kalsu. "I was blown off my feet and flew through the door of the bunker and landed at the bottom of the steps, six feet down, and this tremendous weight crushing me. I couldn't see. I couldn't hear. I had dirt in my eyes, and my eyes were tearing. I rubbed them and I could see again. I pushed off this weight that was on top of me, and I realized it was Bob."[15]

At 5 p.m. on July 21, 1970, James Robert Kalsu died on firebase Ripcord in Vietnam. Less than two days later and a half a world away, at 12:45 a.m. on July 23 at St. Anthony Hospital in Oklahoma, Jan Kalsu gave birth to a baby boy. That afternoon, a knock sounded at the Kalsu front door. Jan's sister opened it thinking she would greet a florist with flowers in celebration of the birth. Instead, an Army officer asked for Jan Kalsu. Sandy Szilagyi,

Jan's sister, told the officer Mrs. Kalsu just given birth at the hospital. Since the soldier needed to inform her personally, he traveled to the hospital to pass along the unfortunate news. Jan Kalsu, on an emotional high having just given birth to a baby boy, thought about her husband's excitement at hearing the news. Her visions of his joy ended abruptly when the army officer walked into the room. Before leaving the hospital to bring her son home, she asked that the birth certificate be updated to name her son James Robert Kalsu Jr.

When he grew up, Bob Jr. traveled to the Vietnam Veterans Memorial in Washington, D.C. Like many Americans, he wanted to search for a name of a loved one on the black gabbro wall. He looked and looked but could not find his father's name. That massive wall lists more than 58,000 names etched in the reflective black granite. They are not listed in alphabetical order so it can be difficult to find a name. Bob Jr. approached a volunteer to get assistance.

"I want to find James Robert Kalsu," he said.

"I can help you with that," the volunteer said, "because it's the most requested name I have to find every day."[16]

The volunteer asked why he wanted to see that name. When Bob Jr. told him that soldier was his dad, the volunteer asked to see his Oklahoma driver's license. Due to the media reports, many people knew of Bob Kalsu and his story. NFL Films did a story on him shown on Veterans Day 1999. *Sports Illustrated* dedicated its July 23, 2001, cover to Bob Kalsu standing in his battle uniform from Vietnam. To honor their 1968 rookie guard, the Buffalo Bills presented to the Pro Football Hall of Fame a plaque recognizing Kalsu as the only active player killed during Vietnam. They placed it in a prominent position so that visitors would see it as they toured the museum.

For many years, pro football historians listed Bob Kalsu as the only pro football player to lose his life in Vietnam. In recent years, they revised the list to include Don Steinbrunner, although Kalsu remains the only active player to die in Vietnam. Steinbrunner, a sixth-round selection of the Cleveland Browns in the 1953 NFL Draft, also had a military commitment due to his ROTC participation in college.

Steinbrunner played offensive tackle in eight games for the Browns his rookie year and then left to fulfill his two-year commitment. After that commitment ended, he considered returning to professional football but decided to stay on full-time with the Air Force. In 1966, he went to Vietnam. On July 20, 1967, the enemy shot down Steinbrunner's C-123 Provider over Kontum, South Vietnam, where he served as navigator. All five crew members died. The 35 year old left behind a wife and three children.

Steinbrunner ended his NFL career once his military career took off. Numerous other players served in our military and then came back to play football. Pittsburgh Steelers running back Robert "Rocky" Bleier interrupted his playing career for a tour of duty in Vietnam. The Steelers did not draft Rocky Bleier until the 16th round in 1968. The captain of the 1966 national champion Notre Dame team had 416 players selected ahead of him in the draft. With limited size and speed, most considered him a long shot to make the team. With hustle and determination, Bleier made the squad and saw action mostly on special teams.

Near the end of his rookie season, he was drafted. This time the U.S. Army called. "And so, in a 24-hour period, I went from being a running back in the NFL to being a maggot in the United States Army, the lowest of the low," Bleier recalled looking back. "My focus basically at that moment was, okay fine, I can be the best soldier I can be."[17]

Bleier hoped he could find a spot in the Army Reserves and not have to go overseas. He knew some other professional football players around the National Football League had located reserve positions and avoided overseas service. Looking back, Bleier said he assumed teams found spots in the Reserves or National Guard for players. He recalled hearing about Packers Paul Hornung and Boyd Dowler going to Camp Randall for their two-week Army Reserve.

In October, Steelers head coach Bill Austin told Bleier they had a problem. He said they could not find him an opening in a reserve unit. In 1968 the draft machine worked overtime and the participation in the war effort ran high. At the time, about five hundred thousand service members served in Southeast Asia. Reserve duty provided one way to avoid serving in Vietnam but those spots grew difficult to find.

Before the 1968 season ended, Bleier reported for service with the Army. He went through basic training and then to Vietnam as an infantry soldier—rough duty. He joined the 196th Light Infantry Brigade whose mission involved looking for the enemy in the Hiep Duc Valley of Vietnam. They spent many long days and nights crawling through rice paddies and jungles. Far from the comforts of home, Bleier had to find happiness in the strangest places.

On August 20, 1969, Bleier patrolled with his fellow soldiers. As they moved through a wooded area toward a clearing separated by two rice paddies, they had to exercise real caution crossing the open ground. As Bleier left the cover of the woods, he heard the sound of machine gun fire. All the soldiers dove for cover. Since Bleier carried the heavy grenade launcher, he needed to quickly get into position and begin firing grenades to provide cover for his comrades. Just as he prepped to get off his first shot, he felt a thud in his left thigh. It didn't particularly hurt, but when he reached down to his leg to check it out, he felt blood. He had been shot in the thigh.

Despite his injury, Bleier managed to fire some grenades at the enemy as machine gun rounds landed all around him. Several nearby soldiers died in the onslaught. It quickly appeared they had enemy soldiers surrounding them. The situation called for a quick prayer. Bleier had a Catholic grade school education and recalled a story about a soldier during World War II who prayed for God to spare his life. According to the story, that World War II soldier pledged he would join the priesthood if God spared his life. Bleier could not pledge a life in the priesthood, but he began to pray anyway.

Minutes later, the medic made it to his position. He told him he would help him get out of there. More shots rang out and the medic took a round in the hand. Bleier had to bandage the medic and together they needed to find their way to the rear to get additional medical attention. The medic and the running back kept low to the ground as they crawled back to the rear of the position. They hoped that spot might provide more cover for injured soldiers. The commanding officer, Captain Tom Murphy, told Bleier he would have to evacuate him so he could get medical attention for his leg injury. No sooner had those words come out than fighting picked up again.

"We held them off and fell back into another wooded area behind the rice paddy," recalled Bleier. "Then they started firing at us again. I was sitting on the side of a knoll when a grenade came in. I didn't see it, but it landed about two feet behind me. It hit another guy real bad and blew me down into a path that ran in front of this knoll. Then another one came in. I saw this one. It hit our C.O. (commanding officer) in the back and rolled without exploding—down onto the path were I was lying."[18]

The blast from the grenade knocked Bleier unconscious. When he woke up, he saw a hole two feet deep where he had been sitting. The explosion caused Bleier to go flying and he landed on Captain Murphy. It left both of them unconscious. His commanding officer woke up and pushed Bleier off of him.

"He had caught it between the legs," recalled Bleier. "He was moaning, having trouble staying conscious. I was lying on my back, looking at him. Then I looked at my own legs and saw the right one quivering uncontrollably. It scared me. I grabbed it to stop the shaking. I felt my pants. They were full of blood. The pain in my right foot pierced me. I could see places on both legs where shrapnel had shredded my fatigues."[19]

Finally, reinforcements came and some men managed to carry those injured who could not walk to a clearing where helicopters would take them to get medical attention. Those who could walk started moving that direction. Neither the commanding officer nor Bleier could walk. They started out on makeshift stretchers made out of poncho liners, but the helicopter pick up location lay roughly two miles away.

The poncho liner ripped and the soldiers tried carrying the men using various methods. Regardless of how they tried to lift the men, it did not allow much progress. After fighting all day, the exhausted men faced terrain rugged with trees, bushes and swamps. They begged Rocky to walk or allow them to drag him through the woods. Neither option seemed suitable. Suddenly another solider arrived.

"Now a guy said he'd carry me fireman style, over his shoulder," Bleier recalled. "I never knew his name, and I don't think he ever knew mine. I did not know anything but nicknames for most of the guys. The Army had a beautiful way of making names seem unimportant, and race, color, creed, and social status. We never looked for any of that in each other. The Army is a great equalizer. I was white; this guy was black. We had each traveled thousands of miles to meet in a jungle. After this night, I would never see him again. We both knew that. Yet, here he was, offering to pick me up bodily and help save my life. That's a special kind of love."[20]

When Bleier woke up in the aid station, he found an Army doctor working on his legs. The doctor carefully picked out shrapnel piece by piece when he noticed that Bleier had woken up. "Rocky Belier?" the doctor asked. "Notre Dame captain?"

Bleier nodded.

The doctor grinned as he said, "I'm from USC. I was at the game you beat us 51–0."[21] About then Rocky began to wonder if he would ever play pro football again. At first, the doctor thought he would have to amputate Bleier's foot. He managed to save the foot but thought Bleier might have a permanent limp. He thought Bleier was fortunate to have his life.

The Army sent Bleier to Tokyo for surgery on his injuries. Recovering in the hospital, he asked these doctors about football. He was told he would never play again. Doctors offered a positive view saying he would be able to walk and assume a normal life despite various leg surgeries and a lacerated kidney. The news hit Bleier hard. "Shortly thereafter, I got a postcard in the mail," Bleier recalled. "Very simple. Two lines. It said, 'Rock, the team's not doing well. We need you. Art Rooney.'"[22]

The bullet had dug a huge chuck of flesh from his left thigh and doctors removed more than 100 pieces of shrapnel from his right side, legs and foot. The doctor said he would be lucky to walk again, but Bleier discounted most of what they told him because he had a dream to play football again.

"I am a breathing example of what you can do if you want to," he said. "I just thought I could play in the NFL. There are parameters, of course, and a certain self-knowledge that's needed. I knew I would never be over 5'10" or run the 40 in 4.4. But I could be stronger than the other players, and in better shape, and I could block better and be more consistent. Goodness, they want consistency in the NFL, somebody they can depend on. I didn't know back then how important that was."[23]

Bleier admitted he had some doubts deep inside, but continued to work hard. When he first started to work out in the spring of 1970, he knew he had a long way to go. He could see that he didn't have any speed to compete with the other athletes on the field. The Steelers put him on the injured reserve list, which gave him another year to get back into football shape. The following year, they put him on the taxi squad. Then in 1972, Bleier played on special teams.

Bleier's dedication and determination in attempting a comeback that seemed impossible impressed his teammates. Joe Greene, All-Pro defensive tackle, said he always saw him in the weight room working out. Greene thought to himself that Bleier would never get back to condition where he could make the team, but the running back continued to work hard. When he changed his clothes, teammates could see purple on his chest, his hips and his thighs from bruises. Greene thought that if Bleier could work that hard hurting as much as he had to be hurting, the rest of the team did not have any excuse.

By 1974, Bleier had cracked the starting lineup as a powerful blocking back. He teamed with Franco Harris to provide a strong ground game for the Steelers. Bleier conquered the odds again by making the Pittsburgh Steelers football squad. He played in four Super Bowls, catching a touchdown pass from Terry Bradshaw that gave the Steelers the halftime lead in Super Bowl XIII. The quarterback on the opposing sideline of that big game also served in Vietnam. Roger Staubach returned to the team in 1969 and won the starting job in 1971.

Sports Illustrated announced Staubach's return home from war in one of those small entries that often can go unnoticed. It appeared just before the start of the 1967 season. "After a year in Vietnam as a supply officer, working 13 hours a day supervising some 200 men and the unloading of 100,000 tons of cargo a month, Lieut. (j.g.) Roger Staubach is back in the U.S. The former Navy quarterback and Heisman Trophy winner has been assigned to the Pensacola Naval Air Station in Florida, a location that he hopes will allow a little more spare-time football."[24]

Staubach did not serve as an infantryman like Bleier, but he has some memories of the bad side of the war years, too. Some of his classmates from the Naval Academy served as marines in Vietnam. "In fact, when I was in Da Nang, I got a radio call from my teammate, Tommy Holton. He wanted to come and visit with me and gave me a hard time, saying 'I am sure you are having a good time there in Da Nang, but I want to see you when I get in,'" recalled Staubach years later. "Then he was shot and killed. So those kinds of episodes were there around me, and we had some classmates that were lost over there."[25]

Staubach had burst on the national scene with the 1962 Army–Navy game. President John F. Kennedy, a former naval officer, attended the game and performed the coin toss. Navy upset Army, 34–14, as Staubach threw for two touchdowns and ran for two more. Although just his sophomore season, it turned America's attention to the Navy signal-caller for the junior season.

That season, 1963, became memorable for other reasons. President Kennedy planned to return to watch the Army–Navy game in person, but was murdered in Dallas just a week before the game. Fans feared the classic game between the service academies would end up canceled out of respect for the president. Instead, officials delayed it until after the funeral. After the tragic events of November 1963, the Kennedy family insisted that the game must go on. Brother Jack (as the family called JFK) so loved the game that he would not have wanted it cancelled, they said.

"I remember the 1963 game being on in the background and that it was more subdued than usual," said Ted Kennedy, brother of the late president. "I believe there was a tribute to the president, but it was a difficult time, and we really couldn't give the game our full attention. Navy won that year. My brother would have liked that."[26]

As commander-in-chief, the president is assumed neutral in games between the academies. Just as former president and West Point graduate Dwight D. Eisenhower pulled for Army, President Kennedy pulled for Navy. He planned to attend the 1963 contest in person, just as he had done the previous season. The plan called for him to sit on the Army side during the first half and the Navy side the second half. "He liked football, but he loved the Army–Navy game," Staubach said. "He was, I would say, a little partial to Navy because he was a Navy guy. He still was commander-in-chief of both sides. He was all set to come to the game. It's a shame, the whole thing."[27]

That 1963 Army–Navy game ended up a much closer battle than some anticipated. Going into the game, Navy had an 8–1 record, while Army was 7–2. Navy lost to SMU in Dallas while Army fell at Minnesota and Pittsburgh. With only about 10 minutes remaining Navy had a 21–7 lead. Army, however, had its own star at quarterback—Rollie Stichweh. Just as Staubach was a dual threat, Stichweh could run and throw, too. Stichweh took the Cadets on a drive for a touchdown and two-point conversion. He even scored the conversion. Then, in more of a fairy tale story, Army recovered the onside kick to keep possession of the ball.

Army had the ball and all the momentum with six minutes on the clock. Another source of worry for the Navy fans among the 100,000 watching the game, Army had the ball on Navy's 49-yard line. Navy had not lost to Army since 1958, had a Heisman Trophy winning quarterback but Army had everything else lined up for them. Forty-nine yards to go with six minutes and 13 seconds left. "We're not going to get the ball back," Staubach worriedly said on the Navy sideline to head coach Wayne Hardin.

Army continued to move the ball on a slow methodical process. It appeared that Staubach's fear would come true leaving the Navy offense stranded without a paddle. Army moved at a snail's pace. As the clock wound down to its final seconds, Staubach stood helpless on the sideline. Watching the Army offense slowly march down the field gave him a hopeless feeling. There was not much he could do to help his team. His Catholic upbringing kicked in and he started to pray. After the game, he said he must have said a hundred Hail Marys.

On third down from the 4 yard line, Navy's defense stopped Army's Ken Waldrop short of the goal line. It seemed to take a long time to unpeel the players and spot the ball again. The seconds continued to click off the clock. Time expired with Army only a couple yards away from the goal. Navy had won the game, climbed to No. 2 in the national polls and would face No. 1 Texas in the Cotton Bowl.

Navy lost its second game of the season—both of them in Dallas, Texas. The Longhorns won the Cotton Bowl, 28–6. Ironically, Staubach later played for the professional team located in Dallas, the site of his only two losses in his Heisman Trophy–winning season. That game marked the last time an academy football team challenged for the national championship.

Roger Staubach played college football at the Naval Academy in Annapolis, Maryland. The winner of the 1963 Heisman Trophy served a tour of duty in Vietnam and joined the Dallas Cowboys in 1969 (Special Collections & Archives Department, Nimitz Library, U.S. Naval Academy).

The Dallas Cowboys selected Staubach as a tenth-round pick in the 1964 draft. They claimed him as a future selection because he had one more year remaining at the Naval Academy. After that last year of eligibility came his military commitment. He did not join the Cowboys until 1969.

Staubach took his military leave during the summer so he could attend Cowboys training camps in 1967 and 1968. He impressed the coaches during those workouts with his athletic ability and his arm. Coach Tom Landry allowed an exception to one of the team's rules and let Staubach take a Cowboys playbook home with him so he could study when he returned to active duty. The team sent him some footballs in Vietnam so he could keep his arm in shape. He still had a huge uphill climb. Landry did not want to play a quarterback in a game until he had two or three years of NFL experience as a backup. If that rule held for Staubach, he might turn 30 before he cracked the lineup.

In Staubach's view, his military and life experiences gave him an edge in dealing with people from various backgrounds. During his service time, he needed to deal with sailors who hailed from all over the country as well as South Vietnamese citizens.

"Roger went out of his way to relate to the black players, and sometimes it was comical," said Bob Hayes. "Once, we were playing cards in training camp, and Roger walked into Jethro Pugh's room when we were listening to a Temptations record. Roger said, 'Oh, yeah, man, the Four Tops sure are good.' He wanted us to know that he was hip. I said, 'Roger, that's not the Four Tops; that's the Temptations.' 'Oh, sure, Bob,' he answered, 'it does sound like the Temps.' Like I said, it was funny, but it also made us black players feel good because (at least) Roger was trying.'"[28]

The Naval Academy proved a good fit for Staubach. An excellent athlete, Staubach earned seven letters in football, baseball and basketball. He really excelled on the gridiron winning the Heisman Trophy his junior season. As a pro prospect, he seemed like a good fit there too. At 6-foot-3 and 200 pounds with a quick release from the pocket and the ability to run, Staubach appeared the ideal candidate for pro football. The only issue coming out of school involved his five-year service obligation.

Color blindness made it impossible for Staubach to serve as a naval line or flight officer after receiving his commission. He had hoped to get into naval aviation or into the Corps. Instead, he went into the Navy as a supply officer and ended up in Chu Lai, Vietnam. His 12-month tour ended just before the Tet Offensive of early 1968.

When his military obligation ended, he wanted to try pro football. Staubach worked hard to stay in shape during his service years so that when his commitment ended in July 1969, he was ready to return to the Cowboys. It was not until midway through the 1971 season that Staubach got a chance to start. That year, he led the Cowboys to a 24–3 victory in Super Bowl VI against Miami. Staubach's tour of Vietnam ended, but the war between the two leagues raged on.

Chapter Eleven

Cease Fire!

American involvement in the Vietnam War continued to increase throughout the sixties until it served as a major issue during the 1968 presidential election. Americans were growing weary of the war. When Richard Nixon took office in 1969, he pledged that he would continue the American effort in Southeast Asia in order to end the conflict and secure peace with honor. The North Vietnamese, however, did not agree to attend peace negotiations until years later. Both sides agreed to the peace plan in 1973. By then, an estimated 2.5 million Americans had served in the war that spanned more than ten years.

Peace came around quicker for the two football leagues. On June 8, 1966, at a press conference at the Warwick Hotel in New York City, another group of combatants announced a cease-fire. Their war had raged on for six long years with plenty of casualties. Some early combatants departed as others joined the fray as the fracas heated up in recent years. Many looked for the hostilities to end and a cease-fire called. Pete Rozelle, Lamar Hunt and Tex Schramm joined to tell the world that the two leagues had called off the fight and agreed to a merger. The agreement had seven major points:

- Pete Rozelle continues as the commissioner.
- The leagues would play a championship game.
- All existing franchises would remain in their present sites.
- Teams would participate in a common draft.
- Two franchises would join by 1968 with the franchise fees going to the NFL.
- AFL clubs would pay the NFL an $18 million indemnity over the next 20 years.
- Inter-league pre-season games would start in 1967 and a single league schedule would begin in 1970.

Reading the list, it may sound like the NFL won. The leaders of the AFL insisted they reached their main goal. They wanted to establish parity with the senior league and they wanted the opportunity to prove it on the field. They said that stood as their main goal all along. As the sixties went on, the quality of the play in the junior league improved and the AFL could not wait for the opportunity to prove it on the field. Soon they would get what they had hoped for—the chance to play against the NFL clubs.

"The two big things we wanted we got—the championship game and pre-season games," Lamar Hunt said.[1] Hunt spoke for all the super competitive men who owned AFL franchises when he said he looked forward to the competition on the field. AFL leaders had asked for a game between the two leagues for years. Joe Foss, the AFL's first commissioner, wasn't shy about challenging the senior league to a duel. As early as 1961, he sent a telegram to Pete Rozelle in hopes of arranging a championship game. The telegram described it as a formal invitation to the NFL to participate in a true world championship football game between the winners of this country's two major professional football leagues. He continued such challenges throughout the sixties.

The 1963 San Diego Chargers featured two Hall of Famers, Lance Allworth and Ron Mix. Quarterback Tobin Rote led the offense driven by backs Keith Lincoln and Paul Lowe. They had a solid defense with two AFL All-Stars, defensive linemen Earl Faison and 6-foot-9 Ernie Ladd. The Bears had a very talented team with many future Hall of Famers: Bill George, Stan Jones, Doug Atkins and Mike Ditka. Both teams had top-notch coaching staffs led by George Halas and Sid Gillman. The trash talking between the two leagues continued. The National League did not intend to accept any of those challenges. Their strategy led them to ignore the other league much like you would ignore a buzzing bee circling around your sweet tea at a summer picnic. To agree to a game would have to give the junior circuit some credibility and they did not want any part of that. It might resemble taking a swat at that annoying bee. You might get stung.

Even the networks got involved. Five months after Foss sent Rozelle the challenge letter came word that NBC offered to donate $500,000 to the Kennedy Memorial Library fund if the two champions would meet on the field in what they called the World Series of Football. NBC made the offer shortly after President Kennedy's assassination when collection efforts aimed at creating a library in the slain president's honor. The assassination still hurt and the appeal attracted attention as the library solicited funds. The NFL declined the offer.

The AFL leadership had requested a game almost as soon as the league began. Football fans just wanted to see how the local team matched up against the NFL teams with national reputations. In short, they wanted the top teams in each league to face off and settle the question on the field. Fans, media, players and coaches all had opinions and debated about which league played the best football. The commissioner of the AFL joined the debate in 1963 in the pages of *Sports Illustrated*. "Much talking has been done of late by the public and the press as to when the American and National Football Leagues will meet in a championship game," wrote Joe Foss in 1963. "I feel strongly that the time has arrived for the inauguration of such an annual game."[2]

Foss suggested that the two teams meet after the 1964 season. *Sports Illustrated* had fun with the challenge. The magazine had two of its writers take sides in point/counterpoint style. Tex Maule, who had worked in the Los Angeles Rams front office before his starting his journalism career with the magazine said the NFL representative would win by "40 to 50 points." AFL commissioner Joe Foss was a guest contributor who argued the AFL point of view.

Had the game happened in 1964, the Buffalo Bills would have faced off against the Cleveland Browns, champions of the old AAFC four consecutive seasons. Some NFL old-timers still considered them a sports carpetbagger team since they originated in the All-American Football Conference. The Bills looked like a NFL team with a tough defense and a ball control offense led by a talented fullback named Cookie Gilchrist and a future politician named Jack Kemp at quarterback. Buffalo Bills guard and co-captain Billy Shaw said he would have welcomed the game. The Bills shut out the high-powered San Diego Chargers, 23–0, in the 1965 championship game and currently ran on all cylinders.

The Bills did not allow the Chargers past the Buffalo 24 yard line all day as they clinched their second consecutive AFL championship. "That was the team that could have really played with the NFL champions," said Shaw. "We matched up really good with them. I'd have loved to have that opportunity."[3]

It took several more years before the winners of each league played one another. The first two clashes between the leagues, initially called world championships, comprised the first two Super Bowls won by the Packers. Vince Lombardi had his team ready to play and, after conclusion of those games, it appeared the NFL had the superior league. The Packers beat the Chiefs, 35–10, in the first game and the Raiders, 33–14, in the second. The AFL, however, won the next two games to even the score with victories by the Jets and Chiefs. By the time of the merger's completion, the leagues sat tied with two Super Bowl victories each.

As the sixties went on, the level of play in the AFL improved. Initially, as a start-up operation they needed to recruit talent. Each year they held their own in the signing wars with the NFL for top caliber talent coming out of college. Subsequently, the AFL molded that talent into good teams. That talent did not come cheap. The increasing cost of talent acquisition due to the competition between the two leagues formed one of the main reasons the merger came about. With teams competing, the price of talent got too steep.

The stress was particularly heated in cities that competed for attention. In New York, the Giants and the Jets competed for every ticket purchased in the city. The Giants consistently made the playoffs as the sixties began. As the decade aged, the Jets improved and the Giants declined. Still competition remained tough and the new league made slow progress. Even the best AFL franchises had trouble. Despite winning the AFL championship in 1962 with a thrilling overtime victory, Texans owner Lamar Hunt packed up and left Texas for the greener pastures of Kansas City.

The New York franchise did not have that luxury. Many believed the AFL would not survive without a New York franchise. Throughout the 1962 season, the New York franchise struggled financially. Alex Kroll, a center and tackle on the 1962 Titans team who later worked as an advertising executive, said, "The Titans of 1962 stand unchallenged as the worst-managed, most-unprofessional professional team of the modern era."[4] Kroll lists numerous reasons why the Titans deserved the worst managed team title. They relate mainly to lack of money and organization. In one cost-cutting move, Harry Wismer ordered general manager George Sauer Sr. to take on the additional duty of backfield coach. That made Sauer head coach Bulldog Turner's boss and employee at the same time.

Wismer gained fame for his poor treatment of his coaches. When he soured of his first head coach, Sammy Baugh, Wismer wanted to get rid of him. Instead of firing him and paying him the final year of his contract, Wismer took the extreme step of moving the training camp location hoping that Baugh would not find it and show up. He did show up and the Titans had two head coaches in camp. Wismer put Baugh in charge of the kickers and punters. The team lost money through the first few years but in 1962 the money started to dry up. Paychecks arrived late. When the checks stopped coming at all, the league took over the team. Other league teams were not rolling in money but, at least, their paychecks did not bounce.

"Before a game in Buffalo, we told Wismer we wouldn't practice unless we got paid," said linebacker Larry Grantham. "He told us we could practice on our own, but if we did, the coaches wouldn't coach. I coached the defense, and guard Bob Mischak coached the offense. We went up to Buffalo on our own, so did the coaches, and we won. The next week, Lamar Hunt showed up, sat at a table in our locker room, asked each guy how much his paycheck was and wrote a personal check for the amount. That's how much he knew the AFL needed a New York team."[5]

AFL commissioner Joe Foss told the media the league did make some progress by 1962. In that summer's College All-Star Game, the AFL had six offensive starters and six defensive starters, one more than the NFL had. In all, however, the AFL had 23 College All-Stars while 29 went with the NFL. The AFL had eight clubs while the NFL had fourteen.

The New York Titans played their last game of the 1962 season at the Polo Grounds in front of only 2,000 fans. They lost, 44–10, to the Houston Oilers and appeared to have reached rock bottom. The league paid Titans players and coaches their last paychecks, as they had since early November. Fan interest dwindled to the point owner Harry Wismer refused to invest any more capital in the team. The league reportedly spent $255,420 to the Titans to keep them running over the second half of the season.[6]

Like the hero on a white horse in a corny Western, a hero came riding to the AFL's rescue. A group led by Sonny Werblin bought the New York franchise from the league for $1 million. They announced that the name would change from Titans to Jets and that the colors from navy blue and gold to green and white. They found their coach in the championship-winning former leader of the Baltimore Colts, Weeb Ewbank. Shortly after Werblin's group took over the club, they announced they had hired Ewbank as head coach and general manager.

The man who had brought two championships to Baltimore came to Gotham with the task of reviving the struggling New York franchise. He felt up to the task. Just as he did in Baltimore, Ewbank's first task centered on finding good players to improve the talent level. Improving the talent level would pay dividends and improve the team's success.

Clearly, the New York Titans had started as one of the weakest franchises in the new league. The situation forced them to play home games in the old Polo Grounds, vacant since the baseball Giants migrated to San Francisco in 1958. They finished with seven wins and seven losses in each of their first two seasons, but dropped to only five wins in the third. Each season, attendance consistently dropped. The franchise seemed headed backward. The players questioned how long it could go on, as things grew steadily worse.

"What was it like playing for the Titans?" asked Larry Grantham decades later. "Well, we dressed in a rat-infested locker room at the old Polo Grounds, and when Wismer announced there were 30,000 people at the games, maybe there were 10,000 people, if that many."[7]

In the early sixties, television started to pay attention to football and the money got bigger and bigger. The AFL got a nice television contract without even having played a game. The 1958 overtime championship went a long way toward starting the attraction. Then, Lombardi took over the Packers and turned Green Bay into the NFL version of David who regularly beat Goliath. Fans loved rooting for the underdog and loved it even more when the underdog stood up to the bully and beat him using a power running game. Some insist that professional sports leagues gain popularity when they have a dynastic team. The league attracts new attention as some watch to see that great team play. A loyal following develops as some fans root for that team while others root against them. The National Football League began reaching maximum popularity by 1963.

In 1963, the NFL received just over $4.6 million from CBS. That represented a huge deal, but with each new deal the numbers kept going up. With increased popularity, owners figured the networks would pay more. Rozelle set his sights on doubling the television revenue to about $10 million per season. He opened the broadcast contract for bids and all three major television networks responded with offers. He opened NBC's bid first and it exceeded the $10 million for which he had hoped. The other offers proved even bigger. ABC offered almost $13 million while the winning bid came from CBS with a $14.1 million per year offer. That meant each team would get about $1 million per year in television rights money. That more than doubled the $360,000 they received the year before.

Some thought the NFL's contract would doom the American Football League. How could they compete financially with big brother with such a lopsided television deal? The AFL needed a big deal to keep pace and had the good fortune that sports programming battle was heating up. NBC still smarting over the lost NFL bid to CBS and still looked for replacement games. They came in aggressively and offered a five-year deal worth $36 million for the regular season and an additional $6.7 million for the championship and all-star games. That meant $900,000 per AFL team, or only 10 percent less than the NFL's huge deal. The AFL kept pace.

The introduction of a new league drove up bargaining power for the players. The AFL struck quickly, signing some talented college players to contracts at elevated salaries. For example, Heisman Trophy winner Billy Cannon from Louisiana State signed a deal with the new league that reportedly would earn him $100,000 over three years, an automobile, and a chain of gas stations.

Cannon originally signed a contract with the Los Angeles Rams before the end of his college career. The Rams asked him to leave the date off the contract so as not to lose his collegiate eligibility. When the Oilers came around with a much better offer, Cannon returned the uncashed bonus check and the contract to the Rams. He signed a new deal with the Oilers immediately after the conclusion of the Sugar Bowl. The Rams sued Cannon in hopes of keeping him from playing with the Oilers. In June 1960, the court awarded Cannon to the Oilers.

Several other big-name college stars also signed with the new league that first season. Cannon's teammate Johnny Robinson signed with the Dallas Texans. Ole Miss standout Charlie Flowers, who originally agreed to play for the New York Giants, took a better offer from the Los Angeles Chargers. Texas Christian lineman Don Floyd went with the Oilers rather than the Baltimore Colts.

The fighting over talent introduced new strategies in the world of sports. In 1964, the NFL created a strategy called Operation Hand-Holding, which involved a conscious effort by the senior league to convince college players not to sign with the junior league. Some called it baby-sitting. The idea, conceived by Los Angeles Rams owner Dan Reeves, consisted of a team of people armed with marketing materials touting the benefits of the NFL. The plan called for this team of sales representatives to establish relationships with college prospects before the draft and then keep them away from AFL officials until they signed a contract with the NFL.

When Pete Rozelle heard of Dan Reeves's plan, he took it leaguewide. He brought Bert Rose, former general manager of the Minnesota Vikings, to New York to run the marketing team. Rozelle put the strength of the league and its many alliances behind the plan. Some of the so-called babysitters came from the advertising firms that populated Manhattan close to NFL headquarters. Scouts from teams and other league officials joined the group. Salesmanship stood as the one main prerequisite to join the squad. They received a gold card that enabled them to hop aboard any United Airlines flight at any time. This, in turn, enabled them to move recruits from city to city to keep them away from the AFL scouts trying to sign the players.

Gil Brandt, who ran the scouting operation for the Cowboys, said each team submitted a list of about 50 players it wanted covered. The squad collected the lists and then assigned the players to the babysitters. Like a shell game on the boardwalk, the babysitters tried to keep the players away from the other competition until they signed a contract. The representatives needed to use their sales approach to win them over for their league.

The NFL developed and ran Operation Hand-Holding for three years prior to the merger. After the NFL rolled it out, their performance in signing those players drafted by both leagues improved. Of the 111 players selected in both 1965 drafts, 79 signed with the NFL, 28 signed with the AFL and four went unsigned.[8] The AFL responded to Operation Hand-Holding with an equally devious plot. The American League found out the names of the babysitters and decided to take them out of action for a time to foil their actions. They invited them all to an organizational meeting of baby sitters in the Pacific Northwest.

"We got the names and addresses of all the babysitters," Al Davis said. "We sent them all a memorandum that on the day of the draft, you are to meet in Portland, Oregon, at 5 o'clock, at a certain motel."[9]

Gil Brandt, the Dallas Cowboys' personnel chief, learned of the plan, warned others of the subterfuge, and thereby foiled the plot. Brandt said he learned of the plan from a player from Oregon, either cornerback Mel Renfro or linebacker Dave Wilcox. He could not remember which one told him. Both players signed with NFL clubs—Renfro with the Cowboys and Wilcox with the 49ers—and eventually made it to the Pro Football Hall of Fame. The AFL wanted to take the babysitters out of action to regain equal footing.

The most famous babysitter case involved Chiefs wide receiver Otis Taylor. Both leagues considered the fast receiver from Prairie View A&M a coveted prize. The tall, fast receiver looked like a solid prospect for pro football. The National Football League sent a stockbroker named Wallace Reed to the campus to pick up Taylor and lineman Seth Cartwright and take them to Dallas for the Thanksgiving weekend. The draft was still days away so the plan was to keep them away from AFL scouts until they could be signed.

The Chiefs started to worry when calls to Taylor's dorm room went unanswered. The Chiefs had a scout named Lloyd Wells who had known Taylor since junior high school. Wells, one of the first full time black scouts in professional football, felt comfortable that his relationship would ensure Taylor signed with the AFL. Wells drove a big Cadillac Eldorado and responded to the nickname "The Judge." He had many connections in college football, particularly within the historically black schools.

Despite their long-standing friendship, Wells started worrying when he could not track down Taylor. He made many attempts to find Taylor, but only ran into dead ends. An extremely outgoing person by nature, Wells had many contacts in many cities. He had worked in the newspaper business previously and began to use those connections to search for Taylor. He needed every one of his contacts to locate Taylor. His search kept coming up fruitless.

"For three days Lloyd hunted for me, checking the hotel registers, talking with every Dallas contact he had," Taylor wrote in his autobiography. "But the NFL was always a step ahead, moving us every day to a different location. On the verge of giving up, The Judge finally made a few calls to Prairie View and then to my mom's house in Houston."[10]

Wells learned the name of a girl in Dallas that Taylor knew. She, in turn, told him of Taylor's location. He immediately rushed to that hotel. Once there, Wells needed to avoid all the NFL representatives surrounding the place. He found a porter who told them that Taylor resided in a room near the pool. Grabbing his camera and a media identification card from his car, Wells ran into the hotel to search for Taylor.

"I'm here from *Ebony* magazine," Wells told one of the babysitters who answered the hotel room door. "I'm here to do a story on Otis Taylor." He flashed one of his press cards and gained access to Taylor.

Once past the sitter, he had to act fast and get Taylor out of the hotel. Talking quickly and quietly, he reminded the young player of all the good times they had and how Taylor could put Wells' job in jeopardy if he did not leave with him. He appealed to Taylor's sense of friendship. He also said that if he came with him, Chiefs general manager Don Klosterman promised him a red Thunderbird. Then at the right time, Taylor and Cartwright climbed out of a window and into Wells's waiting car. As promised, Taylor found a red T-Bird waiting for him when they got to Kansas City. Taylor signed the contract and drove his new car back to Texas.

Some of the stories during these competitive years did not have the hint of espionage like the Taylor story. Some cases just became a matter of beating the other league to the punch. On at least two occasions, Al Davis waited under the goal posts immediately after a bowl game to sign a college star to a contract. The tactic of having the player sign the contract under the goal posts immediately after the bowl game created a public demonstration of getting the deal done at the earliest opportunity after the end of his college career.

In 1962, while an assistant coach with the San Diego Chargers, Davis ran onto the field and signed Arkansas star Lance Alworth after he finished playing in the Sugar Bowl. The 49ers had selected Alworth in the first round (eighth overall) while the Chargers had him as a second-round choice (ninth overall) in the AFL.

In 1965, Davis repeated that tactic when he ran onto the field after the Gator Bowl contest between Florida State and Oklahoma. He located Florida State receiver Fred Biletnikoff and got a signature on a contract. The Detroit Lions of the NFL had also drafted Biletnikoff. During these talent battles, football administrators frequently used a public signing location such as the field of their last collegiate game as a favorite ploy. If the player had signed an undated contract prior to that day, the league could go to court and say the player signed a valid contract with them the first minute of actual eligibility.

All players coming out in the sixties had a choice to make. Some received big money offers by one league or the other. Some players liked the tradition that the National Football League offered. Others saw opportunity with the new league. Some took road trips to visit with the teams and gather additional information before making a decision.

Owners viewed the ever-increasing salaries of rookies as a huge issue. The war between the two leagues had forged a pay scale in which rookies received substantially more than the proven veterans. This became most obvious in Green Bay where Paul Hornung and Jim Taylor paced the Packers' ground game on the way to numerous championships. The talent battle forced the Packers to pay a high price for the futures of Donny Anderson and Jim Grabowski. They would be making more money than Hornung and Taylor.

It caused veteran players on all teams to grumble. The grumbling grew louder and both leagues found themselves facing another foe. As owners worked to limit salaries, players started talking about union representation. The Teamsters arrived in an effort to organize the players. Veteran players listened because they wanted their pay increased to match the rookie's big deals.

When the AFL signed a five-year, $36 million contract with NBC in 1964, they had the money to fund the signing war with the NFL. The AFL's NBC contract carried about five times the value of the original contract with ABC and nearly the same amount per team as the NFL had just received with their new television deal. The AFL package gave each team roughly $900,000. The NFL's television deal provided about $1 million per team. In short, television provided the ammunition for the war.

NBC wanted to make the AFL product worthwhile so they even advanced five AFL teams $250,000 each so that they could compete for player talent.[11] That advance funded the bonuses needed to attract future stars who would improve the product on the field. The network made the investment in the hopes of increasing viewership by improving the level of play.

Once the AFL signed the big-money television deal with NBC, it had the funds it needed to fight dollar for dollar with the rival league. Joe Namath signed with the Jets for $427,000 in January 1965. Reportedly, Green Bay spent more than $1 million on two running backs. Donny Anderson of Texas Tech signed for $711,000 and Jim Grabowski of Illinois joined for $355,000. Tommy Nobis received $600,000 from the expansion Atlanta Falcons after his 1965 collegiate season ended.

Things rapidly spiraled out of control. In the spring of 1966, Rozelle authorized Tex Schramm to meet with Lamar Hunt to discuss the possibility of a merger agreement. Rozelle did not really like the merger concept; he thought some AFL teams sat on the brink of failure. He did not want to bring on board teams in poor financial health fearing it would weaken the whole league. Schramm told him the NFL had teams in similar situation after years of competing for players with ever-rising salaries.

The Namath contract in 1965 set a new record for spending. Behind the scenes, there was talk of a merger. Ralph Wilson of the Bills and Sonny Werblin of the Jets met with Carroll Rosenbloom, owner of the Colts. Sonny was against it and never came to the meeting, recalled Wilson. The Bills' owner went to Florida to meet with the Colts' owner. Some owners on both sides opposed a merger. Cooler heads felt the time had come to end the madness and work towards a merger. A merger meant a common draft and an end to the spiraling cost for unproven players coming out of college.

Those talks got things started. Wilson admitted the merger could not happen at the time but the talks served as the groundwork for the eventual deal. In retrospect, it may have sounded like a simple task to end the fighting and merge the two leagues into one. Not so, according to Ralph Wilson. He said the hostility between the leagues proved too strong initially. During later talks, NFL representatives insisted the AFL owners pay to enter the league, much like an expansion team would do.

That admission fee proved a huge downer for Wilson and the rest of the American Football League. They refused to pay as much as $50 million to join the NFL. They had other issues. The National Football League did not want to accept all the AFL teams. The NFL apparently did not want to accept any AFL clubs in regions that already had NFL franchises. NFL negotiators said the Oakland Raiders and the New York Jets could not join. They insisted those two teams would have to move to other cities or not be admitted at all.

In April 1966, Hunt received a call from Schramm asking if the two could meet secretly to discuss a merger. "We met at the statue of the Texas Ranger inside Love Field that evening and went out in his car in the parking lot," Hunt said. "It was just a feeling that there would be a little more privacy if we did that. It looked very suspicious to have two guys out in the parking lot in the dark."[12]

Hunt said he felt cautiously optimistic that talks could find success. He knew all of the previous attempts over the years had failed. His optimism took a hit due to one of the most unlikely players—a kicker. On May 17, the New York Giants signed Buffalo Bills kicker Pete Gogolak, professional football's first soccer-style kicker. He learned to kick a soccer ball as a youth before his family emigrated from Hungary to the United States. He went out for the Ogdensburg (New York) Free Academy and played tight end. When the coaches asked for volunteers to handle the kicking chores, Gogolak came forward. When he lined up to kick at a 45-degree angle, it surprised the coaches. They hadn't seen anyone kick a football that way before. "I asked the coach to let me try it my way," Gogolak recalled. "When the ball was snapped, I got off a 50-yard kick, but the ball never got higher than three feet off the ground."[13]

He continued to work on it and eventually made his way to Cornell University where he kicked successfully using the soccer style. Despite the success there, no NFL teams drafted him. The Buffalo Bills drafted him on the 12th round of their draft. In his first game with the Bills—a preseason game against the Jets in Tampa, he kicked a 57-yard field goal. The rest of the year, Gogolak hit 65.5 percent of his field-goal attempts and missed only one extra point.

The Gogolak signing created a firestorm between the two leagues. He had played out his contract with the Buffalo Bills during the 1965 season. In 1966, he waited, unsigned, for the Bills to make an offer since they retained his AFL rights. The unwritten rule up until that point prevented a team in one league from signing veteran players from the other league. The Giants challenged that unwritten policy by signing Gogolak to a NFL contract.

The militants in the AFL, led by Al Davis, prepared for retribution. Like the shot heard around the world that started the Revolutionary War, many feared that Gogolak's signing would spark increased hostilities between the leagues. Al Davis had a reputation as a man who got things done. In 1963, he took over a Raiders team that had won just 3 out of 28 games and led them to a 10-win season. When he agreed to take the job, he demanded complete control. He insisted he had neither time nor interest in teaching an owner how to run a professional football team. He was a serious man, especially about football. "Tell him a joke," said a man who used to work for him, "and you'll get a blank look. But if a general manager on another club calls him up and congratulates him on some fast deal he put over, he'll laugh like hell."[14]

All along, Davis wanted to bring the NFL to its knees. He didn't want peace. A student of military history, Davis had already started plotting his battle strategy. He wanted war and aimed at more than simply scoring a few points against the senior league. Gogolak's signing gave him the opportunity he looked for. The NFL had just broken the unwritten rule about stealing each other's players. If they could steal a kicker, he could do more. He devised a plan to raid the senior league's quarterbacks. If successful, it would lessen the quality of play in the senior circuit while improving the junior. It might just work.

Larry Felser, in his book about the merger, wrote that the AFL had a clear plan for the Davis phase. Davis took the commissioner's job with the commitment from the owners that they would build a war chest to fight a recruiting war with the NFL. Every franchise contributed money so that when the opportunity arose, Davis could serve as the AFL's wartime general in the biggest battle between the two leagues. Davis just needed a trigger or spark. Wellington Mara gave him one when he signed Gogolak to a contract. Many in the league could not understand why Mara would do that. Sure, the Giants needed a kicker. They needed a solid kicker who could add points to a suffering offense. The previous season they had hit only 4 of 25 field goal attempts.

The Giants had competed in three straight championship games during the start of the sixties but after the 1963 season, they could do no better than second place and made no playoff appearances. In 1964, they finished with only two wins. Two years later, they managed only one win and one tie. They needed to attract fans by winning some games. The fact the crosstown Jets had Joe Namath playing quarterback for them and attracting all the attention exacerbated the issue. The Giants needed to make their own splash and turn some heads their direction. They did it by hiring the first soccer-style kicker.

The move infuriated the other owners, even the owners in his league. "If you had let me know you wanted a kicker, I would have given you one!" said Carroll Rosenbloom.[15] Rozelle downplayed Mara's actions. In 1964, Gogolak had signed a one-year contract with an option with the Bills. The option had expired so he stood as a free agent, Rozelle reasoned. Ironically, Gogolak made only 58 percent of his kicks for the Giants after hitting 63 percent for the Bills.

Three days after the Gogolak signing, Davis's army made their first advance. His old team, the Raiders, signed Roman Gabriel to a $400,000 contract. Gabriel had not appeared as the top quarterback in the game, but his career appeared promising. The big, strong-armed quarterback and son of a Filipino immigrant entered the NFL as the first Asian American quarterback to start an NFL game. The signing hurt in another way. Gabriel had played for the Rams, the first NFL team on the West Coast. Pete Rozelle rose to the rank of general manager with the Rams.

Shortly after that deal, rumors began to circulate that the Oilers had made 49ers quarterback John Brodie an even bigger offer. Reports claimed Brodie agreed to a $750,000 deal with them. Brodie, another tremendous athlete, never got the notoriety playing with the 49ers that he may have otherwise. A tremendous athlete, Brodie had a second career as a Senior PGA Tour professional golfer after his football playing career ended.

The Houston Oilers also made Bears tight end Mike Ditka an offer. Ditka, another great athlete from western Pennsylvania, starred at tight end for the Bears. Aliquippa High School had won the Pennsylvania state championship in 1955 with Ditka playing both ways. Both Jim Finks at Notre Dame and Joe Paterno at Penn State tried to recruit him, but Ditka chose Pitt for its premed program because he planned to enter the dentistry career field. Can you believe Mike Ditka wanted to be a dentist? That's right, the man who rattled plenty of teeth on the football field intended to fix them instead. Of course, all that happened before he found pro football.

In three quick moves, Al Davis had hit three teams in some of the top media markets in the National Football League. The deals took two experienced and capable quarterbacks away from the two teams on the West Coast along with a popular and rising star at tight end from the Midwest. The moves stood as a big part of an organized effort by Davis to recruit players from the rival league. He wasn't done.

"Using a league wide war chest, Davis set about raiding the NFL's prize quarterbacks, signing them to record-setting contracts and bonuses to induce them to jump leagues," wrote David Harris in his book *The League*, outlining the strategy. "By June, Davis had seven of the NFL's fourteen best quarterbacks prepared to switch."[16]

"It has been said that the offer made to me forced the merger," said Brodie. "This isn't really true. It was typical of what was forcing the leagues together. But mainly it was a matter of lucky timing. Lucky for me. While I was down there in the Warwick Hotel [in Houston], all the merger talks were coming to a head; other men in other cities were talking just as fast, trying to reach an agreement before the talent war got entirely out of control."[17]

All the while Davis waged war, Hunt and Schramm continued their clandestine meetings. The first meeting on April 16 they acted like characters in a spy novel. First they met under the statue at Love Field but quickly moved to cars in the parking garage to avoid observation. Soon, the location moved to their homes, a step up from the parking garage. Like earlier, the major sticking point centered on money. Instead of the $50 million indemnity first proposed, the NFL now looked for an entry fee of $18 million paid over 20 years. The NFL insisted on the fee because they said two AFL teams, New York and Oakland, had encroached on NFL territory. They hoped spreading the payments out over 20 years might make it easier for teams to accept.

The AFL insisted both teams stay in their current locations. Both the AFL Jets and the NFL Giants called New York home, while the Oakland Raiders and San Francisco 49ers sat right across the bay from each other in Northern California. Leaders of these teams generally opposed the merger. They had fought for fans day after day all decade long and passionately argued against a merger. Other owners did not share that passion.

"They don't know how to fight," Davis said of the other AFL owners. "We could have won this thing. We could have wrapped up the whole NFL."[18]

By Memorial Day, the two groups neared an agreement. The NFL offered a plan AFL owners could agree to with some modifications. Lamar Hunt liked what he worked out with Tex Schramm. Next, he solicited the opinion of some of the other owners. First, he met with Bills owner Ralph Wilson and Patriots owner Billy Sullivan. Together they compiled a list of questions and items to clarify.

"He [Hunt] gave me a list of 26 points of differences or additions. Some were minor, some were not," said Tex Schramm. After the meeting with Rozelle over the 26 points, "about a third of Lamar's points were acceptable, another third were not and that left a third to be worked out. Many of the differences involved simple problems of wording. Even now, there is no formal written agreement between the two leagues."[19]

The end agreement created a merger Rozelle did not really want, but accepted anyway. In that way, he and Al Davis might not have seen things too differently. Both of these super competitive men wanted to win. In this case, winning meant beating the other league. Rozelle relented his opposition and finally accepted. A majority of the owners wanted the expensive salary war to end and Rozelle had to listen. Their biggest desire called for a return to financial sanity.

Hunt and the other owners left Davis out of the merger discussions until after they made the decision. "He didn't learn about it until it was announced," said Tex Schramm. "Al was displeased, to put it mildly."[20] Billy Sullivan, president of the Patriots, broke the news of the merger to Davis at a dinner meeting in New York. Sullivan, part of the negotiating committee, felt happy about the upcoming merger. Al Davis was upset. "[I told him] I thought he had abandoned me and personally had sold me out and that we had the thing won and I thought they gave it away," Davis later testified about their meeting.[21]

After only about 90 days as commissioner, Davis returned to the Raiders with an opportunity of running the franchise and getting an ownership piece. He remained furious about the secret negotiations, about quitting the fight and losing the combined commissioner job to Pete Rozelle. That grudge lasted the rest of his life which he spent determined to make life miserable for Pete Rozelle.

Even after the two parties agreed to the merger, it nearly did not happen. Rozelle was well aware Congress would scrutinize any agreement making one league out of two. He was worried Congress would view professional football as a monopoly if the two leagues merged. Rozelle went to work to convince elected representatives otherwise. He managed to get the new combined league exempted from antitrust laws. Senate Whip Russell Long and House Whip Hale Boggs jointly worked the legislation. Both Long and Boggs hailed from Louisiana and wanted to see professional football move to their state. Once Rozelle promised that New Orleans would get an expansion franchise, the legislation approving the merger moved through Congress. Soon after exemption was approved, the owners granted New Orleans an NFL expansion franchise.

Exhibition games in 1967 gave the rival leagues their first chance to face off on the field. The Denver Broncos, not really known as a powerhouse in the American Football League, scheduled games against the Detroit Lions and the Minnesota Vikings. The Broncos had only won four games the previous season. They had not won more games than they lost in any season of play to that point in their history. In fact, of the original eight AFL teams, only the Broncos failed to make it to the championship game at least once. They did not come close.

Lions defensive tackle Alex Karras knew their history and did not like the rivals from the AFL. He made his feeling known publicly. He probably thought on their worst day his team could not lose to Denver. First, that squad played in the American Football League, which he believed had a lower level of competition. Second, the Broncos, one of the worst AFL teams, came off a 4–10 season in 1966. "If we lose to the Broncos, I'll walk all the way home from Denver to Detroit," he snapped.[22] The Lions lost, 13–7. He may have suffered in misery, but he boarded the airplane and flew back to Detroit with the rest of the team.

The Chiefs, having lost the first Super Bowl for the AFL, really wanted to show the senior league they could compete. After Super Bowl I, media members took plenty of shots at the team from Kansas City. *Sports Illustrated* reporter Edward Shrake put it this way: "After watching its best team suffer through that football game that might someday deserve to be called the Super Bowl, the American Football League should at least benefit from a hard but presumably valuable lesson: the AFL is as far behind the NFL as the Chiefs were behind the Packers."[23]

The Chiefs had spent the summer listening and reading about the vast superiority of the NFL and wanted to show people they could play ball, too. They did more than that with a lopsided 66–24 victory over the Chicago Bears. "Every time we turned around we'd score a touchdown," recalled linebacker Bobby Bell years later. "Our mascot was War Paint, a horse. Bob Johnson was riding him. [The horse would circle the stadium at a gallop after every Chiefs score.] Dick Butkus told Gale Sayers, 'hey, we better hurry up and get this game over with because they are going to kill that horse.'"[24]

During that summer of 1967, the exhibition season saw 16 contests between the AFL and the NFL. Preseason games in those days counted for more than they do today. Regulars played more frequently in these games during the sixties than they do today. After those 16 contests, the NFL soundly won the series by a 13–3 count.[25] The series began to tighten up in 1968 and 1969. The AFL actually won the series in 1968, 13–10. The NFL won the series in 1969 with a record of 19–13–1. It might be debatable how much credibility to give to exhibition game results between the two leagues, but in the earliest years, such games provided the only measure available to compare the talent levels of the two leagues. It appeared, however, that the AFL had started closing the gap between the two leagues as the decade of the sixties ended.

Once the hostilities died down, talk of how to coexist in peace warmed. When the two leagues merged, the American Football League name would go away. The National Football League name continued as the larger, combined league. The needed to settle any organization questions prior to the finalization of the merger in 1970. One proposal called for the old AFL teams to live in one conference with the old NFL clubs in another. Initially, Rozelle said he favored that plan.

Rozelle's way, however, created an unequal number of teams in the two conferences. After expansion, 10 teams came from the AFL to join the 16 in old NFL. At the 1969 annual meeting, Rozelle supported a proposal to leave things pretty much status quo. In other words, he supported a league structure where the National teams stayed in one conference and the American in another.

The alternative called for some National teams to join the former American League teams in a conference. Most teams opposed that proposal right off the bat. For example, the Giants, still stinging from battles with the Jets, could not bring themselves to entertain joining up with their hated foes. The merger forced them into the same league, but they refused to play in the same conference.

The second proposal was unattractive because it contained the possibility that the Super Bowl could be played without a representative of the old American Football League. After two Packers victories, talk spread about changing the configuration to make sure the two best teams competed in the big game. Many thought of the Packers last-second victories over the Cowboys as better football than either of the first two one-sided Super Bowls. Meanwhile, Rozelle continued to work on the team alignment for the new league. He visited with owners from the old NFL hoping to convince them to join the upstarts in the American Conference.

Art Modell of Cleveland sat up in his hospital bed. He had a proposal. He would accept the offer of joining the American Conference if Art Rooney would go, too. Modell wanted to keep the home-and-away series with the neighboring Pittsburgh Steelers. He would go with that commitment. That is all it took. Baltimore, Cleveland and Pittsburgh volunteered to move their NFL teams and join the former AFL clubs in the American Football Conference. The remaining NFL teams formed the National Football Conference.

"Carroll Rosenbloom said he'd move his Colts for the money," recalled longtime football reporter Jerry Izenberg. "Art Rooney's Steelers had no money and no clout and had to go. On a long-forgotten morning during those meeting, Art Modell was rushed to the hospital with a bleeding ulcer. That afternoon Rooney and his son, Dan, and Wellington Mara went up to see him. For years, Rooney had counted on his two games with the Browns who were based just up the highway. They were guaranteed sellouts."[26]

The blending of the two leagues brought together the best of both leagues. The National League had proud traditions with stable franchises with long, storied histories. The American League brought new excitement and some refreshing innovations that made the game more entertaining for fans. Some innovations simply aimed to correct some items that fans disagreed with in National League games.

Among the AFL contributions were official time kept on the scoreboard, players' names on the backs of jerseys, the two-point conversion, the vertical passing game, revenue sharing and the integration of African American athletes.

Quarterbacks in the AFL grew more accustomed to playing against the attacking style of defenses that the Raiders and others in the league employed. Joe Namath viewed the Colts' strong-side rotation zone an inviting target. One year later, Len Dawson had great success throwing short patterns against Minnesota's conservative, layback defense. Many NFL teams preferred the zone defense. As the leagues played more games against one another, the styles began to intermix.

The AFL brought professional football to many cities that did not have home action previously. Denver, Houston, Buffalo and Boston got teams as the league added teams to parts of the country starved for football. These cities may not have gotten a team if professional football continued to exist in only one league. Once the merger finally took place, the teams got the opportunity to settle that best on the field argument.

Chapter Twelve

Settle It on the Field

The details of the merger seemed to drag on for a long time. Representatives of the two leagues needed to work out a great number of items before a merger could happen. Then Congress had to approve the merger. Once those lights turned green, the two leagues raced off to play a championship game. They pushed aside the political battles, overcame the time consuming and tricky negotiations and settled down to play the game. Only 223 days came between the merger announcement and the first Super Bowl game.

Many owners wanted to play a final game between the two league champions, especially those in the AFL who wanted to prove they could play the equal caliber to the NFL. They had nothing to lose in challenging the senior league. If they lost, they just fulfilled expectations. "The AFL had been lobbying for a championship game from the beginning since we had nothing to lose," said Kansas City Chiefs head coach Hank Stram. "The NFL had resisted the idea because they had everything to lose. But by 1966, the difference in quality and the two leagues had narrowed to the point where a playoff game became inevitable."[1]

The banter between the two leagues started from the earliest days. George Blanda, who had joined the Chicago Bears in 1949 and played there throughout the fifties, felt sure his new team, the Oilers, could compete with the best in the NFL. Blanda quarterbacked the Oilers to the first two AFL titles in 1960 and 1961. "That first year, the Houston Oilers or Los Angles Chargers could have beaten—repeat *beaten*—the NFL champion [Philadelphia Eagles] in a Super Bowl," said Blanda later. "I just regret we didn't get the chance to prove it."[2]

These discussions dominated any talk about professional football in the sixties. Fans took sides. An AFL fan would claim the Buffalo Bills could beat the Cleveland Browns or the San Diego Chargers could outscore the Chicago Bears. The arguments made for good trash talking. Finally, the champions from the two leagues would face off and settle it on the field.

When the leagues announced the merger at a press conference in New York in June 1966, Hunt sat right next to Pete Rozelle and touted the benefits of the game. "Personally, I think it will be one of the biggest sporting events of the year, every year," he said about the potential face-off. The press conference provided the first sign of any conciliation between the two adversaries.[3]

Once merger plans went public, the idea of a championship game gained momentum. In a letter to Pete Rozelle dated July 25, 1966, Lamar Hunt stressed the need to come up with a catchy name for the matchup. "If possible, I believe we should 'coin a phrase' for the Championship Game…. I have kiddingly called it the 'Super Bowl,' which obviously can be improved upon."[4]

Hunt figured the game would prove popular with the fans, the leagues still needed to win the marketing battle. He wanted something catchy. Something short and snappy, he said. He wanted the name to clearly demonstrate the game's significance and yet short enough to fit neatly in a headline. Rozelle called it "The AFL–NFL World Championship Game." That title went on the game tickets and programs for the first game; it fell well short of Hunt's short and snappy name. Hunt took to calling it the Super Bowl when talking about the game, but he said he would consider any good suggestions for something better. Before anything better came along, however, the less than universally loved name stuck.

The name had come to Hunt while he watched his daughter, Sharron, play with a toy made by the Wham-O company called the Super Ball. The ball, made from synthetic rubber, bounced extremely high. The commercial shown on television during children's programming made it sound like the highest bouncing ball ever made. This terrific ball could fly over a small building with a single bounce. Every kid wanted one. When he started calling the contest the Super Bowl, he said the name would serve the purpose until a better one came along. The official name for the game remained "The AFL–NFL World Championship Game." Other names suggested lacked any real appeal. For example, someone suggested World Series of Football, modeled after professional baseball's fall classic. The 1963 *Sports Illustrated* article proposing the challenge used that name. It really did not fit for football since the gridiron championship consisted of a single contest and not a series of games. NFL commissioner Rozelle liked the Pro Bowl name, but they already used that name for the league's annual All-Star Game.

Despite the fact the leagues could not come up with a suitable name, the networks began to refer to the day of the contest as Super Sunday and the game as Super Bowl. The networks, accustomed to calling all the postseason games in college football "bowl" games, made the leap to Super Bowl easily. The name stuck.

After settling the naming question, the league took up the issue of broadcast rights. Both leagues had contracts that gave exclusive broadcast rights to their championship game to the network televising their regular-season games. CBS held the NFL rights and NBC owned the AFL rights. Both networks insisted on the right to broadcast the new game since they had contracts with their respective leagues that included the championship game. A compromise provided both networks with rights to broadcast that first contest. Each network had its own announcing crew at the game. Ray Scott and Jack Whitaker split the play-by-play for CBS with Frank Gifford providing analysis. Curt Gowdy and Paul Christman formed the NBC team.

Each network paid $1 million for the right to broadcast the game. It seemed like they spent another $1 million promoting the contest. With two networks televising the game, it began to have a special feel. Media flocked to Southern California to cover the game. Reports promoting the game aired on CBS and NBC news and sports programs from the game site to build interest in their telecast. Gowdy and Christman made appearances on the *Today* show and the *Tonight* show.

Rozelle focused his search for potential sites of the first ever game between representative teams from rival leagues to warm weather sites in the Southern United States. He considered both the Rose Bowl and Coliseum in Southern California, as well as sites in New Orleans, Houston and Miami. On December 1, 1966, the league announced the site of the first contest. Rozelle chose the Los Angeles Memorial Coliseum for the first contest. League officials thought it best to find a neutral warm-weather site after recent championship games played out in far less-than-ideal weather conditions. The Ice Bowl played in Green Bay comes to mind. Of course, it came a year after the first Super Bowl. The NFL still considers it the coldest championship game they ever played. Many of the other title games prior to the first AFL–NFL competition also played out in adverse weather. For example, the weather the week prior to the 1960 championship between the Eagles and Packers dropped near freezing and snow ringed Franklin Field in Philadelphia. The temperature improved on game day as it climbed into the forties, but that resulted in less than ideal footing as the field thawed and turned into soft turf.

The following year, Green Bay hosted the championship game. The closer it got to game day, the lower the temperatures sank. Days before the game, local people put hay on the field in an attempt to keeping it from freezing. The temperature sat at just 20 degrees at kickoff. The conditions did not slow the home team as Paul Hornung ran for 89 yards, one touchdown and kicked three field goals while the Packers' defense intercepted Y. A. Tittle four times in a 37–0 rout over the Giants.

The 1962 title game at Yankee Stadium took place in conditions some called barbaric. Temperatures dropped into the teens and the wind gusted to 40 mph. Cameras froze and team benches blew over. "The ball was like a diving duck," said Tittle, who completed 18 of 41 passes for 197 yards. "I threw one pass and it almost came back to me."[5]

The double overtime AFL championship in 1962 played out in monsoon-like conditions in Houston. A front moved in during the game, causing temperature to plummet and winds to gust. It got so bad that Dallas Texans head coach Hank Stram instructed his captain to take the wind instead of the ball as overtime began. The game time temperature only reached nine degrees at Wrigley Field as the Bears and Giants faced off in the 1963 championship game. The bitterly cold day kept a lid on the offenses as the Bears won, 14–10.

The gametime temperature of 34 degrees felt much colder with 15- to 25-mph winds whipping under a (what else) gray December sky in Cleveland for the 1964 title game. Despite the conditions, Municipal Stadium saw a crowd of 79,544, the second largest in NFL title game history at the time. The Browns upset the Colts, 27–0.

The NFL championship returned to Green Bay's Lambeau Field after the 1965 season; the first such game played in January. Several inches of snow fell in the early morning hours, and snow and rain continued throughout the game, turning the field to mud. Year after year, the weather conditions proved less than ideal. Since the championship games always occurred in late December or early January, cold weather seemed guaranteed. Rozelle wanted a neutral site that provided the two teams an environment without weather as a factor in the game.

After the recent poor weather history, Rozelle envisioned a championship game played at a neutral site in warm weather. Having grown up in Southern California, he immediately thought of his home state. Southern California hosted the Rose Bowl game every January 1 and the weather looked very nice, especially to folks living through a snowstorm in the northeastern part of the United States. Rozelle could not book the Rose Bowl in Pasadena, but found an alternative available in Los Angeles.

Thus, the Los Angeles Memorial Coliseum came to serve as the site of the first big game between the two professional football leagues. The huge arena had a large seating capacity. Today, with the tremendous demand for tickets, the big size would provide an advantage. The large stadium gave the commissioner another major worry. He feared the stadium might look empty if the league could not sell all the tickets. Despite his concerns, the commissioner's desire to find good weather conditions and the need to move quickly made the Coliseum the choice.

Rozelle said later he never considered any other stadium for the first contest. The Coliseum sat right in the middle of Southern California with all the glamour and glitz. As a result, many Hollywood actors and stars attended the game. If the television camera panned the spectators, Americans would recognize Henry Fonda, Kirk Douglas, June Allyson, Janet Leigh, Chuck Connors, Danny Thomas, Walter Cronkite, Bob Hope and Johnny Carson. Ten astronauts also attended the game and sat in VIP seating behind the team benches; five behind the Chiefs and five behind the Packers.

Another factor besides the warm weather that made the game appealing. The green grass inside the Coliseum gave the game the appearance of midsummer. Beginning with that first Super Bowl, a groundskeeper emerged who would continue to get the playing surface ready for play for about a half century. George Toma began working on playing fields as a senior in high school. Just like a baseball player working his way from the minors to the major leagues, Toma started as head groundskeeper for the Cleveland Indians' Class-A affiliate in Wilkes-Barre, Pennsylvania, before he took a position as head groundskeeper of the Kansas City Athletics.

When the Dallas Texans relocated to Kansas City in 1963, he assumed their groundskeeper responsibilities as well. He pulled double duty keeping the field in excellent condition for professional baseball and football. Since he kept his fields constantly in fine shape, he attracted the attention of Pete Rozelle. Attending a game in Kansas City, Rozelle marveled over what he called the most beautiful field he had ever seen.

Thus when the two rival leagues agreed to a championship game, Rozelle asked Toma to make sure the playing surface was in the best condition possible. Color pictures of the first Super Bowl game proved his work. The field in the Los Angeles Coliseum held a luscious green grass in perfect shape. For that first game, Toma arrived early, brought a three-by-four equipment truck onto the field, and worked alone. In later years, his crew numbers more than 30 people with expensive equipment filling three tractor trailers.

Toma applied many tricks of the trade to make the natural grass surfaces at the big games look their best and allow the players to play their best. At the first Super Bowl, the Coliseum's Bermuda grass lay at least half dormant in the middle of January so Toma deployed some magic to make it look like it had just benefited from a good spring rain. The night before the contest, Toma sprayed the field with calcium nitrate fertilizer to wake it up from its winter slumber. Watering the food in made the grass turn a beautiful shade of green on game day.

Those early Super Bowl contests helped push professional football into the spot as the number one spectator sport. Television fueled that growth. George Toma's beautiful grass made the game that much more appealing for everyone who tuned in with a color television that day.

After Rozelle checked landscaping off his list, he turned his attention to marketing the game. They set the ticket prices at $6, $10 and $12. For 1967, those prices may have been a little high. The $12 ticket caused Rozelle to worry because at the time most major sports events charged no more than $10. He worried fans might view it as too much for a football game. In the end though, only the $12 tickets sold out. Only some of the less expensive seats remained.

The big game did not sell out. Rozelle had only selected Los Angeles as the site little more than a month before so the NFL had little time to generate local interest in the game. Professional football fans were not used to attending at a neutral site game, something college teams had done for years with bowl games. Until the first Super Bowl, previous pro football championships occurred in the hometown of one of the combatants. Unfortunately, one of every three seats in the Coliseum sat empty despite the crowd of 61,946. The cavernous facility sat nearly 100,000 for football and because of its size appeared nearly empty to the players.

Despite the short time to sell the game, the attendance disappointed Commissioner Rozelle. A regular-season game between the Rams and Packers held just one month earlier in the same site attracted 72,416 fans. A Rams–49ers regular season game in 1957 drew 102,368. A 1959 World Series game accommodated more than 92,000 fans. "The people in Los Angeles didn't attend because they didn't see it as a big game," said Steve Sabol of NFL Films. "Super Bowl I was considered a side show, an afterthought. I had ten tickets and I couldn't give them away."[6]

Some folks make a big deal about the fact the game did not sell out, but the crowd would have filled Lambeau Field. Despite the lack of a sellout, the league earned money for their first attempt at the big game. They earned $2 million from television, $710,000 from ticket sales and about $90,000 from other sources.[7]

Prior to the game, the two leagues needed to work out some details. The leagues had some variations in rules that they employed for games. For example, the AFL used the two-point conversion option after touchdowns, while the NFL only kicked the conversion for one point. The leagues used two different balls. The NFL version, made by Wilson, had a slightly bigger circumference than the AFL ball made by Spalding. The AFL people said the slimmer shape of their ball made it easier to throw.

A less obvious difference involved the keeping of time. The referee and crew on the field kept the official time in NFL games. The AFL preferred to have the official time kept on the scoreboard. They reasoned that everybody would know exactly how much time remained. NFL officials did not want something as important as time controlled by the clock operator hired by the home team.

They thought they had an alternative solution worked out in time for the first Super Bowl. An engineer designed a remote control system so that the field judge could control the stadium clock from the field through a component attached to the hands on the scoreboard clock. They tested the system in the Cotton Bowl in Dallas in a game between the Cowboys and Browns. It worked without fault. They repeated the test in the NFL Championship Game. Again, no issues.

Then, they tested the apparatus repeatedly in the Los Angeles Coliseum in the days leading up to the game. The final test was completed Saturday afternoon. Regardless where the system's creator stood on the field, the hands of the clock moved to his every command. Forward and backward, backward and forward. The leagues felt they were about to enter a new era in professional sports. Not only would they have a key game between the two rival leagues, but also the official time would show up on the scoreboard clock so fans would know how much time remained. With great pride in the technological advances that enabled them to keep official time on the scoreboard, they made a special announcement to the media. League officials were that proud.

"When the Chiefs kicked off a few hours later, the field judge pushed the button in his hand to start the clock and watched in disbelief as one of the wrought iron hands promptly fell off and plunged toward the stands below," said Don Weiss, the NFL's publicity director. "It must have fallen 50 or 60 feet. I can still see it. It looked like a giant spear. To our everlasting good fortune, no one was underneath, and no one was injured. Had there been people sitting in those stands, someone might have been killed."[8]

Later, they learned that metal fatigue caused the accident. Perhaps all the testing needed to configure the hands of the old scoreboard clock caused the metal to wear out. So, to the dismay of league officials, no time showed on the stadium scoreboard. They had hoped for some technological advances improving the fan experience but an unforeseen glitch spoiled the plans. Instead, those in the stands only knew when the referee signaled the quarter end or two-minute warning.

With all the preparation complete, the game came down to a matchup of the Green Bay Packers against the Kansas City Chiefs. It seemed only fitting that the Chiefs, founded by Lamar Hunt, made it to the first Super Bowl. Hunt founded the American Football League, propelling professional football into its golden era. The Packers, led by head coach Vince Lombardi, had turned the Green Bay franchise from doormats of the fifties to dominators of the sixties. Their back-to-back championships at the beginning of the decade gave people across the country a franchise to root for and their victories during the sixties would make the media proclaim them a dynasty.

Each league had its own reputation. The National League, going back to 1920, had history on its side and they were not afraid to remind everybody about it. They had many of the proud traditional franchises people could recall off the top of their heads. The New York Giants, Cleveland Browns and Chicago Bears all had solid histories of winning football.

The American Football League carried a young attitude. Fans quickly tagged them as the non-conformist league. Their players wore their hair long and their coaches scrapped three-yards-and-a-cloud-of-dust for a wide-open style of play involving the pass. Those things attracted Joe Namath to the league in the first place.

The National League preferred an offensive strategy based on massing power at the point of attack. Many of the successful NFL teams from the late fifties and early sixties deployed strong running attacks, often featuring a fullback. Lombardi's offense did not fool people; they overpowered them. They ran the same plays out of the same formations and dared you to try to stop them. The Browns featured the skilled running of their talented fullback Jim Brown. The Giants employed a very physical defense led by middle linebacker Sam Huff and a solid front. The Chicago Bears may not have had speed, but they earned the title of the Monsters of the Midway.

The American Football League also boasted some of the most potent offenses in the professional game. Sid Gillman created an earlier version of the West Coast offense built around offensive players such as Lance Alworth, Paul Lowe, Keith Lincoln, John Hadl, and Tobin Rote. Gillman believed in using the entire field. Hank Stram featured a modern offense with multiple formations, mobile pockets and talented athletes at the skilled positions. New York had the player who would become one of the biggest names in the game by decade end. Early on, the Houston Oilers led by veteran George Blanda won titles.

Rozelle insisted that both teams arrive early for the first contest between the two leagues. He envisioned the teams arriving at least a week early to generate interest and create a buildup to the contest. The Chiefs arrived 11 days before the game. The Packers came four days later, but only after Rozelle insisted Lombardi take his team to California. Lombardi resisted because he wanted to treat it like any other road contest and arrive the day before the game.

Earlier, football fans received a special treat with a championship game doubleheader on New Year's Day 1967. The Chiefs and Bills played at 1 p.m. Eastern with the Packers and Cowboys started at 4 p.m. Eastern in a unique view of future doubleheaders that are common today. The Chiefs defeated the two-time defending AFL champion Buffalo Bills, 31–7, on a muddy field in Buffalo to get the honor of representing the AFL. They topped the league that season with a fast, aggressive defense featuring future Hall of Fame defensive tackle Buck Buchanan and linebacker Bobby Bell. Len Dawson quarterbacked an offense that featured such weapons as flanker Otis Taylor and running back Mike Garrett, the 1965 Heisman Trophy winner.

Despite an impressive performance by the Chiefs in the AFL championship, oddsmakers picked the Packers to win the game. Those in Las Vegas setting the point spread made the Packers a 13-point favorite because they had the more experienced team, had played in more big games over recent years, and had played in the league that some perceived to have the better talent.

On the other side, some in the media said the Packers had started to show their age. They pointed to the ages of the backfield duo of Jim Taylor and Paul Hornung, both 31 years old, and end Max McGee, 34. That factor allowed AFL fans in attendance to hope the game would provide a measure of how much ground the junior league had gained on the senior circuit.

For several years, the AFL teams had collected some good young talent the NFL coveted. The Chiefs, in particular, had some talented young players, particularly among the skill positions. Wide receiver Otis Taylor played in his second year and Mike Garrett started as a rookie. Taylor, a tall, fast receiver, would prove a matchup problem for defenders. Only 5-foot-9, Garrett seemed to come up with the big play when the Chiefs needed it most.

The storyline for the media covering the game quickly developed into one of the youthful Chiefs' complex offense against the veteran but simplistic Packers attack. The boastful antics of Chiefs cornerback Fred "The Hammer" Williamson interrupted those stories. In some braggadocio that could have come from Muhammad Ali's promotion textbook, Williamson predicted the Packers receivers would go down from his "Hammer Tackle."

Officials from both the NFL and AFL would combine to form the six-man officiating crew with three from each league. Norm Schachter, considered one of the best from the National League, served as game referee. When Green Bay had the ball, they would play with the NFL's Wilson game ball, nicknamed "The Duke." When the Chiefs had possession, AFL would use the Spalding JV-5 ball.

Jim Kensil, the NFL's executive director at the time, traveled to Los Angeles to promote Super Bowl I and saw firsthand how the gathering crowd could affect the host city. He based his observations on his attendance at Sunday Mass. Kensil attended Catholic services at a small church in downtown Los Angeles one week before the game. About a dozen people attended the Mass and he noticed that the collection basket seemed nearly empty. On the morning of the game, he returned to the same place, and this time, the church and the collection basket appeared nearly full. It made Kensil think that this game could be the beginning of something big.

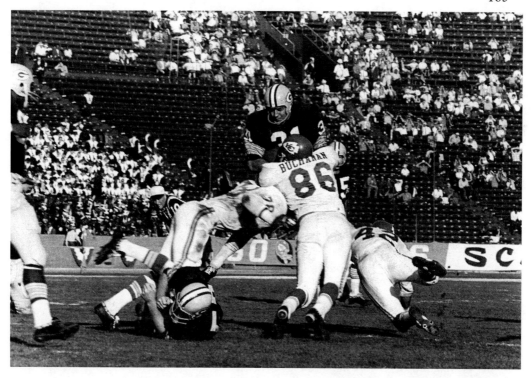

Kansas City Chiefs defensive lineman Buck Buchanan tackled Packers fullback Jim Taylor in the first Super Bowl contest. Buchanan was the first overall selection by the Chiefs in 1963 out of Grambling State University, where he played for Eddie Robinson (Photofest).

Throughout their early history, players and coaches in the American Football League had to hear constantly how their level of competition paled compared to that of the National Football League. Players from the AFL heard that from players in the NFL when they ran into each other off the field. Coaches heard the same talk. It might have discouraged those in the younger league, but hearing it repeatedly created a strong desire for an opportunity to play and prove their detractors wrong.

The game did not involve just the Packers versus the Chiefs. It pitted the NFL versus the AFL. Players and coaches across both leagues sent their best wishes, making the stress rise for both sides, particularly for Lombardi and the Packers. Some of the nervousness may have stemmed from the media attention. Since both networks covered the game, they descended upon Southern California conducting interviews promoting their broadcast that weekend.

"While we had been privileged to play in five NFL championship games over a seven-year span, we had never, ever seen as many people from the national media as were there for the first NFL–AFL Championship Game in Los Angeles on January 15, 1967," said Bart Starr. "It was a strong signal and unreal at that time. Obviously it pales in comparison with today, but in those days it was very large and very significant."[9]

Lombardi refused to let the players take the game for granted so he worked them hard in the week leading up to the game. When Lombardi got nervous, he seemed to work harder with the goal of removing the anxiety. He saw this as an opportunity for some hard work. The extra week between games allowed him to have a mini training camp of sorts.

It was not as long as the regular camp, but certainly every bit as tough. "The price of success is hard work," Lombardi said repeatedly over his career and he believed it.

"The first few practice sessions were reminiscent of training camp back in Wisconsin," recalled tackle Bob Skoronski. "Vince stressed conditioning and, truthfully, a lot of us couldn't understand why at this stage of the year.... Some of us were thinking that Vince might have been concerned about miscalculating the Chiefs. What if they were a lot better than he thought they were going to be? The answer, of course, is to resort to brute strength and power and grind them down. We had to be in shape to do it. We all figured that he was making sure that we were, just in case."[10]

Defensive end Willie Davis said it even more direct. "Coach Lombardi kicked our asses in the practices leading up to the game like he had never done before."[11] Lombardi made the workouts intense. He believed the Packers had everything to lose in that game. He had no desire to go down in history as the coach who lost to the AFL. The Packers had won three championships to that point. Now, he had weight of the entire league on his shoulders as he faced an opportunity to win another.

Hard work only covered half the equation. Lombardi knew very little of the opposition. The leagues did not play any games against teams from the other league. This left him without a measuring stick to appraise the Chiefs. His limited study of them came down to watching three games on film. He may have belittled them with some of his comments, but he wanted to make sure his team knew the importance of the game and stood prepared to win.

He prepared his troops for the biggest game of their lives. "You damn well better not let that Mickey Mouse [American Football] League beat you. It'd be a disgrace, a complete and utter disgrace," Vince Lombardi told his Packers team before the game.[12] The "Mickey Mouse" reference dated back to a comment made years earlier by George Halas of the Chicago Bears. When former Bear George Blanda said the Oilers could compete with teams in the NFL, Halas was incredulous. "The American Football League can't be anything but a Mickey Mouse League," he said.[13]

Everybody had the sense that the game pitted the haves against the have-nots. "We're the kids from across the tracks," Jerry Mays, the Chiefs' defensive captain, said. "We're coming over to play the rich kids."[14]

Lombardi heard from the leadership of the National Football League reinforcing his view that he had the weight of the league on the outcome. They encouraged him to demonstrate the superiority of the NFL to the AFL. "I would want no other general to carry the NFL flag into battle for us," wrote Wellington Mara in a letter stressing the importance of the game. Years later Lombardi said he could relate to the sentiments of NFL leadership.

As the week went on, Lombardi's stress level increased even more. One day after practice, Lombardi read a telegram to the team. It came from George Halas, founder of the Chicago Bears. Normally, Packers and Bears did not get along. Their rivalry dated back to the earliest days of the National Football League. As two of the oldest franchises, they seemed to hate one another. In this case, Halas sounded like a loyal Packers fan. He urged Lombardi's team on in the big game against the rival league. What a first—the leader of the Bears urging the Packers to victory.

On the other side of the field, Kansas City head coach Hank Stram wanted to use that Mickey Mouse comment to his advantage. He also needed to keep his team loose. "I asked our equipment manager to go to the five-and-dime store and get some Mickey

Mouse ears and the Mickey Mouse theme song," said Stram. "When the players walked into the locker room, the equipment guys were wearing the Mickey Mouse ears while the theme song played in the background. I thought what the hell; we'll have a little fun with this and maybe get them relaxed to play like we're supposed to play."[15]

Lombardi wanted to ease his team's stress level. Upon boarding the team bus last for the ride to the stadium, Lombardi could see that his team's tenseness. He looked his team as the driver started to pull away from the curb. "Just a minute," Lombardi told the driver. He stood up and got the players attention. Then he slowly broke into a muted soft-shoe dance. "Go coach, go!" some players encouraged him. Later, Lombardi explained he did what he did to loosen things up. "They were too tight," he said.[16]

As he boarded the bus to the stadium, Max McGee felt tired from his late night. Despite Coach Lombardi increasing the fine for those being caught out after curfew to $5,000, McGee stayed out the whole night. He and his roommate, Paul Hornung, had a reputation for late night adventures and a sense of humor.

"Whenever they'd get to a new city Vinnie would read off the list of bars and restaurants that were off-limits," recalled Tex Maule in *Sports Illustrated*. "Well, they'd get to Chicago on a Saturday and of course the list there was a long one. Once Lombardi read what must have been a list of 200 bars and when he got through, he was furious, just because it had taken so much time to read them. So Max McGee said, 'Jeez, coach, you don't expect me to make all of those places in one night, do you? Next year let's come down on a Friday at least.' Vinnie damn near split a gut."[17]

Hornung labeled their reputation accidental. He played college football at Notre Dame and folks recognized him when he went out to eat in a restaurant, he said. He, however, seemed to enjoy the reputation. His teammate, Max McGee, looked at the Super Bowl as a season-ending trip to Southern California. He viewed it as a paid vacation. It sounded like fun to go to the land of sun and warmth after a long, tough fall and early winter in Wisconsin.

"Max wasn't even thinking about playing," Hornung admitted. "In fact, he didn't even bring his helmet to the game. He didn't have a helmet in his travel bag. After we got back from dinner the night before, Max said, 'Come on, let's go back out.' I said, 'No, I'm staying in. You can do what you want to do.'"[18]

McGee had a plan. Assistant coach Hawg Hanner would make the rounds in the hotel checking to make sure the Packers made to bed by their curfew. Hanner, a former defensive lineman with the Packers, retired after the 1964 season and joined the coaching staff as defensive line coach. McGee knew Hanner would diligently do his bed check on schedule.

When Hanner came around, Max asked his former teammate if he planned to come back to double-check on players. Hanner admitted he would not be back and sarcastically told the two players they were too old to go out anyway.

Despite Lombardi's threats, McGee went out. By his own admission, he did not return until 7:30 Sunday morning. He assumed he would not see any action in the game. He no longer played as a starter. If Lombardi needed a substitute end, he usually called on Bob Long so McGee expected to watch and not play in the game on Sunday afternoon. The Packers deployed two receivers and two backs every snap. The teams took the field and the game began. McGee took a seat on the bench next to some of the injured Packers also not playing. He leaned back into the bench and enjoyed the sun. He even rolled his pants leg up a little to work on his tan.

On the third play of the game, Elijah Pitts, subbing for injured Paul Hornung, ran a play around left end. Boyd Dowler attempted to block Chiefs linebacker E. J. Holub when he reinjured his shoulder forcing him out of the game. He originally suffered the injury during the earlier NFL Championship Game.

"McGee! Get in there," Lombardi yelled. Surprised, tired and, maybe even hung over, McGee, deep down, hoped he would get into the game. He had watched film and liked the matchup between the Packers receivers and the Chief defensive backs. "I've been studying film and I've found me a cornerback," he confided to friends. "I'm gonna have him for breakfast, lunch and dinner."[19] McGee scrambled to locate his helmet. He could not find it and had to borrow one to take the field. He said later that he had forgotten the helmet. He grabbed one from another player and asked equipment manager "Dad" Braisher to go find his helmet.

"Here's McGee on the sidelines," said Bob Long picking up the story. "He's looking around, scurrying around, he starts yelling 'Where's my helmet, where's my helmet?' Someone shouts out, 'Max, you left it in the locker room.' Can you imagine that! He didn't have a helmet."[20]

Nobody knew why Lombardi called for McGee instead of one of the younger ends on the roster, such as Bob Long. McGee played in more games than Long had, but neither caught many passes. McGee caught only four passes during the 1966 season despite suiting up for every game. Although a former Pro Bowl player, his production had decreased of late. Prior to the 1965 season, McGee averaged 36 receptions a year. The choice of McGee over Long might have reflected the stress the coach felt carrying the whole National Football League. He may have wanted his most experienced players on the field.

In a game he did not expect to play, McGee had the game of his life. Some say he should have won the MVP award instead of Bart Starr after catching seven passes for 138 yards and two touchdowns. His best buddy on the team would have voted him the award. "Max should have been named player of the game," said Hornung. "I told Bart [who the media voted MVP] that a hundred times, and he agreed with me. That was the greatest performance by a guy who was out of shape. If Max had not been such a great athlete, he would have had done what he did."[21]

Prior to the game, each team had some films to review so they could familiarize themselves with the opposition. Even with the video, they lacked a good frame of reference since they had zero common opponents. The Packers had three game films and through their study, the Packer coaches and players believed the Chiefs cornerbacks vulnerable. They did not take long to prove out their theory. Max McGee caught the first touchdown of the game as he made an inside move on Willie Mitchell, who attempted to knock the ball down. McGee's strong performance came with most of the snaps against Mitchell.

"They pick out a weak spot and stay with it better than any team I've seen," said Mike Garrett of the Chiefs, who refused to name the teammate he had in mind. Max McGee's big game tells the story: the Packers viewed the cornerbacks as vulnerable. In addition to completing passes against the secondary, they also thought they could run left. On film, Kansas City right defensive end Chuck Hurston appeared vulnerable. Although listed as 6-foot-6 and 240 pounds, Hurston's ulcers had plagued him during the season and he had lost weight. He took the field against the Buffalo Bills in the AFL title game at only 208 pounds. Offensive captain Bob Skoronski played opposite Hurston in the game. "We have nothing to compare them with," said Lombardi. "In watching the movies of their games with other teams in the AFL, we are unable to judge what they are doing since we have never faced an AFL team. It will take us a while to become acclimated."[22]

Before the game, Kansas City cornerback Fred "The Hammer" Williamson did most of the boasting. He held a black belt in karate and boasted he would use his secret weapon during the game. He said he would wield the hammer as a hard forearm chop to the opponent's helmet. He even said he would wear white shoes during the game so people could more easily identify him.

In the fourth quarter, the Packer ran a sweep with Donny Anderson carrying the ball and guard Gale Gillingham leading interference. Williamson approached in attempt to make a low tackle. Gillingham's knee came up as Williamson closed in for the tackle, accidentally slamming into Williamson's chin. Williamson, knocked out cold, left the field on a stretcher. "I hit him with my knee," said Gillingham.

Green Bay Packers receiver Max McGee, who had not planned on playing, caught seven passes for 138 yards and two touchdowns in the first AFL–NFL World Championship Game in 1967. He had only caught four passes during the entire 1966 regular season (Photofest).

"He caught it flush on the head. It's ironic. He was supposed to be the one knocking everybody out, and he's the one who is knocked out."[23]

Noise erupted from the Packers bench when it happened. Players wondered who got hit. "They just nailed The Hammer!" someone said. While Williamson lay on the ground, Fuzzy Thurston stood nearby humming softly the tune "If I Had a Hammer."[24] After football, Fred Williamson went on to a career as a movie actor much like running back Jim Brown. He played similar roles and even appeared alongside Brown in some movies. In 1974, he took Don Meredith's place on *Monday Night Football*.

Many believe a team takes on the personality of its head coach. That certainly seemed true with the winners of the first Super Bowl game. Vince Lombardi displayed an extreme tenseness before the game. He felt the full burden of winning the game for the NFL entirely on his shoulders. His team came out equally tense, playing hard not to lose the game. Yet, some key players appeared overly nervous in the first half. Willie Wood had two opportunities to make an interception in the first half but dropped the ball both times. "We kept complaining the whole first half that the Chiefs were getting too many guys open on passes," said Dave Robinson. "They were running five-man patterns. There was nobody back there for [quarterback Len] Dawson. We didn't blitz in the first half."[25]

At halftime, Lombardi changed that. He ordered his defensive coach Phil Bengtson to get more aggressive. Early in that third quarter, Bengtson called for a "Sam Will dog," so both outside linebackers would rush the passer along with the front four. He wanted to put intense pressure on the Chiefs' quarterback.

Phil Bengtson was the first assistant Lombardi hired when he took over the head job in Green Bay. They coached against each other when both held assistant coach positions; Lombardi an offense coach with the Giants and Bengtson a defense coach with the 49ers. One particular memory stayed with Lombardi. He remembered facing off against Bengtson when the Giants played the 49ers. On December 1, 1957, Bengtson sent his trio of linebackers on blitzes all afternoon. As a result, Giants quarterback Charlie Conerly fumbled five times, losing four of them. The 49ers won the game, 27–17, and Bengtson earned a position with Lombardi.

Early in their tenure with the Packers, Lombardi and Bengtson blitzed heavily. Over time, they blitzed less since Lombardi believed teams used the blitz to cover a weakness in a team's defense. In Lombardi's mind, the blitz constituted a high-risk and low-reward strategy. It left holes in the secondary an offense could exploit. Lombardi knew that quick-release quarterbacks willing to stand in and throw against blitzes frequently beat it. Now he needed a change of pace or a surprise. Something to catch Len Dawson off guard.

At halftime, the score sat at 14–10 with the mighty Packers only slightly ahead of the Mickey Mouse Chiefs. In the press box, some members of the media wondered if the Kansas City Chiefs might turn the Super Bowl into a Super Upset. The AFL champions, just seven years into their professional existence, kept the game close. One score would give them the lead. Neither Lombardi nor his veteran players seemed happy with the halftime score or their first half performance.

"We were a little cautious in the first half," said Willie Davis after the game. "We were concerned with that rolling pocket. We were getting in and then not making tackles, and we weren't blitzing at all."[26]

With the halftime score so close, Lombardi turned up the heat with his defense in the second half. He played much more aggressively. On the first drive of the second half, the Chiefs began to move the ball and crossed the middle of the field into Packers territory. On the fourth play, Lombardi ordered both outside linebackers to blitz Dawson. They hit Dawson just as he released the ball and free safety Willie Wood stepped in front to pick it off. He returned it 50 yards to the Kansas City 5 yard line. Pitts scored on the next play to stretch the Packers' lead to 21–10.

That play stood as the turning point in the contest. The Chiefs, who fared well in the first half, lost their edge after that play.

After the game, Dawson sat at his locker talking with reporters. He said the Chiefs knew that the Packers were not a blitzing team. He said they planned to send the tight end on a drag route into the flat as the first option. The Packers sent more rushers than the Chiefs had left to block. The constant pressure got to Dawson. He could not throw passes with the regular zing. The rushers would hit either his arm or the ball.

"You don't like to think that one play can make that much of a difference," said Hank Stram, "but in this case it did. The interception changed the personality of our attack. Play action and rolls were the things we did best. But when we got behind we had to deviate from our game plan and we got into trouble."[27]

The interception seemed to take the wind out of the Chiefs' sail. It changed the momentum of the contest. The Chiefs kept the game close during the first half, but could not get any traction after that interception. During the third quarter, the Chiefs totaled 12 yards of offense while the Packers scored twice. After the game, folks saw Lombardi walking round the locker room with a cherished prize—the game ball. "The players gave it to me," he said proudly. "It's the NFL ball. It catches better and kicks a little better than the AFL ball."[28]

The reporters all wanted to know his opinion of the Chiefs, now that teams from the rival leagues faced off. Following the general rule of coaching etiquette, Lombardi played it coy about assessing the Chiefs. He wanted to be the gracious winner and answered with a politically correct response about the Chiefs' effort. The reporters continued to press him. They were not going to go away until they got a quote.

Green Bay Packers running back Elijah Pitts take a handoff from Bart Starr during the AFL–NFL World Championship Game in 1967. Pitts played 11 seasons in the league and served two decades as an assistant coach (Photofest).

"That's a good football team, but it is not as good as the top teams in our league," he said finally. Then he grinned and added, "That's what you want me to say and now I've said it. It took me a long time to get that out."[29] Then he ended the exchange with a hearty Lombardi chuckle.

After the crowds left, Lombardi got a chance to sit and think about what had just taken place. Steve Sabol, a cinematographer with NFL Films at the time, had the job of covering Coach Lombardi's press conference. Sabol walked into the coaches' locker room during that quiet moment. Sabol noticed that Lombardi felt so much pressure in the lead-up to the game that he had a problem with his tie after the game.

"At the end of the game, when we went to the locker room to interview Coach Lombardi, he was trying to take his tie off during the interview," recalled Sabol. "But he had knotted the tie so tight, the Windsor knot was about the size of a marble. He kept tugging and tugging. Finally, the equipment manager of the Packers had to come over with a pair of tape shears, cut it off and throw it away. To this day, I think what a great collectible or memorabilia that would be. The tie Lombardi wore at the first Super Bowl. But he had knotted it so tight because he was so nervous, he couldn't get it off."[30]

Many consider the first Super Bowl the best of them all in a similar fashion that some presidential historians call George Washington the best president. No one knew what to expect of the first contest between the two leagues. It turned out a big hit over television with strong ratings. Although one in three seats remained unsold that first game, future years would see those tickets in high demand.

Super Bowl I had the greatest amount of residue from the earlier heated battles between the two leagues. With war wounds fresh, some owners could not accept a merger and wanted to see the junior league taught a lesson. They figured they had the best team to do the beat down, too. The Packers were, without a doubt, the best team in professional football in the 1960s. Five championships in seven seasons proved that. They dominated their league and when it came to head-to-head battles with the AFL, they stood undefeated there too.

The Super Bowl grew into a huge event over time. Pete Rozelle's dream of a weeklong media circus leading up to a classic game eventually came true. Many of the most watched televisions programs of all time are Super Bowl games. Today's Super Bowls are one of the most watched sporting events in the world. It has a potential worldwide audience of an estimated one billion people in more than 200 countries. In the United States, there are 80 to 90 million tuned into the game at any given moment. Recent games have had more than 112 million viewers.

It has taken on a life of its own. People gather together to watch the games, or maybe just the commercials? The whole program catches someone's attention. Halftime has gained fans of its own. One of the top entertainers performs at intermission so nobody is willing to leave their seats.

Halftime shows at the earliest Super Bowl games featured college bands and local performers. As time went on, the shows ramped up, slowly. In 1970, Broadway star Carol Channing and the Southern University band did the honors, marking the start of halftime salutes to everything from Mardi Gras to Motown. Rozelle was a fan of marching bands and balloon drops and those acts dominated the early shows. The biggest acts performed at the more recent shows. Superstar Michael Jackson put on a spectacle in the 1993 game, starting a parade of worldwide superstars such as the Rolling Stones, U2, Prince, Madonna and Paul McCartney.

If you went back in time and witnessed all the empty seats in the first game, you may not have guessed that the game developed into the event it is today. Today, it is the destination for A-list celebrities and Fortune 500 executives. Tickets are hard to come by and friends gather around television sets for a midwinter gathering. The games are some of the most-watched programs in American television history.

While the Chiefs sat in front of their lockers sulking over their lost opportunity, an 11-year-old boy wandered through the Green Bay Packers locker room gathering autographs from the winning team. He collected signatures from Bart Starr, Jim Taylor and Paul Hornung. He even approached Vince Lombardi. "Coach, will you sign my program?" the youngster asked. "I hope your Daddy doesn't spank you for coming in here," Lombardi said as he grabbed the program and signed his name. The boy, Dale Stram, was the son of Chiefs head coach Hank Stram.[31]

The Packers boarded their charter aircraft for their return trip to Green Bay that same night. A dense fog settled over Los Angeles delaying the flight so the team had their celebration dinner in the grounded airplane. That may have been the only thing that went wrong for the Packers all day.

Flash forward to the second Super Bowl and the Packers' nerves seemed much less pronounced. The team having played the Chiefs and gone through the entire process a year earlier, Green Bay had a better position from which to judge the Oakland Raiders.

"I can't honestly say that we were ever afraid of losing to the Raiders, but we did not take them lightly," said linebacker Ray Nitschke. "One thing has happened to the Packers over the last few years. The team we look at in movies in preparation for a game is almost never like the team we meet on the field. Even the last place teams bring a special spirit and dedication to their game with us. I think we had a bad first half against Kansas City because we took them too lightly, but this time we were alerted to the fact that the AFL champion was capable of giving us a tough game for a half."[32]

The Green Bay Packers dominated the first two Super Bowls and left some wondering if the AFL could ever field a team that could compete with the likes of the Packers. Was it a case of one dominating team or just two leagues light years apart in terms of competition? The sports world would soon find out.

Chapter Thirteen

New Generations

Joseph William Namath grew up in Beaver Falls, Pennsylvania, about 28 miles northwest of Pittsburgh. Although western Pennsylvania is not an official region of Pennsylvania, it gained fame for several things. Geographically the region had many steel mills and coalmines. The hardworking immigrants who worked in those steels mills and coalmines called the area home. Most important to football fans, western Pennsylvania produced many of the top quarterbacks (and more than a few other positions) ever to play in professional football. Joe Namath, Johnny Unitas, Joe Montana, Jim Kelly and Dan Marino all grew up as Catholic sons in working-class western Pennsylvania families. Their ancestors came to America seeking a better life for their children. They settled in western Pennsylvania where those tough enough to endure it found ample work. Their families had that inherent toughness.

Do you wonder why western Pennsylvania produced so many top quarterbacks? "I don't pretend to have all the answers," said Dan Rooney of the Steelers and a lifelong resident of the region. "But I do know that the people of our region take their football seriously. They know and love the game. The hard-working people, many of immigrant stock, adopted the game and made it their own. The sport that evolved in western Pennsylvania bore little resemblance to the highbrow college game that came from Princeton and Yale at the end of the nineteenth century. Western Pennsylvania–style football was physically tough, straight-ahead, and hard-hitting, reflecting the often brutal and sometimes violent realities of work in the steel mills and coal mines."[1]

"It's the work ethic, the way people were brought up," said Mike Ditka, who grew up in Aliquippa. "The parents came from the old country and worked in the mills and the mines. People didn't have anything but didn't need anything. They were tough. Were they tougher than they were in Nebraska? I don't know. But they were tough."[2]

Even football moms from western Pennsylvania have opinions why so many good players come from the region. "There's a reason, of course," said Rose Namath Szolnoki, Joe's mother. "It doesn't take a Beaver Falls father—or any father in the valley—much time in the hot mill of one of those steel companies to know he doesn't want his own sons working there if he can possibly help it. Nevertheless, Beaver Falls isn't the kind of place where you can just up and leave. You've got to earn your way out somehow, and for the boys the best way has always been through college, through an athletic scholarship. Bear Bryant has always said that poor boys are easier to coach," being hard players who are "trying to escape."[3]

Namath was the youngest of five children raised by two parents of Hungarian descent. The family settled in the poor end of Beaver Falls, a neighborhood populated mostly by minorities and wedged between the Beaver River on the east and the Pennsylvania Railroad to the west. Seven Namaths shared one bathroom, located in the basement behind the coal burner. His father, John Namath, passed through Ellis Island at age 11 with Joe's grandfather. His mother, Rose Juhasz, was born of two parents who emigrated from Hungry. His dad worked at the Babcock and Wilcox Company steel mill for 40 years as a roller in the number two hot mill.

Western Pennsylvania, in particular the small towns near Pittsburgh, produced many good, tough athletes who performed very well at quarterback position. That history goes back a long way. Johnny Lujack, who quarterbacked three national championship teams at Notre Dame in the forties, came from Connellsville as the first in a line of successful quarterbacks from the area. Shortly after that, the area produced George Blanda and Babe Parilli. More recently, two members of the famous quarterback draft of 1983, Jim Kelly and Dan Marino, came out of western Pennsylvania.

Namath played high school football for Larry Bruno, who had a big influence on Joe's life. Bruno took over before Joe's junior season. Off the field, Coach Bruno performed as an amateur magician. He took his off-field sleight-of-hand skills to the football field. As a coach, he wanted his quarterbacks highly skilled at faking the ball. On a magician's stage, sleight of hand produces the illusion and creates amazement. On the football field, sleight of hand slowed opposition reactions and provided a short-term advantage for the offense. Bruno learned the faking craft from Babe Parilli, who came from nearby Rochester and later played for Bear Bryant at Kentucky. Bruno took extra time with his quarterbacks to pass on the skills of ball faking so that they could master the sleight of hand. Coach Bruno demanded flawless execution of the fake. Those subtle moves took hours of practice time but proved critical in order to freeze the linebacker in a game.

Ever the magician, Bruno trained his quarterbacks to handle the ball in a way that created the illusion on the field. When carrying out a fake, the quarterback put his hand into the back's belly—waist deep, Bruno would emphasize. He would stress waist deep because he wanted the fake to look realistic. Namath took the task to heart. He viewed ball-handling skills like his hustling skills in the pool hall. He had honed his billiard skills his whole life. Now, ideally suited for the task, he took them to the gridiron. Having unusually large hands made the task simpler. Bruno drilled the quarterbacks repeatedly. Namath applied the lessons passed on from the master and developed into a skilled ball handler.

Faking came easy to Joe. He just transferred his billiard hustling skills developed in pool halls to the football field. With practice, Joe got good at faking movement with the football. That time spent at the pool hall did not foster a good reputation on the streets of Beaver Falls.

"Everybody said he was going to be a great quarterback—if you could handle him," Bruno said. "He had a bad reputation. But that was other people's version of Joe."[4] Despite the warnings, Bruno did not see a delinquent. He saw a talented football player, who just needed training and refinement. Along with growing his skills as a quarterback, Joe needed to grow physically. As a junior, he stood just 5-foot-9, 156 pounds.

Pool also taught him angles, which he applied to the gridiron. Joe learned to play the angles on the Brunswick tables as a teen and went on to play the angles on the football field throughout his playing career. Good billiard players also have a coolness about them that allows them to perform at their best under the greatest pressure. Joe brought that same coolness learned hustling pool to his play on the football field. In fact, he loved it. The more pressure the better. He never feared throwing interceptions. He threw plenty of them. Taking risks made him a big stakes gambler on the football field. Namath appeared as the first of many quarterbacks who had a high tolerance for risk on the field, daring to put the football into a tight spot.

Coach Bruno may have seen it a little differently. When he introduced Joe years later at the Hall of Fame, he used the word confidence to describe Joe. "When Joe played for Beaver Falls High School, the entire football team believed whatever play Joe called, they would make it work because they knew Joe had confidence in them."[5]

As a kid growing up, Namath worshipped Johnny Unitas. Local kids followed Unitas's career though high school, college and into the pros. Johnny Unitas came from western Pennsylvania so he was one of them. In high school, Joe asked for number 19 just like his hero. Soon teammates started calling Namath "Joey U" in honor of the famous "Johnny U" from Baltimore. Namath and Unitas had similar upbringings in western Pennsylvania. Johnny grew up in Mt. Washington, a section on the south side of Pittsburgh dominated by row houses. Unitas's parents emigrated from Lithuania; Namath's family came from Hungary. John lost his dad to pneumonia as a young boy. Namath's parents divorced and he lived with his mother. When Unitas started high school, he only weighed 138 pounds. Namath was a late bloomer, too.

As Namath watched Unitas through high school and into college, he most admired his brains. He understood defenses and found ways to exploit them. Unitas took chances and Joe liked that. During Namath's high school years, 1957 through 1960, Unitas led the NFL in touchdown passes.

Through high school, Namath had not enamored himself with the parents in Beaver Falls. He bet, smoked and drank. As noted, he liked to hang out at the pool hall. His playboy ways with women started early, well before he arrived in New York City. In addition, he came from a divorced home, which prompted additional talk among the neighbors growing up in the small town during the fifties. He had gotten a bad reputation, some based on truth and some from exaggerations of the truth.

After his parents' divorce, Joe looked to his three older brothers for male influence. All of them loved and played sports. Joe wanted to follow their example. His oldest brother, Sonny, played as a lineman in high school but enlisted into the military right after graduation. The second son, Bobby, performed well as a quarterback in junior high. Frank, the brother closest in age to Joe, caught in baseball and played on the line in football. The Baltimore Orioles offered Frank a $20,000 bonus to play professional baseball but he accepted a full scholarship to play football for Blanton Collier at the University of Kentucky. Even though his brothers were good in sports, none of them matched Joe's athletic ability.

"Frank was responsible for teaching me the importance of learning from a loss and how to be a gracious winner, with humility," Joe recalled. "You see, Frank is six years older than I am, and I'll tell you, if I had the good fortune of winning a game of stickball or electric baseball or something, I knew not to brag. I mean, not even a little smirk would be a good idea."[6]

"Bob taught me how to throw a football from the ear, shortening the throwing motion," Joe said. He taught me "a different technique than just throwing a stone or throwing a baseball. He drilled me from age six and taught me quite a bit of my coiled-torso throwing motion and emphasis on quick release."[7]

With a family full of boys, Joe's mother, Rose, always wanted a girl. In fact, neighbors who believed in old wives' tales insisted she, when pregnant with Joe, actually carried a girl. Of course, that did not happen. The family adopted a girl Frank's age named Rita. Thus, Joe remained the baby of the family and extremely close to his mother. After the divorce, with the other siblings out of the house, Joe's bond with his mother grew even tighter.

During high school, Namath excelled as a gifted athlete in all sports. "Until my senior year, baseball and basketball were my best sports," Joe said. "Even when I was a senior, I still wanted to play baseball professionally. But the family wanted me to go to college and I guess I agreed with them or else I would have accepted some of the offers I got."[8]

Namath captained his high school basketball team. As a 6-foot-2 guard, he could dunk the ball and was the only white starter on the team. He became close friends with his black teammates. When he quit the team in a dispute with the coach during his senior year, the other four starters quit too. Namath nearly gave up football earlier in high school. "I knew I could play, but coaches put me as the fifth-string quarterback on the varsity," Joe recalled. Each year, the top prospects received an invite to attend a summer camp. Prospects without much chance of helping the team stayed home. Joe hoped to attend, but organizers did not invite fifth-string quarterbacks. "I was still a runt, and I didn't get invited to the Beaver Falls Booster Club varsity summer camp for the high school football team. When you're fourteen years old and your whole life is about trying to make the team, man, it was devastating."[9]

The lack of an invite to the important summer camp convinced Joe to quit football and focus on the other sports. Coaches intervened and convinced him to stick it out. In the fall, he worked himself up from fifth string to third string. Joe's big break came before his junior year when Coach Larry Bruno took over as head coach of the Beaver Falls Tigers football program. Joe responded to Coach Bruno's instruction and the team achieved success. During Joe's senior season, the Tigers finished undefeated and won the state AA championship.

In Joe's development as a quarterback, Coach Bruno took over where his brother left off. He "told me one day in a meeting, told our whole team, 'fellows, if you don't dream about it, it will never happen, but you can't just dream about it, you have to go out and make it happen, you have to work hard.' With that in mind, I dreamt of a high school championship and we won it. We went out and worked for it and got it."[10]

Upon graduation, Joe received offers from numerous major league teams to turn pro in baseball. His mother, Rose, wanted him to get his college education. When it came time to pick a college, Joe knew he wanted to go to school in the South. He committed to play for the University of Maryland as his first choice. His college boards, however, fell a few points short of Maryland's minimum requirements so they did not accept him. Yet, Maryland coaches feared Namath would go to Penn State or another school on the Terrapins' schedule so they put a call in to Alabama, a school not on their schedule. They recommended Joe go to Alabama.

Bear Bryant selected Howard Schnellenberger, one of his less experienced recruiters, to fly to western Pennsylvania to recruit Namath. Bryant picked him because Joe's older brother, Frank, played football at Kentucky in 1955-56 during Schnellenberger's senior year. When he got to Pennsylvania, Schnellenberger found Joe hanging out in front of the Blue Room pool hall. His job was to convince Namath to attend Alabama, which had a head coach, who—in the view of many—had more power than the governor of the state did. Bear Bryant had built a big reputation as a strong disciplinarian and successful coach at Texas A&M and Kentucky before moving to Alabama.

Bear Bryant spoke with a deep gravelly voice. He watched practice from his perch high above in a tower built specifically for the purpose. When he called down to the players and coaches below, his deep voice sounded like a declaration from the heavens. Like all good coaches, Bryant wanted talented players. When the Bear heard about Namath, he wanted him on his team. When Namath arrived for his visit, Bryant summoned him to his tower, where the coach watched practice. Very few people, except for the likes of Governor George Wallace and university president Frank Rose, received invites to that tower but the youngster with the strong right arm received that honor.

Assistant coaches could not recall anybody, not players, coaches, or visiting politicians, ever being invited up to the tower. They could not believe it when this strangely dressed young man with a toothpick dangling from his lips went up the ladder to talk with the Bear. They said it was stranger still when the Bear called down with his bullhorn beckoning him to climb up.

Namath came to the South to play college football during the days of great social change. Growing up in a poor and racially diverse neighborhood, he was shocked by the segregation he found in Alabama. During his drive to campus, Namath saw drinking fountains labeled "colored water" and other blatant acts of discrimination. Having grown up in the poor part of town in neighborhoods made up of poor immigrants and minorities, he expressed surprise by how different things appeared in the South.

"Coming from where I came from, I couldn't believe it," Namath recalled. "Water fountains for whites were painted white, there were different lunchrooms for whites and blacks; blacks had to sit in the backs of buses and whites had to sit up front. I just couldn't understand it."[11]

Namath attended the University of Alabama during the turbulent sixties and encountered a different world for him. He saw firsthand many of the conflicts brewing in the nation at that time. He recalled witnessing history on campus in June of 1963 while registering for class. He joined other students when they heard Governor Wallace had arrived on campus to block a young black woman, Vivian Malone, from going to the state's university. Federalized National Guard troops escorted Malone and another prospective student, James Hood, onto the University of Alabama campus. Governor Wallace attempted to bar them from attending the school intent on keeping his promise to stop integration at the schoolhouse door. Their case represented the civil rights drama playing out across the South that summer. "I'd see her from time to time and say hello," Joe said. "Most of us at school didn't see what all the fuss was about, and while there were some screwballs around (there was a threat and an explosion outside of Vivian's dorm), Vivian completed her schooling."[12] In May 1965, Malone became the first black to graduate from the University of Alabama.

Namath grew up on the other side of the tracks with poor people of all races. He could remember that first trip down South when he first visited Alabama. When he looked out the window of the bus and saw "TUSCALOOSA: HOME OF THE IMPERIAL WIZARD KU KLUX KLAN" he must have thought he had arrived on some other planet. Namath admitted his first sight of Tuscaloosa and the outward signs of discrimination shocked him. "Colored water" just wasn't something he had seen before. Joe felt comfortable with all people. Perhaps his comfort with all races let Namath get a nickname early during his stay in Alabama that he really didn't appreciate.

"In my freshman year, I was sitting in my room doing something and one of the fellas picked up a picture of the Beaver Falls High School football queen and the crown bearer was a black girl. The guy asked, 'Hey, Joe, is this your girl?' and I answered yes, thinking he was pointing at the queen but he was pointing at the black girl. He said, 'Oh, yeah?' and ran out and told everybody he could find that I was dating a black girl; so they started calling me Nigger."[13]

Changes were happening on college campuses across the South. From 1960 to 1962, 28-year-old USAF veteran James Meredith, an African American, applied for admittance to the University of Mississippi. The University, known as Ole Miss, had previously had only white students and faculty. Meredith desperately wanted to attend college in his home state. Mississippi Governor Ross Barnett led the fight to keep him out. On Saturday afternoons during the fall, fans proudly waved rebel flags during football games. Many viewed rebel battle flags as a symbol of racism formed over the slavery debate. The symbolism seemed clear to most. Mississippi had retained many symbols of the Confederate South. They called the football team the Rebels in honor of Confederate soldiers, had a mascot named "Colonel Reb" and played "Dixie" at every game. Despite those symbols, Meredith sought admission to the school. Ole Miss rejected his application. He sued claiming that they had denied him solely because of his race. The case went all the way to the Supreme Court, where the high court ruled that Meredith should be admitted to the school without any further delay. Governor Barnett, son of a Confederate soldier and an Ole Miss graduate, decided to block his enrollment at all costs. Meredith just wanted to attend the state university in his home state. As a result, one determined man faced off against another. Meredith repeatedly tried to go to school and Governor Barnett repeatedly turned him away.

President Kennedy federalized the Mississippi National Guard to work with 170 deputy U.S. Marshals. He went on national television to explain his desire to carry out the Supreme Court decision and allow Meredith to attend the school. Riots broke out pitting the police forces against white students backed by segregationists. Rioters threw bricks and burned cars. Estimates pegged the injured at more than one hundred (various reports disputed the number) and two others, including French journalist Paul Guihard, died. President Kennedy sent in more federal troops to dispel the riots. In the fall of 1962, James Meredith finally registered and attended classes under federal guard. Despite continual harassment, James Meredith eventually graduated from Ole Miss.

Malone's and Meredith's cases stood as prime examples of the rising temperature of the civil rights campaigns during the early sixties. The U.S. Supreme Court ruled in the 1954 *Brown vs. Board of Education* case that separate but equal public schools violated the Equal Protection Clause of the Fourteenth Amendment of the Constitution. In other words, separate but equal made famous in *Plessy vs. Ferguson* did not apply to education. The court said schools needed to integrate. That ruling opened the door for Malone, Hood and others to seek admission to previously white-only universities.

Despite his shock at the racist South, Namath got along with everybody his freshman season at Alabama. Clem Gryska, Namath's freshman coach at Alabama, could not recall any issues with Namath adjusting to life in the South. Gryska said Bear Bryant approached early on and asked about Namath's progress. Gryska said Namath got along with all his teammates, regardless of where they came. Namath had success on the field as well as he led the team to an undefeated freshman season.

Namath started as a sophomore on the varsity at Alabama. He led a team heavy with seniors to a 10–1 record and a berth in the Orange Bowl against a strong Bud Wilkinson-coached team from Oklahoma. The Crimson Tide upset the Sooners, 17–0, in the game. Senior All-American linebacker Lee Roy Jordan made 30 tackles in the game, but Bear Bryant lavished heavy praise on his sophomore quarterback.

Namath continued his progress during the next season before it came to an abrupt end. A scheduled October game against Miami had originally been moved to December in order to be televised nationally but had to be postponed again until the Saturday after the Army–Navy game which was rescheduled following President Kennedy's assassination, giving the Tide a weekend off. Namath spent the off Saturday watching the Army–Navy game on television. Later in the evening, he caught up with his friend Horace "Hoot Owl" Hicks and they crashed some parties along the circuit of frat houses near the Alabama campus. At one point in the evening, they ran into car trouble and Namath got out to direct traffic while the Hoot Owl and others pushed the car. Most everyone on campus knew that Chevy without any doors belonged to the star quarterback. A housemother for one of the sorority houses noticed the car and the commotion. She soon notified the coaches and they told Bryant. On Monday, December 9, Bryant located Namath in the athletic dormitory. He asked Namath about the incident. Bryant said he heard Namath had been drinking and was observed directing traffic. Bryant trusted his source but he wanted to hear Joe's version. He asked the young quarterback if he had been drunk.

"No, sir," Namath said. "I wasn't drunk and I wasn't directing traffic downtown Saturday afternoon."

"You didn't drink at all Saturday?" Coach Bryant asked.

Namath swallowed hard. He could not lie to Coach Bryant. "Yes sir, I did," Joe admitted.[14]

Bryant suspended Namath for the rest of the season and offered him help getting into the Canadian Football League if he chose not to earn his way back onto the Crimson Tide team the following year. People in town put Joe up when he moved out of the athletic dormitory. Even Mary Harmon Bryant, the coach's wife, invited Namath to dinner. His friend, Hoot Owl, felt responsible for hurting Namath's football career since he had invited Joe to go with him to the frat parties. In the end, however, Namath earned his way back on the team and back into the starting lineup for his senior season.

It may have seemed like two men at the opposite end of many spectrums. One had youth; the other had experience. One liked to shave the edges off every rule he encountered while the other enforced the rules as a strict disciplinarian. One represented the old way of doing things while the other blazed a new path.

Namath returned to the Tide football team to play his senior season. Namath started the season strong. Then, in the locker room before the October 10 game against undefeated North Carolina State, Namath did not follow his normal custom of taping his shoes. Before most games, he taped his ankles and shoes, but for some unexplained reason he did not on this day. He usually taped the outside of his shoes with white athletic tape giving his black shoes the appearance of white shoes. They may have looked cool, but he said the tape provided additional support. Midway through the second quarter, Namath took off on a run because he could not find an open receiver. Sprinting in the open field, he collapsed without anyone near him. A teammate approached and Namath said he thought he had hurt his knee.

At first, everyone assumed a minor injury. In 1964, knee injuries relied more heavily on rehabilitation than surgery. The standard practice drained the knee joint of any liquid that collected. If the liquid came out blood red, they operated. They drained Namath's knee and decided not to operate. The treatment plan called for local injections and wrapping in compression bandages with ice packs followed by heat treatment.

Without arthroscopic technology, trainers could not verify the exact problem with Namath's knee. Pain continued for days after the game. The bloody fluid drawn out of the knee joint indicated he had torn something but doctors decided not to perform surgery. Joe struggled with knee problems all season long. The team finished undefeated that year with Joe and Steve Sloan splitting the time at quarterback. As the season ended, Alabama earned the right to play Texas in the Orange Bowl to determine the national champion.

With two top teams facing off with the title up for grabs, NBC Sports decided the Orange Bowl provided the perfect time to highlight college football on primetime television. They would broadcast the game in living color on New Year's Day, 1965. As the first college bowl game broadcast in prime time and in color (not a standard practice to date), it drew an estimated 25 million viewers watching at home. Six days before the game, Namath hurt his knee again. This time he hurt it unloading the trunk of the car. He did not practice much in the days leading up to the game and the coaches questioned if Namath would even get to play in the Orange Bowl.

As he had done during the regular season when Namath could not play, backup quarterback Steve Sloan started the game for Alabama. At the time, Sloan nursed his own knee injury, suffered in the season's final game against Auburn. Texas started strong, jumping to a 14–0 lead early in the second quarter. With Sloan's knee bothering him, Coach Bryant sent Namath into the game. The Alabama team responded. Namath led the Tide to a touchdown that Texas matched before half. At intermission, the score sat at 21–7, Texas in the lead.

Alabama came out strong in the third quarter and reduced the Longhorns' lead to 21–17. As the final minutes ticked off the clock in the fourth quarter, Namath led his team into scoring position at the Texas 6 yard line. They had four downs to get the ball in the end zone. The last play was the critical call. "I called a quarterback sneak, got hit by Texas linebacker Pete Lammons," Namath recalled. "Laying in the pile, looking across the field to the linesman I saw the touchdown signal. Then there was a conference by all the officials, and the linesman who signaled the score backed down. Just like that, I was over the goal line but did not score a touchdown."[15]

Alabama lost the game but Namath ended up with the Orange Bowl Most Valuable Player award. Rarely is a player on the losing team selected for that honor. Namath's valiant effort in leading his team back from a two-touchdown deficit impressed many in the national television audience. Despite the difficult circumstances and playing hurt, officials ruled Namath inches short of victory. Namath insists to this day that he scored on the play.

Professional football scouts took notice. Both the National Football League and the new American Football League had Namath in sight. Al Davis, who first scouted Namath as a young assistant coach with the San Diego Chargers, returned from a scouting trip to Tuscaloosa and told head coach Sid Gillman, "I saw a guy who tips the field."

"What do you mean?" asked Gillman.

Namath "is so good he plays like he's going downhill," Davis said.[16]

Pro talent evaluators, like Davis, saw an excellent athlete with outstanding mobility and a quicker release than anybody playing professionally. Prior to the knee injury, they

Jets Head Coach Weeb Ewbank stands on the sideline with quarterback Joe Namath during a break in the game action. Earlier in his career, Ewbank coached Johnny Unitas and the Colts to back-to-back NFL championships in 1958 and 1959 (Photofest).

timed him at 4.7 seconds over 40 yards. He also possesses a charisma and confidence that got his teammates moving.

When it came time to leave Alabama, Namath said Coach Bryant gave him some advice. He told Joe to make his decision based not just on money but on the kind of people he would end up working with. When it came to money, he told Joe to ask for more than he really wanted so he had room to negotiate.

It appears Namath considered his coach's advice when making his decision. The St. Louis Cardinals in the NFL and the New York Jets in the AFL both drafted him. Namath went with the Jets because of his attraction to Sonny Werblin and coach Weeb Ewbank. Every football fan knew Ewbank coached Johnny Unitas with the Colts when they won two straight championships in 1958 and 1959.

Namath liked the newness of the AFL versus the tradition and structure of the NFL. "The NFL had great players," Namath said. "But everybody seemed to wear their hair a certain way and live up to a very arbitrary 'code of conduct.' They did not seem to have the liberty to be themselves…. I can just imagine how the NFL would have reacted to my white shoes. My feet just feel lighter in white. So, I wore white shoes. I couldn't understand why people made a big deal out of it."[17]

In what turned out as great irony, the New York Giants' 38-year-old quarterback Y.A. Tittle announced his retirement on January 22, 1965, at Mamma Leone's restaurant. Tittle, the star of the New York sports scene, led the Giants to three straight title games in the early sixties. Unfortunately, they made it to the big game, but couldn't win it. After winning it all in 1956, the Giants went to the title game five of the next seven seasons without a victory.

"My three big years with the Giants all ended in the same way: we lost the championship game," Tittle recalled. "I don't know if any team could have whipped Green Bay for the 1961 championship.... They jumped off to a 24–0 lead in the second quarter and we had to try to play catch-up against a very tough defense. It wound up 37–0."[18] The weather was cold and windy in the Yankee Stadium rematch but the outcome was the same for the losing Giants. The third appearance came against the Bears in Chicago. Early in the game, Larry Morris hit Tittle and he felt pain in his knee. In the second quarter, when tackled again he thought someone had stuck an ice pick into that knee. He said that is what it felt like, anyway. The trainers taped the knee at halftime and he tried to play in the second half. Tittle's passes failed to find the target as his knee bothered him. The Bears intercepted five of his passes to claim the title victory.

The Jets appealed to Joe because they appeared as a young team on the rise lead by a solid coach. Meanwhile, the Giants headed backward with aging players and unimpressive coaching staff. To many, Tittle represented the older generation with his high top shoes and balding head. He always appeared older than his age, having lost his hair prematurely. His face showed the lines of experience. With helmet on, he still could play, but sitting there in the restaurant, he looked like a man ready for retirement. He represented times gone by. Later that same afternoon, the future arrived as team officials introduced Joe Namath as the new quarterback of the New York Jets. One team seemed on the way up and the other on the way down.

Like Robert Frost taking the road less traveled, Namath's choice of the AFL made all the difference. He starred as a huge drawing card for the new league playing in the AFL's largest city. Some credit his signing as a major factor in the merger of the two leagues. Sonny Werblin started up his publicity machine to make the Jets a profitable franchise and, at the same time, molding an image of Joe Willie Namath like an artist creating pottery from clay.

He must have seen something in that young player from western Pennsylvania. He signed him without a physical examination. Namath had his knee examined the first time in the men's room at the press conference announcing his signing. Dr. James Nicholas, the Jets' orthopedist, did the exam. Afterward, the doctor sought out Weeb Ewbank and warned him to keep a second quarterback because he feared Namath's career might prove short due to his knee. Not long after the examination, Joe went to Lenox Hill Hospital for surgery on his knee. He had the medial meniscus removed and his medial collateral ligament doubled back and stapled.

"Mr. Werblin had a photographer from *Sports Illustrated* in the operating room— they ran a four page feature on my operation in February 1965," Joe said. "A master at turning out a story, Mr. Werblin knew the importance of having the media on his side. Not by accident, there was an open-door policy to our locker room. And all press rode in the first-class section on the Jet charter planes while the team sat back in coach."[19] Namath was back on the cover of *Sports Illustrated* in July posing at the corner of Broadway and Seventh Avenue.

That magazine with Namath on the cover appeared all over Jets training camp that summer. Jets players could hardly wait to needle their new star quarterback. Some players did it out of good-natured ribbing, but some others seemed just plain jealous of his big payday. One Jet liked seeing his celebrity teammate on the cover. Sherman Plunkett, the big offensive tackle, took one look at the cover and said, "Broadway, yes that's it, Broadway Joe." The nickname stuck. Seeing Namath on the cover of *Sports Illustrated* with the bright lights of Broadway behind him made him think of the name.

Plunkett stood as one of many black players who clicked with Namath. Plunkett, a veteran offensive lineman with the Jets, had come a long way since the Cleveland Browns released him. The Browns had originally drafted him out of Maryland State College, but only a few months later the Army drafted him as well. Plunkett learned how to play offensive tackle from Rosey Grier while playing service ball at Fort Dix, New Jersey. After the service, he joined the Colts where he first met Coach Ewbank.

Plunkett liked seeing his quarterback on the cover of national sports magazines. Articles on Joe Namath were not limited to sports magazines like *Sports Illustrated.* After he moved into a new penthouse atop the Newport East at 370 East Seventy-Sixth Street, the society pages wanted to interview Namath, too. For example, the women's pages of the *New York Times* featured Namath's penthouse. They pictured Joe in an easy chair reading *Catch-22.* "It was old-fashioned movie mag stuff: the star at home. This bachelor pad was straight out of the MCA playbook," biographer Mark Kriegel wrote.[20] His suite featured a llama skin rug that the magazines said looked like dry ice. He had an oval-shaped bed with a mirror suspended above.

The Jets' owner provided numerous tips to Joe, including where to live. He advised Joe to live in the city. The coach had a tip for his star player, too. Ewbank wanted to help Joe get along with his new teammates. When training camp arrived, Ewbank advised Joe not to drive his shiny new Lincoln Continental he received as part of his signing bonus. Weeb thought the picture of him pulling up in that vehicle might prove too much for the other players to endure. Instead, he caught a ride from a photographer for *Life* magazine. The photographer planned to take pictures that would go along with a future profile in the magazine as another of Werblin's publicity efforts.

At training camp, Namath followed the custom of all rookies and stood up to sing the Alabama fight song. The veterans were not interested in that song. Loudly, they began to sing, "There's No Business Like Show Business" and drowned him out. Obviously, everyone had heard about the contract and the nickname Plunkett hung on him. Joe was not your ordinary rookie.

When he left college prior to graduating, Joe's automatic deferment for the draft to Vietnam ended. The war heating up and the increasing number of young men drafted caused concern for all young men his age. Joe knew about military service as his older brother John fought in both Korea and Vietnam. Due to the damage to his knee, the Selective Service classified Namath as unfit for military service. The media put up an immediate outcry: how could he play the very physical game of football and yet not prove fit enough for military service? Some labeled him a draft dodger. Namath could see their point and had mixed emotions.

"If I said I was glad [not to be drafted], I was a traitor," he said. "If I said I was disappointed, I would have been a fool. Kids in college were getting deferments, married guys were getting deferments, people wondered how a football player, a professional athlete nonetheless, could get a deferment."[21]

With the start of the season, draft talk quieted down. Namath did not start at the beginning of his rookie season and that made people talk about the lineup. Ewbank had his reasons for taking Joe along easily. Ewbank figured Namath needed to learn a new offense and he wanted him completely healed from offseason knee surgery before taking the field.

The Jets finished the 1965 season out of the playoff race. The 1966 season proved somewhat similar. The Jets won their first five games. As they began to play teams a second time around, coaches made adjustments in their defenses. The Jets finished 1966 with six wins, six losses and two ties. After the last game, Namath underwent more surgery on his knee. Doctors removed cartilage debris. He also needed to have a ligament rebuilt from his patella tendon. Today, that kind of surgery is similar to an ACL reconstruction.

The next year, 1967, Jets fans' impatience was growing as the clock continued to tick on Weeb's promise to bring a championship to New York in five years. That season would be Ewbank's fifth in New York so fans expectations were high. Teammates and opponents both saw Namath as a special quarterback. "His quickness of release is unmatched," said cornerback Johnny Sample, who played in the league many years and faced all the top signal callers. "He had a great arm. He is extremely accurate, has great distance on his passes, and he can lay the soft one in there when it's needed. Joe has a mind that knows the game of football almost as well as anyone's. He can read defenses quickly and call the right play at the right time. This, added to his passing ability, makes him a truly great quarterback."[22]

On December 17, 1967, the Jets and Raiders faced off at Oakland-Alameda County Stadium. The Jets came into the game having lost their last two games against Denver and Kansas City. The rivalry between the two teams had reached its high point. The Jets handed them their only loss of the season in October. When the rematch appeared on the schedule, the Raiders came into the game with a simple strategy; they would send their talented, quick and ferocious defensive line in on Namath. They planned to hit Joe early and often.

"The quickest way to beat our team was to hurt Joe," recalled center John Schmitt. "We had a love for him we had for no one else. And Ben Davidson was a cheap-shot artist. We had a lot of reasons to hate those guys. They're probably the only team we ever felt that way about. At the time, if I could have run Ben Davidson over with a car and laughed, I would have."[23]

In the third quarter, Ike Lassiter hit Namath so hard in the head that the quarterback reportedly suffered a concussion. "I turned to throw to [George] Sauer on the left, and just as I was releasing the ball—that split-second when my body was most vulnerable— Ike Lassiter delivered a knockout forearm to my face," Namath said afterward. "He bore down on me with a force so fierce that I have no memory of the impact."[24] Namath got the pass off, but it did not get to his target due to the hit. Linebacker J. R. Williamson intercepted it. The turnover set up a touchdown and the Raiders took the lead, 17–14.

In the fourth quarter, Ben Davidson hit Joe Namath with full force, sending Namath's helmet sailing 10 yards away from his body. Officials flagged Davidson for a roughing the passer penalty. The referee marched off 15 yards and signaled a Jets first down. Then he stopped the clock for an injury timeout as Namath still lay on the turf. A teammate collected his helmet and center John Schmitt helped him up. Grabbing the helmet, Namath started for the wrong sideline and his teammates had to turn him around.

In their coverage of the game the next day, newspapers reported that Ben Davidson had shattered Namath's cheekbone in the second half. Most of the articles focused on the physical play of the Raiders and the intensity of the contest. Years later, Namath admitted that Davidson had not hurt his face; it had actually been Lassiter in the third quarter that hurt the quarterback. In the press conference afterward, he wouldn't admit to being injured during the game. "I got my face swollen biting into a steak at breakfast," he told reporters, not wanting to give the opposition the satisfaction of knowing he hurt him.

During the 1967 season, Namath threw for 4,000 yards but also threw 28 interceptions. Nobody in any league had ever thrown for that many yards in a 14-game season. Untimely miscues continued to haunt him. He threw six picks in the 28–28 game against the Oilers that ultimately cost the Jets the Eastern Division title. In another game, he nearly missed the start of the game.

"He came in ten minutes before the game all disheveled," said defensive end Gerry Philbin. "You know he had been out all night long. I called him a prima donna. [Defensive coach] Walt Michaels threatened, if we didn't win the game, he was in trouble. There was a big episode in the locker room. We won the game. He went on to have a good game."[25]

That episode and more like it demonstrated that Joe got away with things that others would not have. "The Jets have come under criticism for having two sets of rules," said Johnny Sample. "That's true, but it wasn't Joe's fault. And he doesn't take advantage of the situation. The problem is really with Weeb. He lets Joe do anything. Weeb might scream and holler at some other player for doing something wrong, but Joe could do the same thing and Weeb would say nothing."[26]

The cozy relationship between Werblin and Namath created serious problems with the rest of the team. One blowup occurred during the weekend of the Denver game in 1967, when the Jets vied for their divisional title and Namath blew the game with four interceptions. After the game, reporters claimed Joe had partied with Werblin until 7 a.m. before the game. Team management saw that Joe needed to settle down and take some responsibility for his actions. They had a strategy for Joe to develop the maturity he needed to succeed in the league. "And so the following year, they came to the players and they said you got to get Joe elected captain," said Philbin. "You got to make him captain because you got to give him some responsibility. When he gets this responsibility, he will show that leadership."[27]

After this season, Joe had his left leg put in a full leg cast from thigh to ankle in an effort heal a chronic case of tendinitis. That strategy didn't seem to work so in March, he went back into surgery. Dr. Nicholas repaired a small tear on Joe's patella tendon and again removed cartilage. During that offseason, that Namath signed his second contract with the Jets. Just as with his first contract, controversy developed over that deal. The controversy involved the timing of the deal.

Patience ran thin across the board. Rumors had it that Werblin had grown unhappy with head coach Weeb Ewbank. Some players expressed displeasure with the situation. Owners squabbled with one another. Then, when Sonny Werblin signed Namath to the big contract without the knowledge of the other members of the ownership group, everything came to a head. They wanted Werblin out so they offered to buy his part of the team. His leaving may have saved Weeb's job.

The new ownership group gave Ewbank a one-year deal. The message seemed clear: If he did not win in 1968, he would be out. With Werblin gone, Ewbank's first action closed the locker room and named Joe Namath a captain. "Being elected captain," Joe said later, "is the most flattering thing a ball player can achieve. Getting a vote from a guy shows that he likes your work ethic. Next to being on a championship team, it's the best honor a player can earn."[28]

The title of captain helped Joe perform better on the field. The Jets started strong with victories over the Chiefs and the Patriots. Then they went to Buffalo to play the Bills, who were not a very good team at the time. Oddsmakers had the Jets as overwhelming favorites to win the game. But in Buffalo's War Memorial Stadium, Joe threw five interceptions (three of which the Bills returned for touchdowns) and the Jets lost. They recovered with a victory over the Chargers. However, inconsistency hit Namath again. Joe threw five interceptions for the second time in three weeks in a loss to the hapless Broncos. The Jets beat the good teams, but stubbed their toes against the weaker teams.

In an effort to gain unity, the players started a no-shaving movement suggested by defensive end Verlon Biggs. Many other athletes in other pro sports have done similar things. While the NFL had a strict rule forbidding facial hair, the Jets played in the AFL. With the beards growing, the Jets kept on winning. They posted a 7–2 record as they went to Oakland to face the Raiders in a rematch of the game in which Joe had his cheek broken.

The game was televised nationally since it featured two top AFL teams with big playoff implications for the season. The previous season the teams faced each other twice. In the first meeting, played at Shea Stadium in New York, the Jets handed the Raiders their only loss of the season. The next time they played at Oakland Coliseum, where the two teams played a very physical game.

Once again, the two teams played an extremely physical, hard-fought game. Between them, they racked up more than 30 penalties. The lead alternated back and forth all afternoon with the teams trading the lead six times by the time they reached the last minute of play. The Jets pulled ahead, 32–29, with a little more than a minute to play. Just as it looked like they would hold on for the victory NBC pulled the plug and television screens on the East Coast watched the children's classic movie *Heidi*.

Before NBC left the game on the East Coast, the Jets kicked a 26-yard field goal to give them a three-point lead. As clock struck 7 p.m. Eastern, NBC switched to the regularly-scheduled programming, despite the fact that the game had not finished yet. The network was contractually obligated to begin the movie at that hour.

After television switched to *Heidi*, Raiders quarterback Daryle Lamonica threw a 20-yard pass to halfback Charles Smith. Then a face mask penalty against the Jets moved the ball to the Jets' 43 yard line. On the next play, Lamonica threw again to Smith, who sprinted all the way for a touchdown. The Raiders took a 36–32 lead with less than one minute left to play.

Earlier in the contest, officials ejected veteran Jets safety Jim Hudson from the game for complaining about a penalty called against him. The Raiders victimized his replacement, rookie safety Mike D'Amato, on those critical plays that led up to the game-winning touchdown.

The Jets' Earl Christy fumbled the next kickoff. He chased it back to the 10 yard line, but could not control the rolling football as it approached his own goal line. Oakland's Preston Ridlehuber scooped it up at the 2 yard line and dove into the end zone. The Raiders had scored two touchdowns in nine seconds.

Several Jets expressed their anger after the game. Assistant coach Walt Michaels and team orthopedist, Dr. James Nicholas, banged on the door to the officials' locker room. "I'm the only team doctor in history ever fined for banging on the door," Dr. Nicholas said later.[29] Both men complained loudly over Hudson's ejection.

NBC had promoted the new version of the children's story *Heidi* in anticipation of a high rating during November sweeps period. The plan called for the movie to air at 7 p.m. Eastern after the conclusion of the football game. NBC executives had decided to stay with the game, but could not get through to the NBC Network control room in New York. The phone lines jammed as some people called urging NBC to air *Heidi* as scheduled while others called urging them to stay with the game. So many viewers called NBC that the switchboard blew.

The widespread reactions to NBC turning off the game showed up on television and in the newspapers. On NBC's nightly news program the *Huntley-Brinkley Report*, David Brinkley reported, "NBC apologized for the error, but by then Oakland had scored two touchdowns in the last minute, had beaten New York, the game was over. The fans that missed it could not be consoled."[30]

The *New York Times* covered the game on its front page. The headline summed it up: "Jets 32, Raiders 29, Heidi 14." Syndicated columnist Art Buchwald wrote, "Men who wouldn't get out of their chairs during an earthquake rushed to the phones to scream obscenities."[31]

The "Heidi Game" may have helped in the movement of football onto center stage. If someone is taking away something from you, it is human nature to get mad and demand it back. A huge outcry against NBC switching to normally scheduled programming erupted, spurred on by the fact the Raiders held up their end by scoring twice in nine seconds to win the game.

As a result, the NFL insisted on adding a clause to their broadcasting contract that guaranteed the complete broadcast of all games in the home markets of the teams. NBC installed a special phone called the Heidi phone to ensure communication between the game site and the network during games.

"Probably the most significant factor to come out of Heidi was, whatever you do, you better not leave an NFL football game," said Val Pinchbeck, the NFL's retired chief of broadcasting. "Ten years earlier, if you did the same thing on a telecast, would you get the same type of an uproar? I do not know. But you sure did at that point in time. It sure let you know that you better not take my football away from me at 7:00 p.m."[32]

David Brinkley appeared on the NBC evening news and said that the error was due to a communication breakdown by "the faceless button pusher in the bowels of NBC." The faceless one, Dick Cline, has been asked about Heidi every anniversary since it happened. "I took exception to that because I wasn't a button pusher," said Cline with a laugh years later.[33]

Cline's instructions said to switch the country to Heidi at 7 p.m. When he received no orders to keep the game on, he made the switch. "I waited and waited and heard nothing," Cline said. "We came up to that magic hour and I thought, Well, I haven't been given any counter-order so I've got to do what we agreed to do."[34]

About an hour after the game, Jets coach Weeb Ewbank phoned his wife in New York.

"Congratulations," she said.

"For what?" he asked.

"On winning," she said.

"We lost the game," he told her.[35]

In the 1968 AFL Championship Game, the Jets would face off against the Raiders in a rematch of the Heidi game. With their early stumbles behind them, the Jets ran a finely-tuned offense as the season neared the playoffs. The team had confidence that their offense could move the ball and score points. The stout defense played stingy. After the Jets beat the Raiders in the rematch of the Heidi Game, the Jets had tremendous confidence.

"I'll tell you the biggest thing we have going for us," Gerry Philbin said. "We have so much confidence in Joe and in our offense. We make mistakes on defense. We made a lot of them today. But Namath is unbelievable. He comes right back. He came to the sideline after the interception and he said, 'we'll get it back…. We'll get it back.' And he did."[36]

Nearly 40 mile per hour wind gusts made gametime temperatures for the championship frigid. By this late in December, the real grass turf at Shea Stadium showed extreme wear. With the grass nonexistent in some places, the wind kicked up dust and trash from the stands and blew it across the field.

Weeb came up with some unique strategy for the game. He opened with four wide receivers, an unusual formation in those days. He wanted the Raiders to play man coverage against his receivers. He believed the Jets' receivers could beat the Raiders' defensive backs one-on-one. A four wide receiver formation just helped push them in that direction. Once they had the Raiders worried about the deep passing game, the Jets ran Matt Snell against them. Despite the windy conditions, the Jets threw the ball 49 times. The wind gusts lowered the completion percentages significantly for both quarterbacks.

The game followed the same physical nature of previous games. Of this one the announcers said, "These two teams don't like each other." In the first quarter, Ike Lassiter hit Namath in the head. Namath had some smelling salts and went back in the game. In the second quarter, Namath had the middle finger on his left hand dislocated. The physical play really wore on the Jets' quarterback. Namath got injections in both knees and the middle finger at halftime.

The game went back and forth. Early in the fourth period, the Jets held a slim 20–16 lead. Namath threw an interception that George Atkinson returned to the 2 yard line. Fullback Pete Banaszak scored and the Raiders went ahead, 23–20.

The Jets were not done. Namath threw a long bomb to Don Maynard. He laid the ball right over Maynard's shoulder as he ran down the field with sprinter speed. Despite the wind, Namath put it right on target. Atkinson could only push Maynard out of bounds, leaving the Jets at the 6 yard line in prime position to take the lead. Namath knew the Raiders would expect a run so he called a play-action pass. He made it through all of his progressions until he looked for his fourth choice. Namath threw a tight spiral about three feet off the ground. Namath made sure that Maynard would catch it or nobody would. Maynard got it and the Jets retook the lead.

The Jets' defense stopped the Raiders. A key fourth-down sack gave the ball back to the Jets. Still, the Jets could not keep the ball so the Raiders got another opportunity. The game ended with Lamonica throwing a lateral to avoid a sack and Jets linebacker Ralph Baker scooping up the ball and ending the game.

After the game, Namath hurt all over. He prescribed "booze and broads" to cure his ills. "I drink for the same reason I keep company with girls," Namath once said. "It makes me feel good. It takes away the tension."[37]

The Jets would travel to Miami to play the Baltimore Colts in Super Bowl III. The media focused on one storyline, which centered on quarterback Joe Namath. The site of Super Bowl III, the Orange Bowl, brought Namath back to where he played one of his best college games. Four other Jets played in that same national championship game. Jim Hudson, George Sauer, John Elliot, and Pete Lammons played for victorious Texas against Namath's Alabama squad.

Just how did Joe Namath impact professional football? Here is one answer you won't hear everywhere.

"You see the way the guys dress here now?" asked guard Dave Herman to a reporter as they both looked at players in sports shirts and casual clothing. Some of them even wore Bermuda shorts. "Joe changed all that," said Herman. "Before Joe got here, everything was cut and dried. Chewing tobacco was a $100 fine. Sonny Werblin had team blazers made up. Matching coat and tie. Then Joe came along…. The first trip he made, he had no coat and tie. Everyone else did. Now you see Joe wearing a coat and tie and nobody else does. Well, Weeb took all that and he changed. He became more liberal. You know and I know that Weeb was ahead of his time. You look up and down this plane now and you don't have guys who can throw the football, but they're all as individualistic as Joe was in 1965."[38]

Chapter Fourteen

Beating Big Brother

Shadows had started to lengthen as the old master picked up a football and gave Colts fans a glimmer of hope. His team lagged behind the upstarts, but teammates had confidence that he could rally them to victory. After all, he had found himself in that position before and he snatched victory from defeat. In the 1958 championship—the game that put the NFL on the map—Unitas led his team on two climactic drives to extend the game into overtime and then ultimately to achieve victory.

Ten years past since that happened. Unitas had more miles on that talented right arm. He suffered through a long season with a painful elbow injury. He tore the ligaments in his right elbow during the last exhibition game that season, forcing him to sit most of the year. He threw only 38 passes all year. His replacement, Earl Morrall, had performed really well. Morrall led the team to a 13–1 record and earned league MVP and comeback player of the year honors. He had a Unitas-like season, throwing for nearly 3,000 yards and 26 touchdowns. The Colts raced through the playoffs defeating the tough Minnesota Vikings, 24–14, and then shutting out the powerful Cleveland Browns, 34–0, in the championship game. That game gave Baltimore some sweet revenge since the Browns handed the Colts their only defeat during the regular season.

Johnny Sample, who had played with the Colts early in his career, considered Unitas the best quarterback ever to play the game. Others held that same assessment. When Sample saw Unitas throw late in Super Bowl III, he could tell immediately that his arm still hurt. He knew Unitas could not throw the ball as he used to do, but he, like the Jets, knew Unitas's calm, cool smarts could inspire the Colts. Robert Liston interviewed Unitas and many other NFL players in the mid-sixties for his book, *The Pros*. During the course of conducting his research, he found that many professional players doubt their abilities at times. Liston said that was not the case with Unitas. He said in a critical situation with one play to win the game, Unitas had supreme confidence in the play call and, more importantly, knew his teammates did, too.[1]

The Colts entered Super Bowl III as a veteran squad with plenty of experience playing in big games. The Jets represented a league still in its first decade of play. The contest pitted old versus young and the media played up the contrast. Even the team nicknames seemed a study in contrast. The colt represented a rugged form of transportation from a bygone era of the old Wild West. Meanwhile, the jet appeared as modern machine with speed and agility. The Jets hailed from New York City led by "Broadway Joe" Namath with all his flash and sophistication. The Colts, led by two lunch-pail quarterbacks, John Unitas and his sub this season, Earl Morrall, represented Middle America. They looked as if they emerged from a 1950s warehouse with crew-cut hairstyles. "John is crew cut and quiet," wrote Tex Maule in *Sports Illustrated*. "And Joe had big hair and a big mouth, but haircuts obviously have nothing to do with efficiency of quarterbacks."[2] Joe Namath's brash confidence and outspoken style led him to say something all coaches don't want to hear coming from their players. His film study led him to conclude that his team could perform well against Baltimore. Everywhere he went people asked about the 18-point spread in the game that said his team had no chance. It made him mad. During the preparation week, the Miami Touchdown Club scheduled its award banquet. Namath was selected Player of the Year. The Jets insisted that Namath attend the dinner to receive his award since he was the first American Football League player to be honored by the group. When a heckler interrupted his acceptance speech, he could not hold back his thoughts any longer. "The Jets will win Sunday," he said. "I guarantee it."[3] The story was reported the next day in the local papers. Coach Ewbank was upset that his star quarterback had provided the ammunition to wake a sleeping giant. It was another sign that the younger generation felt free to comment while the older generation bit the lip.

Despite coming from two different leagues without any interleague play, the Jets and the Colts had a number of ties. More than a handful of Jets had previously played with the Colts prior to joining the AFL club. The former Colts coach, Weeb Ewbank, led the Jets but team also included players such as Johnny Sample, Billy Baird, Curley Johnson, Bake Turner and Mark Smolinski. Ewbank, familiar with the Colts players, recruited many of them to join him in New York. Sample was the Jet most motivated to play against the Colts and the NFL.

In 1970, Sample testified before a federal grand jury that the NFL blackballed him after the 1965 season with the Redskins. He said no team in the league would hire him because they claimed he spoke out against racial discrimination. Of course, he had a reputation for talking constantly on the field and off.

The two head coaches also had a history. Both had their professional start with Paul Brown's Cleveland Browns. Ewbank worked as an assistant coach while Don Shula played defensive back. In fact, Ewbank discovered Shula while on a 1951 scouting trip to John Carroll University and recommended Brown select Shula. Cleveland selected Shula in the ninth round of the draft. Later, Shula played for Ewbank with the Colts. Ewbank released Shula in 1957 when he believed Shula's playing career had ended. Shula played one last season with the Washington Redskins before retiring as a player.

Both teams had defensive assistants with roots in Cleveland. Walt Michaels of the Jets and Chuck Noll of the Colts had played for Paul Brown in Cleveland. Colts defensive coordinator Bill Arnsparger came from Miami University in Oxford, Ohio, the same school for which Ewbank played collegiate ball. There were other similarities. Both teams had strong, veteran defenses. Talented quarterbacks hailing from western Pennsylvania led their offenses. Both teams liked to run the ball, but had effective, dangerous passing games when the quarterback stepped back to throw.

The betting line going into the Super Bowl game pictured the Colts having little difficulty beating the Jets. The Jets were seen as inferior to the Raiders and the Chiefs, the teams that represented the AFL in the first two Super Bowls. Those teams fell to the mighty Green Bay Packers in games only close until halftime. The Jets just barely beat the Raiders in the AFL championship with a late rally while the Colts shut out the legendary Browns. Oddsmakers made the Jets 17 to 20 point underdogs, or as Curt Gowdy said during the NBC telecast, "more than the College All-Stars were against the Packers last August." That may have summed it up. A team comprised of AFL veterans appeared less likely to succeed than a bunch of college players just thrown together in a charity game against the Packers. The Colts opened as 17-point favorites, but by kickoff, the spread climbed to 19½ points.

Strange things started happening at the Orange Bowl. To many fans' surprise the Jets pulled ahead in the game. They had started slowly, but Colts errors helped propel them to an early lead. Then Namath got his offense in gear. His smart play calling mixed runs with passes to keep the drive moving. After a scoreless first quarter, Namath led the Jets on an 80-yard touchdown drive in 12 plays, burning more than five minutes off the clock. The Jets began to take over the game. Morrall, who had such a good regular season seemed to falter. Despite only throwing two interceptions in the previous five games, Morrall's passes lacked his earlier accuracy in the big game. Some of the Jets' three interceptions resulted from strange bounces and deflections, but nonetheless, they stopped drives. Frustrations built up along the Colts' sidelines.

At halftime, speculation grew about a Colts quarterback change if Unitas felt healthy enough to try it. When the teams came back on the field and Unitas starting throwing on the sidelines, speculation grew even stronger. Nearly everyone expected coach Don Shula to make a quarterback change. When the Colts took the field to start the third quarter, Morrall again took the field with the offense to the surprise of many. "We started

the second half saying, 'We've got to keep scoring, and let's hope they don't put Johnny Unitas in the game," Matt Snell remembered. "We didn't know how bad his arm or his shoulder was. And Morrall was having a horrible game."[4]

The Jets led, 13–0, when Unitas finally took the field. The Colts snapped out of the huddle and approached the line of scrimmage with a new vigor. It looked like the Colts believed Unitas had another comeback in him. On third down, Unitas dropped back to throw a down and out pattern to Jimmy Orr. A sideline throw like that one takes arm strength to get the ball to the receiver on target and with enough velocity to prevent an interception. Unitas's ball wobbled and fell incomplete and Baltimore sent the punting team on the field. Namath, who had to

Joe Namath barks out signals at the line of scrimmage during the Super Bowl game against the Colts in 1969. The Jets pulled off one of the biggest upsets in sports history with a 16–7 victory over the heavily favored NFL champions (Photofest).

leave the game briefly on the series before Unitas entered the game, came back in with a renewed vigor as well. He had dislocated his right thumb after his hand hit the helmet of Colts defensive tackle Fred Miller as he finished his follow-through. That pass fell incomplete in Maynard's direction. It occurred on the drive where the Jets took a 13–0 lead.

Namath continued his conservative play calling by running the ball to burn time off the clock. Namath's sprained right hand made it even more important to run the ball. He led the Jets on another drive. This drive stalled deep in Colts territory where Jim Turner kicked his third field goal to give the Jets a 16–0 lead. The Colts ended the third period without crossing into Jets territory; in fact, they did not achieve a first down in that period.

Unitas came back and led the Colts on the drive that most people had expected when they saw him take the field. He drove the team 80 yards culminating in fullback Jerry Hill's 1 yard run over left tackle. The Colts had gotten on the scoreboard and avoided a shutout. That came as small consolation for the fans who hoped for a lot more. The drive had generated a spark of hope, but the clock showed just 3:19 left to play. They needed two scores and it took more than 56 minutes to get on the board the first time.

Everybody in the stadium knew what to expect next. With so much ground to make up, the Colts attempted an onside kick and tight end Tom Mitchell recovered it. Unitas had another chance. "As long as Unitas is in there, this isn't over yet," Gowdy said on the NBC telecast. "Here, Curt, is where John Unitas is absolutely brilliant," Al DeRogatis, his broadcast partner, replied. "He has no peer when it comes to the two [minute drive]— and now exactly three minutes to go in the football game…. He's just brilliant."

Despite the buildup, it turned out too little too late for Unitas. He completed passes left and right, alternating between Willie Richardson and Jimmy Orr. He had the Colts on the move again. Unitas was "coming off the bench to try and save the Colts from one of sports' biggest upsets," Gowdy told the national television audience during the broadcast. The Colts drove deep into Jets territory before the drive stalled. On fourth-and-five on the Jets' 19 yard line, Unitas looked to Orr at the 3 yard line. Al Atkinson, taking a deep drop from his middle linebacker spot, saw it coming. He deflected the ball and the game had all but ended. The Jets needed only to burn the remaining time off the clock to clinch the championship. The Colts used their timeouts in hopes of landing one last chance. By the time they got the ball back, Unitas returned to the field down nine points with only eight seconds remaining. Two meaningless plays later, the game ended in an upset.

The defeat of the crew cut Colts by the upstart Jets signified a changing of the times in sports. The sixties saw many big changes. The decade started with the inauguration of John F. Kennedy as president signaling a generational change in the country. Civil rights struggles and war protests dominated the rest of the decade. Tom Brokaw called 1968 "the volcanic center of the Sixties."[5] Nineteen sixty-eight saw an increase in the debate over the Vietnam War. Protests sprang out on nearly every campus across the country. The debate raged in Washington, D.C. The incumbent president, Lyndon Johnson, decided to retire to Texas rather than running for another term. An army of underdogs raced to replace him in the White House. Then everything exploded. Fatal shots killed Martin Luther King, Jr., as he was standing on a balcony outside of his room at the Lorraine Motel in Memphis. Just two months later, Sirhan Sirhan shot Robert F. Kennedy at the Ambassador Hotel in Los Angeles. Kennedy had just talked of uniting the division that separated the country.

At the inauguration ceremony for President Nixon, former president Lyndon Johnson and President Nixon shake hands at the podium. President Johnson did not run for reelection in part due to the Vietnam War (White House Photographer Oliver Atkins. The Richard Nixon Presidential Library and Museum).

January 12, 1969, stood as the volcanic center of the professional football world. It signified a changing of eras. The high top, crew cut generation gave way to the younger generation, long hair and all. As America changed, professional football changed right along with it.

How could this happen? Strange things happen in our world and strange things happen in sports. At the beginning of the sixties, Richard Nixon served as vice president in an administration some said the country wanted to change. He lost the election to a fresh face representing a new generation. A couple years later, he lost another election, this time for governorship of California. Some thought his political career over, but by the end of the decade, Nixon had moved into the White House. In this decade, strange things happened in sports as well.

The Colts seemed unbeatable. They had only lost twice in the 30 games dating back to 1966. During 1967 and 1968 seasons, they won 26 games and tied two along with those two defeats. Their stout defense had set a new mark for fewest points allowed in a 14-game season with 144 points. That unit had shut out four of the last ten opponents including the Cleveland Browns. In those last 10 games, they had surrendered just seven touchdowns.

Don Shula assembled an all-star coaching staff. His assistants included Bill Arnsparger, who later created the fabled "53" defense that helped the Miami Dolphins dominate in the early seventies, and Chuck Noll, who led the Steelers to four Super Bowl victories later in that decade. With a victory in Super Bowl III, many folks stood ready to name the Colts one of the best teams of all time, if not the best. Shula himself went on to set the record of most wins as a coach by the end of his career.

As Coach Ewbank reviewed film of his old team, he boiled the game down to one simple point, which he stressed repeatedly during the week of preparation. He said they had to neutralize the Colts' pass rush so that Namath had time to read the defense and get the ball to the open receiver. His team needed to put pressure on their quarterback and force some turnovers. As he saw it, action held the key to the game. Ewbank's constant preaching of that one point all week long made an impact on defensive coach Buddy Ryan, future inventor of the Bears' 46 Defense in 1985. Ryan thought if protecting Joe proved that important in this big game, then pressuring the quarterback was the key to defensive football in every game played. Ryan made it the key point in his defensive philosophy.

For Super Bowl III, Ewbank did not prepare any differently from what he did for any game. He always started with pass protection when designing an offensive game plan. So said, Rex Ryan, son of Buddy and an NFL head coach himself. "The first thing Weeb would do to game plan was to talk about protections," Rex Ryan recalled. "He never cared about routes. He never cared about anything else. He wanted to make sure that the line protected Joe Namath. He also was influenced by Y.A. Tittle, who said regardless of how many people you put back into coverage, if he has enough time, he would be able to complete the ball. With that in mind, he went about his business and started attacking people. To this day, I am reminded of that as well."[6]

Bill Curry, who played with Bart Starr in Green Bay and John Unitas in Baltimore, was impressed with Namath when he saw him up close that afternoon in the Orange Bowl. The future head coach said he had not seen a quarterback set up quicker or get rid of the ball faster than Joe Namath. As he watched, he knew Namath's quick feet and release would prove hard to beat, even by a veteran team. The team with many veterans—seven starters had played pro football longer than the Jets franchise existed—went down in the most unlikely defeat. This caught the national media by surprise. In a poll of the media covering the game in Miami, 49 of 55 picked the Colts to win. Tex Maule, who covered the NFL for *Sports Illustrated*, picked Baltimore to win, 43–0. All but five of those who predicted a Colts victory figured on a double-digit victory.

Vince Lombardi, who coached the Packers to lopsided victories in the first two Super Bowl games, privately admitted the Jets had a chance. His primary reason for that admission: quarterback Joe Namath. Lombardi called him a superior quarterback. "I've never seen a quicker release," he said to nobody in particular. That came as high praise from the Hall of Fame coach. Lombardi had watched film of Namath while he prepared to play the Oakland Raiders in Super Bowl II and found his quick release and strong arm impressive. Throughout the sixties, Lombardi faced the top quarterbacks in the NFL. He assessed Namath as equal to the best in the established league. "His arm, his release of the ball," Lombardi repeatedly said, "are just perfect."

Sports Illustrated writer Tex Maule saw Tex Schramm, president of the Cowboys, before the game. Maule asked if he wished his team were representing the NFL in the big game. "I guess so," Schramm said after a short delay. "Certainly, you always want to be in the big game, but I think the AFL is going to win a Super Bowl before long and I had just as soon not be the team to lose."[7]

In the end, Unitas failed to pull off another of his famous last-minute drives to win Super Bowl III. When he first took the field, the Jets took notice. "I can envision Unitas coming in as if it were yesterday," said Dave Herman, who had the task of blocking Bubba Smith in the Super Bowl. "I saw him play when I was a kid, and when I saw him trot onto the field that day my heart stopped for about ten seconds. Here we go now, I thought. We all knew what he had done in the past. He had had so many, many outstanding games. But as soon as we saw there was little to no improvement in their offense, I kind of forgot about it and relaxed."[8]

John Unitas and Joe Namath presented an interesting contrast in quarterbacks. Namath wore white shoes when nearly everybody else wore black. Unitas's black high top shoes more resembled those on the feet of coaches than players. The clean-shaven Unitas wore a crew cut while Namath, famous for his facial hair, wore his hair long. In fact, Namath received $10,000 to shave his Fu Manchu in a live television commercial just a month before the Super Bowl. Unitas, married with a family, seemed quiet and reserved versus the vocal and outgoing Namath, one of the nation's most eligible bachelors.

Any true football fan could pick out Unitas's bow-legged gait with a quick glance at his shadow. Those same fans could easily pick out Namath's silhouette. Those bulky steel braces that made his uniform pants bulge at the knees left little doubt. He had the most famous knees in football. If the knee braces did not give it away, the stooped shoulders would. In fact, both Unitas and Namath shared their poor posture. Namath, however, had a backpedal all his own. He nearly turned around and ran back into a throwing position.

These two quarterbacks played central roles in the changing of the guard in the NFL and professional sports in general. In the fifties and early sixties stout, very physical defenses dominated professional football. The AFL brought more speed into the game and it opened up offenses with deep passes thrown downfield. Namath served as the ideal quarterback to lead the new game. His arm let him get the ball deep to speedy receivers creating the home run play that could break the game open and keep fans cheering.

In the end, this is why Super Bowl III has proven so significant in pro football history. It marked a changing in the eras between one in which

Edwin "Buzz" Aldrin salutes the flag of the United States on the lunar surface during the Apollo 11 mission to the moon. He was the second man to walk on the moon after Neil Armstrong. Both men were aboard Apollo 11 (NASA).

President Richard M. Nixon welcomes the Apollo 11 astronauts aboard the USS *Hornet*, after the historic Apollo 11 lunar landing mission. Already confined to the Mobile Quarantine Facility (MQF) are (left to right) Neil A. Armstrong, commander; Michael Collins, command module pilot; and Edwin E. Aldrin Jr., lunar module pilot (NASA).

physical power, disciplined play organized around a strong running game and stout defense dominated to one where the use of speed and athletic ability made the game much quicker and explosive. This game matched the physical, zone-oriented Colts against the more athletic and quicker Jets.

"When the 20th Century's top 10 sports events are ranked in order of their impact on America, it's easy enough to name the top three," wrote Bob Oates of the *Los Angeles Times*. "They are the U.S.–Soviet Union hockey game at the Lake Placid Olympics in 1980, the long-count Dempsey–Tunney fight in 1927, and Super Bowl III, the 1969 football game that created a new kind of national holiday."[9]

Just weeks after Apollo 12 proved Americans could go back to the moon, the AFL could do what some hardline NFL fans would not have thought possible: they proved it could repeat as Super Bowl champion. At the beginning of the decade, it appeared as if the Americans were behind the Soviets in the space race. By decade's end, the United States had landed astronauts on the moon. The U.S.S.R. successfully soft landed on the moon in 1976.

Chapter Fifteen

Keepers of the Flame

During the fifties in southern New Jersey, Ed Sabol went to work every day selling overcoats. He did not really like it, but he had a family to support. So, off to work he went. "In fact, I used to tell my wife all the time it was like going to the dentist every morning," Ed said.[1]

Friends lovingly called him "Big Ed." He loved films, football and family. Big Ed's fun started after the normal workday ended. He loved watching director John Ford's movies and Fred Astaire and Gene Kelly musicals. When not at the movies, he spent time with his family. His family consisted of his wife, Audrey, son Steve and daughter Blair. Big Ed attended all the kids' events. He watched his son, Steve, play football. When he did, he brought the Bell & Howell film camera he received as a wedding present in 1940 and recorded the action. Afterward, he supplemented the video with the tunes of John Philip Sousa or Woody Herman. Steve's teammates frequently came over to the house and watched their exploits while munching on cookies and apple cider.

As much as he disliked selling coats, he loved making films of his son's football action. Big Ed dreamed about finding a way he could do this for a living. His dreams found him wondering how he could combine his love of football and movies while still supporting and making time for his family. Could he really find a way where he could blend these things into one profitable business? Was it possible?

Ed Sabol loved movies and the theater his whole life. He went to the Ohio State University on a swimming scholarship after an undefeated swimming career at Blair Academy in Blairstown, New Jersey. He claimed three interscholastic swimming records; one of which he took from Johnny Weissmuller. Of course, Weissmuller won five Olympic gold medals in swimming and played Tarzan in the movies. Being Jewish, Sabol had no interest in competing in Nazi Germany. He may not have swum in the Olympic Games, but he found theater.

At Ohio State, the acting bug bit Sabol. He left Ohio and headed to Broadway, where he landed a part in a play co-produced by Oscar Hammerstein called *Where Do We Go from Here?* When Sabol looked back, he said Hammerstein produced some great musicals but this one closed after two weeks. Sabol also performed on and off Broadway with vaudeville acts such as the Ritz Brothers.

Ed Sabol had a full life. His biography has a Forrest Gump sound to it. He did it all from Olympic-caliber swimming to Broadway plays to encounters with some of the most famous people in the world. Sabol served as a rifleman under General George S. Patton in World War II, landing on Utah Beach and fighting the Battle of the Bulge in the Hurtgen Forest.

Ed Sabol wanted more out of life than selling overcoats. Fortunately, his father-in-law sold the apparel business and the Sabols got some money. Ed made a sort of bucket list and one of the items was to travel to the Orient. Off went Ed and Audrey to Japan. Cross that off the list. Another item called for him to learn to fly a plane. He crossed that one off the list, too. On a trip to Bahamas, he flew his plane with one hand and worked the Bell & Howell camera with the other. This resulted in a film he sold to the Bahamas Development Board as a way to attract tourists to the islands. Returning home, he observed the building of a Howard Johnson motel and filmed the construction. Using time-lapse technology, his movie showed the motel springing to life in living color. He sold that film, too.

Then Big Ed saw an announcement in the paper stating the NFL had put the film rights for the 1962 championship game up for bid. He recognized this as his big opportunity and he knew he had to bid. He found out the previous winning bid of $2,500 and decided he would double it to $5,000. In 1962, Big Ed formed his own little film company. He named it Blair Motion Pictures after his daughter. He did not have any experience other than filming his son's games, but he had confidence.

As Ed watched previous football highlight films, he told himself he could do better. Rather than shooting in black and white, he used color. They played marching band music; he would use music with a wider appeal. They used corny language to describe the play like, "Milt Plum pegged a peach of a pass to become the apple of Coach George Wilson's eye." His scripts would enhance the visual images without distracting. At times, the words would slow down or disappear so they did not distract from the action. Finally, but most important, Sabol looked to the film itself. Sabol believed he could make the images better. The previous producer, TelRa Productions, used one single high camera in the stands. Sabol envisioned more cameras at non-standard locations to get richer video.

He bid on the project and came in with the highest bid. Unfortunately, commissioner Pete Rozelle had not heard of Blair Motion Pictures and appeared reluctant to award the project to an unknown. Sabol arranged a meeting with the commissioner. He had sold the Bahamas and Howard Johnson films, but his only experience filming football consisted of his teenage son's games. Sabol put his selling skills into use. Using all the tools he knew from those years selling overcoats, he sold the commissioner on Blair Motion Pictures during a three-martini lunch in Manhattan. He convinced Rozelle that his brand-new company could do the job. Ed called his son, an art major and fullback on the football team at Colorado College, and told him about the job. "He said he could see by my grades that all I'd been doing for the last four years at Colorado is playing football and going to the movies," said Steve Sabol. "So he said, 'I think that makes you uniquely qualified for this job.'"[2]

Game day presented additional trouble for the film crew. The crew from Blair Motor Pictures arrived at Yankee Stadium with eight men in their twenties with cameras in their hands ready to film a game. In contrast, today NFL Films takes more than one hundred people to Super Bowls today.

The young film crew arrived excited about this new adventure. As they stepped outside, their excitement turned to fear. In one of the coldest days ever for a NFL title game, temperatures dropped into the low teens with a brisk 40 mile per hour wind blowing. In such low temperatures, the film broke, the cameras stopped working and the cinematographers got frostbite. The film crew started bonfires in the baseball dugouts so the cameras and the photographers could thaw out. Steve said his dad became so nervous that he spent most of the day in the men's room with diarrhea. Even the walkie-talkies they brought to keep the photographers all linked together did not work right. Instead of hearing each other, they heard cab companies and workers at construction sites.

As Sabol saw it, the 1962 championship game had a classic storyline with big city New York facing off against the league's smallest city, Green Bay. Sabol got into his Cessna airplane and filmed some shots of the New York skyline. He traveled to Green Bay to take film of the small Wisconsin town with paper and food operations. These shots framed the story and opened the film. The game had some good storylines. Native New Yorker Vince Lombardi came home to Yankee Stadium to lead his Packers against the team that gave him his professional start. He served as the Giants' offensive coordinator prior to getting the Packers job.

The players in the 1962 championship felt the pain of the poor playing conditions firsthand. After the game, Giants quarterback Y. A. Tittle sat tired and dejected in front of his locker. Still wearing the long underwear from the game, he seemed to be waiting for the feeling to return to his extremities. Tittle just starred at the floor as he thought through the struggles of the day.

"The wind was impossible," Tittle told the reporters gathered around his locker. "You wouldn't believe what it did to that football. One time it would sail way past my receiver; the next time it would dip and flutter."[3] Ed Sabol agreed with the player's assessment. He, too, would have preferred better weather conditions. He finally had a chance to achieve his dream and he confronted terrible conditions. Those weather conditions caused endless problems. He felt certain he had a disaster on his hands. The film crew had dumped the frozen film into a tangled mess inside a laundry basket. Sabol looked down and saw a laundry basket full of frozen spaghetti.

That reaction proved only temporary. Steve Sabol said his father refused to quit or let the poor weather conditions demoralize him. After a lifetime spanning Broadway shows and Olympic-caliber swimming, he was not going to quit that easily. He had to be tough to serve in General Patton's army during World War II. About the same time the Sabols and crew filmed the title game, Darryl Zanuck came out with a movie about D-Day called *The Longest Day*. As he endured the frigid conditions, Big Ed saw that day as the longest day of football that he had ever experienced. Instead of calling the film *The 1962 Championship Game*, Sabol called it *Pro Football's Longest Day*. That started a tradition where NFL Films presented sports with a movie twist.

The film premiered at Toots Shor's restaurant on West Fifty-First Street in Manhattan. The location made a great choice since many of the media considered it one of their favorite watering holes. Numerous celebrities and athletes also came to the bar often. The New York media gathered in the bar ready to watch the film. Some Giants players even showed up in anticipation. With the projector ready, the lights went out and the film started playing. About 10 minutes into the show, a loud crash echoed through the room and the film immediately stopped. A waiter had crashed into the projector, knocking it onto the floor. A tray of hors d'oeuvres went flying. Someone turned the lights on so that Ed and Steve Sabol could get everything set up again.

"Rozelle never skips a beat," said Steve Sabol, continuing the story. "He brings up Frank Gifford, Del Shofner and Alex Webster and he's holding a press conference about their thoughts on the game they are about to see in film while we're cleaning up the mess and getting the film out of the crab legs. By the time the film was ready again, we have a fascinated audience. Only Pete could have done that. It could have been a disaster."[4]

By the end of the film, Sabol knew he had a big hit. Commissioner Rozelle loved it. He could not stop talking about the film. Rozelle wanted to create a mystique for the game and he left thinking the film left exactly the image he wanted. Big Ed took the film on the road with Giants receiver Del Shofner. They visited American Legions, Kiwanis Clubs and other community centers where they showed the film. Sabol told tales of making the movie and Shofner would answer questions about the game and sign autographs. Despite the game's poor weather conditions, the film was a success and Rozelle liked their work. Ed Sabol bid on the next two title games, doubling his bid every year.

The 1963 rights cost $10,000 and doubled to $20,000 in 1964. Ed Sabol could see that the prices were climbing too high too fast. He proposed that the league buy Blair Motion Pictures and take it in house. Rozelle liked the idea because he wanted control over the league's image. Ed even had the new name already picked out: NFL Films. The commissioner urged the owners to agree with the concept. The owners ponied up $20,000 each for a total investment of $280,000. That purchase got each team an annual highlight film and the league one of the championship game.

The purchase did not thrill all the owners. The Colts' penny-pinching Carroll Rosenbloom reportedly pulled Sabol aside after the purchase and told him to never come back and ask for another penny. Sabol and crew never did. At first, George Halas picked away at the films, finding fault with nearly everything. He did not like the montage editing. The 1965 Bears highlight film showed quarterback Rudy Bukich throwing a ball in Wrigley Field then cut to the Los Angeles Coliseum where Mike Ditka caught it. Halas wanted to know how they pulled that off. Halas, nearly as frugal as Rosenbloom, looked for reasons he could use to convince others the investment was not the right call.

Sabol recalled another incident with Halas, who grew infuriated when he saw a 1967 NFL Films clip that showed a gun-toting Bears fan in the stands. "[Halas] insisted, 'Those are not Bears fans! We don't have people like that coming to our games.'" Sabol said he remedied it by selecting some closeups of Washington fans and splicing those into the Bears films.[5]

All that happened in the days before NFL Properties saturated the audience with team shirts and jerseys. NFL Films could not pull that off these days. Outside-the-box thinking helped them succeed in those early days. Some owners were not early fans but eventually they came around. George Halas wrote the Sabols an emotional letter saying because of NFL Films, "the history of football would forever be preserved on film and not by the written word a la baseball."[6]

The Sabols had to convince another key stakeholder, Vince Lombardi. After Lombardi saw Steve Sabol's first highlight film for the Packers, he called Ed Sabol to complain about the arty close-ups. He wanted to know who was responsible for the film. "My son," Ed Sabol told him. "How old is your son? Seven?" asked Lombardi. Steve was 23 at the time. Over time, Lombardi also turned into a believer in NFL Films.

"The biggest champion among owners who often come to Big Ed's defense was Art Modell," said David Plaut, NFL Films senior producer and a 35-year veteran of the company. "He also was steeped in show business. He had that background. He often had to beat back the cries of dissent from some of the more traditional owners and say, 'Look, you really don't understand what they guys are doing. They're helping us sell the game.'"[7]

Even though that first experience was not the best, Sabol knew what he needed to do and he had a vision. He wanted to present football as a Hollywood movie director might tell a story in a film. The Sabols saw their task as combining the four main elements—photography, music, sound and voice into one cohesive vehicle. The combined package would entertain viewers like no sports film had ever done before.

"His whole theory was to show football the way Hollywood portrayed fiction," said Steve. "My feeling was to show the game the way I had experienced it as a player, with the snot flying and the sweat spraying and the eyes bulging. We merged those two viewpoints and that's how the style of NFL Films emerged."[8]

The Sabols's vision of NFL Films seemed obvious after a few minutes of watching. The tight shots of a spiraling football spinning for 20 or 30 yards downfield through the air, the sweat dripping from a beard and the vapor escaping from a huddled mass of men shivering on a bitterly cold day truly displayed the game. Later, they wired players and coaches for sound to give viewers the feel of playing in the game. They kept the scripts tight and used baritones for added emphasis in the video, but never took away from the action shots.

The Sabols went to the extreme with every aspect of their films. Just as Lombardi strove for perfection in his team's performance, the Sabols drove for quality in their production. Their passion drove them to do everything possible to improve the product. They used film, rather than videotape, to preserve the best visual images possible. Ed Sabol believed video would not produce as crisp an image and he insisted on the highest quality photography possible. When they filmed a project, Ed Sabol told his cinematographers to let the film run like water. He did not want the cameras to miss anything.

They hired an entire orchestra to produce original music for the films. They were the first to put microphones on players and coaches to capture sound of the game. They heard the voice they had waited to hear. They wanted just the right talent to voice their scripts. Most sports films of the day used sportscasters. John Facenda, a Philadelphia news anchor, became the voice of NFL Films until his death in 1984. "I felt that in order to make our films memorable and different, the script was going to be decreased, which meant that the voice that was used to read the script would be even more important," Steve Sabol said.[9]

NFL Films put all the component parts together with the documentary titled *They Call It Pro Football*. Commissioner Pete Rozelle watched the film and said, "For the NFL to prosper, it has to succeed on television and, in order for the NFL to succeed on television, it needs a mystique. It needs a certain style. It needs an image. And the film that I just saw will help us create that image." The film stood as the first to put all the elements Sabol wanted into one film.

The film opened with the statement "It starts with a whistle and ends with a gun." All the elements that made NFL Films a hit went into that film. The Sabols matched great shots with thrilling music and the thunderous voice of John Facenda. In reality, that film served as a primer for the novice football fan. It talked about everything we like about the game with minutes dedicated to the linemen, the quarterbacks and all the positions. Although produced in 1966, it did not show on television until 1969. Even then, you only saw it if you got up early. It aired early in the morning on one of those time slots common for infomercials today.

"It was the first montage editing," Sabol said as he began to tick off all the innovations he and his dad put into the film. "It was the first use of theatrical music. It was the first time anyone wired a coach for sound in a game. It was the first time that cameras shot ground level slow motion. It was the first time a camera stayed on the quarterback after he released the ball. It was the first time a reverse angle was ever used. Prior to that, all cameras were always put on the same side of the field."[10]

The Sabols recruited Yoshio Kishi, a Japanese film editor, to add a unique style to the presentation of the game action. The editing in the film was critical, Steve Sabol explained. Previously, highlight tapes showed entire plays from the snap of the ball to the completion of the play. The Sabols believed they did not need to show the entire play; instead, they could show the very best of countless different plays. For example, a show on a talented running back might show clips from a half dozen runs during a half-minute segment. This was the element called montage editing.

Academy Award–winning director Ron Howard said in an interview with the *New York Times* in 2000 that NFL Films changed the way movies were made. "Lots of different images," he said. "Images on images. Using the slow-motion, combined with the live action. The hard-hitting sound effects, juxtaposed against incredible music, powerful music, creating a really emotional experience for the viewer."[11] Steve Sabol recalled director Sam Peckinpah telling him that he got the idea for the classic slow-motion gunfight scene in the 1969 movie *The Wild Bunch* after watching a NFL Films Super Bowl highlights film.[12]

Most folks rightfully believe NFL Films played a major role in increasing the popularity of football. In 1960, pro football sat as the third favorite sport, at best. Baseball still claimed the top spot as America's favorite pastime. College football, with a huge following across the nation, came next. Professional football had not clicked yet, but NFL Films pushed it along the path to popularity.

The film gave newcomers to the game and opportunity to learn something. If you knew it already, you have to see the game from perspectives not seen before. Slow motion, color, extreme close-up views; all stood as part of the film's appeal. Real sound from the game, great music and stirring narration added to the tremendous images to form a wonderful documentary film. NFL Films earned more than one hundred Emmys while under the Sabols' direction. According to the NFL Films website, Steve Sabol held direct responsibility for more than 40 of those. He received the Lifetime Achievement Award in 2003. NFL Films has preserved the visual history of professional football. *Sports Illustrated* called the enterprise "perhaps the most effective propaganda organ in the history of corporate America."[13] Art Modell said NFL Films sold the "beauty of the game."[14]

The innovative techniques NFL Films deployed are commonplace today. Today, we are used to seeing very long or very wide shots of the action. Wireless microphones take the fans right on to the field to hear the players and coaches. Broadcast television producers copied the use of actual sound in telecasts. They also shot action in super slow motion and played orchestra music to add extra drama. The Sabols presented football on film as Hollywood would show a motion picture.

Those concepts made NFL Films what it is today. In addition, it contributes to making the NFL what it is today—the most popular sport in the land. Pete Rozelle foresaw the day when professional football at the top of American sport. Television and NFL Films, in particular, propelled professional football along that journey. They provided the NFL with a mythology that sparked interest and helped the sport grow.

NFL Films worked due to the collaborative genius of the father-and-son combination of Ed and Steve Sabol. Ed, the founder, entrepreneur and visionary, launched the company. Steve used an artist's eye and mind to determine how best to show the game of football. Ed imagined football as a story with plots and subplots, much like a dramatic movie.

Steve had the innovation and creative talents to transform his dad's vision into the distinctive look that NFL Films made famous.

NFL Films developed a strategy for covering a regular-season game with three cameras. Sabol has a name for each role the cinematographers play: the tree, the mole and the weasel. "A tree is the top camera," said Sabol. "He's on a tripod rooted into a position on the 50 yard line in the press box and he doesn't move. A mole is a handheld, mobile, ground camera operator, with a 12 to 240 mm lens and he moves all around the field and gives you the eyeball-to-eyeball perspective. A weasel is the cameraman who pops up in unexpected places, to get you the telling storytelling shot the bench, the crowd, and all the details."[15]

Steve Sabol worked as the weasel when he started shooting for NFL Films. That role left with him with unique memories of football games. "I filmed the first fifteen Super Bowls and never saw a play," he said. "But I could tell you what kind of hat Tom Landry was wearing, how Vince Lombardi was standing in the fourth quarter, if Bob Lilly has a cut on the bridge of his nose. Those were the things that I remember in the Super Bowl."[16]

Ed Sabol summed his life philosophy to son Steve this way: "Tell me a fact and I'll learn. Tell me the truth and I will believe. But tell me a story and it'll live in my heart forever."[17] Steve Sabol listened; he was a masterful storyteller.

"Alfred Hitchcock once said, 'drama is really life with the dull parts cut out,'" continued Steve Sabol. "When you look at what we were doing is taking a game that requires three hours to play but only has 12 minutes of action. We take that 12 minutes, condense it, focus it, distill it, add music to it and sound effects, and edit it. What we do should be more exciting…. What we do is embellish the game and draw out the story lines, which in certain ways can be just as emotional to some people as the outcome itself."[18]

Ground level cameras brought a unique perspective that television viewers normally did not see. The dramatic soundtrack and stirring narration made the dramatic images come alive. By mid-decade, NFL Films documentaries would provide viewpoints not seen elsewhere. The networks soon copied those techniques.

"Storytelling is basically done through the editing," said Steve Sabol. "It's the cameraman's job to come back with as much material storytelling shots, action shots as he possibly can." At that point, editing becomes "so critical, and it's one of the most overlooked art forms or disciplines in filmmaking. Most people don't understand editing; they understand writing, they understand music, they understand cinematography. But when it comes to editing film and the selection and order of shots, that's the key to storytelling."[19]

Early on, NFL Films played at team events or at various local organizations such as the VFW or Kiwanis. Then television took over and ordered a highlight package that aired on the Saturday prior to all the Sunday games. That happened in the days before the all-sports cable networks came on the air and before the Internet. These highlight packages gave fans the only chance to see the top plays from the previous weekend. NFL Films highlight reels offered something new, fresh, and immediately popular and quickly became a frequent choice in sports programming.

The Sabols created that popularity with the use of slow motion photography with tight close-ups of players and views not often seen by football fans in the past. He brought out the majesty of the visual with the use of the deep baritone voice of John Facenda and the orchestral music composed specifically for NFL Films by Sam Spence. Facenda read the script Steve prepared. After reading just a short while, he stopped reading. Facenda came from the news business where the scripts used full sentences. He quickly learned the NFL Films script did not always use complete sentences.

Words needed to supplement the images on film without taking anything away. Facenda's deep voice produced words that resonated with power and passion. Meanwhile, Spence's music relayed urgency and danger. Actual game sounds made it more authentic. We could hear the voices of coaches and the grunts of players.

The earliest sports highlight films used military-style march music to accompany the film. Steve Sabol said they wanted to improve on that concept. They found Sam Spence and came up with their own unique sound. Years later, they released a collection of that music on compact disc, featuring such hits as "Sunday with Soul" and "Head Cracker Suite."

After they hired Spence and had the music composer settled, they began to look for the rest of the components. Ed and Steve Sabol liked to hire former football players. They felt former players really understood the game and could anticipate the action on the field, putting them in a good position to record the events. A prime example, Phil Tuckett, had played with the San Diego Chargers and first met Ed Sabol while in training camp attempting to make it to another season. Tackett knew as a marginal player he had to fight hard every year to get one of the last spots on the roster. He did not make much money playing football and supplemented his income by painting houses, working construction, teaching school as a substitute and writing for a small San Diego newspaper.

During the summer of 1969, Ed Sabol first discussed opportunities with Tuckett at training camp. Sabol visit the camp while putting together a feature on what happens on NFL sidelines during games. Tuckett approached him at lunch, told him he could write and showed him a clipping of an athlete's diary he had written for *Sport* magazine. Sabol said he had a job for Tuckett once his playing career ended.

"I certainly didn't have any background in filmmaking or photography at that time," said Tuckett. "I had a B.A. in English [from Weber State University in Ogden, Utah]. As far as I knew, I would write scripts and that would be it. Then when I got here, Ed Sabol said, 'Listen we didn't hire you just as a writer. We want you to edit, and shoot a camera someday.' In other words, I'd do the same work as everyone else there."[20]

The Chargers cut Tuckett from the team that summer. When he got the news, he said, he called Ed Sabol and accepted. Tuckett had a long and very successful career at NFL Films. He started as a camera operator but before he left 38 years later, he added writer, director and producer to his resume. He personally won 14 Emmys and played a major role in winning 30 more for his projects there. His project included such films as *Lost Treasures*, *America's Game* and *Autumn Ritual*.

If you polled a group of fans of professional football, you would find that every one of them has a favorite NFL Films moment. One often cited comes from the Super Bowl IV highlight film. The game featured the Kansas City Chiefs against the Minnesota Vikings. The AFL Jets had won the previous Super Bowl when, as some NFL fans put it, the Colts failed to take advantage of their opportunities. The Chiefs wanted to prove it was not a fluke and that the AFL could do it again.

The Chiefs came to the game led by a short, dapper man named Hank Stram. Folks knew Hank for two things, not necessarily in this order: (1) his inventive, imaginative offense and (2) his style of clothing. You could easily find him on the sideline on Sunday. He always dressed to the nines. He wore shirt and tie but loved to top it off with a Kansas City Chiefs red vest and dark blazer.

It did not take long to see why the Sabols chose to put a microphone on Stram over Vikings coach Bud Grant. One quick glance revealed big differences between the quiet Grant and the extremely outgoing Stram, who strutted up and down the sideline like a peacock. That day he wore a black blazer, black tie, red vest and matching silk handkerchief. He never stopped talking during his strolls up and down the sideline. Conversely, some people called Coach Grant "The Great Stone Face" behind his back.

NFL Films' microphone caught Stram's running monologue. It provided pure entertainment. "Way to go, boys!" Stram cheered on his players. "Just keep matriculatin' the ball right down the field!" followed immediately by "Just keep negotiating that ball down the field." At one point, when Vikings defenders appeared confused by the Chiefs' offense, Stram offered, "Look at 'em, boys. They're running around out there like it's a Chinese fire drill!"

Then came probably the most famous play in Super Bowl history. Along the sideline, Stram send Gloster Richardson in with the call. "Sixty-five toss power trap." Then Stram turned to the players on the sideline. "We're going to call sixty-five toss power trap," he said. "Watch this now, boys! Watch this now! This thing just might bust wide open." As the play unfolds, Dawson hands the ball to Mike Garrett, who runs through a huge hole in the line and into the end zone. The Chiefs had a 16–0 lead and Stram had time to brag. "How about that, boys? Huh? How about that?"

The rest is history, as the cliché says. That play call became part of the NFL lore that NFL Films built. The company used techniques that had not been used before in sports programming. They also translated to movies shown in theaters. They became an important part of the media explosion that began in the sixties.

Chapter Sixteen

Instant Replay

In 1960, ABC shocked the television world with its high bid for the coveted college football package. At the time, ABC struggled as the distant third-place network. As a result, they attracted mavericks and people with little fear of risk. One of those hires had significance unknown at the time. The network hired Roone Arledge to produce college football games and that move changed the way we watched sports on television. He had innovative ideas that brought the pageantry of college football into living rooms across the country. Like NFL Films, Arledge wanted to entertain, feeling he might attract casual viewers in addition to the devoted fans. Arledge pioneered the use of the hand-held camera to get shots that viewers at home had not seen before. They could pick up fans in the stands, cheerleaders on the sidelines and screaming coaches running onto the field.

A $3 million bid by ABC in its pursuit to take over television production of NCAA college football in 1960 shocked the television world. The bid surprised folks because that network had "a financially disastrous one-year stint" with college football in 1954 and never seemed to have funding to compete for top programming. Sports served as the stepping-stone ABC needed to increase its viewership as a network. Winning the bid stood as a clear victory for the struggling network.[1]

ABC, however, needed some things to fall into place in order to win the contract. It got some good financial backing when NBC cancelled its long-standing and popular *Friday Night Fights* sponsored by the Gillette Safety Razor Company. Gillette had increased their market share in shaving products from 16 percent in the 1930s to more than 60 percent after sponsoring sporting events on radio and television. A big believer in advertising, Gillette attributed a large part of their expanding market share to their advertising on sports programming. They began to look for another place to spend their large advertising budget.

The *Gillette Cavalcade of Sports*, the company's biggest program on NBC, featured various sports including baseball, football and boxing. Their most popular show aired boxing bouts on Friday nights. The program had immense popularity with Gillette's target audience. Nevertheless, by 1959, ratings began to slip and NBC wanted to replace the programming. Gillette, which credited sports programming for their growth in market share, feared the loss of the linchpin of their advertising programming. Therefore, Gillette approached ABC. They offered ABC $8 million in advertising if ABC let them sponsor their existing Wednesday night boxing series.

Eight million dollars?

For the struggling network, that amount of money equated to winning the lottery. It exceeded what ABC had bid on sports in all its years of existence combined. That capital provided the funding ABC needed to compete for top of the line programming. With Gillette's budget commitment, ABC could bid on NCAA football (then on NBC) and the baseball game of the week (then on CBS). Winning such programming would provide a terrific boost to a last place network.

Wanting NCAA football and winning those rights seemed like another thing all together. ABC kept the Gillette deal secret to sneak up on the other networks. NBC had held the NCAA football rights since 1952. Edgar Scherick and Tom Moore handled the bidding for ABC. They figured that CBS would not bid since they had just won the NFL rights. Meanwhile, Tom Gallery represented NBC. Scherick's knowledge of the industry and his competitors paid off.

"Scherick's instincts told him that Gallery would have two, maybe three, sealed envelopes in his pocket," Bert Sugar wrote in his book about ABC Sports. "If there was no one present from the other two networks, he would drop the envelope with the low bid on the table, probably containing no more than the standard 10 percent increment over the previous $5 million bid. However, if his antennae were stimulated or he spotted a recognizable member of the alien forces, he would hand over another envelope containing a larger bid."[2]

The key, they figured, would be to send someone unknown to the other network officials to the bidding process. They selected Stan Frankel, the assistant controller for ABC. They described Tom Gallery so Frankel could watch him and take his action based on what Gallery did. At bidding time, Gallery looked around and seeing no one he recognized, put a sealed envelope on the table. After that envelope hit the table, Frankel walked to the front of the room and put in his bid.

The action shocked the NCAA representatives. It must have surprised Tom Gallery, too. ABC won the bid to telecast NCAA football games. The perennial last-place network won perhaps the most significant programming deal of the day, next to professional baseball. That deal put ABC on the path to sports broadcasting prominence.

When Lamar Hunt created a new football league in 1960, it needed to find a television partner. Harry Wisner, an announcer who had done Notre Dame football games and had directed sports for the ABC Radio Network, worked with Lamar Hunt in an attempt to locate a network to cover the games in the new league. They met with NBC and CBS without success. They met several times and the estimates are that the first-year rights to the AFL went for an estimated $400,000.

Roone Arledge got his broadcasting start when the fading DuMont Television Network hired him after graduating in 1952 from Columbia University. Before long, the Army drafted him and by the time he left the service in 1955, DuMont had folded and Arledge went looking for a landing spot. He earned his first producer credit for a NBC children's puppet show called *Hi Mom* with Shari Lewis. That show earned him his first Emmy in 1959. *For Men Only*, loosely based on *Playboy* magazine, came next. A pilot was filmed but was not picked up for production.

The rejected pilot caught the eye of Edgar Scherick, then the head of a company called Sports Programs Inc., which functioned as the sports programming arm of ABC. Scherick needed someone to help produce the package of college football games he had just acquired for ABC. The idea intrigued Arledge, but leaving NBC presented a huge risk. NBC was an accomplished network and the offer came from a place mockingly nick-named "Almost Broadcasting Company."

Two technological changes made Arledge's timing perfect. Ampex Corporation introduced videotape in 1956 opening possibilities for instant replay and slow motion. In the late forties, Dr. Frank G. Back invented the revolutionary Zoomar lens, which allowed zooming in for a close-up and zooming out for a long shot without losing focus. It became widely used over the fifties. The second major event helping sports broadcasters came in 1962 when Telstar went live. Communication satellites gave them flexibility to air distant events, which blurred the lines between local and national. Prior to the sixties, sports viewers saw little more than local contests.

Most media historians credit Arledge with many of the technologies we take for granted today in television sports programming such as instant replay, slow motion, and advanced graphics. The technology changes gave him the opportunity to personalize the view of sports American see. He brought us the "Hi, Mom" shots from the sideline as well as the feature stories of the competitors that enable viewers to know them as people as well as athletes. Viewers got to know Olympic competitors due to the snapshots ABC showed during the broadcast.

Arledge set out to "utilize every production technique.... To heighten the viewer's feeling of actually sitting in the stands and participating personally in the excitement and color" of the game. "We will have cameras mounted in jeeps, on mike booms, in risers or helicopters, or anything necessary to get the complete story of the game. We will use creepy peepy camera to get the impact shots that we cannot get from a fixed camera."[3] Arledge wanted to get that close-up of the coach after a player made a critical error, along with a close-up reaction shot of the player. He wanted viewers to see the strain on the referee's face when making a controversial call as well as the spectator in the stands feeling the pain or exhilaration of his team in action.

Networks had room for improvement in the way they broadcast football on televi-sion. Most broadcasters placed camera high in the stadium and worked hard to catch all the action from that vantage point. Without ground or end-zone cameras, they shot the game from a very wide angle on a single camera at the 50 yard line. Without the high definition television we all love today, the players looked like little tiny objects with num-bers on their back.

"Television and pro football, which grew up together, were about to make each other's fortunes," wrote Phil Patton in *Razzle Dazzle*. "In a little more than a quarter cen-tury, television turned a barely respectable blue-collar game into a major form of enter-tainment. Watching professional football on television gained a unique status; it became the thing that more Americans did as a group than any other. Football helped television realize its mass dramatic appeal. Never did medium and message operate more closely together."[4]

During the summer after ABC's first season of college football, Arledge continued thinking of ways to improve the product. While in Tokyo to acquire the rights to the Japanese All-Star baseball game, he attended a movie. He witnessed a slow motion scene that made him think, "What if we could do the same with football?" It served to open Arledge's imagination to numerous possibilities. "We could view the whole game differ-ently," he concluded.[5]

Upon his return, he met with ABC engineer Bob Trachinger. He told him of his idea. The engineer had given the idea some thought on his own. He told Arledge he had an idea how to do it. In short, he planned to replay taped action on an orthicon camera tube and tape it again with another camera running at half speed. During halftime of the Texas–Texas A&M football game on Thanksgiving Day 1961, slow motion made its debut. Arledge planned to show the scoring plays at halftime. Arledge had not counted on the lack of explosive plays during the game. The sluggish first half had only score, coming on a field goal. Arledge went with the plan and showed the field goal in slow motion. The audience saw something never seen before.

The following week Arledge had more to work with. In a game against Syracuse, Boston College quarterback Jack Concannon broke loose for a 70-yard run. During the halftime break, analyst Paul Christman, a former quarterback, described every move as viewers saw Concannon again weaving down the field at half speed. Announcers reminded viewers that Concannon had not broken away again. They just showed the play from the first half over again using new technology.

Two years later, CBS director Tony Verna refined the process and improved it. ABC had shown the replays during the halftime break, not immediately following the live action. Verna showed action from the delayed Army–Navy game in slow motion immediately after it had occurred live, as we are accustomed to seeing today.

"The techniques we'd introduced had jacked up ratings—and the bid price on the next NCAA contract," said Roone Arledge. "[ABC president] Leonard Goldenson judged the new figure too rich for ABC and CBS took over" the college football contract.[6] In Arledge's view, CBS did not just pick up the contract, but they adopted many of the techniques ABC introduced.

Tony Verna had experimented with technology to bring instant replay to television. Although TV had video recorders in the early sixties, they used the technology primarily to tape delay broadcast programs to the West Coast. The large, non-portable machines forced sports producers to limit highlights to halftime when they could show them from the studio where the large video recorders stayed.

Ironically, President Kennedy's assassination and the media coverage immediately after prompted the changes Verna made. NBC broadcast live transmission of Jack Ruby shooting accused assailant Lee Harvey Oswald as officials moved him from the jail in Dallas. Two television cameras from NBC's WBAP-TV captured the action live, but CBS's KRLD-TV recorded it. This led the networks to an attempt to immediately play back a significant event that had aired live. The shooting occurred at 11:21 a.m. Central time and the first replay came on NBC at 11:30. They considered the delay of just nine minutes quick.

The tapes of the Oswald shooting served as an extra incentive to climb over the many obstacles preventing airing replays at sporting events. The video recorders of the day, about the size of big deep freezers, weighed 1,200 pounds. In addition to the weight and bulk, they proved difficult to move because they operated with vacuum tubes, which broke easily when jostled. Verna, however, wanted to show replays right after the live action happened. He wanted to do it as part of the broadcast. To reach the goal, Verna had to get one of those large machines out of the main control room in New York City and drive it 90 miles south to Philadelphia for the Army–Navy game.

"Those days," he said, "CBS kept its fourteen Ampex VTR-1000s housed on the seventh floor in the main terminal building of New York's Grand Central Station. Since a tape on a news van would not be available to me, I had to get my hands on one of the machines. More than just that Ampex VTR-1000 machine had to be transported. Each machine came in two parts: the huge recording machine and the large electronics cabinet that housed the racks of large vacuum tubes, which supported it."[7]

Verna continued, "Because the tape machines couldn't synchronize immediately, the engineers spliced a test-strip of prerecorded tape to the front of the newly recorded material they were about to put on the air. What they used was an old 'I Love Lucy tape'—they called it 'Lucy Leader'—as the pre-roll so that they could tweak the images of Desi and Lucy into synchronization to get the new recording up to speed and ready for airing."[8]

Verna wanted to make the synchronization happen quickly so he could show the play again before live action began again with machine not designed to work that way. "I knew we couldn't control the video so I conceived the idea of using audio tones that I could insert on-the-fly during the live action of the game," he said. "The conception of an audio-alert was needed so that I could hear the state of the tape's playback distortion as it rolled back through its heads while trying to reach the right speed for synchronization. By analyzing the audio tones we inserted I was able to calculate exactly what the tape was doing during the lengthy eight to ten seconds of indecipherable video hash it was transmitting."[9]

Verna's bosses at CBS told him not to promote the instant replays early in the telecast just in case they couldn't get it to work. Verna told the announcing team in the cab on the way to the stadium what he had planned but otherwise stayed silent. His original plan required them to catch Roger Staubach on a scramble and show it again to the national television audience. Early on, he tried to get his experimental technology working but each time it failed.

Lindsey Nelson did the play-by-play and Terry Brennan added the color commentary as Navy took a 21–7 lead. The game had nearly ended and Verna had not gotten the opportunity and technology to mesh. Games involving the service academies frequently were hard-fought battles until the final whistle. Army trailed by two scores, but they had not given up. They mounted a long drive and as they approached the goal line, Rollie Stichweh faked a handoff to the tailback and took the ball off tackle himself for a touchdown.

"It was an isolation that George Drago had caught on his camera and which John Wells immediately rewound and then hit the play button," Verna recalled. "And during the seven to ten seconds, while the pre-roll played back, I heard the tones strengthen, and lo and behold, clean video came up. My technical director, Sandy Bell, punched it up while I shouted into Lindsey's ear, 'This is it!'"

When the replay hit the screen to the national television audience, Lindsey shouted into his microphone, "This is not live! Ladies and Gentlemen, Army did not score again."[10] Graphics with the words "video tape" appeared on the screen. The phrase instant replay had not come into common use nor had the practice of seeing a key play over again.

Verna worked to improve the technology that he used for the second time when Navy, ranked second in the nation, lost the national championship in the 1964 Cotton Bowl to first-ranked Texas, 28–6. Verna had hoped to capture a magnificent run by Staubach in the first contest but did not. He missed in the bowl game as well. The Texas defense kept Staubach in check during the Cotton Bowl game, just as Army had done.

The first use of instant replay in a professional game occurred just a few days after the Cotton Bowl. The two second-place teams played in the now defunct NFL Playoff Bowl in the Orange Bowl. Bart Starr led the Packers over the Cleveland Browns, 40–23.

In that otherwise ordinary game, Verna used isolated instant replays that had the camera focused tight on receivers and linebackers to provide viewers with something they had not seen before.

The most famous early replay from a NFL game in the sixties came during the Ice Bowl championship game between the Cowboys and Packers. The wind chill brought the temperature to minus 46 degrees as the Packers held the ball at the goal line. The Packers called their last timeout before the third-and-goal play. Verna expected a pass in the end zone. He told camera operator Herman Lang to focus tightly on Bart Starr as he left the huddle and then to pan right and pick up the flanker, Boyd Dowler, prior to the snap of the ball.

That is when Lang ran into issues. The cold weather made his cameras freeze. Lang kept his composure and held the camera on Starr, who faced him from his position in the end zone. Starr took the snap and the offensive line fired forward. Jerry Kramer slammed into Jethro Pugh hard and, with the help of center Ken Bowman, opened up enough room for Starr to go across the goal line and fall into the end zone. The weather actually helped the network catch one of the most famous plays in NFL history. The play aired repeatedly with Kramer's name mentioned every time. The instant replay made him one of the most famous linemen in America and he titled his best-selling book *Instant Replay*.

Tony Verna was ahead of his time when it comes to technology. He always looked for new equipment that would improve the broadcast. He predicted the introduction of videocassettes, widespread use of satellites to transmit live events around the world and the development of the Steadicam, a camera that could move without shaking the image. These innovations happened in the 1970s.

Arledge may not have used instant replays first during a broadcast, but he sure made the most of it. Everything he did worked toward bringing out the human side of sports. Instead of turning the camera on at the sporting event and hoping not to miss a play, Arledge wanted more out of television sports. He wanted to humanize sporting events by letting viewers get up close to the participants. "When I got into it in 1960," said Arledge, "sports amounted to going out on the road, opening three or four cameras and trying not to blow any plays. They were barely documenting the game, but nobody cared because the marvel of seeing a picture was enough to keep people glued to their sets."[11]

Arledge turned the game telecast into a complete broadcast. He advocated replacing the halftime show with a highlight show from the studio. Then, he wanted any lull in the action filled with a prerecorded interview or profile of a player or coach. Isolating cameras on one particular player enabled the announcers to have video along with their commentary explaining what happened in the previous play.

The network recognized and appreciated Arledge's work. By 1964, they appointed him vice president of ABC Sports. By 1968, he took over as the president of the sports division. Arledge did not limit his innovations to football. He soon brought his innovative ideas to other ABC programming. He created a sport anthology show called *Wide World of Sports* that aired on Saturday afternoons. The show brought various sporting events to the public attention. It debuted on April 29, 1961.

The first show featured the Penn Relays from Philadelphia and Drake Relays from Des Moines, Iowa. They originally created the show to fill the gap created when football season ended and baseball season started. They planned to cover events that many Americans had never seen before. They showed demolition derbies, surfing, and firefighter competitions. ABC cameras took Americans out west to watch a rodeo and to Mexico to show some thrilling cliff diving. Preliminaries for traditional Olympic events the public only saw once every four years, such as figure skating, skiing and gymnastics, also received coverage.

The show featured its own stirring, brassy theme music interrupted by host Jim McKay saying, "Spanning the globe to bring you the constant variety of sport, the thrill of victory and the agony of defeat, the human drama of athletic competition.... This is ABC's Wide World of Sports." The show aired for three decades from 1961 to 1991 with a personal touch for all events. The show treated all events, no matter how mundane or bizarre, as seriously as sports more familiar to Americans.

Roone Arledge brought the sports anthology to a whole new level by bidding for and winning the rights to the Olympic Games. In 1964, ABC televised the Innsbruck Winter Olympics and four years later the summer games from Mexico City famous for the drama of the black athletes John Carlos and Tommie Smith raising their gloved fists on the medal podium.

During Arledge's tenure with ABC Sports, that network became synonymous with Olympics coverage. Arledge personally produced all 10 ABC Olympic broadcasts shown on the network. He was the first television executive and one of the very few Americans to receive the Medal of the Olympic Order from the International Olympic Committee. In 1989, they inducted Roone Arledge into the Olympic Hall of Fame. Arledge used sports to increase ABC's prominence as a network, but sports and television did not always seem like a match made in heaven.

The marriage of football and television came with some bumps in the road. The earliest days of television nearly scared pro teams away. The Los Angeles Rams became the first NFL team to televise all its home games. As the Rams searched for additional revenue streams and for ways to increase football's popularity, the Admiral Television Company approached with a proposal to broadcast all the home games to the local Los Angeles market. At the time, technology did not support broadcasting games back to Los Angeles live from the East Coast.

The Rams considered it a good deal as long the gate attendance did not drop. They averaged nearly 50,000 a game during the 1949 season with their entertaining team challenging for the championship. The potent Rams offense featured quarterbacks Bob Water-field and Norm Van Brocklin tossing footballs to receivers Tom Fears and Elroy Hirsch. The team forecasted an increase of about 10 percent because their Los Angeles rivals, the AAFC Dons, dissolved in 1950. In short, prospects looked good for increased attendance. As an insurance policy, they got the Admiral Corporation to agree to compensate the team for attendance short of the ten percent target.

The season ended with a championship for the exciting Rams. Despite the success, attendance decreased nearly 50 percent from 49,854 per game to 26,804.[12] Based on the agreement, the Admiral Corporation owed the Rams $307,000 to cover the cost of the attendance drop. One could only conclude that televising home games caused the decline at the gate. As further evidence, they cite the fact that the Rams played the Bears in a home playoff game not broadcast in Los Angeles and 83,501 fans showed up.

In 1951, the Rams only televised their road games and attendance rebounded to about 44,000 a game. Since television comprised such a small part of team revenue compared to ticket and related stadium revenue, the NFL started a policy of blacking out home games to the local market, which they defined as the area within 75 miles surrounding the team's home city. In 1953, the U.S. District Court upheld as legal the NFL's policy of blacking out home games.

"When our attendance had gone down over 50 percent in 1950, we knew that televising home games wouldn't work," said Tex Schramm, general manager of the Rams at the time. "We'd gained more fans but also furnished such a strong example of what would happen if home games were televised that Judge Allan K. Grimm in the U.S. District Court approved the entire blackout feature of the league's television contracts. The Grimm decision was one of the most important ones ever made and is still in effect today. I testified in the case, and the thing that made it happen was that we actually had all the facts and figures and didn't have to cope with outside influences lobbying against us. Judge Grimm just made the decision, and that was it."[13]

Schramm had a personal connection between football and television. He joined the Los Angeles Rams as publicity director in 1947 and worked his way up to general manager. Before he joined the Rams, he had earned a journalism degree from the University of Texas and worked as a sportswriter for the *Austin American-Statesman*. Despite his position as a football executive, he never lost his connection to the media. On Sundays, you could always find Schramm hanging with members of the media in the press box. There he basked in his element. After the game, he held court, taking questions from the assembled media. He followed the same set-up during training camp. Schramm entertained questions from media with an after-practice J&B Scotch in his hand.

Schramm left the Rams for a position in television with CBS Sports in 1957. His background at CBS showed him the true potential of sports on television. He saw what TV could do and brought that love of the medium with him when he began to build the expansion Dallas Cowboys from scratch. Even so, he did not ignore other media. He established the *Dallas Cowboys Newsweekly*, whose circulation quickly reached 100,000. Then he set out to develop the largest radio network of any team in the league. By the late seventies, he had 225 stations in 19 states. They even had Spanish-language stations in several states and across Mexico.

Meanwhile, commissioner Pete Rozelle wanted to increase the games popularity using television. Ultimately, he wanted to get his product into the prime time spotlight. He struggled to convince the networks to share his vision. Eventually, he got them to agree to a three-game experiment with games on consecutive weeks in October 1969. CBS broadcast two and NBC aired the other.

ABC, left out of the experiment, strongly desired a prime-time football package. Tom Moore originally proposed airing NFL games on Friday to replace their fading boxing programming. Traditionally, Friday nights belonged to high school and college football. The NCAA did not like the concept. At the time, NCAA executives did not want to deal with a network that also produced professional games. The executives felt their broadcasting partner should not carry professional football at all. That frustrated Roone Arledge, who wanted a piece of the NFL pie. Getting the NCAA to agree represented just one of the hurdles Arledge needed to cross. Meanwhile, Rozelle had his own issues to deal with.

Rozelle also had to make sure that Congress did not think the NFL planned to encroach on times generally reserved for high school and college sporting events. That meant that Pete could not sell a Friday or Saturday night package. He viewed Monday night as the next best alternative.

After the test, neither CBS nor NBC expressed interest in the Monday Night package

Pete Rozelle offered to sell. They had strong entertainment programming schedules already in place on Monday. Roone Arledge, at ABC, however, expressed an interest. ABC had an anemic slate of Monday night programs that consistently lost viewers to the rival networks. With NBC and CBS out of the picture, a mysterious new bidder arrived on the scene. When Pete Rozelle started shopping the package to the sports network owned by reclusive billionaire Howard Hughes, it gave Arledge more ammunition. He told ABC executives that many affiliates—he estimated as many as one hundred—might drop the ABC Monday night programming slate of entertainment programs and sign up for Hughes's football package.

The idea that many of their affiliates might abandon the network programs in favor of sports brought them around. ABC put up $25.5 million to the NFL for the Monday night games. Only then did Arledge tell NCAA president Walter Byers about the deal. As expected, Byers protested. Arledge countered with the promise that ABC would not promote NFL games during NCAA telecasts or use the lead NCAA football announcer, Chris Schenkel, on Monday nights. They agreed.

Once he secured the NFL deal, Arledge needed to sell it to the American public. Arledge thought that in order to sell any sports at night, the telecast needed to appeal to more than just the hard-core fan. He would need to reach out to the casual fans, both men and women, to give the show hopes of attracting the evening entertainment audience. In other words, he needed an entertainment program and not just a pure sports telecast. He wanted people to tune in regardless of what teams played.

Arledge had a plan to make *Monday Night Football* successful on a work night. Some doubted if people would watch football during prime time with work and school the next day. Would they pass on their favorite comedies? In order to attract and maintain viewers, Arledge knew he needed an announcing staff that could entertain as well as inform.

His first choice would actually work as the third man in the booth. He envisioned a play-by-play man along with an analyst that most networks used but his fresh idea added a third person. The man he had in mind was Howard Cosell, who had gained prominence covering Muhammad Ali's fights and his legal battles over his draft status. Cosell, a very controversial figure in sports reporting, would, in Arledge's opinion, attract and hold the audience.

Cosell gave up a lucrative law practice in the fifties to enter broadcasting. At first, he gained some local fame with ABC Radio in New York. Some producers did not want to use him on national broadcasts due to his regional accent. He continued to work and eventually gained a spot on *Wide World of Sports* with various spots including interviews with Ali.

Depending on your point of view, Cosell was either the most liked or most hated broadcaster of his day. The reason depended upon whom you asked. When people used adjectives to describe the ABC commentator, the words most often used included arrogant, opinionated, and loudmouthed. Those adjectives are not the ones we all strive for. He could be brilliant and maddening at the same time.

Arledge's first choice for the analyst role, Frank Gifford, still had a contract with CBS. Gifford recommended his friend Don Meredith, who he thought would do great in the role. Arledge asked Gifford to have Meredith call him. The former Cowboys quarterback got the job as the second man in the booth. Many Americans knew Meredith only as a football player as he had not done any broadcasting at that point.

He had a rough start in the booth, but his quick wit and folksy charm made him a natural choice. Meredith often came out with statements that fans may have thought but would not say aloud. Dandy Don's spontaneous and funny statements endeared him to fans. Once, when the ABC cameras caught Bud Grant glaring at his team out on the field, Meredith burst into song. "You are my sunshine, my only sunshine," he sang in his unique twang.

It came as no surprise since Meredith used to start singing old country and western tunes in the huddle to his Cowboys teammates during a particularly stressful game. He liked to have fun and he dealt with the stress of a game through humor or music. Or both.

As Cowboys quarterback, Meredith took a lot of heat in the media. In a 1965, the Browns and Cowboys battled in a close contest in the Cotton Bowl in Dallas. The Cowboys lagged one touchdown behind but had driven the length of the field and had a first down on the 1 yard line. The fans and the Cleveland Browns expected the Cowboys to try a dive play into the center of the line. Instead, Meredith threw the ball into a group of players that the Browns' middle linebacker intercepted. The Cowboys lost, 24–17. The next day in the *Dallas Morning News*, Gary Cartwright started his game recap story with, "Outlined against a grey November sky, the four horsemen rode again. You remember them: death, pestilence, famine and Meredith."[14]

When he joined *Monday Night Football*, Meredith had no polish as an announcer. That stood as part of the appeal Arledge saw in him. Soon all America pulled for him in his weekly verbal spats with Howard Cosell. Even Cosell could see it playing out. After their first rehearsal, he had a message for Meredith. "Middle America will love you," Cosell told him. "Southern America will love you…. You'll wear the white hat, I'll wear the black hat."[15]

His sparkling, fun-loving personality caught attention right away. Meredith referred to himself as Jeff and Hazel's baby boy from Mount Vernon, Texas.

He soon earned a reputation for bursting out in a song when the game grew decidedly one-sided. "Turn out the lights, the party's over," he'd sing. "They say all good things must end. Call it tonight, the party's over and tomorrow starts the same old thing over again." He sang that Willie Nelson song as a signal that the game's fate seemed pretty much decided.

With two-thirds of the team selected, Arledge felt he needed a balance between the brash eastern lawyer and the southern football star. He found that person in college football play-by-play man Keith Jackson. He grew up on a farm in Georgia before enlisting for the Marines at 16. Upon his return, he attended Washington State on the G.I. Bill. Initially a political science and criminology major, he soon switched to broadcasting. He developed his own language broadcasting college games on ABC. He described the Rose Bowl as "the granddaddy of them all," offensive linemen as "the big uglies" but his best came when the excitement of the game picked up. "Whoa, Nellie!" he exclaimed.

Jackson served as the "straight man" among the broadcast trio. He had to put up with the squabbles between Howard Cosell and a rookie color man, Don Meredith. He never knew what to expect when it came to working with those two, but he recalled one cold Monday night. "It was 28 degrees in Philly and Cosell had been drinking for three hours," he said. "Howard did throw up all over Meredith's cowboy boots."[16]

Just as Arledge needed to convince his bosses to take on the Monday night package, Rozelle needed to convince ownership. They had reservations about what a Monday might do for ticket sales. In-stadium turnout still formed an important revenue source. Monday night would not earn like a Sunday afternoon. Art Modell, a member of the television committee, volunteered to host the first contest. "Let me take a chance in Cleveland," he told the commissioner with one provision. "Just give me the Jets."[17] He knew that the Jets had the league's biggest star, Joe Namath, and the league's biggest television market. Modell's gamble resulted in the largest crowd to see a game at Cleveland Municipal Stadium as 85,703 fans showed up to see history made.

With his three-man booth settled, Arledge took steps to make the game much more appealing to viewers than the typical Sunday afternoon contest. He brought more cameras to the game than the other networks typically brought to a Sunday telecast. He deployed at least 10 cameras at every contest. He bragged he had the whole field covered. It all functioned as a continuation of Arledge's philosophy of bringing the game to the fans. Just as he had done with college football previously, he wanted to show more than the other networks did on Sunday. Other than Olympic coverage, Arledge was most well-known for *Monday Night Football*. In its first season, the weeknight football broadcasts earned a 35 share and, by season's end, helped ABC climb to number two ahead of NBC.

In 1994, *Sports Illustrated* compiled a list of 40 individuals who had the greatest impact on the world of sports during the past four decades. It might surprise some, but Arledge fell third on the list. The first two came without surprise: Muhammad Ali and Michael Jordan. Four years earlier, a *Life* magazine poll listed Arledge among the "100 Most Important Americans in the 20th Century."

As the decade of the sixties headed to the seventies, the influence television held over the game increased. Even traditionalist Vince Lombardi could see that the times were changing. "Considering the money involved, we do have to put forth some cooperation with television," said Lombardi. "If they ask us to start a little later so more people can see the game, we have to cooperate somewhat. We can't be penny-wise and pound-foolish. Given today's budgets, there wouldn't be a single franchise left in the National Football League without television."[18]

Another old-time football coach agreed with Lombardi. "We think television exposure is so important to our program and so important to this university that we'll schedule ourselves to fit the medium," said Bear Bryant, Hall of Fame coach at Alabama. "I'll play at midnight if that's what television wants."[19]

Pete Rozelle spoke candidly in numerous interviews about the key role television played in the growth of the sport. He said he doubted the American Football league would have survived without television. He predicted that half of the franchises would cease to exist without the funding received from television. Last, the Super Bowl would not be the huge event it is today without television. Without the revenue from television, the NFL could not meet the demand for higher wages, better pensions, and the rising costs of everything it takes to run a professional sports league.

While television has not asked Alabama to kick off at midnight, it has made some demands on the sport. During the 1967 Super Bowl in Los Angeles, they needed two kickoffs at the start of the second half because NBC remained in commercial when the Packers first booted the ball to the Chiefs. Contrast that with a network employee having to masquerade as a drunken fan to interrupt play at the 1958 title game. Time has changed for the sport and for television.

Chapter Seventeen

The Dream

As he lay dying in his hospital bed in 1970, a weary Vince Lombardi struggled. A fighter, even in his current weakened state, he had grown up believing you never gave up, even if the fight seemed impossible. You fought the good fight. You never quit. That is what he always told his players.

During his entire adult lifetime, Vince Lombardi was always in charge. Only this time, he fought an enemy he could not overpower. In the past, he achieved success by sheer will, grit, hard work and determination. Such actions meant nothing to this enemy as Lombardi battled colon cancer. Relentless, the cancer wore him down. It made him weak, too weak to fight the other enemy he faced.

That other enemy haunted him at night when his dreams took over.[1] He had controlled everything in his successful career as a head coach and general manager in the National Football League. That control led his team to five league championships in seven seasons, including three in a row. No team in modern history has won three consecutive championships. The Green Bay Packers did due to Lombardi's long reach and tight grip over everything.

"He decided how many stripes of what width and color he wanted on the jerseys," said his longtime assistant coach Phil Bengtson. "He told the janitor where to move the water cooler, and gave instructions for the nameplate on his door to read 'Mr. Lombardi,' not 'Coach Lombardi.' To the first veteran who came in asking to be traded to a winning team, he retorted, 'This is going to be a winning team.' If it smacked of dictatorship, then that was what was needed."[2]

Stuck in a hospital bed, Lombardi struggled to survive and for the control that he could not summon. He tossed and turned restlessly in that hospital bed on the sixth floor at Georgetown University Hospital. His wife, Marie, insisted she stay with him. She spent most days and nights at her husband's side. Sometimes she slept in a room across the hall where she heard him struggle through the night. During the eerie quiet of the night, his dreamy shouts would break the silence.

In 1967, Lombardi toured the country giving speeches he viewed as warnings for the country. The protests occurring all over the country frightened him. Young people burned draft cards in protest of the war in Vietnam. He saw the protests as a breakdown in authority and the moral code he accepted as doctrine. Lombardi's players called him "Old Man." Lombardi saw it as a hard-earned badge of honor that served as a source of pride. Since he considered his players his family, he took it as a term of affection. He was, in fact, only 57 years old as he tried to sleep in that hospital bed. Not an old man in terms of the calendar, he appeared older stuck in that hospital bed where his illness aged him.

"Joe Namath!" he shouted from his dream. "You're not bigger than football! Remember that!"[3]

The words startled Marie and left her uneasy. She saw how the dreams affected her husband. His tossing and turning increased as he struggled with some inner demons, almost as if bound by imaginary shackles.

Beyond the illness, the decade of the sixties had aged him. The changing times took a hard toll on his soul. Lombardi saw the derogation of the moral fiber of the country. His league and his game changed, too. During those dreams, Marie Lombardi said he called out the name of quarterback Joe Namath. With his long hair and modern attitudes, Namath stood as a symbol of the changing times of the sixties.

Lombardi, born and raised a traditional Catholic, was a man who learned the catechism and followed its teachings proudly. He could recite it. He tried to live it and the tenets of the Ten Commandments. He saw daily Mass as a requirement if he hoped to keep on the right path. Religion provided order against the chaos of the outside world. The church provided authority and structure against the undisciplined and unruly war raging in the sixties. He did not like what he saw. The young generation pushed the limits using freedom as their pass card. It just was not freedom in the patriotic spirit of the revolution. Lombardi saw this freedom as superficial and excessive. It challenged the moral standards he followed.

He saw the demonstrations in the streets as challenges to the authority of the organized world. The freedom young people supported through demonstration attacked the structure and core of the country. Lombardi believed in order, discipline and obedience, which were virtues driven into his soul at a young age. The changing times made him shudder. Those so-called individual freedoms challenged everything Lombardi held dear.

One person in particular epitomized the changing social times in Lombardi's view. Joe Namath symbolized that lack of order and newfound freedom in America. Lombardi did not doubt the young quarterback's impressive athletic abilities. He could throw the ball like no other. He had a quick release and a strong arm. Even the coach marveled at Namath's gifted throws. His ability to throw that deep ball with impressive accuracy could ruin a defense's confidence. He even did it against the best defenses.

Off the field however, Lombardi believed Namath's actions and those of others like him undermined the country's moral fiber. More than crumbling values and decaying morals troubled Lombardi as he lay in that hospital bed. The game he loved with all his heart had started changing. Football provided regimen, structure and order. Successful teams thrived on discipline, which was one of the things that attracted Lombardi as a player to the game.

Football games, fixed in length, gave teams just 60 minutes to impose their will on the opposition and clinch victory. One hundred yards stretched from goal line to goal line. Teams had only four opportunities to do something with the ball or surrender it to the opposition. A simple game really. Lombardi said so publicly. "Blocking and tackling," Lombardi said. "If you do those two things better than the opposition, you win the game."[4]

Nevertheless, things began to change. In the mid-sixties player salaries escalated. The competition between rival leagues drove the inflation. The players started earning more than the coaches did. With money came power. Lombardi felt coaches needed to run things, but that was not the case anymore. Namath's $427,000 contract in 1965 had changed all that.

It was not just a number on a piece of paper. Namath's salary proved so much more than that. That one signature changed so many things. It changed the game forever. Could Vince Lombardi handle that change?

While the Lombardi family would not admit it, but maybe Vince Lombardi left at the right time. Although he had no choice, at 57 Lombardi seemed too young to lie dying in a hospital bed, and yet seemed too old to handle the rapidly changing world outside of that hospital.

The game he had loved so long now broke his heart. As he called out in the middle of the night, he pleaded for consistency.

"Why can't they stay the same?"

It would not stay the same. The sixties proved a time a rapid change in the country and huge change in football. Changes in society reached every aspect of life, particularly in pro sports. A prime example, minorities slowly received more opportunities in America and those changes moved even faster in the sports world.

Labor unions played prominent roles in the business world, but had not in the sports world. That changed as the country moved through the sixties and into the seventies. Unions formed in professional sports and took a larger role in professional sports. As did television.

The black and white programming people watched at the start of the decade yielded to color. At first, televised sports stood as a weekend fare, but soon started seeing the primetime. Before the decade ended, television insisted Lombardi's team kick off again because they had not returned from commercial yet. Clearly, television exercised growing power over the game. Television and professional football grew together into dominant structures on the sporting landscape.

Through television, the country saw leaders assassinated and riots in the streets over wars and social injustice. Concurrently, football fans witnessed the game's leaders—the biggest innovators of the sport—pushed aside in the name of progress. As the world changed, the National Football League changed right along with it, all of which happened too fast for Vince Lombardi.

Chapter Eighteen

Closing

For young people growing up during the sixties, the highlight of the decade came in 1969 when a team that symbolized that younger generation put the older generation in its place during Super Bowl III. The leader of the Jets, Joe Namath, spoke his mind and gave little respect to the opposition. Just when many thought the old folks would send junior to time-out, he backed up his boasts with actions and won the game.

"Namath was in a different class," said John Madden, the former Oakland Raiders coach and later an Emmy-winning TV analyst. "One time I was leaving the house for a Jets game and my wife said, 'You have to stop Namath today.' I said, 'Yeah, I know. That's all we talked about all week.'"[1]

That brief discussion between husband and wife came before the game in which Ike Lassiter and Ben Davidson hit Namath all day long as he attempted to pass. On one play, the Raiders rolled the quarterback and his helmet went flying off his head. Namath suffered a broken cheekbone after one of the Raiders hit him hard in the head.

"Helluva game, we wound up winning," continued Madden. "I came out of the locker room afterwards and my wife was standing there, really mad. First thing she said was, 'You didn't have to hurt him.' She didn't care that we won the game; she was mad that we whacked Joe. I said, 'but that's part of stopping him.'"[2] After the game, Madden told the assembled media what tremendous respect he had for the quarterback. He said Namath had a reputation as a pretty boy, but he didn't play like a pretty boy. Madden said in all his years as a professional sports, only once did he go to the other team's locker room to shake a player's hand. He did that with Joe Namath. Despite the constant pressure, Namath got up and kept throwing touchdowns.

Quarterbacks and quarterbacking seems much different today. Completion percentages are much higher in today's horizontal passing offenses in which the passes are much shorter and easier to complete. Many times today, the receiver runs across the field directly in front of the quarterback. Other times, the pass goes to the back in the flat or to a receiver on a bubble screen. All those are short passes, with high completion percentages. Namath, in particular, played in a vertical passing game. He threw the ball deep to take advantage of receiver Don Maynard's speed.

"Joe was the best passer I ever saw," said Maynard. "Joe didn't play for stats, he played to win. I see quarterbacks today throw 4-yard passes on third-and-15. It goes in the books as a completion, it looks good in the stats, but it doesn't accomplish a damn thing. I never saw Joe throw a ball short of the sticks. If he needed 12 yards for a first down, he threw it 15. When he got inside the 20, he went for the end zone. He got some picked off, but he also made a lot of big plays that won games."[3]

While Namath's arm and quick release served him well, his knees gave him problems his entire professional career. With his playing days over, Namath sat back and discussed his career. "I never played a down of pro football healthy," Namath said years after his playing career ended. "Not one down."[4]

Namath's first surgery came before he had even suited up for the Jets for the first time. Orthopedic surgeon Dr. James Nicholas examined him in the men's room at Toots Shor's, the site of his introductory news conference. That first surgery came on the right knee injured in college and occurred only three weeks after he signed his substantial contract. He had two more operations on his knees before the Super Bowl victory and one afterward.

While the star quarterback of the decade endured surgeries to keep him on the field, the best known coach of the day ended the decade with health issues of his own. During the summer of 1970, as Vince Lombardi prepared for his second training camp with his Washington team, he admitted to friends he didn't feel well. On June 27, he entered the hospital for surgery; doctors removed a tumor and a section of his colon. On July 10, he left the hospital with the public thinking he had returned to normal activities as he went to an owners' meeting in New York and a rookie scrimmage in Baltimore. On July 27, he returned to the hospital for additional surgery.

"He lay in his bed at Georgetown University Hospital, looking so drawn and tired, the intravenous needles feeding his right arm and hand," said Jerry Kramer, recalling his visit to see Coach Lombardi. "He motioned for me to come up on the left side of the bed. I went up to him and squeezed his hand, trying to say without words all the things I wanted to say, how much I had learned from him, how grateful I was, how much I loved him."[5]

Bill Curry, who played center for Lombardi and later coached college football, visited Lombardi in the hospital, like many of the players. "He was in a state I had never seen him in before: helpless, vulnerable, diminished, and no longer larger than life," said Curry. "He was gray and his body was emaciated. There were tubes protruding from his right arm. It was hard to believe this shell of a human being was Vince Lombardi."[6]

Coach Lombardi squeezed Curry's hand and made one simple request. "You can mean a great deal to my life if you will pray for me,"[7] he said.

Backup quarterback Zeke Bratkowski joined Bart Starr in a trip to see Lombardi in the Washington hospital after a Saturday preseason game in Milwaukee. "He was emaciated and weak, no longer vibrant," observed Starr of Lombardi. "He obviously didn't want anyone to see him in that condition, and after speaking with us a few minutes, asked his wife, Marie, to tell us he wished to be alone. Zeke and I left quietly, unable to talk until we reached the airport."[8]

On September 3, Lombardi passed away due to colon cancer. His death shocked the football world. It came roughly two months after doctors gave Lombardi the diagnosis. The Green Bay Packers gained fans across the nation as the team dominated play during the sixties. At the end of the decade, Lombardi moved to the Washington team and appeared to have that team on track towards improved performance before his illness struck. He became coach of the Redskins in February 1969 and led them to a 7–5–2 record, their first winning season in 14 years. The following summer, he was ill.

They took his body to Gawler's funeral parlor in Washington, D.C and then to the Abbey funeral home in New York City for viewing. On Labor Day 1970, mourners filled the streets of New York City. Thousands stood in silence behind the police barricade across from St. Patrick's Cathedral. Coaches and owners from all over the league came to the church to say goodbye. Players and officials from the Giants, Packers and Redskins paid their respects.

"Cardinal Cooke did the [funeral] Mass, and I was one of the readers," said Father Tim Moore, who first hired Lombardi at St. Cecilia High School. "The number of people at St. Patrick's Cathedral that day was incredible. The two biggest funerals ever held there were those of Bobby Kennedy and Vince Lombardi. I remember the 30 limousines going down the Garden State Parkway to the cemetery in Middletown. We exited and got on Route 35, and there were all these kids lined up and down that road, wearing football jerseys, some of them crying. At the cemetery, people placed footballs near his grave. I did the ceremony. It was very hard not breaking down."[9]

"The saddest part of his death was his players," said Harold Lombardi, Vince's brother, with tears welling in the corner of his eyes. "You could see the sadness inside of them. He was amazing; he really was amazing."[10]

The motorcade drove to New Jersey, where Vince would have his final resting place. All along the path, people gathered along the side of the road as if for a head of state. The morning of September 3, 1970, started with rain falling in Green Bay, as Paul Harvey took to the airwaves and delivered an on-air eulogy of the world's most celebrated coach. Harvey was a nationally syndicated radio broadcaster heard across the country at the time.

"It is a grey day in Green Bay, Wisconsin, a city which shouted itself hoarse for the teams of Vince Lombardi today speaks his name in whispered prayers," began Harvey. "The sun always shown on Packer Sundays; they called it Lombardi weather. They said the town ran on Lombardi time—15 minutes ahead of everywhere else. And elsewhere, in an era where many sought to deify the common man, some of us continue to thrill to the accomplishments of the uncommon ones—Rockne, Leahy, Bud Wilkinson, Bear Bryant and the incomparable Vince Lombardi."[11]

People across the country reacted to the news. Paul Harvey was just one who felt sorrow that morning. He felt for the football fans of the NFL's smallest city.

"In an era of something for nothing, prop up the underdog, pull the punches, wars for indefinite objectives then somebody in Vince Lombardi's uncompromising determination to be the best could not alone inspire us all, but he made the citizens of one city stand real tall," said Harvey. "With the kind of unanimous local pride that we use to feel nationally you'd hear local folks say, 'I live in Green Bay.'"[12]

Lombardi restored civic pride in Green Bay as well as hopes for a better tomorrow in Washington, D.C. He would be missed in many cities in between. As the sixties wore on, some said the Lombardi magic had worn thin. Some said that new magic came from players like Joe Namath, not older men standing on the sidelines. Lombardi's passing, at the end of the decade, signaled another change in the country, just like the sixties as a whole had done. America was a little less autocratic and players like Namath tested their newfound freedoms each day.

Chapter Notes

Introduction

1. Editors of Time-Life Books. *Turbulent Years: The 60s (Our American Century)*. Pages 22–24.
2. "R.C.A. Plans to Double Output of Color TV Sets, Sarnoff Says." *New York Times*. February 18, 1960.
3. Walter Bingham. "A War on Ferocity." *Sports Illustrated*. November 11, 1963. Pages 18–23.
4. Wesley Lowery. "The Activist Minds." *Sports Illustrated*. December 19, 2016. Pages 53–60.
5. See "The Soft American." *Sports Illustrated*. December 26, 1960 Pages 18–23 and "The Vigor We Need." *Sports Illustrated*. July 16, 1962.
6. "The Beatles Arrive in New York." History. com. November 24, 2009.
7. Dave Anderson. "Namath Takes if Off—at $10 a Clip." *New York Times*. December 12, 1968.

Chapter One

1. Wright Thompson. "Vince Lombardi Lived Here." *ESPN*. January 31, 2011.
2. Bob Oates. "Lionel Aldridge: A Long Journey and Happy Days; Former Packer Is Back on His Feet." *Los Angeles Times*. October 27, 1987.
3. Dave Robinson and Royce Boyles. *The Lombardi Legacy*. Page 232.
4. Ibid.
5. Jennifer Briggs. *Strive to Excel*. Pages 131–2 as quoted in Mike Towle. *I Remember Vince Lombardi*. Page 146.
6. Mike Towle. *I Remember Vince Lombardi*. Page 188.
7. Jerry Kramer. *Instant Replay: The Green Bay Diary of Jerry Kramer*. Page 49.
8. John Wiebusch. *Lombardi*. Page 16 as quoted in Mike Towle. *I Remember Vince Lombardi*. Page 180.
9. Jerry Kramer. *Instant Replay*. Page xvii.
10. Mark Kriegel. *Namath: A Biography*. Page 10.
11. Ibid.
12. Paul Zimmerman. *The Last Season of Weeb Ewbank*. Page 63.

13. William Johnson. "Ararararararargh!" *Sports Illustrated*. March 3, 1969. Pages 28–33.
14. Gene Wojciechowski. "Lombardi Turned Packers into Winners." *ESPN*. February 3, 2006.
15. Donald T. Phillips. *Run to Win*. Page 142.
16. Ibid. Page 144.
17. NFL Films. *America's Game: 1966 Packers*.
18. Jerry Kramer. "We Played for Lombardi." *Life*. September 11, 1970.
19. Vince Lombardi Jr. *What It Takes to be #1: Vince Lombardi on Leadership*. Page 92.
20. John Rovi. "And Yes, Vince Lombardi Said It." *Mind Your Business*. December 8, 2011.

Chapter Two

1. Ralph Bernstein. Associated Press. "Commissioner Bert Bell Dies, Leaving Void in Pro Football." *Ludington Daily News*. October 12, 1959.
2. The Pro Football Hall of Fame. "Bert Bell: The Commissioner." *The Coffin Corner*. Vol. 18, No. 3 (1996).
3. Richard Whittingham. *What Giants They Were: New York Giant Greats Talk about Their Teams, Their Coaches, and the Times of Their Lives*. Pages 176–77.
4. Ibid.
5. Tom Farley. "Riot at Yankee Stadium." *The Coffin Corner*. Vol. 21, No. 4 (1999).
6. Stuart Leuthner. *Iron Men*. Page 156.
7. Al Silverman. *It's Not Over 'Til It's Over*. Page 115.
8. Myron Cope. "A Life for Two Tough Texans." *Sports Illustrated*. October 20, 1969.
9. Lou Sahadi. *One Sunday in December*. Page 157.
10. Ibid. Page 113.
11. Ibid. Page 136.
12. Jack Cavanaugh. *Giants Among Men*. Page 85.
13. Gary Cartwright. "Tom Landry: Melting the Plastic Man." *Texas Monthly*. November, 1973.
14. Jack Cavanaugh. *Giants Among Men*. Page 26.
15. Dave Anderson. "His Championship Seasons: Ewbank Reflects." *New York Times*. September 18, 1994.

16. Barry Gottehrer. *The Giants of New York*. Page 261.

17. Paul Zimmerman. "Total Package." *Sports Illustrated*. September 5, 1994. Pages 66–70.

18. Lou Sahadi. *One Sunday in December*. Page 96.

19. Stuart Leuthner. *Iron Men*. Page 3.

20. Bob Herzog. "When Colts Beat Giants in 1958, Modern NFL Was Born." *Newsday*. December 27, 1988.

21. Jack Cavanaugh. *Giants Among Men*. Page 175.

22. Mike Towle. *Johnny Unitas: Mr. Quarterback*. Page 136.

23. Lou Sahadi. *One Sunday in December*. Page 124.

24. *USA Today*. September 12, 2002 as quoted in Mike Towle. *Johnny Unitas: Mr. Quarterback*. Page 131.

25. Ted Brock and Larry Eldridge Jr. *25 Years: The NFL Since 1960*. Page 23.

26. Dan Manoyan. *Alan Ameche: The Story of "The Horse."* Page 231.

27. John Steadman. "Colts' Preas Was a Quiet Catalyst of Victory in '58." *Baltimore Sun*. November 15, 1998.

28. Bob Herzog "Sudden Life Excerpt: Made for TV." *Press Box Online*. Issue 132. December 2008.

29. Josh Katzowitz. *CBS Sports*. "Remember When: 'Greatest Game Ever Played' still impacts NFL." December 27, 2013.

30. Jack Cavanaugh. *Giants Among Men*. Page 183.

Chapter Three

1. Sam Farmer. "A Crew Cut Above." *Los Angeles Times*. September 12, 2002.

2. Rob L. Ruck, Maggie Jones Patterson, and Michael P. Weber. *Rooney: A Sporting Life*. Page 287.

3. Mike Klingaman. "Unitas' First Pass Wasn't a Bears' TD." *Baltimore Sun*. October 21, 2006.

4. Michael Mink. "Johnny Unitas Willed His Way To Football's Heights; Be Resilient: From Gridiron Reject to Baltimore Colts' Star Quarterback, His Iron Determination Helped Him Pass Them All." *Investor's Business Daily*. January 14, 2005.

5. Ed Gruver. *From Baltimore to Broadway*. Page 46.

6. Mike Towle. *Johnny Unitas: Mr. Quarterback*. Page 89.

7. Tom Callahan. *Johnny U*. Page 68.

8. Bob Griese. *Perfection*. Page 165.

9. Mike Towle. *Johnny Unitas: Mr. Quarterback*. Page 107.

10. Ted Lewis. "Lenny Moore: Streak's Longevity Impressive." *The Advocate*. October 8, 2012.

11. Ed Gruver. *From Baltimore to Broadway*. Page 36.

12. Robert Liston. *The Pros*. Page 45.

Chapter Four

1. Bill Walsh. *Finding the Winning Edge*. Page 6.

2. His record is listed as 3,202 points to 339 points against in Tex Maule. "A Man for This Season." *Sports Illustrated*. September 10, 1962, and 2,393 to 168 in Ernie Palladino. *Lombardi and Landry*. Page 35. Palladino states his 1940 team outscored its opponents, 477–6.

3. John Keim. *Legends by the Lake*. Page 19.

4. Ernie Palladino. *Lombardi and Landry*. Page 35.

5. https://case.edu/ech/articles/c/cleveland-panthers.

6. Alan Ross. *Browns Glory*. Page 15.

7. www.profootballhof.com/news/franchise-nicknames/.

8. Terry Pluto. *When All The World Was Browns Town*. Page 46.

9. Tony Grossi. *Tales From the Cleveland Browns Sideline*. Page 3.

10. Jack T. Clary. *The Gamemakers: Winning Philosophies of Eight NFL Coaches*. Page 21.

11. Terry Pluto. *When All The World Was Browns Town*. Page 241.

12. Bernie Parrish. *They Call It a Game*. Page 102.

13. Jack T. Clary. *The Gamemakers: Winning Philosophies of Eight NFL Coaches*. Page 18.

14. Andrew O'Toole. *Paul Brown*. Page 238.

15. Jeff Miller. *Going Long*. Page 267.

16. Paul Brown, with Jack Clary. *PB: The Paul Brown Story*. Page 277.

17. Jon Morgan. *Glory for Sale*. Page 69.

18. George Cantor. *Paul Brown: The Man who Invented Modern Football*. Page v.

19. Jack Newcombe. *Sport*. December 1954 as quoted in Andrew O'Toole. *Paul Brown*. Page 196.

20. Tom Callahan. *Johnny U*. Page 264.

21. Jim Brown, with Myron Cope. *Off My Chest*. Page 7.

22. William C. Rhoden. *New York Times*. "When Paul Brown Smashed the Color Barrier." September 25, 1997.

23. Ibid.

24. Paul Grossi. *Tales From the Cleveland Browns Sideline*. Page 17.

Chapter Five

1. Editors of Time-Life Books. *Turbulent Years: The 60s (Our American Century)*. Page 70.

2. Manning Marable. *Race, Reform and Rebellion* as quoted in Gary Younge. *The Speech: The Story Behind Dr. Martin Luther King, Jr.'s Dream*. Pages 16–17.

3. John Lewis. *Walking with the Wind* as quoted in Gary Younge. *The Speech: The Story Behind Dr. Martin Luther King Jr.'s Dream*. Page 18.

4. Nick Bryant. *The Bystander*. Page 194.

5. Jeffrey J. Miller. *Rockin' the Rockpile*. Page 252.

6. Ibid.

7. John Wawrow. "Cookie Gilchrist, Bruising Fullback in Old AFL Days, Dies at 75." *Washington Post*. January 13, 2011.

8. John Keim. *Legends by the Lake*. Page 109.

9. Michael MacCambridge. *America's Game.* Page 109.

10. Mike Freeman. *Jim Brown.* Page 155.

11. Tim Layden. "Why Jim Brown Matters." *Sports Illustrated.* October 6, 2015.

12. Jim Brown, with Steve Delsohn. *Out of Bounds.* Page 60.

13. Ibid. Page 61.

14. Bob Hayes. *Run, Bullet, Run.* Page 103.

15. Ibid.

16. Ibid., page 104.

17. Cody Monk. *Legends of the Dallas Cowboys.* Page 83.

18. Tex Maule. *The Pro Season.* Page 12.

19. Jim Brown, with Myron Cope. *Off My Chest.* Page 30.

20. Jim Brown, with Steve Delsohn. *Out of Bounds.* Page 55.

Chapter Six

1. Robert S. Lyons. *On Any Given Sunday.* Page 302.

2. Chad Millman and Shawn Coyne. *The Ones Who Hit the Hardest.* Pages 36–37.

3. Mickey Herskowitz. *From Cannon to Campbell.* Page 24.

4. Peter King. "The AFL." *Sports Illustrated.* July 13, 2009.

5. Bob Oates. "10 Years on the Road to Glory." *Los Angeles Times.* July 17, 1990.

6. John Pirkle. *Oiler Blues.* Page 26.

7. Tracy Thibeau. "Seventh Son of a Seventh Son." *The Coffin Corner.* Volume 37, Number 1 (2015).

8. Ken Rappoport. *The Little League That Could.* Page 102.

9. John Eisenberg. "A Football Interloper's First Gust of Success." *New York Times.* December 15, 2012.

10. Joe McGuff. *Winning It All.* Page 74.

11. Robert H. Boyle. "The Underdogs Have Made It." *Sports Illustrated.* November 12, 1962. Pages 18–23.

Chapter Seven

1. Ed Gruver. *Nitschke.* Page 190.

2. David Maraniss. *When Pride Still Mattered.* Page 245.

3. Dave Klein. *The Vince Lombardi Story.* Pages 9–10.

4. Vince Lombardi, with W. C. Heinz. *Run to Daylight!* Page 42.

5. Vince Lombardi, with W. C. Heinz. "Secrets of Winning Football," in Mike Bynum (editor), *Vince Lombardi: Memories of a Special Time.* Page 133.

6. David Maraniss. *When Pride Still Mattered.* Page 161.

7. Jerry Kramer. *Jerry Kramer's Farewell to Football.* Pages 44–45.

8. Jennifer Briggs. *Strive to Excel.* Page 25.

9. Frank Gifford. *The Whole Ten Yards.* Page 182.

10. Chuck O'Donnell. "The Game I'll Never Forget." *Football Digest.* March 1, 2001.

11. Frank Gifford. *The Whole Ten Yards.* Page 181.

12. "Sport: Vinnie, Vidi, Vici." *Time.* December 21, 1962.

13. Tom Landry. "Vince Lombardi." *Sport.* December 1986. Page 5.

14. Bob Berghaus. *The First America's Team.* Page 98.

15. David Maraniss. *When Pride Still Mattered.* Page 241.

16. Dave Klein. *The Vince Lombardi Story.* Page 108.

17. Steve Cameron. *The Packers!* Page 102.

18. Vince Lombardi. "*ESPN SportsCentury.*"

19. "Giants–Packers Title Games in '61 and '62 Part of NFL Lore." Associated Press. January 18, 2008.

20. Ed Gruver. *The Ice Bowl.* Page 30.

21. David Maraniss. *When Pride Still Mattered.* Page 434.

22. Allen Barra. *The Last Coach.* Page xx.

23. Michael O'Brien. *Vince.* Page 292.

24. Sally Jenkins. "Vince Lombardi: The Coach That Still Matters 40 Years after His Death." *Washington Post.* September 7, 2010.

25. Dave Brady. "'I Will Demand a Commitment to Excellence,' New Chief Says." *Washington Post.* February 7, 1969. Page D1.

26. K. Shelby Skrhak. "Greatness Beyond the Gridiron." *Success.* December 12, 2010.

27. Sirius Radio interview. September 28, 2011.

28. Jennifer Briggs. *Strive to Excel.* Page 39; Mike Towle. *I Remember Vince Lombardi.* Page 114; Bart Starr. *Starr: My Life in Football.* Pages 46–47.

29. Vince Lombardi. *Run to Daylight!* Page 64.

30. Ibid.

31. Roy A. Clumpner. "America's Unknown Leader of the Sixties: Lombardi." *NASSH Proceedings 1973.*

Chapter Eight

1. Claire O'Neil. "Charles Moore, Photographer of the Civil Rights Movement, Dies at 79." *National Public Radio.* March 16, 2010.

2. Originally quoted in *Newsweek*, October 15, 1962 as quoted in Alan Levy, *Tackling Jim Crow*, page 120 and Ben Bradlee, *A Good Life: Newspapering and Other Adventures.* Page 203.

3. Mark Newgent. "Bobby Mitchell Comes to Washington." *Washington Examiner.* June 16, 2009.

4. Thomas G. Smith. *Showdown.* Pages 52–53.

5. Ibid. Page 32.

6. Thomas G. Smith. "Outside the Pale." *Journal of Sports History.* Page 256 as quoted in Charles K. Ross. *Outside the Lines.* Page 41.

7. Thomas G. Smith. "Outside the Pale." *Journal of Sports History.* Page 256.

8. Charles K. Ross. *Outside the Lines.* Page 44.

9. Michael MacCambridge. *America's Game*. Page 18.

10. Woody Strode. *Goal Dust*. Page 155.

11. Michael Oriard. *Brand NFL*. Page 212.

12. Vince Lombardi Jr. *What It Takes to Be #1: Vince Lombardi on Leadership*. Page 87.

13. John Keim. *Legends by the Lake*. Pages 44–45.

14. Ed Gruver. *Nitschke*. Page 49.

15. William C. Rhoden. "At Some NFL Positions, Stereotypes Create Prototypes." *New York Times*. December 11, 2011.

16. Ibid.

17. Ken Crippen. "Where Are They Now: Marlin Briscoe." *National Football Post*. December 13, 2013.

18. Ibid.

19. Mike Towle. *Johnny Unitas: Mr. Quarterback*. Pages 176–77.

20. William Gildea. *When the Colts Belonged to Baltimore*. Page 217.

21. Gale Sayers, with Fred Mitchell. *Sayers: My Life and Times*. Pages 16–17.

22. http://www.homeofheroes.com/DG/07d_brian.html.

23. Scott Simon. *Home and Away*. Page 102.

24. http://www.homeofheroes.com/DG/07d_brian.html.

25. Bill Curry. *Ten Men You Meet in the Huddle*. Pages 160–61.

Chapter Nine

1. "Pete Rozelle Interview." Academy of Achievement. May 15, 1991.

2. Ibid.

3. Frank Deford. "Heirs of Judge Landis." *Sports Illustrated*. September 30, 1974.

4. Ibid.

5. Leonard Shecter. "Does Pete Rozelle Run Pro Football? Ask Joe Namath." *New York Times*. August 17, 1969. Page SM30.

6. Neil Steinberg. "He Could Always Move Merchandise." *Sports Illustrated*. July 27, 1998.

7. Ibid.

8. Frank Litsky. "Larry Kent, 86, Marketer of NFL Merchandise." *New York Times*. July 27, 1999.

9. Idid., and Michael Oriard. *Brand NFL*. Page 179.

10. "Pete Rozelle Interview." Academy of Achievement. May 15, 1991.

11. Bruce Weber. "Alex Karras, All-Pro N.F.L. Lineman Who Also Starred as an Actor, Dies at 77." *New York Times*. October 10, 2012.

12. Gary Mihoces. "Longtime Lion, Actor Karras Dies at 77." *USA Today*. October 10, 2012.

13. Douglas Brinkley. *Cronkite*. Page 272.

14. "Pete Rozelle Interview." Academy of Achievement. May 15, 1991.

15. George Bozeka. "Pete Rozelle and the Kennedy Assassination." *The Coffin Corner*. Vol. 34, No. 2.

16. John Kennedy. "The Soft American." *Sports Illustrated*. December 26, 1960. Pages 14–17.

17. Associated Press. "Commentary: A Nation Grieves as the NFL Plays On." *Santa Fe New Mexican*. November 23, 2013.

18. Jeffri Chadiha. "Football's Forgotten Choice." *Sports Illustrated*. September 24, 2001.

19. Jeff Davis. *Rozelle: Czar of the NFL*. Page 211.

20. Michael MacCambridge. *America's Game*. Page 187.

21. Jeff Davis. *Rozelle: Czar of the NFL*. Page 214.

22. Walt Garrison and Mark Stallard. *"Then Landry Said to Staubach…"* Page 12.

23. "Pete Rozelle Interview." Academy of Achievement. May 15, 1991.

24. Tim Sullivan. "Rozelle Put Pro Football in Nation's Fabric." *Cincinnati Enquirer*. December 8, 1996.

25. Ibid.

26. Bob St. John. *Tex!* Page 207.

27. http://www.baseball-almanac.com/humor7.shtml.

Chapter Ten

1. David Halberstam. *The Powers That Be*. Page 514.

2. Ibid. Page 515.

3. Mike Wright. *What They Didn't Teach You About the '60s*. Page 110.

4. Walter Cronkite. *A Reporter's Life*. Pages 255–56.

5. Don Oberdorfer. *Tet!* Page 159.

6. Howard Zinn. *A People's History of the United States*. Page 485.

7. Muhammad Ali. *The Soul of a Butterfly*. Page 18.

8. Robert Lipsyte. "Prophets," in Jay Lovinger. *The Gospel According to ESPN*. Page 32.

9. Mikal Gilmore. "How Muhammad Ali Conquered Fear and Changed the World." *Men's Journal*. February 5, 2015.

10. Martin Gitlin. *Powerful Moments in Sports*. Page 106.

11. Michael Ezra. *Muhammad Ali: The Making of An Icon*. Page 143.

12. Tim Layden. "Ali: The Legacy." *Sports Illustrated*. October 5, 2015. Pages 60–67.

13. William Nack. "A Name on the Wall." *Sports Illustrated*. July 23, 2001. Pages 60–72.

14. William Nack. *My Turf*. Page 258.

15. Todd Anton and Bill Nowlin. *When Football Went to War*. Page 82.

16. Jeff Snook. *"Then Bud Said to Barry, Who Told Bob…"* Page 108.

17. NFL Films. *America's Game: 1978 Pittsburgh Steelers*.

18. "The Bleier Percentage." *Notre Dame Scholastic*. May 2002. Page 10.

19. Rocky Bleier and Terry O'Neil. "Rocky Bleier's War." *Sports Illustrated*. June 9, 1975.

20. Ibid.

21. Ken Rappoport. *Profiles in Sports Courage.* Pages 128–29.

22. Todd Anton and Bill Nowlin. *When Football Went to War.* Page 228.

23. Rick Telander. "Local Boy Makes Good." *Sports Illustrated.* August 11, 1986.

24. "People." *Sports Illustrated.* August 28, 1967.

25. John Ingoldsby. *Armchair General.* "Roger Staubach: An Interview with the Super Bowl XLV Chairman." January 2010.

26. Senator Edward M. Kennedy. "Foreword" in Michael Connelly. *The President's Team.* Page 11.

27. Gary Mihoces. "How Sports Changed in the Aftermath of the JFK Assassination." *USA Today.* November 22, 2013.

28. Bob Hayes. *Run, Bullet, Run.* Page 135.

Chapter Eleven

1. Jack Horrigan and Mike Tathet. *The Other League.* Page 30.

2. "The Two Pro Football Leagues Must Meet." *Sports Illustrated.* December 16, 1963.

3. Mark Gaughan. "Could '64 Bills Have Won 'Super Bowl' against Browns?" *Buffalo News.* May 29, 2005.

4. Alex Kroll. "The Last of the Titans." *Sports Illustrated.* September 22, 1969.

5. Dave Anderson. "Blue and Gold, Then Green and White as the Titans Became the Jets." *New York Times.* October 14, 2007.

6. John Hogrogian. "The Titans Become the Jets." *The Coffin Corner.* Vol. 13, No. 5 (1991).

7. Dave Anderson. "Blue and Gold, Then Green and White as the Titans Became the Jets." *New York Times.* October 14, 2007.

8. Pete Williams. *The Draft: A Year Inside the NFL's Search for Talent.* Page 47.

9. Jarrett Bell. "From Upstart to Big Time, How the AFL Changed the NFL." *USA Today.* June 30, 2009.

10. Otis Taylor. *The Need to Win.* Page 47.

11. Jarrett Bell. "From Upstart to Big Time, How the AFL Changed the NFL." *USA Today.* June 30, 2009.

12. David A. F. Sweet. *Lamar Hunt.* Page 64.

13. Dave Anderson. *The Story of Football.* Page 116.

14. Dave Goldberg. "Football War Ended with Merger 25 Years Ago." Associated Press. June 9, 1991.

15. Larry Felser. *The Birth of the New NFL.* Page 50.

16. David Harris. *The League.* Pages 62–63.

17. John Brodie. *Open Field.* Page 127.

18. Larry Felser. *The Birth of the New NFL.* Page 68.

19. Tex Schramm. "Here's How It Happened." *Sports Illustrated.* June 20, 1966.

20. David Harris. *The League.* Page 62–63.

21. Ibid.

22. Dave Anderson. "The Broncos' Climb from Nowhere." *New York Times.* January 27, 1998.

23. Edwin Shrake. "Still A Long, Rough Road Ahead for the AFL." *Sports Illustrated.* January 30, 1967.

24. Bobby Bell interview on the Talk of Fame Sports Network. December 4, 2015.

25. http://www.pro-football-reference.com/blog/?p=4086.

26. Jerry Izenberg. "People Have It Wrong about Art Modell; He was a Good Man Who Should be in the Football Hall of Fame." *Newark Star-Ledger.* September 6, 2012.

Chapter Twelve

1. Harvey Frommer. *When It Was Just a Game.* Page 37.

2. Ed Gruver. *Nitschke.* Page 156.

3. Ross Greenburg Productions. "Episode IV." *Star Spangled Sundays.*

4. Michael MacCambridge. *America's Game.* Page 237.

5. Richard Rothschild. "Cold Weather Title Game Has Come Full Circle for NFL." *Sports Illustrated.* January 30, 2014.

6. Harvey Frommer. *When It Was Just a Game.* Page 164.

7. Don Weiss. *The Making of the Super Bowl.* Page 122.

8. Ibid. Page 126.

9. Ken Leiker, and Craig Ellenport. *The Super Bowl: An Official Retrospective.* Page 32.

10. Martin Ralbovsky. *Super Bowl: Of Men, Myths and Moments.* Page 9.

11. Willie Davis. *Closing the Gap.* Page 236.

12. Ken Leiker, and Craig Ellenport. *The Super Bowl: An Official Retrospective.* Page 32.

13. Ed Gruver. *The American Football League: A Year-by-Year History, 1960–1969.* Page 60.

14. Michael Beschloss. "Before the Bowl Was Super." *New York Times.* January 24, 2015.

15. Matt Fulks. *100 Things Chiefs Fans Should Know & Do before They Die.* Page 17.

16. Harvey Frommer. *When it Was Just a Game.* Pages 158–59.

17. John Wiebusch. *Lombardi.* Page 50.

18. Ken Leiker and Craig Ellenport. *The Super Bowl: An Official Retrospective.* Page 147.

19. David Maraniss. *When Pride Still Mattered.* Page 393.

20. Adam Lazarus. *Super Bowl Monday.* Page 148.

21. Bud Lea. *Magnificent Seven.* Page 124.

22. Edwin Shrake. "Still a Long, Rough Road Ahead for the AFL." *Sports Illustrated.* January 30, 1967.

23. Bud Lea. *Magnificent Seven.* Page 127.

24. Mickey Herskowitz. "Super Bowl I," in *The Super Bowl: Celebrating a Quarter-Century of American's Greatest Game.* Page 50.

25. Harvey Frommer. *When It Was Just a Game*. Page 199.

26. Tex Maule. "Duel For Superiority." *Sports Illustrated*. July 7, 2011.

27. Mickey Herskowitz. "Super Bowl I," in *The Super Bowl: Celebrating a Quarter-Century of American's Greatest Game*. Page 50.

28. Ray Didinger. *The Super Bowl: Celebrating a Quarter-Century of America's Greatest Game*. Page 52.

29. Michael O'Brien. *Vince*. Pages 179–80.

30. Bob Wolfley. "Early Super Bowls Fondly Recalled." *Milwaukee Journal Sentinel*. January 28, 2006. Page 2C.

31. "People." *Sports Illustrated*. January 30, 1967.

32. Ray Nitschke, and Tex Maule. "Champions on the Way Up." *Sports Illustrated*. July 15, 1968.

Chapter Thirteen

1. Dan Rooney. *Dan Rooney: My 75 Years with the Pittsburgh Steelers*. Page 39.

2. Rich Cohen. *Monsters: The 1985 Chicago Bears and the Wild Heart of Football*. Page 98.

3. Rose Namath Szolnoki. *Namath: My Son Joe*. Page 6.

4. Mark Kriegel. *Namath: A Biography*. Page 33.

5. Larry Bruno. Pro Football Hall of Fame presentation speech for Joe Namath. 1985.

6. Joe Namath, and Shawn Coyne. *Namath*. Page 39.

7. Ibid. Page 38.

8. Stephen Randall and the Editors of *Playboy* magazine. *The Playboy Interviews: They Played the Game*. Page 303.

9. Joe Namath, and Shawn Coyne. *Namath*. Page 44.

10. Pro Football Hall of Fame induction speech.

11. Stephen Randall and the Editors of *Playboy* magazine. *The Playboy Interviews: They Played the Game*. Page 306–7.

12. Joe Namath, and Shawn Coyne. *Namath*. Page 67.

13. Stephen Randall and the Editors of *Playboy* magazine. *The Playboy Interviews: They Played the Game*. Page 307.

14. The story appears in numerous books including Joe Willie Namath with Dick Schaap. *I Can't Wait Until Tomorrow … 'Cause I Get Better-Looking Every Day*. Page 185; Namath and Coyne. *Namath*. Page 83 and Randy Roberts and Ed Krzemienski. *Rising Tide*. Pages 304–5.

15. Joe Namath, and Shawn Coyne. *Namath*. Page 103.

16. Keith Dunnavant. *America's Quarterback*. Page 171.

17. Joe Namath, and Shawn Coyne. *Namath*. Page 123.

18. Y. A. Tittle, and Tex Maule. "Year of Agony and Decline." *Sports Illustrated*. August 30, 1965.

19. Joe Namath, and Shawn Coyne. *Namath*. Pages 129–31.

20. Mark Kriegel. *Namath: A Biography*. Page 192.

21. Joe Namath, and Shawn Coyne. *Namath*. Page 134.

22. Johnny Sample. *Confessions of a Dirty Ballplayer*. Page 154.

23. Andy Martino. "No Love Lost between Jets and Raiders." *New York Daily News*. October 25, 2008.

24. Joe Namath. "It's a Hard Game." NFL.com. December 3, 2006.

25. NFL Films. *America's Game: 1968 New York Jets*.

26. Johnny Sample. *Confessions of a Dirty Ballplayer*. Page 155.

27. NFL Films. *America's Game: 1968 New York Jets*.

28. Joe Namath, and Shawn Coyne. *Namath*. Page 175.

29. Gerald Eskenazi. "25 Years Ago, Namath Was a Star; but 'Heidi' Ruled the Airwaves." *New York Times*. October 10, 1993.

30. Dennis Deninger. *Sports on Television*. Page 52.

31. Art Buchwald. "Heidi Fans' Next Game: Swiss Alps vs. Super Bowl." *Los Angeles Times*. November 24, 1968.

32. "Heidi Bowl." Raiders.com. December 2, 2013.

33. Milton Kent. "TV Executive Turns Back the Clock on 'Heidi' Game." *Baltimore Sun*. November 12, 1998.

34. Josh Dubow. "Heidi Changed the Way Television Covered Football." *Amarillo Globe-News*. November 13, 1998.

35. Gerald Eskenazi. "25 Years Ago, Namath Was a Star; but 'Heidi' Ruled the Airwaves." *New York Times*. October 10, 1993.

36. Bill Gutman. *Miracle Year, 1969*. Page 79.

37. Mark Kriegel. *Namath: A Biography*. Page 189.

38. Paul Zimmerman. *The Last Season of Weeb Ewbank*. Pages 219–20.

Chapter Fourteen

1. Robert Liston. *The Pros*. Pages 48–50.

2. Tex Maule. "Say It's So, Joe." *Sports Illustrated*. January 20, 1969. Page 10.

3. Mark Kriegel. *Namath: A Biography*. Page 268.

4. Jeff Miller. *Going Long*. Page 305.

5. Tom Brokaw. *Boom*. Page xv.

6. Talk of Fame Network interview. December 1, 2014.

7. Tex Maule. *The Pro Season*. Page 202.

8. Bill Gutman. *Miracle Year, 1969*. Page 97.

9. Bob Oates. "The Top 10 Sports Events: Olympic Hockey Game, Dempsey-Tunney Fight, Super Bowl III: Best of the 20th Century." *Los Angeles Times*. April 2, 1995.

Chapter Fifteen

1. Rebecca Leung. "NFL Films, Inc: Father-Son Team Establishes Gold Standard for Sports Photography." *CBS News*. August 25, 2004.

2. Mike Kupper. "Steve Sabol Dies at 69; President of NFL Films." *Los Angeles Times*. September 18, 2012.

3. Don Smith. *The Quarterbacks*. Page 107–8.

4. Jerry Izenberg. *Rozelle: A Biography*. Page 208.

5. Thomas Danyluk. "Steve Sabol—President, NFL Films." *The Coffin Corner*. Vol. 23, No. 1. (2001). Page 4.

6. Steve Sabol. "Pro Football's Own Mythmaker: How I Did It." *Inc.* February 2006. Pages 98–100.

7. Josh Weir. "Ed Sabol, Hall of Fame Class of 2011: Ed Sabol's Relationship with Pete Rozelle Played a Big Role in the Birth and Growth of NFL Films." *Canton Repository*. August 3, 2011.

8. Jonathan Tamari. "Ed Sabol Could Become Part of the NFL History." Philly.com. February 2, 2011.

9. Edward B. Driscoll Jr. "The NFL Films Model." *Videomaker*. January 2004.

10. DailyInterview.Net. "Steve Sabol—President of NFL Films." January 26, 2008. http://dailyinterview.net/?p=99.

11. Steve Almasy. "Through Ed Sabol's Lens, the NFL and Its Players Became Mythic." *CNN*. February 4, 2011.

12. Douglas Martin. "Steve Sabol, Cinematic Force for NFL, Dies at 69." *New York Times*. September 18, 2012.

13. Travis Vogan. *Keepers of the Flame*. Page 5.

14. David Litsky. "This Is NFL Films." *Money*. September 1, 2002.

15. Edward B. Driscoll Jr. "Shooting Sports: The NFL Films Model." Videomaker.com. January 1, 2004.

16. Ibid.

17. Conor Orr. "With NFL Films, Ed Sabol Gave Football a Hollywood Touch." NJ.com. February 5, 2011.

18. Thomas Danyluk. "Steve Sabol—President, NFL Films." *The Coffin Corner*. Volume 23, Number 1. (2001). Page 4.

19. Edward B. Driscoll Jr. "Shooting Sports: The NFL Films Model." Videomaker.com. January 1, 2004.

20. Maria Gallagher. "Film Pro Has a New Game Plan: His Life's Taken on a New Focus; Sports Cameraman Is Shooting Stars." Philly.com. January 25, 1993.

Chapter Sixteen

1. Ronald Austin Smith. *Play-by-Play*. Page 103.

2. Bert R. Sugar. *"The Thrill of Victory": The Inside Story of ABC Sports*. Page 50.

3. Michael Oriard. *Brand NFL*. Page 25 and Ronald A. Smith. *Play-by-Play*. Page 105.

4. Phil Patton. *Razzle Dazzle: The Curious Marriage of Television and Professional Football*. Page 4.

5. Roone Arledge. *Roone: A Memoir*. Page 38.

6. Ibid. Page 39.

7. Tony Verna. *Instant Replay*. Page 9.

8. Ibid. Pages 4–5.

9. Ibid. Page 200.

10. Ibid. Page 14.

11. Roone Arledge. "Television, by Roone Arledge." *New York Times*. December 7, 2002.

12. Overall attendance decreased from 205,109 in 1949 to 110,162 in 1950.

13. Bob St. John. *Tex!* Page 190.

14. Tex Maule. "When the Booing Stopped." *Sports Illustrated*. September 26, 1966. Page 32.

15. Howard Cosell. *Cosell*. Pages 278–79.

16. Chris Erskin. "Whoa, Nellie! Keith Jackson Talks Cosell, College Football and Cotton." *Los Angeles Times*. September 10, 2013.

17. Dennis Deninger. *Sports on Television*. Page 55.

18. William Johnson. "TV Made It All a New Game." *Sports Illustrated*. December 22, 1969. Page 86.3.

19. William O. Johnson Jr. *Super Spectator and the Electric Lilliputians*. Page 28.

Chapter Seventeen

1. The story of the dream sequence come from David Maraniss. "When Football Mattered." *Esquire*. September 1997. Pages 80–83.

2. Jonathan Rand. *The Year That Changed the Game*. Page 31.

3. David Maraniss. "When Football Mattered." *Esquire*. September 1997. Pages 80–83.

4. Bob Berghaus. *The First America's Team*. Page 1.

Chapter Eighteen

1. Ray Didinger. "25 Years Later, They Remember Namath, Now Off-Broadway Joe as Family Man At 50, Is Forever Tied to Super Bowl III." *Philadelphia Daily News*. January 25, 1994.

2. Ibid.

3. Ray Didinger. "25 Years Later, They Remember Namath, Now Off-Broadway Joe as Family Man At 50, Is Forever Tied to Super Bowl III." *Philadelphia Daily News*. January 25, 1994.

4. Dave Anderson. *New York Times*. "Joe Namath Receives a Brand-New Pair of Knees." May 3, 1992. Section 8, Page 3.

5. Jerry Kramer. "We Played for Lombardi." *Life*. September 11, 1970. Page 53.

6. Bill Curry. *Ten Men You Meet in the Huddle*. Pages 101–2.

7. Ibid. Page 102.

8. Bart Starr. *My Life in Football*. Page 54.

9. Ian O'Connor. "St. Vincent's in Lombardi Image, Packers Have a Prayer." *New York Daily News*. January 10, 1996.

10. NFL Films. *A Football Life: Vince Lombardi, Part II*.

11. https://www.youtube.com/watch?v=jEYUgHV9320.

12. https://www.youtube.com/watch?v=jEYUgHV9320.

Bibliography

Books

Ali, Muhammad, with Hana Yasmeen Ali. *The Soul of a Butterfly: Reflections on Life's Journey.* New York: Simon & Schuster, 2004.

Anton, Todd W., and Bill Nowlin. *When Football Went to War.* Chicago: Triumph Books, 2013.

Arledge, Roone. *Roone: A Memoir.* New York: Harper Collins, 2004.

Barra, Allen. *The Last Coach: A Life of Paul "Bear" Bryant.* New York: W. W. Norton & Company, 2006.

Berghaus, Bob. *The First America's Team: The 1962 Green Bay Packers.* Cincinnati: Clerisy Press, 2011.

Bradlee, Ben. *A Good Life: Newspapering and Other Adventures.* New York: Simon & Schuster, 1996.

Briggs, Jennifer. *Strive to Excel: The Will and Wisdom of Vince Lombardi.* Nashville: Rutledge Hill Press, 1997.

Brinkley, Douglas. *Cronkite.* New York: Harper Collins, 2012.

Brock, Ted, and Larry Eldridge Jr. *25 Years: The NFL Since 1960.* New York: Simon & Schuster, 1986.

Brodie, John, and James D. Houston. *Open Field.* Round Rock, TX: Houghton Mifflin, 1974.

Brokaw, Tom. *Boom! Voices of the Sixties: Personal Reflections of the '60s and Today.* New York: Random House, 2007.

Brown, Jim, with Myron Cope. *Off My Chest.* New York: Doubleday, 1964.

Brown, Jim, with Steve Delsohn. *Out of Bounds.* New York: Zebra Books, 1989.

Brown, Paul, and Jack Clary. *PB: The Paul Brown Story.* New York: Atheneum, 1979.

Bryant, Nick. *The Bystander: John F. Kennedy and the Struggle for Black Equality.* New York: Basic Books, 2006.

Callahan, Tom. *Johnny U: The Life & Times of John Unitas.* New York: Crown Publishers, 2006.

Cameron, Steve. *The Packers! Seventy-five Seasons of Memories and Mystique in Green Bay.* Lanham, MD: Taylor Publishing Company, 1993.

Cantor, George. *Paul Brown: The Man Who Invented Modern Football.* Chicago: Triumph Books; 2008.

Cavanaugh, Jack. *Giants Among Men: How Robustelli, Huff, Gifford, and the Giants Made New York a Football Town and Changed the NFL.* New York: Random House, 2008.

Clary, Jack T. *The Gamemakers: Winning Philosophies of Eight NFL Coaches.* Chicago: Follett Publishing Company, 1976.

Coenen, Craig R. *From Sandlots to the Super Bowl: The National Football League, 1920-1967.* Knoxville: University of Tennessee Press, 2005.

Cohen, Rich. *Monsters: The 1985 Chicago Bears and the Wild Heart of Football.* New York: Farrar, Straus and Giroux, 2013.

Connelly, Michael. *The President's Team: The 1963 Army–Navy Game and the Assassination of JFK.* Minneapolis: MVP Books, 2009.

Cosell, Howard. *Cosell.* New York: Playboy Press, 1973.

Cronkite, Walter. *A Reporter's Life.* New York: Alfred A. Knopf, 1996.

Curry, Bill. *The Men You Meet in the Huddle: Lessons from a Football Life.* New York: ESPN, 2009.

Davis, Jeff. *Rozelle: Czar of the NFL.* New York: McGraw-Hill; 2008.

Davis, Willie, with Jim Martyka and Andrea Erickson Davis. *Closing the Gap: Lombardi, the Packers Dynasty, and the Pursuit of Excellence.* Chicago: Triumph Books, 2012.

Deninger, Dennis. *Sports on Television: The How and Why Behind What You See.* New York: Routledge, 2012.

Didinger, Ray, Mickey Herskowitz, Kevin Lamb, Bill McGrane, Phil Musick, and Shelby Strother. *The Super Bowl: Celebrating a Quarter-Century of Amerzica's Greatest Game.* New York: Simon & Schuster, 1990.

Dunnavant, Keith. *America's Quarterback: Bart Starr and the Rise of the National Football League.* New York: Thomas Dunne Books, 2011.

Eisenberg, John. *That First Season: How Vince Lombardi Took the Worst Team in the NFL and Set It on the Path to Glory.* Round Rock, TX: Houghton Mifflin Harcourt, 2009.

Ezra, Michael. *Muhammad Ali: The Making of an Icon.* Philadelphia: Temple University Press, 2009.

Felser, Larry. *The Birth of the New NFL: How the 1966 NFL/AFL Merger Transformed Pro Football.* Guilford, CT: Lyons Press, 2008.

Fortunato, John. *Commissioner: The Legacy of Pete Rozelle.* Lanham, MD: Taylor Trade Publishing, 2006.

Freeman, Mike. *Jim Brown: The Fierce Life of an American Hero.* New York: William Morrow, 2006.

Frommer, Harvey. *When It Was Just a Game: Remembering the First Super Bowl.* Lanham, MD: Taylor Trade Publishing, 2015.

Fulks, Matt. *100 Things Chiefs Fans Should Know & Do Before They Die.* Chicago: Triumph Books, 2014.

Garrison, Walt, and Mark Stallard. *"Then Landry Said to Staubach..."* Chicago: Triumph Books, 2007.

Gifford, Frank, and Harry Waters. *The Whole Ten Yards.* New York: Random House, 1993.

Gifford, Frank, with Peter Richmond. *The Glory Game: How the 1958 NFL Championship Changed Football Forever.* New York: HarperCollins, 2008.

Gildea, William. *When the Colts Belonged to Baltimore: A Father and a Son, a Team and a Time.* Round Rock, TX: Houghton Mifflin Harcourt, 1994.

Gitlin, Martin. *Powerful Moments in Sports.* Lanham, MD: Rowman & Littlefield, 2017.

Gotterher, Barry. *The Giants of New York: The History of Professional Football's Most Fabulous Dynasty.* New York: G. P. Putnam's Sons, 1963.

Griese, Bob, and David Hyde. *Perfection: The Inside Story of the 1972 Miami Dolphins' Perfect Season.* Hoboken: Wiley, 2012.

Grossi, Tony. *Tales from the Cleveland Browns Sideline: A Collection of the Greatest Browns Stories Ever Told.* New York: Sports Publishing, 2012.

Gruver, Ed. *The American Football League: A Year-by-Year History, 1960–1969.* Jefferson, NC: McFarland, 1997.

_____. *From Baltimore to Broadway: Joe, the Jets, and the Super Bowl III Guarantee.* Chicago: Triumph Books, 2009.

_____. *The Ice Bowl: The Cold Truth About Football's Most Unforgettable Game.* Ithaca, NY: McBooks Press, 2005.

_____. *Nitschke.* Lanham, MD: Taylor Trade Publishing, 2002.

Gutman, Bill. *Miracle Year, 1969: Amazing Mets and Super Jets.* New York: Sports Publishing, LLC, 2004.

Halberstam, David. *The Powers That Be.* New York: Alfred A. Knopf, 1979.

Harris, David. *The League: The Rise and Decline of the NFL.* New York: Bantam, 1986.

Hayes, Bob, with Robert Pack. *Run, Bullet, Run: The Rise, Fall, and Recovery of Bob Hayes.* New York: Harper & Row, 1990.

Herskowitz, Mickey. *From Cannon to Campbell: An Illustrated History of the Houston Oilers,* Corpus Christi: Gulf Coast Graphics, 1979.

Hornung, Paul, and William F. Reed. *Golden Boy.* New York: Simon & Schuster, 2008.

Horrigan, Jack, and Mike Rathet. *The Other League: The Fabulous Story of the American Football League.* Chicago: Follett Publishing Company, 1970.

Izenberg, Jerry. *Rozelle: A Biography.* Lincoln: University of Nebraska Press, 2014.

Johnson, William O. Jr. *Super Spectator and the Electric Lilliputians.* Lincoln, NE: Little, Brown, 1971.

Karras, Alex, with Herb Gluck. *Even Fat Guys Cry.* New York: Holt, Rinehart & Winston, 1978.

Keim, John. *Legends by the Lake: The Cleveland Browns at Municipal Stadium.* Akron, OH: The University of Akron Press, 1999.

King, Peter, Will McDonough, and Paul Zimmerman. *75 Seasons: The Complete Story of the National Football League, 1920–1995.* Atlanta: Turner Publishing, 1994.

Klein, Dave. *The Game of Their Lives, 50th Anniversary Edition: The 1958 NFL Championship.* Lanham, MD: Taylor Trade Publishing, 2008.

_____. *The Vince Lombardi Story.* New York: Lion Books, 1971.

Kramer, Jerry. Edited by Dick Schaap. *Jerry Kramer's Farewell to Football.* New York: The World Publishing Company, 1969.

Kramer, Jerry, and Dick Schaap. *Instant Replay: The Green Bay Diary of Jerry Kramer.* New York: Doubleday, 1968.

Kriegel, Mark. *Namath: A Biography.* New York: Viking, 2004.

Lazarus, Adam. *Super Bowl Monday: From the Persian Gulf to the Shores of West Florida: The New York Giants, the Buffalo Bills, and Super Bowl XXV.* Lanham, MD: Taylor Trade Publishing, 2011.

Lea, Bud. *Magnificent Seven: The Championship Games That Built the Lombardi Dynasty.* Chicago: Triumph Books, 2002.

Leiker, Ken, and Craig Ellenport. *The Super Bowl: An Official Retrospective.* Winnetka, IL: Rare Air Media, 2005.

Leuthner, Stuart. *Iron Men.* New York: Doubleday, 1988.

Lewis, John, with Michael D'Orso. *Walking with the Wind: A Memoir of the Movement.* New York: Simon & Schuster, 1998.

Liston, Robert. *The Pros.* New York: Platt & Munk, Publishers, 1968.

Lombardi, Vince, with W. C. Heinz. *Run to Daylight!* Englewood Cliffs, NJ: Prentice Hall, 1963.

Lombardi, Vince, Jr. *What It Takes to Be #1: Vince Lombardi on Leadership.* New York: McGraw-Hill, 2000.

Lovinger, Jay. *The Gospel According to ESPN: Saints, Saviors and Sinners.* New York: Hyperion, 2002.

Lyons, Robert S. *On Any Given Sunday: A Life of Bert Bell.* Philadelphia: Temple University Press, 2009.

MacCambridge, Michael. *America's Game: The Epic Story of How Pro Football Captured a Nation.* New York: Random House, 2004.

Manoyan, Dan. *Alan Ameche: The Story of "The Horse."* Madison: University of Wisconsin Press, 2012.

Marable, Manning. *Race, Reform and Rebellion: The Second Reconstruction in Black America, 1945–1990.* Jackson: University Press of Mississippi, 1991.

Maraniss, David. *When Pride Still Mattered: A Life of Vince Lombardi.* New York: Simon & Schuster, 1999.

Maule, Tex. *The Pro Season.* New York: Doubleday & Company, 1970.

McGuff, Joe. *Winning It All: The Chiefs of the AFL.* New York: Doubleday & Company, 1970.

Miller, Jeff. *Going Long: The Wild 10-Year Saga of the Renegade American Football League in the Words of Those Who Lived It.* Chicago: Contemporary Books, 2003.

Miller, Jeffrey J. *Rockin' the Rockpile: The Buffalo Bills of the American Football League.* Toronto: ECW Press, 2007.

Millman, Chad, and Shawn Coyne. *The Ones Who Hit the Hardest: The Steelers, The Cowboys, the '70s, and the Fight for America's Soul.* New York: Gotham Books, 2010.

Monk, Cody. *Legends of the Dallas Cowboys.* New York: Sports Publishing LLC, 2004.

Morgan, Jon. *Glory for Sale: Fans, Dollars and the New NFL.* Baltimore: Bancroft Press, 1997.

Nack, William. *My Turf: Horses, Boxers, Blood Money and the Sporting Life.* Boston: Da Capo Press, 2003.

Namath, Joe, and Shawn Coyne. *Namath.* New York: Rugged Land, 2006.

Namath, Joe Willie, with Dick Schaap. *I Can't Wait Until Tomorrow … 'Cause I Get Better-Looking Every Day.* New York: Random House, 1969.

Oberdorfer, Don. *Tet! The Turning Point in the Vietnam War.* Baltimore: The Johns Hopkins University Press, 2001.

O'Brien, Michael. *Vince: A Personal Biography of Vince Lombardi.* New York: William Morrow, 1987.

Olsen, Jack. *The Black Athlete: A Shameful Story: The Myth of Integration in American Sport.* New York: Time-Life Books, 1968.

Oriard, Michael. *Brand NFL: Making and Selling America's Favorite Sport.* Chapel Hill: University of North Carolina Press, 2007.

O'Toole, Andrew. *Paul Brown: The Rise and Fall and Rise Again of Football's Most Innovative Coach.* Cincinnati: Clerisy Press, 2009.

Page, Joseph S. *Championships Before the Super Bowl: A Year-by-Year History, 1926–1965.* Jefferson, NC: McFarland, 2010.

Palladino, Ernie. *Lombardi and Landry: How Two of Pro Football's Greatest Coaches Launched Their Legends and Changed the Game Forever.* New York: Skyhorse Publishing, 2011.

Parrish, Bernie. *They Call It a Game.* New York: The Dial Press, 1971.

Patton, Phil. *Razzle Dazzle: The Curious Marriage of Television and Professional Football.* New York: Dial Press, 1984.

Phillips, Donald T. *Run to Win: Vince Lombardi on Coaching and Leadership.* New York: St. Martin's Griffin, 2002.

Piascik, Andy. *Gridiron Gauntlet: The Story of the Men Who Integrated Pro Football in Their Own Words.* Lanham, MD: Taylor Trade Publishing, 2009.

Pirkle, John. *Oiler Blues: The Story of Pro Football's Most Frustrating Team.* New York: Sportline Publishing, 2000.

Rader, Benjamin G. *In Its Own Image: How Television Transformed Sports.* New York: The Free Press, 1984.

Ralbovsky, Marty. *The Namath Effect.* Englewood Cliffs, NJ: Prentice-Hall, 1976.

_____. *Super Bowl: Of Men, Myths, and Moments.* Portland: Hawthorne Books, 1971.

Rand, Jonathan. *The Year That Changed the Game: The Memorable Months That Shaped Pro Football.* Washington, DC: Potomac Books, 2008.

Randall, Stephen, and the Editors of *Playboy* magazine. *The Playboy Interviews: They Played the Game.* New York: M Press, 2006.

Rappoport, Ken. *The Little League That Could: A History of the American Football League.* Lanham, MD: Taylor Trade Publishing, 2010.

_____. *Profiles in Sports Courage.* Atlanta: Peachtree, 2006.

Robinson, Dave, and Royce Boyles. *The Lombardi Legacy: Thirty People Who Were Touched by Greatness.* Louisville, KY: Goose Creek Publishers, 2009.

Rooney, Dan, as told to Andrew E. Masich and David F. Halas. *Dan Rooney, My 75 Years with the Pittsburgh Steelers and the NFL.* Boston: Da Capo Press, 2007.

Ross, Alan. *Browns Glory: For the Love of Ozzie, the Toe and Otto.* Nashville: Cumberland House Publishing, 2005.

Ross, Charles K. *Outside the Lines: African Americans and the Integration of the National Football League.* New York: New York University Press, 1999.

Ruck, Rob, Maggie Jones Patterson, and Michael P. Weber. *Rooney: A Sporting Life.* Lincoln: University of Nebraska Press, 2010.

Sahadi, Lou. *One Sunday in December: The 1958 NFL Championship Game and How it Changed Professional Football.* Guilford, CT: Lyons Press, 2008.

St. John, Bob. *Landry: The Legend and the Legacy.* Nashville: Word Publishing, 2001.

_____. *Tex: The Man Who Built the Dallas Cowboys.* Englewood Cliffs, NJ: Prentice-Hall, 1988.

Sample, Johnny. *Confessions of a Dirty Ballplayer.* New York: The Dial Press, 1970.

Sayers, Gale, with Fred Mitchell. *Sayers: My Life and Times.* Chicago: Triumph Books, 2007.

Shropshire, Mike. *The Ice Bowl: The Green Bay Packers and Dallas Cowboys Season of 1967.* New York: Donald I. Fine Books, 1997.

Silverman, Al. *It's Not Over 'Til It's Over.* New York: The Overlook Press, 2002.

Silverman, Matthew (managing editor), Bob Carroll, Michael Gershman, David Neft, and John Thorn. *Total Football II: The Official Encyclopedia of the National Football League.* New York: Harper Collins Publishers, 1997.

Simon, Scott. *Home and Away: Memoir of a Fan.* New York: Hyperion, 2000.

Smith, Don, editor. *The Quarterbacks: Original Stories of Pro Football's Greatest Quarterbacks*. New York: Franklin Watts, Inc., 1963.

Smith, Ronald Austin. *Play-by-Play: Radio, Television and Big-Time College Sport*. Baltimore: The Johns Hopkins University Press, 2001.

Smith, Thomas G. *Showdown: JFK and the Integration of the Washington Redskins*. Boston: Beacon Press, 2011.

Snook, Jeff. *"Then Bud Said to Barry, Who Told Bob...": The Best Oklahoma Sooners Stories Ever Told*. Chicago: Triumph Books, 2008.

Starr, Bart, with Murray Olderman. *Starr: My Life in Football*. New York: William Morrow & Co., 1987.

Strode, Woody, and Sam Young. *Goal Dust: The Warm and Candid Memoirs of a Pioneer Black Athlete and Actor*. Lanham, MD: Madison Books, 1990.

Sugar, Bert Randolph. *The Thrill of Victory: The Inside Story of ABC Sports*. New York: Hawthorne Books, 1978.

Sweet, David A. F. *Lamar Hunt: The Gentle Giant Who Revolutionized Professional Sports*. Chicago: Triumph Books, 2010.

Szolnoki, Rose Namath, with Bill Kushner. *Namath: My Son Joe*. Birmingham, AL: Oxmoor House, 1975.

Taylor, Otis, and Mark Stallard. *The Need to Win: Football from My Own Heart*. New York: Sports Publishing LLC, 2003.

Time-Life Books. *Turbulent Years: The '60s (Our American Century)*. New York: Time-Life Books, 1998.

Towle, Mike. *I Remember Vince Lombardi: Personal Memories of and Testimonials to Football's First Super Bowl Championship Coach as Told by the People and Players Who Knew Him*. Nashville: Cumberland House Publishing, 2004.

_____. *Johnny Unitas: Mr. Quarterback*. Nashville: Cumberland House Publishing, 2003.

Verna, Tony. *Instant Replay: The Day that Changed Sports Forever*. Beverly Hills: Creative Book Publishers International, 2008.

Vogan, Travis. *Keepers of the Flame: NFL Films and the Rise of Sports Media*. Champaign: University of Illinois Press, 2014.

Walsh, Bill, with Brian Billick and James Peterson. *Finding the Winning Edge*. Champaign, IL: Sports Publishing Inc., 1997.

Weiss, Don, with Chuck Day. *The Making of the Super Bowl: The Inside Story of the World's Greatest Sporting Event*. New York: McGraw-Hill, 2003.

Whittingham, Richard. *What Giants They Were: New York Giant Greats Talk about Their Teams, Their Coaches, and the Times of Their Lives*. Chicago: Triumph Books, 2001.

Wiebusch, John, editor. *Lombardi*. Chicago: Triumph Books, 1997.

Wiggins, David K., editor. *Out of the Shadows: A Biographical History of African American Athletes*. Fayetteville: University of Arkansas Press, 2008.

Williams, Pete. *The Draft: A Year Inside the NFL's Search for Talent*. New York: St. Martin's Griffin, 2007.

Wismer, Harry. *The Public Calls It Sport*. New York: Prentice-Hall, 1965.

Wright, Mike. *What They Didn't Teach You About the '60s*. San Francisco: Presidio Press, 2001.

Younge, Gary. *The Speech: The Story Behind Dr. Martin Luther King Jr.'s Dream*. Chicago: Haymarket Books, 2013.

Zimmerman, Paul. *The Last Season of Weeb Ewbank*. New York: Farrar, Strauss and Giroux, 1974.

_____. *The Thinking Man's Guide to Pro Football*. New York: Dutton, 1971.

Zinn, Howard. *A People's History of the United States*. New York: Harper Perennial Modern Classics, 2015.

Newspapers & Magazines

The Advocate
Amarillo Globe-News
Associated Press
The Baltimore Sun
Buffalo News
Canton (OH) Repository
Cincinnati Enquirer
The Coffin Corner
Dallas News
Esquire
Football Digest
Houston Chronicle
Inc.
Investor's Business Daily
Life
Los Angeles Times
Ludington (MI) Daily News
Milwaukee Journal Sentinel
Money
New York Daily News
New York Times
Newark Star-Ledger
Newsday
North American Society for Sport History (NASSH) Proceedings, 1973
Philadelphia Daily News
San Antonio Express News
San Jose Mercury News
Santa Fe New Mexican
Sport
The Sporting News
Sports Illustrated
Texas Monthly
USA Today
Wall Street Journal
Washington Examiner
Washington Post

Websites

www.achievement.org
www.theadvocate.com

www.armchairgeneral.com
www.baseball-almanac.com
www.bengals.com
www.cbsnews.com
www.cbssports.com
www.DailyInterview.net
Dave Softly Mahler radio show, www.950kjr.com/
    podcast/softy, February 4, 2011
Encyclopedia.com
ESPN.com
www.foxsports.com
www.history.com
www.homeofheroes.com
www.jfklibrary.org
www.landscapeonline.com
www.lbjlibrary.org
www.medium.com
www.mensjournal.com
Mind Your Business, www.rovi.usglassmag.com
NFL.com
www.nationalfootballpost.com
NJ.com
www.npr.org

Philly.com
www.pressboxonline.com
www.profootballhof.com
www.profootballresearchers.org
www.pro-football-reference.com
www.nixonlibrary.gov
www.raiders.com
Sirius radio, "NFL Network" channel.
www.success.com
www.talkoffamenetwork.com
www.timesfreepress.com
www.videomaker.com
www.youtube.com

Films

ESPN. *ESPN SportsCentury*, 1999.
NFL Films. *A Football Life* series, 2011–Present.
NFL Films. *America's Game* series, 2011–Present.
NFL Films. *NFL Films Presents* series, 1985–Present.
NFL Films and Ross Greenburg Productions. *Star
    Spangled Sundays*, 2013.

Index

Index